In Search of the Donnellys

In Search of the Donnellys

Second Revised Edition

Ray Fazakas

Order this book online at **www.trafford.com**
or email orders@trafford.com

Most Trafford titles are also available at major online book retailers.

Printed in the United States of America.

ISBN: 978-1-4669-1299-1 (sc)
ISBN: 978-1-4669-1300-4 (e)

Trafford rev. 02/02/2012

 www.trafford.com

North America & International
toll-free: 1 888 232 4444 (USA & Canada)
phone: 250 383 6864 ♦ fax: 812 355 4082

Robert Donnelly died in 1911 in Lucan where his traces could still be found when the author first visited the village in 1964.

CONTENTS

Illustrations

To Beverley

Preface

The Donnelly Album, first published in 1977, told how and why a vigilance committee of neighbors massacred several members of the Donnelly family in the early morning hours of February 4th, 1880. The victims included James and Judith (or Judy, Julia, Johannah) Donnelly, their two sons and a niece of the old man. They died at the hands of their fellow church members in their log house on a road known as the Roman Line near the village of Lucan in the County of Middlesex about fifteen miles north of London, Ontario. Two other sons had died not long before, one in seemingly mysterious circumstances that are still argued about to this day, and another in a barroom squabble. The new priest of St. Patrick's parish was implicated in the massacre to the extent that, when circumstances drove him to oppose the Donnellys shortly after his arrival in the community, he founded a so-called property protective association that quickly evolved into the vigilance committee. Its own members called it the Peace Society.

While the research for that first book covered a period of about fifteen years, its publication was merely an incident in my ongoing search for all details connected with the Donnellys and the community in which they lived and died. This new book, *In Search of the Donnellys*, does not retell the story but approaches it from a different angle: it recounts my personal adventures in searching for the information on which the story is based from the beginning of my investigation. While I stand by the original telling, the new information fills in some gaps, expands some areas and, I hope, further accounts for some of the controversy which continues to surround this fascinating bit of North American folk history with Irish roots.

The first revised edition added some interesting elements such as the ultimate fates of Maggie Thompson, Sam Everett and the parents and siblings of Johnny O'Connor as well as the discovery of the Protestant connection in Ireland of the Donnelly family. This second revised edition re-organizes the previous material and includes intriguing new information about Bridget Donnelly and her family back in Ireland, Emma Rees of the Salvation Army, as well as new information about the Keefes and others. It also includes several new photographs that have recently come to light.

Swamphenge
Beverly Township, Ontario
September 1, 2011

Chapter 1

Kelley's Revival

Hot summer days always remind me of the Donnellys. Perhaps it is because my first awareness of them came on such a day. The year was 1962. While my wife Beverley shopped I waited in the car with my two-and-a-half year old son David and baby daughter Sandra. Barely listening to the voice on the car radio, I was almost dozing off when the words from the speaker suddenly riveted my attention:

> This latest study traces to Ireland the origins of the blood feud between the Donnellys and their neighbors.

The review continued in which the words "massacre," "vigilance committee," "fellow Roman Catholics" and "parish priest" electrified me.

For months after that hot summer afternoon I recalled the words heard over the airwaves. Occasionally as I slept, the Donnellys appeared in my dreams: the mother and father jumping up startled when the men rushed in; the manacled son hurling himself through the mob and out the front door; those waiting outside clubbing him to the ground and dragging him back in. Log houses, back country kitchens, coal oil lamps, cast iron stoves, dusty country roads, Sunday Mass, the priest's confessional, the Donnellys themselves and my childhood memories all tumbled together in my dreams.

In the main, however, the story was pushed to the back of my mind. Two years later with the birth of our third and last child, Derek, our customary weekend trips to the summer cottage were seriously curtailed by the daunting task of getting three small children ready for a four hours' drive and a short boat trip across the water to our island cottage in Haliburton. One weekend my wife and I were looking forward to a quiet couple of days at home when a small pocketbook in the racks of a neighborhood store caught my attention. Curiously, although it must have been around magazine and book racks for years, I had never previously noticed it. The book was *The Black Donnellys* by Thomas P. Kelley.

Thomas P. Kelley, Jr. was born in 1904. The senior of the name was a traveling carnival huckster known as The Fabulous Kelley.[1] He called his snake medicine Banyan Oil and flogged the cure-all by means of an old-time medicine show which made circuit tours of North America as late as the 1930s.

Thomas P. Kelley

In 1925 Doc Kelley's medicine show made a very successful tour of southwestern Ontario—in later years Tom Kelley, Jr., referred to it as "that golden season"—when it visited the towns of Stratford, Clinton, St. Marys, Mitchell, Seaforth, Parkhill, Strathroy, Ingersoll and Exeter. In that last-mentioned village, it made a one-week stand.[2]

That week in Exeter, young Thomas P. Kelley met and fell in love with a teen-aged girl named Edith Preszcator. Although he continued traveling with the medicine show

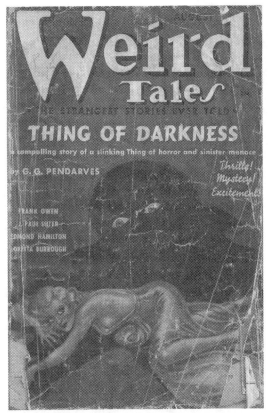

One of the pulp fiction magazines which published Thomas P. Kelley's weird and wonderful stories.

for several more years, he kept in touch with Edith until ten years later he returned to Exeter to claim her as his bride. By this time, the elder Kelley had died, the medicine show days were over and Kelley was making a living writing imaginative stories for the pulp fiction magazines which were popular at the time.

In my collection is one of those magazines called *Weird Tales* published in August 1937. In it is a 20-page tale called *The Last Pharaoh* by Thomas P. Kelley. The writing is pedestrian at best and sloppy at worst. Pierre Berton knew Kelley in those days and tells of meeting him on the street one morning in Toronto. As they walked along, Kelley suddenly stopped and said, "Excuse me, Pierre, but a great title for a story just popped into my head." It was something like *Prince Charming Meets Medusa* or a title equally bizarre. Kelley rushed off. Later that evening,

Berton happened to meet Kelley again on the street.

"Well," Kelley announced, "I've finished it."

Berton was mystified. "Finished what?" he asked.

"Why, that story. You remember, I thought of the title this morning. After that, the rest was easy. I'm going to take it to the publisher tomorrow."

Berton told me this was Kelley's common writing technique: first, think up a good title then quickly write the story to match it. Some of this technique no doubt went into his writing of *The Black Donnellys*. In bits and pieces Kelley had learned an outline of the story of the Donnelly murders from his wife. Her hometown of Exeter was, after all, the northern terminus of the stagecoach line that the Donnellys had operated and while the story may have been ostensibly forgotten in Lucan and Biddulph it was well remembered outside those places.

Following World War II the pulp fiction magazines were branching out into stories of true crime and Kelley began to think he could wring a little story out of those bits and pieces. He later recorded his thoughts on the beginnings of his book:[3]

> I well recall back in the summer of 1945, when my wife and I drove up to Lucan's St. Patrick's Church and the adjoining graveyard, that no one in the vicinity seemed to know where the Donnelly plot and tombstone was, and apparently cared less. But we finally found the grave of the Donnellys, neglected and knee-deep in long grass. And I little thought, as I first looked at the tombstone, that I was destined to write the two books that would make that tombstone a veritable Mecca for thousands of Canadians as well as Americans and even people from abroad . . . .

Thus Kelley's sense of place in history, in his own mind at least, was well fixed. In July of 1946 a magazine called *True Crime* published one of his first stories on the subject. Later that year in September came another, this time in *Real Crime*. One sentence, which will give the reader an idea of the depth of Kelley's research so far, reads:

> Sometime after the death of John Donnelly, as he sat in a neighboring farmhouse, a rifle bullet whistled in through a window and Patrick Donnelly plunged forward, limp and lifeless upon his face.

To put this in context, I am not aware of any incident in the history of the Donnelly family to which this statement could possibly relate. Patrick Donnelly, of course, died in his bed of natural causes.

By this time, however, Kelley knew he was on to a good thing and decided to do a little more research. The next time his story was published was in *New Liberty* magazine of September 6th, 1947. The article was one and one-quarter pages in length and the reading time—stated immediately below the title—was 8 minutes and 5 seconds. Throughout, it mentioned James Donnelly's six sons—there were in fact seven—and perhaps for the first time and I think only once it referred to the family as "the Black Donnellys".

Kelley was now working up a head of steam over the story. What he knew of it up to this time, besides the scraps of information told to him by his wife, he appears to have gleaned from some of the Toronto newspapers such as the *Mail* or *Globe*. Of these, however, he could only have looked at the first week's issues following the massacre. He now decided to go into the subject in greater depth.

When I met Lewis Needham, he had recently retired as an instructor from the Ontario government's police training school in Aylmer. Earlier in his career, he was one of only four detectives in Ontario working at the central Criminal Investigation Bureau at Queen's Park in Toronto. Lewis Needham remembers seeing Thomas P. Kelley and his wife coming in 1952 to the library in the legislative building. In that

This marker stood over the graves of the Donnellys for 75 years—from 1889 to 1964—and was removed within days of our first visit to the scene.

3

Two of Kelley's informants were Joe and Jim Kennedy, shown here with their sister, Sarah, in front of the house built by their father, Big Jack Kennedy, a leading member of the Peace Society and Will Donnelly's brother-in-law.

library were books entitled *Famous Canadian Trials* by Albert R. Hassard published in 1924 and *Canadian Murders and Mysteries* by W. Stewart Wallace published in 1931. In the latter was a chapter entitled *The Lucan Murders* and in the former a chapter entitled *When Biddulph Seethed With Crime*. To further his research, Kelley read both these chapters.

How do we know this? Simply because of the dozen or so factual errors in the two accounts, Thomas P. Kelley incorporated into his own soon-to-be-published book *The Black Donnellys* every single one of them.[1]

Before completing his *magnus opus*, however, Kelley went to stay for three days and nights at the Donnelly homestead then farmed by Joe Harrigan. During his sojourn he even interviewed some living persons. The son of William E. McLaughlin of the Roman Line remembers Kelley coming to their farm for information. McLaughlin told him that as he had been born in 1895 he

knew nothing of the story first hand but to go and see old Joe and Jim Kennedy on the eleventh concession of Biddulph. They were the sons of Big Jack Kennedy, William Donnelly's brother-in-law, who had played a prominent role in the events.

At the time of the massacre, however, Joe Kennedy was only five years old and his brother Jim had not yet been born. Perhaps the only first hand recollection of the events of 1880 which Joe Kennedy carried into his later years was that of accompanying his mother on a visit to his father in the London Jail in the winter of that year. Joe used to tell the story that when the jailer called for the visitors to leave, he wept and clung so fast to his father's legs that the kindly jail official allowed him and his mother to stay in the cells overnight. The story may be true for Jailer Joseph Lamb paid dearly for his concession when it came to light. He was fired. Grouchy Ryder and James Maher

4

In an upstairs room of the front tower of the venerable London courthouse, the old records of the nineteenth century gathered dust before being rescued by Dr. Edwin Seaborn.

helped to move his family and effects to the village of Lucan where he opened a grocery store. Lamb died soon after.

Joe and Jim Kennedy spun some fanciful tales for Kelley and it was they who gave him the supposedly inside information as to the events on the night of the murders. Kelley also talked with Jack Casey, the longtime resident of Biddulph and sometime constable of Lucan. He also went to Glencoe in the southwestern part of Middlesex County to see the Curries, sons of Jenny Donnelly. He had a drink with them but, according to Jenny's son Mike, they refused to disclose to the one-time medicine show huckster anything they may have known.

From its first publication in 1954, Tom Kelley's *The Black Donnellys* was a wild success. It has been reprinted many times. It was also published in serial form both in Canada and in Ireland where it appeared in the Irish *Independent* from April 17th through to May 29th, 1955. In later years and perhaps with some justification, Kelley wrote:

> . . . it gives me great satisfaction to know that it was I, and I alone, who first brought the attention of that violent feud back to the attention of the outside world, after it had been forgotten for more than seventy years. That I accomplished with the writing of my two books, *The Black Donnellys* and *The Vengeance of the Black Donnellys*.[2]

To criticize Kelley's book, *The Black Donnellys*, is easy. The writing is casual, sloppy and replete with slang. A very little checking soon shows the research to be so skimpy as in spots to vanish altogether. In those parts the author turned to invention. Similarly, conversation is conjured up wholesale. Some opponents of Kelley's work were vociferous in their opposition. "That book should be burned!" James Reaney once vehemently declared to me.

Despite its many faults, however, Kelley's book is nonetheless a fascinating read in that it created the legend of the family. Perhaps unwittingly, the author attached a kind of heroic proportion to their swashbuckling antics. For their audacity and boldness alone one cannot help but admire Kelley's Donnellys as he painted them with his broad and careless brush. The father, James, feared no one. Wicked Johannah cackled in delight at her sons' diabolical acts of vengeance. In bare knuckles no one ever bested the fearless son Tom. And then there was Clubfoot Bill, the cunning genius whose evil plotting brain prevailed for so long against their hapless neighbors. To be sure, all were stage caricatures—or were they?

Orlo Miller was a youth when he first heard of the Donnellys, but like so many Londoners he allowed an outsider like Kelley to write the first modern telling of the story. I do not count the four or five pages of a chapter in Miller's book, *A Century of Western Ontario*, which was published in 1949. This was a brief account based on the skimpiest of investigation. A couple of small examples to illustrate the dearth of research will suffice. Miller states that after Donnelly killed Farrell, he was at large for two years—it was just one year. He states that on the night of the murders the vigilantes arrived at the Donnelly house on horseback—they were all on foot.

It is curious that in 1936 Orlo Miller helped to retrieve a great cache of documents discovered by Dr. Edwin Seaborn in an upstairs room of the front tower of the old London courthouse. Many were legal documents filed in the nineteenth century with the county clerk of the peace. For the most part the papers related to the early criminal cases of Huron and Middlesex counties. Although the cache of papers ended up in the Regional Collection of the University of Western Ontario[3] in London, it was years before the library was able to catalogue them.

Orlo's book, *The Donnellys Must Die*, was first published in 1962 as a direct response to Kelley's book of eight years before. Miller's book is a superbly written account, much more factual than its predecessor, and it sets out for the first time the involvement of the parish priest, Father John Connolly, in the founding of the association or society which in one form or another was responsible for the massacre of February 4th, 1880. It was a review of this book on the radio in 1962 which first got me intrigued with the story. When I finally obtained a copy, I prepared

and sent to Orlo an index for which he expressed his gratitude and which he incorporated into the softcover edition. I visited Orlo after his move to Mitchell, Ontario and we had a grand discussion of the Donnellys and their story.

Although there is no denying that Miller's book was carefully and well written, its shortcomings must also be dealt with. Tiresome polemics abound on its pages. My law partner at the time had much less patience with them than I.

"It reads too much like a lawyer's argument," was his surprising comment, coming as it did from a practitioner of the law, albeit one who was no advocate of legal sophistry. "Enough argument," he said he found himself saying as he read the book, "Let's get on with the story."

True, the text pointed out again and again that the Donnellys were unjustly persecuted and that they were not nearly as bad as their enemies painted them. Their murderers, went the thesis, were a lot worse. The surviving Donnellys, the book argued, were martyrs to a legacy of slander perpetrated against them by their enemies and their progeny for the latter, after all, had the numerical advantage. Although Orlo in his book brought the Donnelly story down to earth and rooted it in reality, I nevertheless admit to having felt a vague sense of unease about it.

Assisting Orlo in his research for the book was Alfred Scott Garrett, better known as just Scott. Orlo told me himself that he was his secret contact. Scott Garrett was a well-known local amateur historian from the Lucan area who took an interest in the Donnelly story long before anyone thought of writing a book about it. For years he wrote articles for the London *Free Press* on many topics of local interest—but not the Donnelly story. At the time it was very much a taboo subject in the community.

Scott Garrett was suspicious of most written sources. In a letter to Spencer Armitage-Stanley,[4] he wrote:

The entrance from London to the village of Lucan in 1964.

I must admit that I cannot get up much enthusiasm over the court records, as they are full of perjured testimony. And I am not greatly influenced with the contemporary newspaper accounts that appeared in the days following the tragedy and the trials. They were hastily written by newspaper men mostly unfamiliar with the territory or its people, and are full of misspelled names, gross exaggerations, misrepresentations of facts and Lord knows what else.

Part of Scott Garrett's dilemma, in my view, was being too close to the subject. Although I agree with him that the court records contain perjured testimony and the newspaper accounts contain many errors, to ignore these sources is a mistake. And while he relied instead on the word-of-mouth, we all know how unreliable that can also be, especially with the passage of years to dim the memory. Moreover, it is difficult to write impartially about the parents and grandparents of individuals whom you have

befriended and who have entrusted you with their private confidences.

7

Chapter 2

The Scene of the Crime

Unlike Scott Garrett, when I began my own inquiries I knew none of the families involved in the incidents. Beyond the secondary sources, however, I began a wide correspondence with descendants of those connected with the story. Finding these people was sometimes very difficult. Often, when they were found, there was no assurance that they would volunteer any information. More often they simply had none to offer.

While information imparted by word-of-mouth from generation to generation is useful it is also, as we all know, notoriously unreliable in its details. Nevertheless, I welcomed such stories and remain grateful to this day to those who allowed me to receive every single one of them, no matter how far-fetched or fanciful. Every story handed down by word-of-mouth is, in my opinion, of some value and part of our oral history. Often it takes only a certain amount of reflection upon the version handed down before the proverbial grain of truth—a tangible relation to something more real—is found. In addition to the accounts of others, of course, I sought out the contemporary records such as court documents and newspaper accounts for, unlike Scott Garrett, I could not dismiss them out of hand.

And then there is the matter of a thesis. An academic once told me that my book, *The Donnelly Album*, had a lot of information but lacked a theory. Without even thinking, I quickly retorted that I would rather have no theory than the wrong one. Upon reflection, however, I realized that as I did my research I had no intention of formulating a grand thesis. And even as I write now, I feel that as far as this story at least is concerned, there are far too many theories. I myself have heard lots of them, some by academics.

Most of them are just that—theories—often with little substance. One of the problems with formulating a thesis and then marshalling the facts to support it is obvious. It is all too human to tend to omit or even forget those inconveniently awkward bits which do not support your thesis.

When, for example, I reviewed the files which Orlo Miller had gathered in preparing

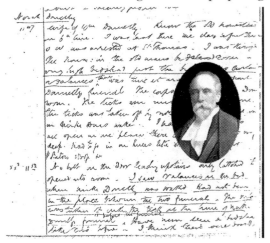

A page from the bench notes of Justice Featherston Osler (shown inset), on which he begins to note the testimony of Norah Donnelly at the second trial of Jim Carroll.

to write *The Donnellys Must Die*, I found a letter written by Charles M. Macfie of Appin, a person of standing within the community as he had been at one time a member of the Ontario legislature. In it he stated that Will Donnelly had been a model citizen while a resident in Appin. While Orlo chose to include this part of the letter in his book, it was merely a postscript. The letter itself mentioned some less savory aspects of the Donnelly family such as Tom Donnelly's son born out of wedlock and Will's son, Jack, contributing to his mother's giving up the hotel business in Appin because Jack's hand was "heavy on the till". As these facts did not fit in with Miller's thesis, he simply omitted them.

While Scott Garrett trusted neither the newspapers nor the legal documents, the essential truths of the story in their most complete form are found in those sources.

St. Patrick's Church in 1964 with the little house of the groundskeeper in left foreground.

True, the statements found in them are not gospel truths. Newspaper errors, I have found, can be corrected from other sources. And even now the perjured or at least suspect statements in the testimony of witnesses can often be spotted.

One must also keep in mind the particular nature of testimony for court purposes: it is made not for the historical record but solely for the purpose of making a legal finding as between parties in conflict. Court testimony is only for the purpose of imposing a sanction for certain conduct, be it punishment as in a criminal case or, between parties in a civil matter, to decide who shall bear the burden of a loss by way of damages or the forbidding of certain actions or enforcing certain rights.

The weekend following my reading of Kelley's book, Beverley and I packed up our little family and drove off in search of whatever faint traces might be left in Biddulph Township of the Donnellys. The date was August 7th, 1964 and again it was a hot summer day. As we came over the crest of the last hill from London City approaching Elginfield, the elegant spire of St. Patrick's Roman Catholic Church loomed up in the distance.

Coming closer, we slowly approached the churchyard until we could make out the lettering on the sign standing at the corner of the grounds. It read:

St. Patrick's Catholic Church
Biddulph
Sunday Masses
8:30 and 11:00 A.M.
Confessions
7:30 – 9:00 P.M.
Established in 1845

Behind the sign was a tiny house, almost a shack—the home, we later discovered, of the church caretaker—and still within the churchyard stood a little yellow brick schoolhouse. Again, we did not know it at the time but learned later, that this was once the site of the Andy Keefe Tavern.[1] And the little school had been erected through the efforts of Father John Connolly during his long years of tenure at St. Patrick's following the Donnelly affair.

From the corner, a gravel road ran north past the front gates to the church. This was the Roman Line. Almost in awe, we turned to enter this road and in a moment came to the front gate of the churchyard. A concrete walkway led to the doors of the church itself. Through those doors, we imagined, the Donnelly boys had gone: some to be married, others to be buried. Through those very portals James and Johannah—only later did I learn she was more commonly known as Judith or Judy—had walked to perform their spiritual duties. And later, their burned corpses or what remained of them were carried out in a plain wooden box containing also the ashes of their son Tom and the niece Bridget. There in the sacred ground beside the church they were laid to rest forever. Or were they?

As we contemplated the large No Trespassing sign at the gate, suddenly the front door of the church opened and out came a man walking straight toward us. He wore a long black robe and around his neck the Roman collar of the Catholic priest. The crucifix at his side swung vigorously from its chain as he strode nearer and nearer. He was scowling and I admit I was intimidated. We had not got out of the car and as the engine was still on it was a simple matter to press the accelerator and move on before the priest could reach us. But as we slowly drove off, we noticed for the first time the caretaker of the grounds who, it seemed to us, was deliberately scratching away at the fence near the gate with what seemed to me a grim little smile on his face.

While from the road we could see many other tombstones bearing such now familiar names as Toohey, Carroll, McLaughlin, Maher and Quigley, we could not pick out the marker, which appeared on the front cover of Kelley's book. This was understandable, for the Donnelly marker was in the last row but one at the rear of the churchyard cemetery.

Later I discovered, however, that if we had gone into the little cemetery that day, it would have been one of the last times that we could have seen the now famous tombstone standing on its original site. It was only a matter of days before the stone was removed and hidden from sight. The pastor, Father Bricklin—it was he who had come scowling toward us—had lost all patience with the floods of visitors. Taking matters into his own hands, he ordered the grave marker removed. Immediately rumours of its fate abounded. Was it smashed to smithereens? Was it driven off to a remote location and secretly buried? Was it in the church basement? Later I learned from one of the men who helped take it down that day that it was lying intact but in its separate pieces only a few feet away from its original resting place in the large shed at the rear of the churchyard.

From St. Patrick's we drove north along the Roman Line. Guided by a large-scale topographic map on which I had carefully plotted the exact location of the Donnelly homestead (one of the few accurate statements of fact in *The Black Donnellys*), we soon knew we were approaching the Donnelly farm itself. This blood-stained plot of land, the north half of lot 18 in the sixth concession, was a parcel of fifty acres.

Biddulph Township in this area is almost completely flat. The sky seemed vast and foreboding and the Roman Line was silent, hot and sultry as we drove slowly along the gravel road. Signs of the old pioneer homesteads were fast disappearing. Not one in ten houses, barns or orchards was left from the days of the Donnellys. Several of these, standing derelict in the lonely fields, would also soon disappear. No believer in psychic phenomena, yet I felt the silent heat more oppressive and ominous as the Donnelly farm came into view.

Fortunately, the buildings were still there. To be sure, they were not those of a hundred

The Donnelly Schoolhouse, with the Fazakas family picnicking in front.

years before but they seemed old enough. I later learned that the house was in fact the one rebuilt by the surviving Donnellys in 1881 only a few feet from the spot where their parents, brother and cousin had perished. And, a few years following the massacre, Bob Donnelly had lived there for a time after returning from Glencoe before finally moving into the village of Lucan. The land itself remained in the Donnelly name for many long years after he and his surviving brothers and sister had died.

We had brought a picnic lunch and as it was then about mid-day, my wife suggested we stop and spread a blanket at the roadside. This we did, just beyond the farm in front of a little brick schoolhouse, which stood forlorn and abandoned a few feet off the roadway. The schoolyard was overgrown with weeds. At the front peak of the little building a small wooden cross, slightly askew, signified that it had been Catholic in denomination.

Later I learned that this was the Donnelly Schoolhouse built on a corner of the Donnelly farm itself. The original log school, I later learned, had been built in 1851 and first opened to classes in 1852. The schoolyard had been enlarged by a deed to the trustees and signed by Jim Donnelly himself while serving his time in Kingston Penitentiary. In February 1878 the log school burned down and was replaced by the frame structure, which stood before us, the walls of which had been later veneered over with brick.

Between the little school and the roadway we spread our blanket under the shade of a tree. Our six-week-old son, Derek, sat propped in his seat while his sister, Sandy, two and one-half, played in the grass with her five-year-old brother, David.

Although I had been telling my wife little bits of Kelley's book, she herself did not yet know the story and was therefore bemused at my apprehensions when a truck drove by.

The Cedar Swamp Schoolhouse in 1964 with its bell, belfry and front porch intact.

The driver, an elderly man, barely glanced in our direction but the name on the door of the vehicle was clearly visible. It read: "T. TOOHEY."

"Beverley, did you see that?" I said excitedly when the truck was well out of earshot.

My wife was perplexed.

"That was a Toohey truck! Do you realize who that is?" I said. "Why, the Tooheys were leading members of the Vigilance Committee. Maybe their descendants don't like tourists skulking around here like this."

While Beverley laughed at my temerity, I confess to feeling sensitive to this day about intruding on the privacy of the Catholic Settlement of Biddulph. Perhaps it explains the circumspection with which I began to gather information about the Donnelly story. In the months and years that followed, I avoided in most cases the direct approach. Others tried it and were coldly, if not rudely, rebuffed. It was much better, I felt, to be unobtrusive.

From the Donnelly farm site we drove east to the Swamp Line of Biddulph. There we saw the Cedar Swamp Schoolhouse. Below its belfry, the date of its erection in 1874 was clearly proclaimed. Here in the summer and fall five years after that date, the Peace Society of Biddulph were wont to meet and hatch their little plots against the one family in their parish whose members had become anathema. The building itself was a bit grander than the Donnelly School, which I later learned, had not been used since about 1939. Classes in the Cedar Swamp School, on the other hand, had continued until just the year before we first saw it. Along with St. Patrick's School near the church, these were the only schools of the Catholic Settlement of Biddulph.

From the Swamp Line we doubled back to the village of Lucan. According to the sign at its entrance, the population was 900. The number was 300 less than it was during the heyday of the Donnellys. Lucan was a typical small village in rural Ontario. Many old buildings still lined its main street. Several, we felt, went back to at least the 1880s and one, I later learned, was the last home of Bob Donnelly. The Central Hotel at the centre was still thriving but we could see few other signs of the Donnellys in Lucan that day. Over the years, however, I was able to find traces of them in the village even into our own time.

Chapter 3

Jim the Father

One morning I found in the mail a fattish envelope containing a document made in Kingston Penitentiary on Saturday, July 22nd, 1865. Written on this paper were Jim Donnelly's answers to the Liberation Questions[1]— that is the title by which they were headed.

When he was asked if he thought the threat of imprisonment was a deterrence to crime, Donnelly gave the following answer:

> Cannot say. He never heard the like before his misfortune. Dreaded his God more than earthly punishment.

How did he feel when he was first jailed at Goderich?

> The effect was very serious, when reflecting on his unfortunate crime.

But while he may have felt deserving of punishment, Jim Donnelly did not consider himself a criminal of the order of his fellow inmates in Kingston. When asked if he had seen any cruel treatment inflicted upon prisoners in the penitentiary, he replied:

> Have not, nor half so much as many of them deserved.

To the question, Do you think the system adopted in the institution together with the religious instruction tends to reform the prisoners? his answer was:

> Thinks every trouble and pains are taken with them and in many cases without effect.

When asked whether he saw the other prisoners manifest feelings of revenge against the prison staff, he said:

> Has heard the like, and very wrongfully.

As to his own soul, James Donnelly said that as a child the only religious instruction he received (and by implication all that he needed) was given to him by his parish priest.

James Donnelly, Sr., as sketched by author.

And while in prison he met with his clergyman twice a year. On those occasions he would have made confession of his recent sins, been given his penance and received the blessing of the priest.

Did he think his imprisonment had been beneficial from a moral or religious standpoint? His reply was:

> Not more so than before he came here.

The family of James Donnelly always maintained that his conviction for murder was the result, in the words of his son Will, "from an unlucky stroke he gave in liquor".[2] The historical record, however, is quite the

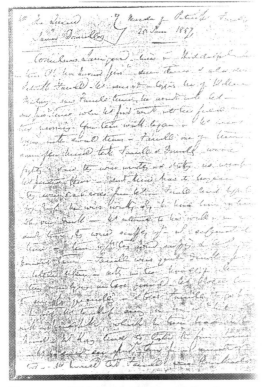

First page of Chief Justice Robinson's bench notes on the 1858 trial in Goderich of James Donnelly for the murder of Patrick Farrell.

And William Maloney testified, "Farrell was drunk—Donnelly let on to be a little high—heard Farrell say before he got the blow that he had enough and would fight no more—think it was Donnelly's intention to pick a quarrel with someone when he came to the bee more than to help to do anything."

Even more damning, however, were Jim Donnelly's own words. Chief Justice John Beverley Robinson recorded them in the notes made in his bench book at the trial for murder in Goderich the following year.[4] Donnelly uttered the words over the body of his victim.

"Pick up this fellow Farrell," he said, "He deserved this five years ago. My children will have satisfaction when I'm in my grave."

Patrick Ryan testified from the witness box at the trial that he heard those words spoken by the accused man. They were addressed, according to Ryan, to the young man named Cornelius Lanigan. Lanigan at the time lived near Farrell and had that morning accompanied the latter to the logging bee.

Other witnesses also testified at the trial of hearing Donnelly speak words to much the same effect immediately after he struck the fatal blow. The bench notes of Chief Justice Robinson recording the testimony of Michael Carroll state:

> Witness heard Donnelly say that it was either 3 or 5 years before that he wished to get back— & that his children would have satisfaction when he prisoner was in the grave.

The judge also recorded Martin Mackey's evidence as follows:

> He [Donnelly] said to witness, 'There's your friend for you now and it's five years ago that he had a wish to do the deed.'

Towards the end of the Crown's case, Mackey was recalled to the witness stand, and testified further as recorded by the trial judge:

> Mackey again—Heard prisoner say this before he went that it was five years ago he had a dispute over that & that he thought he 'had satisfaction'.

opposite. There seems little doubt that James Donnelly, as concluded by the coroner's jury, "feloniously, willfully and of his malice aforethought, did kill and murder" Patrick Farrell.

The killing of Farrell took place on Thursday, the 25th day of June in 1857 at William Maloney's logging bee on the Roman Line of Biddulph Township. Malice aforethought, the essential element of murder, can be deduced from the testimony of at least three of the witnesses at the adjourned inquest[3] held at Patrick Flanagan's Victoria House.

Cornelius Maloney testified, "Deceased was lying down at the time—Donnelly was well able to walk about when he gave the blow—I saw Donnelly leave the field after the deed—he did not stagger any."

Michael Carroll stated in his testimony: "I considered that Donnelly tried most to keep the quarrel going."

Though a man of few words, those which Jim Donnelly did utter, tended towards hyperbole and exaggeration. After Donnelly's return from prison, Jack Casey remembered his coming over to his father's farm one day. Casey had grown up near the Donnellys as his father, Thomas Casey, owned the adjacent farm to the south until Donnelly lost the south half of his homestead. As a near neighbor still—only the lost acreage now intervened between the two farms—Jim Donnelly came over to the Caseys that day to help out in the slaughter of a pig for the pantry. After the carcass had been prepared and hung, Thomas Casey asked Donnelly to stay for the evening meal. The heads of everyone at the table were still bowed for the blessing when Jim Donnelly startled them all by declaring, "I believe in only one God and that's Jim Hodgins. He saved me from the gallows."

During those seven years in Kingston, Jim Donnelly had plenty of time to reflect on his misfortune, as he called it. One of the Liberation Questions posed to him within days of his release wanted to know to what he attributed that misfortune. His answer appeared to acknowledge his deserving of punishment:

> Liquor and passion—for killing a man, but merely the effect of passion.

And what was it like for Donnelly during those seven long years in Kingston Penitentiary? Again, we do not have to guess but can look at the historical record. Donnelly seems to have been a fairly well-behaved prisoner and well-liked by his keepers. The punishment most efficient in maintaining discipline, he thought, was the chain. But the chain was not for him. Other than the confinement itself, he said he had not received further punishment of any kind. To the contrary, he said he never experienced bad treatment by the custodians, and stated:

> He has found them kind to himself. Mr. Whyman who is dead and gone underwent great fatigue and was very kind to him as well as to many others.

The punishment register belies Donnelly's denial of ever receiving punishment in prison as it discloses that several times he was put on bread and water and deprived of his bed. The disciplines were variously for talking—the prison was at the time run on the silent system—or laughing, quarreling while working, refusing to go back to work, for not using a clean shirt left in his cell and for having a vest made from a blanket.

Donnelly found the prison sufficiently well heated and ventilated, although he thought the size of the cells—at that time, two feet and six inches wide by six feet and eight inches long—were "small enough". The food was satisfactory and he found it good. Clothing and bedding were adequate.

Outside (top) and inside (bottom) of one of the original log-lined cells of the Goderich Jail.

Sheriff John McDonald who on August 5 and 6, 1858, escorted James Donnelly by train from Goderich to Kingston Penitentiary.

They did, however, send many letters. They were probably written by Will, the most literate of the boys. The warden read them to Jim Donnelly.

Aside from those two visits and the letters and whispered news or rumors brought by freshly arrived prisoners, he heard nothing from the outside world. But thoughts of freedom on the other side of those high stone walls could not be dimmed.

Donnelly entered the penitentiary on August 6th, 1858 and remained the full seven years. He learned no trade or other occupation there. When asked if he thought he was better qualified to earn a livelihood than when he came there, he answered:

> Is not so well qualified as before he came here being further advanced in years.

Prior to his imprisonment, he said, he had earned his living by "hard Farm Labour" and "will return to his farm labour".

The Liberation Questions from Kingston Penitentiary were a prize but long before that document came to hand and in the days following our first visit to the scene, I began in earnest to search for the real Donnellys. The reference library in Hamilton yielded up a couple of old newspaper clippings and an old *MacLeans Magazine* article. As Kelley's version of events seemed obviously one-sided, I thought perhaps sources of the time would give the arguments on the other side. Old newspaper files were often available on microfilm and I began to pursue them. In my naivety I was surprised to learn that newspapers of the middle and late Victorian age had few pictures and no photographs whatsoever. In the Exeter *Advocate*, for example, the first photograph or half-tone picture—the illustrations we see in our newspapers every day—was published only on October 20th, 1910.[5]

It is true that the newspapers of 1880 such as the Toronto *Mail* and *Globe*, the Hamilton *Spectator* and the London *Free Press* and *Advertiser*, published likenesses of Mr. and Mrs. Donnelly and their sons Tom and Will

The worst privation, he thought, was "the confinement to the cells on Sundays".

He admitted, too, that the presence of visitors who came to gawk at the prisoners for entertainment or for a mere social outing "often tried his feelings as well as those of other convicts".

Did the prisoners nevertheless hold conversations among themselves?

"They do when they get the chance," Donnelly answered, adding that the most talk he ever heard in prison was in the Roman Catholic chapel. And while there may have been mutterings among some of the prisoners against the staff, he knew of no plots being formed against them.

Although the family in Biddulph could ill afford the expense of visiting trips to Kingston, Mrs. Donnelly may have made a couple of them during her husband's sojourn.

as well as John in his coffin. They also published portraits of Jim Carroll, Martin McLaughlin, John Kennedy and others. Such pictures, however, were all engravings or woodcuts transferred to the printed page. Illustrations in the local newspapers previous to the second decade of the twentieth century were almost all engravings or line drawings of this kind.

I soon found some original issues of the London daily newspapers held by the London Library as well as the Regional Collection of the University of Western Ontario. Then one day I happened to be in the town of Simcoe on business and dropped in at the offices of the Simcoe *Reformer* newspaper. Upon inquiring about old back issues, I was directed to a rear room where I found many issues of the Waterford *Review*. This newspaper yielded important details concerning the trial of William Lewis charged with the murder of Michael Donnelly. The stabbing of the young man—he was then only 28—took place in Waterford, Ontario on December 9th, 1879, a few weeks before the massacre at the homestead. Lewis, the newspaper reported, was convicted of manslaughter and sentenced to five years in Kingston Penitentiary. The newspaper editor thought the conviction should have been for murder.

Again, I once happened to visit a backcountry site between the cities of Hamilton and Cambridge known at the time as Wentworth Pioneer Village and later as Westfield Heritage Village. A bundle of old newspapers in a corner of the printing shop caught my eye. Looking more closely, I saw they were the discarded issues of the Exeter *Times* newspaper from the Donnelly era. They were privately owned. Years later I purchased those newspapers from their owner. Now in a bound volume, they included the 1881 issues reporting the trial of James Carroll for the murder of Judith Donnelly.

While the newspaper reports were helpful, much more exciting were the actual documents of the time sometimes containing the very handwriting or signatures of individuals long dead. In the Regional Collection in London was a great treasure trove of such documents from the earliest settlement days by the Europeans of Huron and Middlesex Counties. Biddulph Township, the home of the Donnelly family, was originally in Huron County as part of the great Huron Tract of the Canada Company. In 1863 its citizens chose to take their township out of Huron and join it to Middlesex County. The change was legally effected in 1865. The Regional Collection therefore contains many documents relating to the history of both counties. Included among them were box upon box of tax and assessment records, municipal government documents and papers in countless legal proceedings both civil and criminal. Among the last were informations laying charges, summonses to persons accused, subpoenas to witnesses, sworn statements of complainants as well as those of witnesses and decisions of the various courts from the assize judges of the high court to the lowly local justices of the peace. The parties to

James Donnelly, Sr., as sketched by Robert Harris in 1880, based on descriptions by his survivors.

some of these cases were, of course, the Donnellys themselves.

The Regional Collection also included the correspondence over the years of Charles Hutchinson, the Middlesex county crown attorney for many years both before and after the Donnelly tragedy. From letters exchanged between Hutchinson and Æmilius Irving, retained by the government in 1880 to prosecute the alleged murderers of the Donnellys, we now know that the Crown retained the services of a private detective named Armstrong. Described by Hutchinson as "an intelligent, reliable old man," Armstrong first claimed to have found a blood-stained set of clothing near a little place called Florence, southwest of London, and it was suggested that the Caswell boys who lived near this place had secreted the clothing on their return from "up home" in the first week of February. The Caswells had formerly lived in Biddulph which they always referred to as "up home" and they had never forgotten the persecution inflicted upon them—as was supposed but never proved— by the Donnellys of Biddulph.

William Donnelly did not credit Armstrong's tale. "The Caswells are Orangemen," he said, "and the Catholics of St. Patrick's would never have trusted them." I personally believe Will was right.

Another private detective whom the Crown officials relied on was George Washington Clay, a sometime constable in the environs of London. First, in snooping around the Catholic Settlement, he found a bloodstained frock and a pair of pants in a pile of manure on the farm of James Maher on the Roman Line where James Carroll had made his home upon his coming to Biddulph. As a result of this find, Mrs. Maher and the hired man of the family, an old pensioner named James Shea, were arrested. Again, the bloody clothing came to nothing and Mrs. Maher and Shea were soon released.

Detective Clay then traced to Detroit a man who claimed to have been present at the massacre and knew all about it. Clay wrote to Hutchinson from Detroit and the latter sent a man after him but Clay in the meantime had gone to Cleveland. There the supposed witness whom Clay had been chasing revealed himself as a sometime driver on the Lucan to London stagecoach. He said his name was Hyland and that he had worked for Flanagan. Again, Hutchinson checked the lead with William Donnelly. Donnelly said he knew no one by that name who had driven stage. The crown authorities thereupon dropped the matter. Their decision was reinforced by suggestions that the clothes found at Maher's had been put there by Clay himself.

Curiously, however, the papers still on file at the Regional Collection in London reveal that there was indeed a man who had been a driver for Flanagan's stagecoach who went by the name of Franklin B. Hyland. Hyland had testified against Thomas, James and John Donnelly when they were charged with the burning of Patrick Flanagan's stables in Lucan in October 1875. He so signed his name on the deposition he made in the case. Five years later, however, no one remembered this.

Much of what we know about the Donnelly story comes from depositions made in court cases. A deposition, such as an affidavit, is simply a statement in a court proceeding, which has been reduced to writing and sworn to under oath. It is, in other words, a short note of what the witness said, often not word-for-word but nevertheless containing the gist of his or her testimony. The depositions were often written by the presiding magistrate, justice of the peace or the coroner presiding at an inquest. What sometimes makes them more interesting is that some of the justices of the peace were themselves barely literate. For example, Patrick McIlhargey who heard in his court some of the petty litigation arising out of the troubles in and around Lucan in the 1870s, would write—and the quotation is given without spelling corrections—the following:[6]

View inside the main gates of Kingston Penitentiary in the nineteenth century.

Province of Canada

Patrick Keeffe, of the township of Biddulph, county of Middlesex, has come before me this day & sayeth that he is not gilty of the charge laid against him by William thorp, & that he does verley blive that it is for the purpose of extorting money & for no other purpose the above charge was being made.

Taking and sworing on the 17 february 1879 at biddulph.

[signed] Patrick Keeffe

P. McIlhargey, J.P.

The charge by Thorpe in this case was for the rape of the complainant's wife.

As longhand can rarely keep up with the spoken word, the handwriting in some cases is barely decipherable. By contrast, the writing of William Porte, the village postmaster who was sometimes engaged by the Lucan justices of the peace to record the evidence was in a classic, almost copperplate, hand which is instantly recognizable from its wide, well-formed letters.

And there are caches of papers other than in London. In Toronto I found a store of papers in the basement of Osgoode Hall. Here the assize notebooks of the High Court judges—the so-called Red Books—lay untouched for decades. They were at the time not open to the public without special permission from the Chief Justice of Ontario. This finally granted, it turned out that the basement had in the meantime been flooded and the Red Books had been packed off for storage until renovations to the venerable old structure could be made. Finally after many months of waiting, they were returned and I was allowed to look at them. Among those I inspected were the trial notes of Justice Matthew Cameron in the case of William Lewis tried for the murder of Michael Donnelly, Justice John D. Armour's notes on the first trial of James Carroll and the notes of Justices Featherston Osler and Cameron again on Carroll's second trial.

Jack Casey in 1936 at his home on Alice Street, Lucan, and (inset) as a young man.

Chapter 4

Mother Judy

I had often wondered about the validity of this statement made about the character of the matriarch of the Donnellys of Biddulph:[1]

> [T]here has been built by the family's detractors a whole body of false legend picturing her as the evil genius of the family, a backwoods Lady Macbeth implacably urging her browbeaten husband and sons on to ever greater and even more outrageous deeds of rapine and cruelty. The portrait is absolutely without basis and an unspeakably vicious and wanton tampering with the facts.

One person who knew Mrs. Donnelly well was Jack Casey whom I have already mentioned. He was born in 1863 to Thomas Casey and Ellen Heffernan and grew up on the farm south of the Donnelly homestead. The property was immediately adjacent to the Donnelly homestead in the early days and it was only the loss of Donnelly's south fifty acres which caused a separation between the two farms. When the two were still clearing the fronts of their respective lots, Tom Casey and Jim Donnelly had only one horse each. They thereupon teamed them up and took turns plowing each other's fields. The two families always remained friends. Even after the Caseys moved into Lucan in 1878, Jack Casey would return often to the Roman Line to work as a hired man.

Following the tragedy in 1880, Jack Casey left his native land for Detroit and then Cleveland. In the 1930s he returned to Biddulph and worked for several years as a hired man for the Hodgins families. When Casey retired from hard labor and settled down on Alice Street in Lucan with his third wife, Wilhelmina Hodgins, he served as the Lucan constable even at the advanced age of 85 years. He died in 1958 at 95 years of age.

In his later years he would often return to play cards with his former employees, the Hodgins families, with whom he had become close friends. Always a great raconteur, Casey told many stories of his early days on the Roman Line. One who heard those tales was Arnold A. Hodgins, son of Eli Hodgins. And while it is not surprising that Jack Casey spoke often of the Donnelly family, what is a little surprising is that almost invariably he spoke well of them. They were not, according to him, heartless monsters devoid of human feelings. The boys were fun-loving Irishmen and, yes, they were fond of a good fight.

Although Jack Casey died four years

Mrs. Donnelly

before publication in 1962 of Orlo Miller's *The Donnellys Must Die*, Arnold A. Hodgins read the book and then wrote Miller a letter[2] stating that the facts set out in the book more or less accorded with the version of the Donnelly story as related over the years by Jack Casey except in one instance. In that one instance, wrote Hodgins, the two versions differed sharply.

What the point of difference was Hodgins did not specify, but I have discovered it from different sources. One such was William Kilmer, born in 1924 on a farm outside Clandeboye and raised in and around Lucan. Bill Kilmer was only one of many persons to whom I spoke or communicated with over the years who confirmed that, according to Jack Casey, Mrs. Donnelly was a hellion.[3] That was Casey's way of describing her. It was she who kept the pot boiling, who insisted that her boys left no slight unanswered or wrong unavenged and constantly urged them at every turn to defy their enemies.

This was the opinion of Jack Casey who knew Mrs. Donnelly well. He said these things and many others, not with malicious intent but simply as his own personal observations. According to Casey, Mrs. Donnelly—he never heard her called Johannah but only Judith or Judy—had many admirable qualities. She was strong not only physically but in character and prepared to stand up against overwhelming odds. Fiercely protective of her children when they were left vulnerable and defenseless by their father's flight and later imprisonment, she refused to sink into despair but sprang immediately to his defense. Without stint or pause, she immediately shouldered the heavy burden of maintaining the backwoods farm which at that time was barely cleared enough of its forest cover to support a growing family. She made payments on the farm and continued to feed and clothe the children though the youngest, Janey, was barely out of the suckling stage. In addition, she embarked upon vigorous campaigns, first to save her husband from the gallows, and then to have him released from the penitentiary before his term had ended. The first efforts were successful, the second failed. Government records show that in 1860 she forwarded a petition to have the balance of his term of imprisonment remitted. When this was denied, she caused another to be sent in 1862. It, too, was denied.

"When you and all the rest of the boys were children," she once told her son Will, "I often took the light at midnight to look at you taking a happy sleep, full of the hope that I might live to see you all men."[4]

Shortly after her death, her daughter wrote:[5] "James [my husband] told me that William has preserved one of the bones of my poor mother's arm and if so when he comes to St. Thomas let him bring it with him so that I may kiss the loving arm that never failed to throw its protection around and provide for all of us in the darkest days of our need."

For a female of that Victorian age, Judith

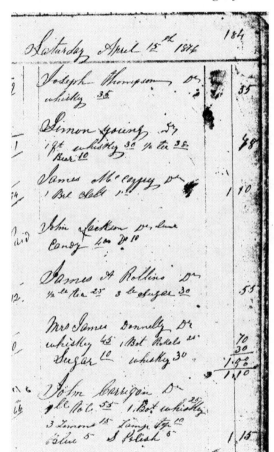

Mrs. Donnelly's purchases from Lucan grocer, Patrick Bruin, as shown in his ledger book.

Donnelly had a forward and brash demeanor. Although it endeared her to many of her sons' youthful companions, it made a bad impression on so-called respectable members of society. Nevertheless, she had a big heart for those who were friends of the family. She greeted those warmly and treated them well. The young men of the neighborhood admired her masculine will and she inspired

Mrs. Patrick Whelan

towards her in particular rather than to her husband or to the old couple together.

There seems little doubt that Judith Donnelly was a hard talker. On October 16th, 1878 James Carroll was making a sworn complaint before the London Justice of the Peace, John Peters.

"Their mother called me a son of a bitch, a thief and a rogue," he swore.[7] Later, he added the epithet "blackguard" to the list.

Many stories are told of Mrs. Donnelly's penchant for "jawing" at someone who had displeased her. Mrs. John Carroll, a near neighbor who lived across the road from her on the Roman Line said that following the Peace Society's invasion of the Donnelly homestead in search of the Thompson cow in September 1879, Mrs. Donnelly came out on the road later that day. She was in a passion and seemed particularly incensed at Jim Ryder, son of Grouchy, whom she had considered up to that time a good friend.

She told Mrs. Carroll: "I'll go out on the road and meet young Grouch, put a blush on his face and make him lie back in his grand buggy."[8]

Years before, John Cain had wanted to sell his farm—the same fifty acres of land lost by Donnelly to Michael Maher—but the prospective purchaser was scared off. According to Cain, he saw Mrs. Donnelly confront the man on the road. Although he could not hear the words spoken, he saw her "jawing" the man, implying that she was scaring him off with threats.

Other neighbors who knew Judith Donnelly well were the Whelans. Patrick Whelan and his wife, Anne Cooney, were early settlers in Biddulph who first took up a farm near the church. One year after the birth of their daughter Theresa in 1862, they sold the farm and moved to a new place on the Roman Line, which happened to be directly opposite the Donnelly homestead. At this time Mrs. Donnelly was struggling to raise her own family and hang on to the farm until her imprisoned husband completed his sentence. Little Theresa Whelan grew up

in them a fierce loyalty. Jim Feeheley, for example, stated on his cross-examination that he went over to the Donnelly place on the evening of February 3rd, 1880 within hours of the massacre "merely to sympathize with Mrs. Donnelly"[6] over her tribulations arising out of the charge of arson then pending against her and her husband. It is true his stated motive on this occasion may not have been genuine, yet it shows Feeheley's relationship to her as a close friend: it was not strange for his sympathy to be directed across the road from the Donnellys. She and her parents and brothers helped out the Donnellys from time to time and were in turn helped out by them. Although they traded hands at harvest time it was true, as Mrs. Whelan said, that "the boys would sometimes have a tiff".

On the very Christmas before the tragedy, Mrs. Whelan was friendly enough to be found visiting in Mrs. Donnelly's home.

Theresa Whelan

There was an easy but careful familiarity between them, and she usually called her Mrs. Donnelly rather than the more familiar Judith or Judy by which, for example, Mary O'Connor of Lucan addressed her. It was Mr. and Mrs. Patrick Whelan and their daughter, Theresa, then 17, who met young Johnny O'Connor the night he scrambled over to their home from the burning log house across the road where the flames were then licking up to the dead or dying Donnellys. And it was Theresa's hat that O'Connor wore home to Lucan that morning.

Theresa's daughter, Mary Antaya, told me what her mother and grandmother thought of Mrs. Donnelly, having got to know her well during the sixteen or so years they lived across the road from her. She was, they said, the energy behind not only the family's success in their early years but also its great misfortune later. In their view, it was Judith Donnelly who encouraged her sons in their reckless escapades. When she became aware of some devilment they might be planning, not only did she fail to berate them for undertaking it but admonished them not to fail in its implementation.

Mrs. Whelan said that she well remembered the time that one of the boys was accused of shooting at the Lucan constable, Sam Everett. It was Tom or Bob, she said, who was going out to do the job but dressed in another's clothes.

Coins excavated from the site of the Donnelly house.

"If it has to be done, then do a good job of it," were the words that Mrs. Whelan said she heard Mrs. Donnelly tell her son.

One quiet Sunday afternoon on the Whelan farm, Theresa and her brothers had some young friends over from up the road to play cards when Mrs. Donnelly happened to drop over.

"I'm surprised at you, Mrs. Whelan," she said in her busybody way, "letting the young people play cards on a Sunday."

Stung by the rebuke, Mrs. Whelan answered sharply, "Well, Mrs. Donnelly, at least I know what my children are up to."

From Theresa Whelan's daughter I also learned the answer to a little nagging puzzle about Judith Donnelly's physical appearance. Many times I had heard it said by someone whose mother or grandmother had known her that "she was shifty-eyed", "she would not look you straight in the face" or "you could tell from looking at her she could not be trusted". The truth is that Mrs. Donnelly

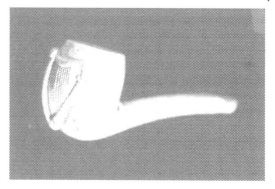

Mrs. Donnelly's pipe.

suffered from a condition known as strabismus—a congenital defect in which one of the six eye muscles is weaker than the others resulting in the eye wandering off the mark, usually to the outside. A person with this condition appears not to look you in the eyes.

One more person who had a strong opinion about Judy Magee's character was Catherine Currie. Catherine was not her sworn enemy but twice related by marriage: she was sister to James Currie who had married Jenny Donnelly as well as to Annie Currie who had married Bob Donnelly. Her opinion of Mrs. Donnelly, as related by her daughter,[9] was this:

> Mrs. Donnelly was the brains as well as the trouble-maker of the family. She was the she-wolf who put the boys on the wrong track. Although she was a handsome woman, even in her later years, she had terribly strong eyes. And when she got mad, she could become very mean.

Over the years, I have heard much the same opinions of Mrs. Donnelly's character expressed not by descendants of the vigilante families but by those who were at least neutral between the protagonists or outside the feud altogether.

Physically, Mrs. Donnelly was not a heavy-set woman but rather "tall and raw-boned" in the words of one woman who knew her, and "lean and rangy" in the words of another.

"I could tell it was her lying near the kitchen door by the length of her limbs," said Patrick Whelan when he looked into the burning house.

Her grandson, Mike Currie, seldom volunteered information about his grandmother but on one rare occasion he did say that she was taller than her husband Jim. And in one of his more expansive moments of reflection he offered the further observation: "My grandmother smoked a clay pipe—and it had an Irish harp on it." Such information was, of course, learned from his mother.

Mrs. Donnelly as she has come down to us from unflattering verbal portraits painted by unsympathetic authors like Thomas P. Kelley.

Chapter 5

Land and Religion

In the bench notes of Chief Justice Robinson written in Goderich at the trial of James Donnelly for murder, an allusion was made to a dispute between Donnelly and Patrick Farrell three or five years prior to the fatal logging bee held on June 25th, 1857. At the trial the widow of the victim, Sarah Farrell, testified that the dispute was over a parcel of land.

Land was at the root of most disputes in the Catholic Settlement of Biddulph. And it was land that entangled Jim Donnelly not only with Patrick Farrell but with another who became his bitter enemy, one Michael Maher. Except for his lawsuit to oust Donnelly from the south half of his homestead, for years I could find little trace of Michael Maher in Biddulph. Then in 1994 a new genealogical magazine, *Irish Roots*, published my brief article on the Donnelly story, which I wrote specifically to arouse interest among descendants of the families of the Catholic Settlement in Ireland as well as in the United States and Australia[1] where the new magazine began to have a wide circulation.

Soon I was corresponding with several individuals from those places. One was Sharon Linares of Cleveland, Ohio who had been researching her own family. She wrote that it seemed like a coincidence but her great great grandfather had once settled in Canada. His name was Michael Maher and his farm was located at lot 18 in concession 6 in a township called Biddulph. The lot and concession numbers jumped out at me from her letter and I knew immediately this Michael Maher was the same man who had ousted Jim Donnelly from one-half his homestead in 1856. From Sharon and her uncle, Frank Maher of California, I learned that Michael Maher had been born in the townland of Cloonanagh in Ireland being in the parish of Dunkerrin, which was the birthplace of Judy Magee. Maher also emigrated to America about the same time as Donnelly and perhaps his wife and child. He did not, however, find his way immediately to Biddulph, for in 1844 Maher married Ellen Woods in Halifax, Nova Scotia. The couple then spent time in Vermont and Connecticut but 1852 found them in a one-storey log cabin in the township of Westminster south of the city of London, Canada West. Here they kept a small tavern or store and by this time had three children aged 6, 4 and 2. From Westminster, Maher moved his family to London Township and in 1856 purchased from John Grace, of the same place, the south half of lot eighteen in the sixth concession of Biddulph. This was the homestead of James Donnelly.

Frankly, I am not at all certain how the dealings between James Donnelly, Patrick

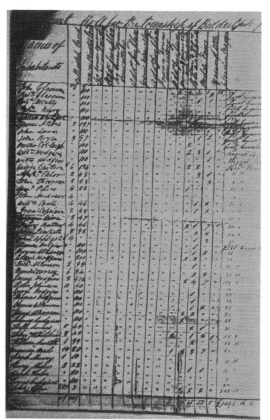

This 1835 assessment roll is one of Biddulph Township's earliest.

Farrell, Michael Maher and John Grace are intertwined. With one's present incomplete knowledge of the facts, therefore, one can only speculate. My present belief is that there were at least two parcels of land involved. In

for on the books of the Canada Company a lease had been issued to him in 1843.

Whoever the legal owner was, the township property assessor showed Donnelly as owner of the entire one hundred acres in 1845, the whole parcel at that time being like most of the other lots around it still covered with forest. A little later, Donnelly may have learned of Fogarty's claim. As he had not yet gone to reside on the lot, he appears to have abandoned it on account of the unclear title. Instead, in 1847, Donnelly laid claim to lot 21 in the seventh concession, which was a little further south and across the road from his original choice. That year John Grace, not a settler but a non-resident land speculator, may have acquired Fogarty's rights as he was then shown as the assessed owner of lot 18 in the sixth.

James Donnelly, Jr., in working clothes as a hired man of the Hodgins family, is the only known photograph of the eldest son, taken by an itinerant tintype artist.

When Patrick Farrell appeared in the Catholic Settlement looking for land upon which to settle his family, he appears to have made an agreement with Donnelly to buy the rights to lot 21. On the strength of this deal, Donnelly agreed to swap rights with Grace in return for his first choice of land. Under this arrangement, Donnelly would get possession of his preferred lot 18 in the sixth and Grace, the land speculator, would obtain lot 21 in the seventh with the added bonus to the latter that there was already a buyer for this lot, Patrick Farrell. Thus Donnelly took possession and in 1848 was assessed as the

1845 upon his first becoming acquainted with the Canada Company lands in Biddulph Township, James Donnelly laid claim to lot eighteen in the sixth concession. The story goes that James Hodgins, then acting as agent for the land company, directed Donnelly to this particular lot, which had supposedly been abandoned by the previous claimant. That person appears to have been Patrick Fogarty,

This is a charge of threatening laid by Michael Maher against Jim Donnelly, Jr.

owner of lot 18 in the sixth while Grace was assessed for lot 21 in the seventh concession.

Shortly afterwards, Patrick Farrell brought his family to Biddulph. He soon discovered that not only did Donnelly have no legal claim to the parcel which he purported to sell to him—except a certain repute in the neighborhood—but that there was available a lot which looked to have better prospects. The new lot—number 20 in the seventh concession—lay directly across the sideroad from the one that Donnelly claimed to have sold him. Farrell quickly threw over the agreement with Donnelly and just as briskly made an agreement with the Canada Company for its lot 20, and here on this new lot Farrell settled down.

The bargain between Donnelly and Farrell had probably been oral only and therefore not legally binding. Its repudiation by Farrell infuriated Donnelly. It put into jeopardy the latter's own bargain with Grace over lot 18 in the sixth. Donnelly took a pot-shot at his now sworn enemy. Farrell hauled Donnelly up before the magistrates who put him on his bonds to keep the peace.

In the meantime Grace was also aggrieved as he no longer had vacant possession of the lot to which he held the paper rights— Donnelly had moved in as soon as he had made the deal with Farrell—and with Farrell taking up the new lot, he no longer had a buyer for the one he had obtained from Donnelly in the exchange. Naturally then, Grace also repudiated the transaction he had made with Donnelly over lot 18 in the sixth. He sold one-half of it to his neighbor in London Township, another newcomer to the area named Michael Maher. When Donnelly refused to vacate, Grace and Maher both brought legal action for eviction.[2] The proceedings were eventually compromised by Donnelly's agreeing to give up the south half of lot 18 to the newcomer Maher and paying or promising to pay Grace for the north half. This was the situation when Jim Donnelly met and killed Patrick Farrell at William Maloney's logging bee on June 25th, 1857.

Michael Maher took possession of the south half of lot eighteen, but even though his next-door neighbor was eventually apprehended and sent to Kingston Penitentiary, his tenure on the Roman Line was an uneasy one. On August 16th, 1864 Maher went before the justices of the peace to complain that James Donnelly, Jr., then twenty-three years old, had threatened to "take the life of the said complainant before long and that he would shoot him". Not long afterwards, with the prospect of the senior Donnelly about to return home, Michael Maher decided to pack up his family and leave. First he attempted to sell the farm to his cousin, James Maher, of Stephen Township. The Donnellys refused to allow it. Eventually they permitted a very young man named John Cain to occupy the place but continued to nurse the resolve once more to hold all of the original soil of their homestead. Michael Maher moved his family to Bay City, Michigan and there he died the following year.

The close proximity of the birthplaces of both Michael Maher and Judy Magee—the same parish of Dunkerrin—brought up another issue, which had bothered me for

29

Tombstone of Michael Maher in Bay City, Michigan.

years. How true was the assertion pronounced over and over again by authors and others, often with little or no evidence, that the feud between the Donnellys and their enemies had been brought over from the old country and specifically from Tipperary?

Perhaps because of these stories, for many years I felt an undercurrent in the Donnelly story that I was unable to put my finger on. In a nutshell, the Donnellys often seemed to conduct themselves as if they were half-Protestant. I cite the following examples: (1) The story which over the years I have heard several times of the boys rolling into a Catholic dance and one of them, John or Will, confronting the little band and demanding they play *The Protestant Boys*, a well-known Orange tune. When the band members demur, Donnelly pulls out a pistol and fires a shot into the ceiling, after which the band is soon playing the requested melody. (2) At harvest and other appropriate times on the farm, the family did not mind helping out the Orangemen such as the Kent, Haskett and Cornish families in Biddulph and Usborne. (3) As late as January 1880—a week

or two before their deaths—at least one Orangeman was standing bail for James and Judith Donnelly on the Ryder barn-burning charge. (4) Robert is not a common Irish Catholic given name—at least among the Irish Catholics of Biddulph Township[3]—yet here it is in the Donnelly family. (5) Patrick Donnelly and his first wife, Mary Ryan, were married in St. James *Anglican* Church in Biddulph. (6) Of the five Donnelly boys who took wives, three of them did not hesitate to marry Protestant girls.

In the early years of my research, I attributed these seeming anomalies to the assertion by Zackariah McIlhargey that Mrs. Donnelly had been a Protestant. Zack, a Biddulph Old Boy, had told this to Spencer Sceli who relayed it to me. Zack was a young man of twenty-seven when the Donnellys were murdered. As his parents had been friendly with the family, he himself knew every one of them and his story therefore seemed credible. Something must have been lost in the re-telling, however, as new information came to light that proved

Zackariah McIlhargey

30

Mr. Wm. Ashbury, who died on the Market Square on Tuesday, was a full first cousin to James Donnelly, who was murdered in Biddulph on the 4th of February, 1880. Mr. Donnelly's mother was a full sister to Mr. Ashbury's father.

The London *Free Press* item of Thursday, September 5, 1889 mentioned in the text.

beyond all doubt that Judith Donnelly had been born, raised and remained a Catholic her entire life. The theory had to be revised. For a time then I attributed the suspicious conduct to the aggressive reaction of the family to at least some degree of ostracizing which naturally followed the conviction for murder of the head of the family. But I bore this theory uneasily.

Then out of the blue one day[4] came the revelation that Mrs. Donnelly was indeed a member of a Protestant Orange family after all. It was not, however, the *wife* of James

William Ashbury

Donnelly who came from an Orange Protestant family but his *mother*.

This startling revelation came to light in a small item of the London *Free Press* of Thursday, September 5th, 1889 which stated:

> Mr. Wm. Ashbury, who died on the Market Square on Tuesday, was a full first cousin to James Donnelly, who was murdered in Biddulph on the 4th of February 1880. Mr. Donnelly's mother was a full sister to Mr. Ashbury's father.

In Goodspeed's 1889 *History of the County of Middlesex*, I found a biography of William Ashbury, part of which reads at page 720 as follows:

> William Ashbury, capitalist, is the oldest man in point of residence in London, Ont., and is a native of the County of Tipperary, Ireland. At an early day he was deprived of a father's care by death, and he came with his mother and brothers and sisters to Canada, and settled in London in 1833 . . . .

At the time of Ashbury's funeral, the London *Advertiser* of Wednesday, September 4, 1889 reported that:

> His blacksmith shop was on Dundas street about where McPherson's dry goods store is now, and next stood Mr. James Gillean's book store.

William Ashbury who began his working life as a blacksmith but later became a real estate salesman, had no children but left as his heirs several nephews and a niece. He died a wealthy man, reported by the newspaper to be worth over $100,000—an enormous sum in 1889. He died of a heart attack while strolling with his two pet dogs through the London market.

I confess I was at first skeptical of this startling discovery. Upon checking my Irish notes, however, I found that in the years 1837 to 1844 there were indeed mentions of Ashburys in or around Borrisokane in either the Outrage Reports at Dublin Castle or in the newspaper that reported the news of the area. Some of these little mentions are as follows:

. . . Finnoe Townland of Rodeen . . . Robbery of Arms . . . 2nd instant three men armed . . . came to the house of Thomas Ashbury, gatekeeper to Joseph Falkner, Esq., of Rodeen . . . placed Ashbury on his knees . . . took away two guns and a shot pouch . . . J. H. Bracken, Chief Constable Borrisokane, January 4, 1837 [*recte*, 1838] . . . since writing the foregoing report, the Police stationed at Kilbarron brought in three men . . . one of them named Meara, has been fully identified by Ashbury and his wife . . .
(Outrage Reports, 1838, Tipperary 14415C)

From our Borrisokane Correspondent. House-breaking—Plunder of Fire Arms, and Robbery. On last Wednesday . . . house of Mr. Thomas Ashbury, of Rodeen, was broken into . . . Mr. and Mrs. Ashbury were both at the fair of Borrisokane.
(Nenagh *Guardian*, September 28, 1838)

On Sunday night last about 9 o'clock, some countrymen were going home from Borrisokane, one of them to all appearances tipsy, shouted for an Orangeman in passing Robert Ashbury's house, at the same time the fellow stooped for a stone and threw it . . . left a deep impression in the door. Charles Ashbury, the son, had a narrow escape . . . Ashbury's house is in the suburbs of Borrisokane.
(Nenagh *Guardian*, September 3, 1845)

William Ashbury, of London, Ontario, appears to have been born about 1815,[5] which conforms nicely with the date of birth of his first cousin, James Donnelly of Biddulph, supposedly born in 1816. We know, too, from his biography in Goodspeed that William Ashbury's father, brother of James Donnelly's mother, was dead by 1833. This father could have been born around 1780 or thereabouts as his widow, who came to Canada with her children was listed as 78 in the 1861 census of London. She was 88 in the 1871 census and presumably born about 1783. Although Mother Donnelly, nee Ashbury, must also have been born before 1800, there is a lot yet to be discovered about the Ashbury family.[6]

As first cousins, it is not unlikely that William Ashbury and James Donnelly were familiar with each other as they were growing up in Borrisokane or its adjacent townlands. Ashbury was about 17 when he arrived in London, Canada West, where he remained the rest of his life. His early blacksmith shop was on Dundas Street close to the London market and it is likely his residence was adjacent or very close by. William Donnelly's daughter, Jo-Anna, told Scott Garrett that the first house the Donnellys occupied in Canada in the mid-1840s was opposite the London market on Dundas Street. It is therefore logical to assume that on his arrival from Ireland, James Donnelly may have looked up his first cousin in London and that the latter

John Ashbury's marker in Jerseyville Cemetery, Ancaster.

accommodated the new arrivals. The first house which the Donnellys occupied in Canada may well have been one supplied by Jim's cousin, William Ashbury, opposite the London market. It is even possible that William Donnelly, born in London in 1846, was named after William Ashbury.

32

Derrinvohill House, near Borrisokane, the residence of the Donnelly family in 1823.

If that is so, while the Ashbury and Donnelly families may have been close at first they appear to have drifted apart in later years. What may have happened is that the relatives in Ireland may have informed the Ashburys in Canada that Donnelly had fled his native land under a cloud. Then when he was later convicted of the murder of Patrick Farrell and sentenced to be hanged, the paths of the two families fell forever apart. The only glimmer of the close relationship came shortly after the death of William Ashbury in 1889 when someone let slip the secret. My hunch is that it was the nephew who came rushing back from Chicago upon hearing of his rich uncle's death. Whoever let out the secret was soon hushed up for it was never again referred to in public.

I find it curious that William Ashbury's heirs lived in places like Campbellville, Oakville, Beverly, Waterdown, Carlisle, East Flamborough and Ancaster, near where I happen to live.[7]

A small confirmation of the supposed identity of the parents of Jim Donnelly as claimed by the Ashbury family came to light when a baptismal record from Borrisokane parish turned up not long before publication of the second revision of this book. In this record, a Michael Donnelly was baptized on September 30, 1823. The father of the child was John Donnelly and the mother's maiden name was Ashbury, her given name being illegible in the original record. The residence of the parents was shown as Derinavola. There is little question that the name of the place written in the record as Derinavola is in fact Derrinvohill which is very close to Borrisokane. Derrinvohill is the name of a townland and a fairly substantial stone house which sits upon it. It is also a name which will come up again in Chapter 15. I speculate that the parents of the child Michael were also the parents of James Donnelly of Biddulph.

Chapter 6

Toohey Trouble

There is little doubt that County Tipperary in the nineteenth century was notorious for its violence. It was called "the cockpit of the country" and had always been a thorn in the side of Robert Peel. He had served at Dublin Castle as the Chief Secretary of Ireland, the *de facto* governor of the country, and in 1829 he wrote:[1]

> My opinion is decidedly in favour of putting down by any means (justifiable of course in the eyes of the law) the insurrectionary spirit of Tipperary. That county is by far the most troublesome county in Ireland . . . .

The Nenagh *Guardian* newspaper reported many occurrences in the parishes of North Tipperary of serious injuries and even homicides that arose out of trivial incidents. In the year 1838, for example, the newspaper told of a couple of men who were severely beaten at Kilmastulla, in one of those parishes. The report stated:[2]

> P. Hayes's skull was so severely fractured he was not expected to recover—FOR REFUSING TO DRINK O'CONNELL'S HEALTH!!

In the first half of the nineteenth century, at the time of this occurrence, Daniel O'Connell was the great popular hero of the Irish Catholic masses. Whenever he passed through North Tipperary on the way to his ancestral home in County Kerry, all work came to a standstill, as everyone had to gather on the streets to watch his coach pass by. O'Connell came from a prominent Catholic landed family of County Kerry and became a very successful criminal lawyer and political activist. He organized the Catholic Association and raised funds by requiring each peasant to pay a penny a month in dues. O'Connell made every priest in Ireland an honorary member and to show their appreciation, each Sunday the priests cajoled their parishioners to pay those dues, the so-called Catholic Rent, and passed them on to O'Connell's organization. The vast sums so raised enabled O'Connell to give up his lucrative law practice in order to devote his full energies to the Catholic cause.

After the Glorious Revolution in England of 1688, which included the banishment of the Catholic Stuart line from the kingdoms of England, Scotland and Ireland, Catholicism in Ireland was suppressed by the enactment of a series of statutes known as the Penal Laws. The laws severely discriminated against Catholics in fields of inheritance, land-owning, entry into the professions and the like. Priests were required to register and their number was limited. Although the penal laws were allowed to wane after many decades, remnants of the penalties under them persisted into the first part of the nineteenth century.

One of these was, in effect, a prohibition against Catholics sitting in Parliament. In 1828 O'Connell made a frontal attack on the legal obstacle by running for a seat in the House. Elected, he refused to take the required oath denouncing his own religion and was forbidden to take his seat. The people elected him again. The following year the government headed by the Duke of Wellington and Robert Peel, grudgingly gave in by passing the Emancipation Act. George IV, defender of the Protestant faith, was furious. When O'Connell entered the room in which the monarch was holding his levee, the king spat out the words, "There is O'Connell! God damn the scoundrel!"

Scoundrel or not, O'Connell had gained a victory and for a period of years collaborated with the Whigs against the Tories of Peel. The Englishman and the Irishman hated each other. Almost from the first, O'Connell referred to him derisively as "Orange Peel". Peel's smile, O'Connell said, reminded him of "the silver plate on a coffin". For years they traded insults and once, in 1815, Peel challenged O'Connell to a duel. The ground could not be in England or Ireland as dueling was illegal in both countries. Peel stipulated France and went there to await his opponent—but he waited in vain. O'Connell's enemies sneered that he had deliberately got himself arrested to prevent the meeting with Peel, and the circumstances indicate there may be some truth in this. On the other hand, earlier that year O'Connell had killed another opponent in a duel and he had no further stomach for that gentlemanly barbarity.

The popularity of Daniel O'Connell in Ireland was still at its height when, just before the great famine of 1845 to 1849, James Donnelly and Judy Magee, like thousands of others emigrated to Canada. Despite his popularity, the Liberator could not single-handedly change the course of history to give the young couple and their first child a good enough future in the old land. When they and the other thousands left for America, they took with them their language and their culture including the customs, morality and superstitions of their homeland.[3]

Those Irish from North Tipperary also brought with them their religion. In Biddulph, the Roman Catholic parish of St. Patrick's was soon established. The year, as declared on the sign which we saw posted there on our first visit, was 1845. That the society in that parish had lost none of the turbulent spirit of Tipperary, however, is exemplified by an incident, which occurred there in 1850. The event was the wedding of Patrick Toohey and Catherine Tierney.[4] The pastor of the parish, Father James O'Flynn, boarded with the family of Patrick Nangle whose home stood across the road from the church, which may then have been under construction and not yet finished. In mid-November the father of the bride, Cornelius Tierney, sent over to the priest the marriage fee of one British sovereign, which was then equivalent to five dollars. On the prescribed day the young couple, accompanied by the wedding crowd, presented themselves at Nangle's house for the ceremony to take

Daniel O'Connell, the champion of the common people and the "uncrowned King of Ireland" sported this luxurious whig to hide his baldness.

place. O'Flynn first called the youthful pair alone into the house. He informed them that the marriage fee was nine dollars and he would require four dollars more. The young man went outside to inform his father, Dennis Toohey, Sr.

The father had been born in Tipperary in the year of the rebellion of 1798. He had in the Old Country suffered, as he saw it, not only the injustices of English law but what he considered the exorbitance of his own parish priests. He was outraged at the demand for the higher fee. He herded his son—now surrounded by his brothers Timothy, Michael and Dennis, Jr.—back to the door, accompanied by the bride's father, Cornelius Tierney and the latter's brother, Thomas Tierney. The priest met them at the door with cane in hand.

"They came to bully me into compliance with their wishes," he later deposed in his complaint, "and to force me by threats to marry a couple for any fee they pleased, contrary to the law of the diocese." The crowd protested that nine dollars was too much for a marriage. The priest remained

The bridal couple of this chapter, in later years, are Patrick Toohey, seated on the right, with the hand of the bride, Catherine Tierney, on his shoulder. Behind Patrick is his sister, Julia Toohey, widow of Charles Keefe. Seated on the left is the groom's brother, Timothy Toohey, and standing behind him is his wife, Mary Ryder.

had to take hold of his own brother, Thomas, as if to push him away from a direct confrontation with the priest. At the same time he said, "Father, I want no disturbance. I will give you my note rather than see my daughter not married. Please marry them as steady as ye can."

"No," replied the priest, "I want Mr. Toohey's note."

"I will not give it," Toohey declared. "My word is good enough."

The crowd then pushed into the house. The priest ordered them out. The senior Toohey then retorted, "I will not go out as this is not your house. It is Pat Nangle's house."

Father Flynn thereupon lost his temper. "I will not be run over by a factious mob," he cried. He raised his cane to strike the older man but the knob of the cane struck the low-beamed ceiling and broke off. The priest then seized hold of old Toohey to try to push him out. Toohey's sons, however, jumped in and took hold of the priest.

"Marry them or give back the money," old Toohey cried out.

adamant. The older Toohey then offered to let the priest keep the sovereign already handed over if he would accept his promise of payment of the priest's board to Nangle in the amount of four dollars. The priest, not trusting Toohey's word, refused.

The wedding party then stiffened and began to look belligerent. The bride's father

The rest of the crowd interfered to part them. Finally, Dennis Toohey, Sr., shrugged and turned. He left the house and the others followed. They finally agreed among themselves that a note for four dollars would be drawn up and signed by the groom's father. To witness it they called young Tom Nangle out from a field behind his father's house where he had been working.

With note in hand and accompanied by young Nangle, Patrick Toohey the groom and his brother, Dennis Jr., went back inside and were followed by the bride and her father. As they handed the note over, however, Dennis Toohey, Jr., muttered something under his breath.

The priest took umbrage. "Get out!" he cried.

Young Toohey was not to be cowed that easily. "My father says to marry the parties or give back the money," he said.

"No," said the priest, "Get out!"

The bride's uncle, Thomas Tierney, then rushed into the house in great passion and demanded the priest return the money. He refused, and told them again to leave the house. They stood their ground. Once again the priest raised his cane, but young Dennis Toohey turned just in time for the knobless stick to strike him on the back.

"I will hit one of you each day if I have to," the priest cried.

The men then grabbed hold of the priest and young Toohey wrested the cane from his hand, broke it in two over his knee and threw the pieces to the floor.

Meanwhile, when the rest of the crowd outside heard the ruction start up again they flew through the door and another grappling match ensued. Finally, when emotions had subsided, the priest agreed to perform the ceremony on condition that only the bride and groom and the two formal witnesses remained in the house. The demand was complied with and the marriage proceeded.

Upon its conclusion, the groom dropped to his knees and begged the priest's forgiveness.

"Begone with ye, ye rascal," the priest replied, striking him in the face with his fist.

The next day Father O'Flynn went to the justices of the peace in Irishtown and laid charges of assault against the men. The charge against the bride's father, Cornelius Tierney, was withdrawn but the others were convicted and fined. Thus ended one of the first marriage celebrations in the Catholic Settlement of Biddulph.

Before the decade of the sixties was out, the Tierney family left Biddulph for good.[5] Like so many others, they sought free land in the American Mid-West following the conclusion of the great Civil War in that country. A few years ago I ran across a descendant in St. Paul, Minnesota, who sent me a photograph of the grave in Fort Dodge, Iowa of Cornelius Tierney, father of the 1850 bride. Naturally I would have liked a photograph of the man himself but, alas, such a picture was not known to exist. What did turn up, however, was a photograph of the wedding couple, Patrick Toohey and Catherine Tierney, in their later years, which is here included.

Who actually invented photography is apparently a moot point but the two who claimed the invention shortly before 1840 were Louis Daguerre of France and William Henry Fox Talbot of England.[6] Daguerre made photography practical by making exposures of only several minutes and using gas vapors to develop the image on a polished plate of silver. Following the offer of a generous lifetime pension, the French government persuaded Daguerre to disclose the secrets of his invention to the world at large, which he did—except in England where he took out a patent just days before the disclosure in Paris.

While the new discovery engaged and fascinated the upper classes, it took about a generation before the new art reached the common people such as your ancestors and mine. After the introduction of improvements such as better lenses and cameras, wet collodion plates, development

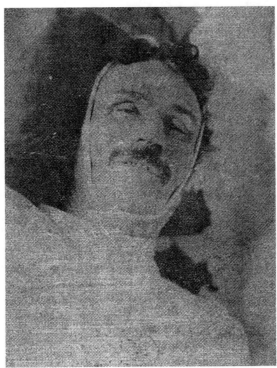

John Donnelly, like his father, was apparently not
photographed in his lifetime. This coffin photo was
made by Lucan photographer, John S. Thom.

by liquids rather than vapors, introduction of the smaller and cheaper *cartes de visites* and innovations such as the tintype, the new art spread like wildfire.

By the 1860s every little village seemed to have its own portrait gallery. Even an insignificant railway flag-stop such as the village of Granton, in 1868-69 advertised the studio of Samuel Caswell. By this time the next stop, the bustling village of Lucan, also had such an artistic establishment. Alfred Smart operated a studio there for about five years and many of the early personages of Lucan are by him. By the 1870s, almost everyone had had his or her likeness made—everyone, that is, except the odd person like James Donnelly, Sr. He, out of either superstition or neglect, failed even to have a *carte de visite* or a cheap tintype made of his likeness. As a result, we have to rely for his appearance on an artist's impression based on descriptions given by his surviving children. There are three such sketches extant, all made by Robert Harris, who had just turned thirty when he was dispatched to Lucan by the Toronto *Globe* to cover the Great Biddulph Tragedy. His fame and fortune came later. Harris painted the well-known picture of the Fathers of Confederation, which hung in the parliament buildings in Ottawa until the original was destroyed in a great fire.

Contrary to some current belief, then, photographs at the time the Donnelly boys were growing up in Biddulph were common. But when I first began my investigation of the story, few could be found. Almost no one in and around Lucan had ever seen a likeness of any member of the family. Only after persistent hunting did photographs gradually come to light. This if nothing else, I felt, would make my own book on the Donnelly story different and more interesting. For, as Alice said before embarking upon her adventures in wonderland, "What use is a book which has no conversation or pictures?"

38

Chapter 7

The Last Donnelly

My search for the true story of the Donnellys encompassed not only the unearthing of written records but also the attempt to find individuals who may have had knowledge of stories handed down by word-of-mouth. Such individuals would include, of course, descendants of the Donnellys themselves as well as their contemporaries. Many of those descendants, scattered today throughout North America, did not usually jump out of the bushes at you. And when I first began my searching and for many years thereafter, the internet or anything like it did not exist. The individuals I was looking for usually had to be tracked down by co-relating current-day news items with old records and then writing many letters. Occasionally those letters were answered. In many cases the trail led to the United States but only sometimes was there a reward of new information at the end.

How difficult it is to piece together disparate pieces of data is illustrated by a story told by Mona Schmitz who came to visit us from Lyons, Ohio because of her interest in the Donnelly story. Mona's maiden name was Donnelly and her family came from the Toledo area. In Munroe County, Michigan—once part of Ohio—during searches of her own roots, Mona found a James and Johannah Donnelly giving birth to children in the nineteenth century close to the same time as the couple of the same name on the Roman Line of Biddulph.

Almost all the Donnellys in the United States with whom I came in contact searched for links between their families and the famous Canadian Donnellys of Biddulph. One can imagine the connections sought in the future by Donnellys descended from James and Johannah of Munroe County. Obstacles will be that the mother's maiden name was Malloy and not Magee; that it was in the wrong place, Michigan, not Ontario; the wrong time—births of the children were in the 1880s and 1890s, not the 1840s and 1850s. It is amazing, however, how often putative descendants can blithely ignore such details.

My first break came when one day a Mr. Leo Corrigan telephoned me. He was quite sure, he said, that his mother, whose maiden name was Donnelly, was connected to the Biddulph family but he could not prove it. Could I help? After several weeks of investigating, I satisfied him that his mother came from a family who settled in Peel County, Ontario. Surprisingly, however, although the family had no connection with the Roman Liners, it nevertheless had a connection with the Donnelly story after all.

The Donnellys of Peel County had intermarried with the Bench family, also of Peel, and it turned out that Peter Bench was the schoolteacher at the Cedar Swamp School at the time of the Donnelly murders. His daughter, Marie Bench, lived in St. Catharines, Ontario. When I contacted her, she told me how her father had passed down stories of his going to the school in the morning and knowing immediately that the Peace Society had met the night before because the kindling he had prepared for the next morning's fire was burned and he had to prepare the kindling afresh. She also told how in later years her father had become a near neighbor of Patrick Donnelly in St. Catharines, and how he would duck inside on a Sunday morning when he saw Pat coming along the street. Even in his later years, he wanted little to do with the Donnellys. She also showed me letters of recommendation written on behalf of her father by James Harrigan, the school trustee, and Father John Connolly, the parish priest.

In the course of his own investigations prior to contacting me, however, Leo Corrigan had found a genuine grandson of Patrick Donnelly, and he told me about him almost as an afterthought. The grandson of

Margaret and Tom Newman with the author in front of the new Donnelly marker.

Patrick was Tom Newman, also of St. Catharines, Ontario.

When Leo gave me Tom's name and telephone number, I admit I was excited. This would be my first live contact with the family. When I called him, however, I soon discovered that while Tom was friendly enough, he had little enthusiasm for looking into his family's background. The attitude of reticence—so typical of most of the genuine Donnelly descendants whom I eventually tracked down—may well have been passed down from the previous generations.

For example, Tom Newman's mother once wrote to Scott Garrett as follows:[1]

> 17 Glenridge Avenue
> St. Catharines,
> My dear Mr. Garrett,
> Yours of October 10th received asking for information regarding my father Patrick Donnelly. He died May 18 1914 at the age of 65 years and is buried in Lake View Cemetery, Thorold, Ontario. My father never fully recovered from the effect of his terrible sorrow over the deaths of his people and a good many articles written about him have been incorrect. I sincerely wish we wouldn't continue reading any other articles about it. Would you think we could sue any of these writers for libel.
> Hoping to hear from you again,
> Sincerely yours
> Mrs. A. G. Newman.

Despite the lukewarm response, Tom agreed that I could come for a visit. My wife and I drove up, and Tom introduced us to his charming wife, Margaret, and those of his seven boys and two daughters who were still at home. Tom and his brother Bob had lived in the Niagara area all their lives. They had known about the black chapter in their family's history as far back as they could remember, but had kept it quiet. While even Tom's children were not aware of their relationship to the so-called Black Donnellys, the older offspring were thrilled to learn of it.

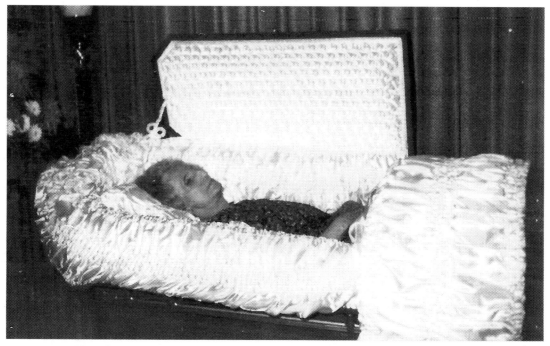

Mary (Mayme) Donnelly (1886-1970) was the last surviving child of Patrick Donnelly.

When Kelley's book, *The Black Donnellys*, came out in 1954, Tom said he and his brother were so upset at the portrayal of the family they consulted a lawyer friend with a view to taking legal action. The legal man listened to their complaint with great sympathy, but when several months passed without their hearing from him, they pressed him about it. He then confessed to having done nothing. He had even lost the copy of Kelley's book that they had left with him. As the lawyer seemed less than enthusiastic about pursuing the case, they dropped it.

In the weeks following our first meeting, I kept urging Tom to join me on a visit to Biddulph. Strangely, it seemed to me, he had never taken the trouble to go there. Eventually it was his wife Margaret who generated the enthusiasm. Prodded by her, Tom finally worked up a lukewarm interest in the story and promised to call me if, he said, he could ever find the time to make the trip. Frankly, I thought he would never call. Surprisingly, however, one day the telephone rang and it was Tom. He said he and Margaret would like to go up to Biddulph and Lucan. The following Sunday my wife and I drove them up and we toured the area. We visited Lucan and Biddulph, St. Patrick's Church and Cemetery, the Cedar Swamp Schoolhouse, the homestead on the Roman Line and the Donnelly Schoolhouse.

The little Donnelly School still stood on the north-east corner of what had been the family's homestead. As we walked about in the schoolyard, I talked about his great grandparents' frequenting the little building when the parish priest came to celebrate mass and especially to make his Easter visitation. When he heard this, Tom's enthusiasm quickened. Suddenly he began to look around for a loose brick or other article to take back home as a souvenir. "It's too late, Tom," I laughingly told him, "I've already got everything."

From Tom I learned that the various branches of descendants of James and Judith Donnelly gradually lost touch with each other. Tom told me as much as he could about his mother, his uncles and his aunts—the children of Patrick Donnelly—but of the other branches he knew very little. On paper

41

Jack Donnelly's reply to his cousin, Tom Newman.

I had myself traced some of them but my attempts to contact them had failed.

Then one day Tom called me again. "I have to tell you, Ray, that my Aunt Mayme died recently in Detroit. Even though we had not heard from her for years, I was down as her nearest next-of-kin so I arranged her funeral. Unfortunately, however, I could not attend. But I have just now received the account from the undertaker and with it he sent the Mourners' Book. Poor Mayme must not have been in very good circumstances nor could she have had many friends. There was only one man—with his wife—who came to the visitation or attended the funeral."

"Who was that?" I asked.

"He signed his name Jack Donnelly. Do you have any idea who that might be?"

Once again, I admit that that was one of the most exciting moments in my quest of the Donnelly story. From my previous research I knew immediately who Jack was.

"That's Will's only surviving son," I told Tom excitedly. "We must go and see him right away."

As before, however, Tom was less than enthusiastic about going all the way to Detroit to meet a long-lost cousin. He nevertheless said he would ask his wife Margaret to write to Jack in his name. She did, and the letter reads:[2]

St. Catharines, Ontario
October 13, 1970
Dear Mr. Donnelly.

The past March of this year my Aunt Mayme Donnelly passed away in Detroit, Michigan.

42

Aunt Mayme, Uncle Matthew and John and my mother Anne were children of Patrick Donnelly who settled in the Niagara Peninsula after leaving Lucan county.

My brother Bob and myself (Tom) were Aunt Mayme's only survivor, and therefore received her records, etc.

We thought Aunt Mayme was the last Donnelly and were therefore surprised and pleased to see your name on the Perry Funeral Home visitor book. However, with the surprise came many questions on your ancestry, and if you would know of any other surviving Donnellys.

My mother Anne Donnelly married Arthur Newman in 1919. She passed away in 1951 at age 64. Aunt Mayme, Uncle Matthew and John had lived in Detroit most of their adult life. Uncle John died in the early 1940s, and Uncle Matt about four years ago. My wife and myself have seven sons and two daughters. One is named Patrick for his grandfather, another Matthew, William, Thomas.

We would be very happy to hear from you, and any information you might have on Donnelly relatives, living or deceased. Would it be possible sometime to have a personal conversation with you.

We thank you for your time, and anxiously wait to hear from you.

In due course Jack Donnelly of Detroit replied and Tom and Margaret were kind enough to give me his letter. It is reproduced here in this book.

Once more I urged Tom, "We must go and see this man. He is your cousin but very elderly. If we wait too long we may lose the only opportunity we will ever have to talk with him."

Again, Tom was reluctant. He was busy with his work, his children were growing and needed attention and he just did not know when he could find the time to make a trip to Detroit. But he said he would call me if he did.

After waiting several weeks, I took matters into my own hands. One late afternoon I packed an overnight bag and, accompanied by my older son David who had just turned twelve, we drove west. We took a room for the night in Windsor. Next morning we had breakfast, drove through the tunnel to Detroit and began to look for the home of Jack Donnelly.

The address we sought was not far from the downtown area but as we approached it we saw more and more the charred and blackened remains of what had been buildings. Large black patches bore silent testimony to the violence of the race riots there of just four years before. Over the entire forlorn area an oppressive silence hung in the early morning air.

When we found the apartment building, it was bolted up like a fortress. A man inside the front door eyed us with apprehension but finally decided we were harmless and let us enter. We found the apartment and knocked. After a long wait, the safety chain inside rattled, the doorknob turned and the door opened an inch. Part of a face appeared through the crack.

A gruff voice said, "Yes?"

"Are you Mr. Jack Donnelly?" I asked, hoping that the trepidation in my voice would not be too much noticed.

The answer was not at all friendly, the sound seeming to come from deep within the man's chest. "Yes—what do you want?"

The moment was critical. A false move now would forever lose the opportunity of a lifetime. I am sure my voice shook. "Mr. Donnelly," I said, "I'm a friend of your cousin Tom in St. Catharines. You wrote to him recently. Can we come in?"

There was a very long pause. For an eternity, it seemed, the issue hung in the balance. I wondered whether our trip would come to nothing after all.

"Just a minute," he finally said.

The door closed and there was a wait so long I thought it would never open again. Later I realized that while it was nine o'clock in the morning in Windsor, it was only eight o'clock in Detroit.[3] We had got the Donnellys out of bed.

At last the door opened again. "C'mon in," the man said. For years I had been searching for this person, the sole surviving member of the Donnelly family bearing the

Jack Donnelly and his wife in their 1921 wedding photograph.

name. Now at long last he was standing in front of me.

When I met him, Jack Donnelly[4] was a vigorous 86 years old and his wife Effie was several years younger. She had donned a housecoat and he had pulled on a pair of pants but was still in his undershirt. It was a real intrusion to come in on them so early in the morning for they had not even had breakfast. At first the atmosphere was uncomfortable and the conversation stiff, but it was not long before everyone became more relaxed. Having my twelve-year-old son

David with me probably did not hurt my prospects with them. We talked for several hours.

Jack remembered his father, William Donnelly, very well for he was thirteen when he died, almost the same age as my son David who was with me on that memorable visit. Having been bed-ridden for the final few months of his life, Jack's father had by then had to give up the fiddle but his son did remember his picking it up once or twice nonetheless. He also recollected his father boasting that shortly after his marriage he had hardly a penny in his pockets. But he borrowed two hundred dollars from a local doctor, Jack said, and bought a stallion. Inside of two years he was earning two thousand dollars a year in stud fees.

"Oh, the Donnellys were enterprising," his wife chimed in.

Jack Donnelly had grown up in Appin and after the death of his father helped out in running the hotel and later lived for a while in London. In 1921 he and Effie, a Pittsburgh girl, were married. They had met while working in a market, they told me, and for eight months they lived in London and then moved to Pittsburgh where they remained for twenty-five years. There they had been good friends with Billy Conn, the boxer who had fought two exciting championship matches with the great Joe Louis in the 1940s. Finally the couple moved to Detroit where I met them. They had been living in that city for the previous twenty-five years before our meeting. Strangely, though living in the Motor City, Jack Donnelly had never owned or driven a car. Having spent most of his life as a bartender at private clubs, he retired at the age of seventy-five. Rarely did he drink liquor himself and when he did it was in moderation. Both Mr. and Mrs. Donnelly now enjoyed watching professional wrestling on television and it was with some difficulty that I kept steering them off this subject and back to something which to my mind was far more important: Jack's memories of his father, his mother, his uncles Pat and Bob and his aunt Jenny.

When we touched upon the great tragedy of his family, Jack's voice rose: "My father and his brothers were ambitious, wore fine clothes and got along very well in the world. But their enemies just couldn't stand this. They were jealous, and in the end they killed them because of it."

Mrs. Donnelly added: "When my husband's father married Norah Kennedy, all six of his brothers stood up with them. The priest said he had never seen such a handsome bunch of fine young men."

After breakfast Jack got dressed, went out for a newspaper and returned in a few minutes. With more prompting on my part, he spoke of his younger days. For extended periods, he said, he lived with his Uncle Pat in Thorold and with his Aunt Jenny near Glencoe. I noticed that when he relied on his own personal knowledge, his recollection of the past was excellent. The later address of his Uncle Pat in St. Catharines, for example, was exactly right. When he spoke of the early history of the family in Biddulph, however, he relied on what was told him by his mother. The latter, Norah Kennedy, survived until the year 1937 and died in a London hospital.

As I was interested about possible Toledo relatives, I asked Jack about his grandfather's brother or other possible relatives he may have had in Toledo. He shrugged off the question with a brief reference to an uncle who drowned when the car he was attempting to start with a crank had inadvertently been left in gear. It lurched forward and threw him into the water where he drowned. He was reluctant to provide further details and I got the distinct impression there were really none to offer. I did not press him on the subject.

After several hours of conversation, Jack surprised me by suddenly asking, "Have you ever seen a picture of my father?"

From the bedroom he brought out the family pictures. Among the photographs he allowed me to copy was a picture he himself took of the famous tombstone in St. Patrick's churchyard on the Roman Line, while another photograph shows him standing beside it with his wife and his sister Nora.

One of the most surprising things Jack told me was that no one had ever before interviewed him about his family. At the time I found it hard to credit the statement, but after his death his widow repeated the assertion at the second meeting I had with her. Upon reflection, however, the circumstance was fairly easily explained. The tragedy, as it was called, was not often

45

referred to within the family during the years that Jack was growing up. At that time he lived in the Appin and Glencoe area where his relatives the Curries were one of the long established and very respectable families. One of them, James, was the husband of Jenny Donnelly and they had a large family of twelve children. Out of respect or perhaps fear—for she was reputed to have as hot a temper as her father—Jenny's antecedents were seldom mentioned in the district. Later, when Jack and his wife lived in Pittsburgh and then Detroit, no one in the circles that they frequented, made any connection with those other notorious Donnellys in Canada even if the story had been known in those places. It was a subject that just never came up. It was, moreover, not a topic which Jack himself or his wife would ever have introduced into conversation. The interview that day in Detroit then was the only one Jack Donnelly ever gave.

His wife, Effie Ahara, was born in 1896. She knew nothing about her husband's family until many years after they were married. Then on a visit back to Jack's mother in London in the 1930s, she heard the story alluded to and was troubled. She asked her husband and his mother to elaborate. When they told her the truth, she could hardly believe that it was in the arms of her own mother-in-law that John Donnelly, her husband's uncle, had died on the early morning of February 4th, 1880. And, worse still, among the murderers was Norah Kennedy's own brother. The revelations were a shock to Effie Ahara.

When we parted on that memorable day in Detroit, Jack and Effie shook our hands warmly. Although I had hoped to see them both again, it was not to be. Jack died less than two years later in April 1973. On his death, the name died with him. As they had no children, Jack was therefore the last descendant rightfully to bear the famous surname of James and Judith Donnelly of the Roman Line of Biddulph.

Although I did not see Jack again, a couple of years after his death Effie Donnelly decided to make the trip from her home in Detroit to Hamilton. She must have heard—I myself did not tell her—that I had in my home a collection of documents and artifacts relating to the Donnelly family. It is true that over the years I began to refer to the part of the house where I stored those items as my Donnelly Room. I first heard she was in town when a friend who worked at the Y.W.C.A. telephoned me. Effie had taken a room there. As she wanted to come for a visit, I arranged to pick her up and brought her to my home. We had supper and again we talked for hours.

Effie Donnelly told us what she knew about the rest of Jack's family. Living in London, Ontario was Ione Powell, a daughter of her late husband's sister, Joey. Joey was named Jo-Anna or Johannah after her grandmother although she sometimes used the name Josephine. As a teenager Joey had gained local renown as an accomplished horse rider. Effie also said that Joey's son, Jack Clay, lived in Toronto but was in poor health. Later I learned of Jack's two marriages and came to be in touch with his only child, a son Michael, from his first marriage to a Walkerton girl. After dinner we took Mrs. Donnelly down to the Donnelly Room. When she viewed the pictures, artifacts and records that I had acquired over the years, she seemed almost in a daze as if she did not know what to make of it all. As for her husband's own pictures, she said, she had given them all to his nephew, Bill Lord, who lived in Levack, a small town near Sudbury, Ontario. Bill Lord, or Charles William Lord to give his full name, was the son of her late husband's other sister, Norah.

Again, we parted as friends. Four years later, however, and a couple of years after publication of *The Donnelly Album*, Effie Donnelly heard about the book. Although apparently she did not read it, she was displeased. Deciding to do something about it, she picked up the Detroit telephone book

**Effie Donnelly, in 1979, when interviewed by a Windsor
Star reporter.**

and found a lawyer by name of Vince Paul
Donnelly.

"It seemed like a name I could trust," she
said, and made an appointment to see him.

When she introduced herself to the
lawyer, he teased her. "There are Donnellys
and there are Donnellys," he said, "And then
there are the Black Donnellys."

"Well," she said, "you're looking at one of
them—the Black Donnellys, that is."

What legal advice the lawyer gave her I
can only guess, but he must have sensed the
historical significance of the event for he
persuaded her to be interviewed by a
newspaper across the river.

"To me it was important," Vince Paul
Donnelly is reported to have said. "I mean,
that is part of Canadian history and it would
be too bad to see the last of a great clan die
without having been recognized, because
here she is living—right in Detroit, right
across from you."

Effie Donnelly was now not happy with
having met me and with our visits back and
forth. "Fazakas arrived unannounced," she
told the Windsor *Star* staff reporter who went
over to her home to see her. "He wrote some
pretty terrible things. He started taking
pictures and so on and promised he wouldn't
write anything derogatory."

For years Jack Donnelly had kept from his
wife the dark secret in his family background.
"He didn't say anything to me about it," she
said, "because he just wanted to forget it.
The whole family was that way. They were
disgusted with the whole thing."

Effie, too, now wanted to forget the story.

"That's it now. No more interviews. You
can tell your readers I don't want to talk to
anybody about it any more. That's it."

And she did not want her address made
known. The reporter noted, however, that
her home was in a bleak downtown
apartment building among neighborhood
rubble, derelict buildings and vacant lots. It
sounded very much like the same place I had
visited a few years before. This was the last I
heard from or about Effie Ahara Donnelly
except that about a year or two later I
received a telephone call from another lawyer
in Detroit. He was calling on her behalf and
we simply chatted, but during the

conversation he did make an oblique suggestion that I might want to share with his client the supposedly huge profits from the sale of *The Donnelly Album*. Mrs. Donnelly died shortly after.

Following my visit to Detroit to see Jack, I looked up the last two surviving sons of Jenny Donnelly. Through years of correspondence, I had learned that Patrick and Michael Currie were living in Chatham and Glencoe respectively and found their addresses. In Chatham, by mentioning to Pat Currie when he came to the door that I had visited with his first cousin in Detroit, he asked me to come in and introduced me to his wife.

We sat in the living room and during our chat they told me they had lost contact with Cousin Jack many decades before. Their own children had in the meantime all grown up and left home. Mr. and Mrs. Currie told me that they, too, did not advertise the fact that they were related to the Donnellys of Biddulph. On the other hand, they did not hide from it either. But they said they resented the lies spread about their family and wanted to protect their children from them.

By way of example, Mrs. Currie related the story of one of their daughters and her male friend. The two were not serious about each other or intending to be married but merely dating on a regular basis. When they broke up, however, he tried to hurt her feelings by referring to the Donnelly affair.

"Why," he told her sarcastically, "your people are written up in the public library."

One can only hope their daughter realized she was well rid of such a person.

"Do you know," Pat told me, his voice—like Jack's—rising at the mention of the tragedy, "my people who were killed up in Biddulph were not criminals or anything like that. They had a clean record. Why, not one of them had ever been convicted of anything before they were murdered."

Silently, I suppressed my astonishment at such a sweeping statement. And although Pat

and his wife were not hostile, they were not warm either. As we parted, Pat said, "I don't want you to take a picture of my house. I haven't got much but if you do, I will sue you with every penny I've got."

It was not long after this that I also met Pat's brother, Mike Currie. He was then living in the house just outside Glencoe in Ekfrid Township to which the family had moved in 1912. His mother, Jenny Donnelly, had died here four years after the move. My efforts with Mike were rocky. His own nephew, Jenny's grandson, confided to me that Mike was not easy to approach or get along with. Like his uncle Bob Donnelly, who was once described by the crown attorney Charles Hutchinson as "his own worst enemy," Mike brought much of his misfortune upon himself. He became estranged from his wife and children and for many years lived the life of what could almost be described as a recluse. I confess his appearance when I first laid eyes on him startled me, as he was unkempt and his clothes from head to foot seemed to be in tatters. Later I learned that for weeks he seemed to live on a supply of bananas and bottles of rye whiskey brought to him from the village on an almost daily basis by a kindly neighborhood youth. As I quickly learned, Mike was brusque, outspoken and intemperate in his language; it is little wonder that he alienated many of those who attempted to approach him in a friendly manner. In the end he was fortunate that his brother Pat stood by him, and saw to it that he spent his final years in a comfortable nursing home. Michael Currie died in 1984. Pat survived for a further ten years.

While my contact with Michael was a little tempestuous, after all was said it was not without some success. An enthusiast of the Donnelly story with whom I kept in constant touch took it upon himself to befriend Mike. Over the years, through him, I obtained valuable information and photographs of the family.

Chapter 8

Tales from Toledo

At about two o'clock in the early morning hours of Saturday, January 4th, 1913, Dr. Peter Donnelly, a very popular physician practicing in Toledo, Ohio, left the Toledo Club, got into his new Cadillac touring car and drove off the end of Madison Avenue into the Maumee River. His body was not pulled out until the afternoon and whether his death was an accident or a suicide was not discovered. For a week, the tragic death of the popular physician was featured on the front pages of the Toledo *Blade*. On the day of his large and conspicuous funeral, all city offices were closed.

The account of the fatal accident was mentioned in some of the Canadian

Front page of the Toledo *Blade* of January 4, 1913

49

newspapers. Its write-up in the *Free Press* of London, Ontario read as follows:[1]

Fate Pursues the Donnellys of Biddulph.
Grandson of Murdered Family is Killed in
Auto Accident.
Grim Tragedy of 1880 that Stirred London.
Brutal Butchery is Recalled in the Death of Dr.
Donnelly of Toledo.

Toledo, Jan. 10—Dr. Peter Donnelly, who met a tragic end here through his auto plunging into the Maumee River, was a grandson of the Donnelly family who were foully murdered in Biddulph Township, near London, Ontario, on the night of February 4th, 1880 . . . He seldom talked about the grim event of 30 years ago . . . The doctor . . . was much dissatisfied with the result of the trial of some of the alleged vigilants in the Assize Court at London . . . .

The account, which is only partly reproduced above, was inaccurate in several details. The complete version stated, for example, that two men who were in the vehicle with the doctor, escaped. There is no question, however, that the victim was alone in the car.

William Donnelly's widow, Norah, responded to the news item with the following:[2]

I saw the account in your paper of the death of Dr. Donnelly, of Toledo, who was said to be a grandson of James Donnelly, who was murdered in the Biddulph tragedy. Dr. Peter Donnelly was a son of Patrick Donnelly, who came to Canada from Tipperary, Ireland, in May 1858, and who stayed with his brother, James in Biddulph for some time. He then went to Toledo, where he entered into the hotel business. Later he married in Toledo, and he and his family have resided there since.

Years later Norah's daughter, Nora Lord, also referred to the brother of James Donnelly, Sr., when on July 24, 1969 she wrote:

Grandpa Donnelly's Brother came to Canada with him, but went to the States and settled in Toledo. They never kept in touch, but a man from my home town, met a lawyer in Toledo, Donnelly by name, red hair as follows us, and the image of Uncle Mike's Jim.

From Toledo, I managed to obtain a half-tone photograph of the Toledo lawyer

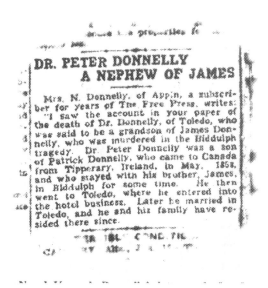

Norah Donnelly's letter to the London *Free Press*.

referred to by Nora Lord. His name was Cyril E. Donnelly. Further investigation revealed that he was the son of Judge Michael Donnelly of Napoleon, Ohio, who was the brother of Dr. Peter Donnelly who drowned in the Maumee River in 1913.

On a trip to Toledo in the spring of 1983, my wife and I found that Dr. Peter Donnelly was 44 years of age when he drowned. His older brother James had begun practicing medicine in Toledo before him. Another brother was the Michael mentioned in the previous paragraph who became a lawyer and later a judge and was the father of Cyril E. Donnelly, also mentioned above. A third brother, Patrick, stayed on the home farm. The father of all these men, however, was not Patrick—as one might have expected by attempting to reconcile the stories—but Peter Donnelly, Sr., a pioneer of the Toledo district. According to *A History of Northwest Ohio*, published in 1917, the elder Peter Donnelly was born in County Galway in 1814 to Michael Donnelly and Bridget Glynn. He married Alice O'Hearn[3] of Tipperary. The account goes on:

In the spring of 1837 Peter Donnelly came to America with his brother John. They landed in Quebec, Canada, but soon afterward started

Cyril E. Donnelly
Mr. Donnelly, 52, of 4031 North Lockwood Avenue, has practiced law in Toledo since 1915. He is married and has two children.
The attorney has lived in this community 24 years. He is a member of the Eagles' Lodge. Mr. Donnelly attended St. John's University, Toledo, and obtained his law degree at the University of Michigan. He is a member of St. Agnes' Church.

From the Toledo *Blade* of August 8, 1942.

for Detroit and subsequently came to Toledo. Peter Donnelly was employed on the Maumee Canal for several years, and it was with the earnings from this occupation that he came to Henry County in Washington Township and bought eighty acres in section 36 of Washington township.

The homestead in Washington Township remained in the Donnelly name well into the twentieth century.

This Peter Donnelly, father of Dr. James, Dr. Peter and Judge Michael, who came from Ireland is listed in the 1860 census of Ohio in Henry County, Washington Township. Also listed in the same place is John Donnelly, Sr., implying that he had a son bearing the same first name. I speculate that this senior John Donnelly may well be the brother referred to in the account quoted immediately above. And it is possible, I suppose, that another brother may have been James of Biddulph although this is unlikely in view of the divergence of the two lines as we shall see.

The fate of either of the two Johns noted above, however, may have been noted in a brief report in the Toledo newspaper in 1881:[4]

A Queer Incident.
About 4 o'clock yesterday afternoon a man named John Donnelly met his death by drowning in the Maumee. He was crossing the Union Bridge alone, when for some unaccountable reason he fell into the river below. The bridge tender and several bystanders who saw him fall ran to his rescue, but he had gone down for the last time before they reached him. Search was at once commenced for the body but as yet it has not been recovered.

Donnelly was a peddler by trade, and had resided in the City for some time. Whether he was intoxicated or not is unknown as yet.

Speculating a little bit more, it may have been this John who as a peddler accustomed to travelling about, made frequent trips between the Toledo area and Biddulph. Perhaps it was he who assisted Judy Donnelly on the Roman Line farm when her husband had been sent to prison after the commutation of his sentence for murder and to whom Norah Donnelly was referring in 1913.[5] And the drowning in the Maumee River in 1881 may have been the one to which Jack Donnelly of Detroit and his mother some 50-odd years before him were referring. It may somehow have got confused with the drowning of Dr. Peter Donnelly in 1913, which echoed it. It seemed curious that we had gone to Toledo to discover the details of one drowning of a Donnelly in the Maumee River in Toledo and turned up two.

There are other difficulties with Norah Donnelly's letter to the *Free Press* in 1913. First, she is clearly wrong regarding the name of Dr. Peter Donnelly's father. She says it was Patrick but there is no question it was the Peter Donnelly who settled as a pioneer in Washington Township, Ohio. Second, her statement that James Donnelly's brother entered into the hotel business in Toledo has to be questioned. The Toledo city directories commencing in 1858 list no Donnelly as the proprietor of a hotel. The closest that anyone of that name comes to be associated with a hotel is Edward Donnelly, a bartender for Joseph DeVries in 1889-90 and a John Donnelly, a porter at the Boody House in 1891. Can this be considered as being in the hotel business?

Continuing with my findings in Toledo, a John Donnelly, laborer, is first listed in the city directories in 1860. He appears to be the same person listed in one or two of the following years. One can speculate that it was this man, not his son of the same name, who was listed in the Washington Township census as John Donnelly, Sr., and that it was he who was a peddler and therefore often away from the district. It was possibly he who was drowned in 1881 and who may have been the brother of Peter of Washington Township and even perhaps James of Biddulph. John Donnelly, porter at the Boody House, may then have been his son.

While none of this proved very conclusive, further discoveries confused the issue even more. After returning home, I broadcast letters to all the Donnellys in the Toledo city directory seeking information. One response led to an exchange of letters and then one day in October 1983 a car bearing Ohio license plates pulled up in front of our house in Hamilton. Out stepped one who I thought was the spitting image of Tom Donnelly. This person was handsome with light blonde straight hair, a large but well proportioned frame and smooth, light-complexioned skin. Tom Donnelly would have looked like this, I thought, except for one thing. The person was a woman. Becky Donnelly had driven down from her home in Toledo with her aunt, Dorothy Donnelly Cawthorn, for the purpose of exchanging information. Dorothy was like the other line of genes in the Donnelly blood: small and quick, with an inquiring mind and agile tongue.

It turned out they were descended from Thomas Donnelly who was born in Ireland in 1808 and died in Toledo in 1886. With his wife, Catherine O'Brien (1818-1893), he had emigrated from the town of Woodford, County Galway. Woodford is directly across the Shannon from North Tipperary. The tradition in the family—but it was only a tradition—claimed kinship with Dr. Peter Donnelly who drowned in the Maumee River in 1913.

During our trip to Toledo, I had thought to investigate another connection of the Donnelly story with that city, namely, the ultimate fate of James Feeheley. Shortly after the massacre in Biddulph, James's father, Michael Feeheley, better known as Mick, made a visit to friends in Saginaw. There he died of a sudden. According to his sons, James and William, Mick Feeheley had not himself been implicated in the deadly plot against his former friends—he was, after all, one of only two men who testified on behalf of Jim Donnelly at the latter's trial for murder in 1858—but he claimed to have intimate knowledge of those who were. Mick was in fact related to many of them through his wife, Bridget Cain.

Ever the opportunist, Mick Feeheley's plan after the murders was to rent the Donnelly farm from the survivors and to defy any of the Peace Society to try to run him off it. The tragedy, which befell his neighbors, seemed a godsend, he thought, by enabling him to get more land. He may even have considered raising cash by blackmailing his guilt-ridden neighbors to enable him to buy the Donnelly place outright and at a bargain price for he knew the survivors would never sell to a Vigilant family. All came to nothing, however, when Mick died unexpectedly in Saginaw.

For years I had searched for a descendant of the Feeheleys without success. Then one Saturday afternoon in August 1977 I received a telephone call from John J. Feeheley of Detroit. He and his brother Bill had seen *The Donnelly Album*. It had aroused their curiosity enough to make a trip to Canada. At St. Patrick's Church in Biddulph someone had told them where I lived and they wanted to come for a visit.

James Feeheley's last home in Toledo, Ohio.

The next day the Feeheley brothers arrived with their wives and children. Jack and Bill were the sons of William Feeheley of Saginaw who was in turn the son of William Feeheley of the Donnelly story. Both had been born and raised in Saginaw. They were intrigued to learn for the first time of their grandfather's role in the events in Biddulph almost a century before.

Although they knew nothing of their grandfather's brother, James Feeheley, the brothers' Aunt Margaret remembered an "Uncle Jim" coming to her door one day in about the year 1925. Because he believed Margaret's newly married son Jim was named after him, he went out and bought the young groom and his bride a new bedroom suite. That was about all the Feeheleys of Saginaw remembered of James Feeheley of the Donnelly story.

I later learned that after James and William Feeheley had been extradited from Michigan, charged with the murder of the Donnellys and then released on bail—the authorities in London having virtually abandoned all hope of ever obtaining a conviction—the brothers returned to their work in the iron foundries of Saginaw. In 1883 James Feeheley married a good Catholic girl named Elizabeth O'Reilly but little else is known about this marriage. He soon tired of working as a blacksmith and took up the butcher business. At first he worked as a meat peddler making rounds with a wagonload of fresh meat and visiting more or less regular customers. Then he became a meat packer and distributor selling carcasses wholesale. Travelling frequently between East Saginaw and Toledo, by 1898 he is found marrying once more, this time a widow named Mary Neville. He then settled permanently in the city of Toledo, acquiring a plentiful supply of worldly goods and gradually moving up his residences from the poorer areas of the city to the more affluent. Although I did not find out what happened to his first wife, the second was the widow of a well-to-do meat merchant of Toledo, which did not hurt his prospects. He himself had no children but his second wife Mary had a son and daughter by her first marriage.

James Feeheley died in Toledo in 1932. The newspaper notice of his funeral reads:[6]

> Funeral services for James J. Feeheley, 75, of 322 Logan street, who died Thursday, will be in the Coyle & Son funeral home at 9 A.M. Saturday and in the Immaculate Conception Church at 9:35 A.M. Burial will be in Calvary cemetery. Mr. Feeheley was formerly general agent in Toledo for Armour & Co.

Meanwhile, James Feeheley's brother William remained in Saginaw and married a Biddulph girl, Julia Keefe, daughter of an old crony of the Donnelly boys, Daniel Keefe. William Feeheley died in 1926 and is buried in Mount Olivet Cemetery in Saginaw, the last resting place of many former Biddulphers.

Back in Biddulph, the Feeheley homestead on the Roman Line eventually came into the hands of Joe Mitchell, who had married Eliza Jane Keefe. The young couple chose to live on the old Feeheley place because it was immediately south of the farm of Eliza Jane's parents, Robert Keefe and Mary Ryan. A daughter of Joe and Eliza Jane was Mary, who told me her mother once wondered aloud why their house was set so far back from the road. Eliza Jane's mother finally gave her the answer: there used to be a low-lying swamp between the house and the road. "That's where Feeheley had his shanty," she added disdainfully, implying that anyone with any sense would not have built there. The remark was a tiny indication of the low esteem in which the Feeheleys had come to be regarded by members of the community after their departure from Biddulph, including those who, like the Keefes, sympathized with the Donnellys.

Grave marker in Toledo, Ohio

Julia Keefe, who married William Feeheley. Both were born in Biddulph.

Chapter 9

The O'Connors

When we made our trip to Toledo in 1983, I was unaware that there was at least one other important connection of the Donnelly story with that city. That was Johnny O'Connor, the only survivor of the massacre at the homestead. Over the years, I had heard many different versions of his later life[1] and I wrote many letters trying to contact his descendants, if any. All had been to no avail. One of the more reliable of sources, I felt, was Alice McFarlane. On November 19th, 1946, she had presented her paper on the Donnelly murders to the London and Middlesex Historical Society. Miss McFarlane had pencilled a note in the margin of her paper reminding herself to inform the audience that Johnny O'Connor was at that time living near Detroit. He would then have been eighty years old. But, alas, when she wrote to me she could tell me nothing more. Nevertheless for years, skimpy as it was, this was for me the most authentic information of the later whereabouts of the young boy who survived the massacre at the Donnelly homestead.

When I had almost given up hope, one Sunday morning in 1997 I met Bill Kilmer at one of Lucan's first Heritage Days. Bill introduced himself and told me he had met Johnny O'Connor in Toledo on two different occasions in 1934. He apologized for not remembering more details of the two meetings, but said he was only ten years old at the time. Nevertheless, the meetings had left a strong impression on him and he remembered some details clearly. Although Bill had to hurry off the day we met, I managed to get his address and wrote him shortly after asking him to set out in writing everything he could remember of those meetings with John O'Connor. Upon receipt of his reply, I arranged a visit and my wife and I drove up to his home on Nottawasaga Bay to obtain, if possible, even more information.

Bill Kilmer was born in 1924 on a farm at Clandeboye. His mother had been a close friend of Lina Hodgins, a native of London Township, and the two families visited back and forth for decades. Lina first married an older man in the States and when he died she became well off financially. She then married Billy Huggins, an American several years her junior. They came to London Township and the Kilmers and Huggins families renewed their friendship. The two families remained close even after Bill and Lina Huggins went back to the United States to live in Toledo with Lina's uncle, William Bernard Hodgins. I had known about Hodgins for many years

Johnny O'Connor, photographed by Lucan photographer, John S. Thom, two days after the tragedy.

55

for he had been raised in or near Lucan and had married Mary Hines. She happened to be a sister of Nellie Hines who had married Michael Donnelly.

It was at the home of William Bernard Hodgins who operated a wagon works and then garage in Toledo that Bill Kilmer met John O'Connor on two occasions in 1934. O'Connor would then have been sixty-eight years old. Bill Kilmer remembers seeing him on the first occasion in the living room. He was of medium height and medium build, not slight nor heavy but with a good, wiry physique. He would have been about the same height as Bill's father, five feet and eight inches, with graying hair. He was quiet spoken and of a retiring disposition.

At that first meeting he seemed a little shy and not very talkative, but the second meeting was during a meal in the dining room where he seemed more relaxed. On this occasion he talked about the Donnelly murders, and Bill clearly remembered his naming Buckshot Ryder,[2] Toohey and Ryan as well as several others who were among the mob. Bill could not remember the other names. But the one thing he did recall clearly to the day he told me was O'Connor's insistence that the parish priest was implicated. And while he did not remember the exact words O'Connor spoke that day, the impression left on the wide-eyed ten-year-old boy was that according to O'Connor the priest was actually present at the massacre.

While I cannot credit the part of Father Connolly's being actually present at the murders, I believe Bill Kilmer's story generally. I was able to verify several of the incidental circumstances of the story which he related, including the exact location of the Hodgins house in Toledo. One other detail that Kilmer remembered was that O'Connor did not use that name. It was something similar but he could not recall what it was. It may have been Cochrane, or possibly Conners, or some other similar sounding name.

Shortly after the tragedy, County Crown Attorney Charles Hutchinson moved Johnny O'Connor and his parents out of Lucan and into the city of London. A few weeks later, the O'Connor house in Lucan where the rest of the family were living burned to the ground, in all likelihood the work of an arsonist. Even though the father also owned the house on the adjoining parcel, lot 32 on Francis Street, the remaining members of the family were brought to the city to join their parents.

Following the Carroll trials, Michael O'Connor sold the now vacant lot on Francis Street on which the family home had stood but kept and rented out the house on the adjacent property. The family can be followed for a few years in London. They seemed to move about frequently and for a short time kept a store on Richmond Street. Michael O'Connor, the father, died on January 5th, 1884 at his residence at 283 Simcoe Street. In 1886 Johnny, listed as a plumber, was living at 204 Bathurst Street with his brother Patrick, a laborer working at McClary Stoves. Johnny returned to Lucan in 1888 in all probability to arrange with William Porte for the collecting of the rent on the remaining O'Connor house on Francis Street in the village. Porte noted in his diary:[3]

> Wed. Nov. 7/88
> The notorious Johnny O'Connor came here by stage from London last evening. I mean him of Donnelly Tragedy renown . . .
> Thurs. Nov. 8/88
> . . . O'Connors was in the office today for an hour or so. I never mentioned tragedy to him. He is now 21 years of age . . .

I speculate that O'Connor, having turned 21,[4] came up to see Porte about transferring into his own name the Francis Street property in Lucan. He may have convinced his mother to make a deed to him in return for which he would look after her the rest of her life. If so, this transfer may have later caused a rift between him and his siblings. That year John

Mary Hastings O'Connor, in 1891, with her daughters, Mary Ellen (Nellie) on left, and Catherine Elizabeth (Lizzie) on right.

being collected by Porte was not for their mother but for their brother John.

The year following, on December 29, 1891, the mother, Mary Hastings O'Connor, died. Johnny brought her remains back to London for burial beside her husband in a plot at the rear of St. Peter's Cemetery. The London *Free Press* of Monday, January 4, 1892 noticed the event in the following words:

> The remains of Mrs. Mary O'Connor arrived here Friday evening from Detroit, and the funeral took place on Saturday from St. Peter's Cathedral, where High Mass was offered. Mrs. O'Connor was the mother of Johnny O'Connor, of Donnelly murder fame. The young man has grown quite a bit since that event, and looks exceedingly well.

O'Connor was listed as working as a laborer at Hyman's in London.

Not long after, the entire family moved to Detroit, Michigan. In 1889 John, his mother and two brothers are listed in the directory of that city as living at 190 Mount Elliott Avenue. Patrick appears to have worked at about this time as a seaman on the Great Lakes. It seems curious to me that on Friday, September 26th, 1890, back in Lucan William Porte made the following note in his diary:[5]

> Miss Nellie Connors was here today from Detroit. After McKinnon rent.

This may well have been the time that Johnny's siblings discovered that the rent

O'Connor was twenty-five years old at this time. Upon return to his home in Detroit, he continued to live in that city for a time residing at different addresses, and was variously listed as a laborer or teamster.

Not long before completing the manuscript of the first revision of this book, *In Search of the Donnellys*, my friend Randy White found what he and I had been seeking for many years—not, unfortunately, Johnny himself but at least the final location of his two brothers and at least two of his three sisters. They all ended up living near each other in the city of Duluth, Minnesota, where they spent the remainder of their lives.

John's youngest sister, Lizzie (baptized as Catherine Elizabeth) had married Dennis Connors in Detroit. When he died not long after the marriage, the young widow went to join her sister, Nellie (baptized Mary Ellen) who by this time had gone to live in Duluth. Lizzie married Frank Scott in Superior, Wisconsin in 1895 and they went back to live in Duluth where she had two children, Earl and Maxine. Lizzie's husband Frank Scott turned out to be a habitual drunkard and wife-beater and after divorcing him, she brought up her two children by herself. Later in life she was was married once more to a man named Frank Lesler. She died in 1946.

Lizzie's daughter Maxine grew up in a free and easy lifestyle and gained a reputation as "a dance hall girl". She had a son, Cameron, born out of wedlock. Cameron grew up and married a girl named Emma and they had a long and happy marriage with several children. Shortly after Cameron died, Randy White finally located his widow Emma in Duluth, Minnesota. Neither she nor her husband knew anything about the Donnelly story. She shared with Randy all the information she had about the O'Connors and even gave him some original photographs of the family, including one of Mary Hastings O'Connor, the mother.

The middle sister, Nellie, had married Michael Frederick Kenney in London and had two girls, Lillian and Agnes. Nellie and Michael separated and a son Freddie was later born to Michael Frederick and another woman. Without a proper family, the son Freddie had an unhappy childhood, spent time in prison and when World War I came along was rejected by the armed services of his own country. He then came to Canada and joined the Canadian Expeditionary Forces, went overseas and was killed in France in 1918. Nellie also married again, this time to Levi Mason, and had more children. Levi later committed suicide and Nellie herself died in 1940.

Patrick O'Connor, Johnny's youngest brother, did not remain a seaman on the Great Lakes for long as he soon joined his sisters Nellie and Lizzie and brother Thomas in Duluth. For a time not long before he died he was the caretaker at the Duluth jail but died unmarried in 1911 of tuberculosis contracted in a hotel where he lived for a time. His obituary mentioned his brother John as one of his surviving siblings. This appears to be the last mention of John by the family, except for a brief one-word jotting set out on some skimpy notes on a single sheet of paper made by his great nephew, Cameron. The note failed to specifically indicate his relationship within the family.

In London, after the Carroll trials, John and his brother Patrick got into a fracas with another London youth. Their brother, Thomas, though very close to John in age, missed this excitement. Thomas held various jobs in Duluth during his working years and kept a small garden plot outside the city where he would take the children of his sisters as a kind of summer treat. In his later years he lived with his sister Lizzie. He did not marry, died in 1942 and is buried in Duluth.

It strikes me as strange that aside from his being included as a survivor of Patrick in 1911, there was almost no other mention of John in the family stories left by his sisters Nellie and Lizzie and by his brother Thomas. I speculate that a rift developed between John and his siblings, probably over the transfer into John's name of the Francis Street property in Lucan when he turned 21, and the siblings lost contact with each other, especially as it seems John continued to collect the rent from that property for many years after. He was listed by the village assessor as owner of the property until about 1898.[6]

I must confess that after many years of searching for the ultimate fate of Johnny O'Connor, I have not succeeded. It is, however, possible that he was the retired seaman who died in Cleveland, Ohio in 1936. The following particulars are extracted from his Ohio death certificate:

This tintype from the O'Connor family is believed to be of Lizzie on left and Bridget on right.

Name:	John Connors
Place of death:	City of Cleveland
Residence:	1701 Lakeside Street
Sex, race, status:	Male, white, single
Date of birth:	February 4, 1860
Age:	77 years 2 months
Occupation:	Seaman, unemployed
Years worked in this occupation:	40
Last worked:	1930
Birthplace:	Detroit, Michigan
Father:	Unknown
Mother:	Unknown
Informant:	County Morgue Records
Cause of death:	Acute myocarditis
Contributory cause:	Alcoholism
Burial:	Highland Park
Undertaker:	S.W. Raus & Son 5040 Broadway

This John Connors was buried in an indigent plot in the cemetery without a marker and no next of kin are listed in the cemetery records.

Admittedly on skimpy evidence, I speculate that this deceased person may be the John O'Connor of the Donnelly story.

His birth date of February 4th—the day of the Donnelly massacre—strikes me as odd. Was this a date obtained from a calendar in the room where he died? If it is our John, the place of birth as Detroit is incorrect, of course, but he did live in that city for a time. And being a seaman for 40 years may account for his not being able to be located from about 1890 onwards, despite years of searching and following down many false leads. He was, of course, seen in 1934 in Toledo by Bill Kilmer as I have related. And the fact that the seaman who died in Cleveland in 1936 appears to have retired from his occupation in about 1930 fits well with his making trips to Toledo and Lucan in the years immediately following. Until better evidence comes to light, therefore, this John Connors who died in Cleveland in 1936 is a likely candidate to be the John O'Connor of the Donnelly story.[7]

A question that is often ruminated over by followers of the Donnelly story is whether James Carroll had actually seen Johnny O'Connor sharing the bed with old Mr. Donnelly, and if he had, why then had the vigilantes spared him?

Based on the available evidence, I personally believe that Carroll did indeed see the boy. O'Connor himself testified that when he went to hand the old man his coat which he had been using as a pillow, Carroll was standing at the doorway to the bedroom with candle in hand. The boy held the coat out to the old man and said, "Here it is."

Carroll looked right at the youth and must have heard him. "Carroll saw me in bed," O'Connor moreover stated in the witness box at the inquest. "He looked right at me, and I saw him looking right at me for a while; he did not speak to me."

This accords with the testimony given by Patrick Donnelly at the extradition hearing of the Feeheleys in Detroit in 1881. Referring to the supposed confession made by William Feeheley, the question and answer were as follows:[8]

Thomas O'Connor

Mr. Finney—Did William say anything about seeing Johnny O'Connor there?

Witness—He said they saw him, but that he was thought not old enough to do anything about it.

In truth, the killers that night acted recklessly. They were aware, for example, that others could and did in fact see them that night. John Doherty saw them as they passed westerly along the side road towards Grouchy Ryder's outlying place, the old farm of Patrick Farrell on Lot 20, concession seven. John Whelan, along with William Feeheley and Martin McLaughlin's hired man, Mike Welch, who was probably with them looking out from behind Whelan's fence, saw them. And William Donnelly's neighbors at Whalen's Corners, John Walker and William Blackwell, could easily have seen and probably did see many of them. Blackwell, in fact, admitted as much to the schoolteacher, Frank Morley, that very morning although he could not be persuaded to repeat the statement to the police. Many others, too, could have and probably did see

them as they tramped along the roads of the Catholic Settlement. It was not a particularly cold night and their faces would not have been shrouded up, but the members of the Peace Society were hell bent on their fatal mission and were oblivious to all risks.

I believe that in the minds of most of the forty or so men in the group that night, there was embedded the idea of a confrontation and intimidation but not necessarily murder. They all remembered the hanging up of Billy Atkinson by Hugh McKinnon's vigilance committee in Lucan two or three years before when Billy was roughly treated but survived the ordeal with only a bruised neck. A hardened few at the core of the Biddulph Peace Society, however, probably knew that death would rear its ugly head before the night was over. Among these could be counted men such as Grouchy Ryder, James Maher, James Carroll and Michael Carroll.

As for some of the details of the events that night, I personally do not believe that Bridget was raped or that any of the victims were decapitated. Nor do I believe that the

Michael and Mary O'Connor's unmarked plot in St. Peter's Cemetery in London, Ontario at the paper and spade in mid-picture.

bodies were mutilated except as would occur as a matter of course during the beatings with weapons such as clubs and bludgeons, pitchforks and shovels. The evidence, which survives is that at least, two of the victims, Tom and his mother, may still have been breathing when Johnny O'Connor ran past the one and stepped over the other. Hence, in the weeks, months and years, which followed, many of the mob members doubtless reconciled the matter with their own consciences and perhaps with their priest in the confessional in their own peculiar fashion. Why, they had killed no one. It is true they had beaten parties, a common enough occurrence in St. Patrick's parish, but were not the victims still alive when they left? Even at Will's place, no member of the mob saw the dead body of John immediately after the shots were fired. While such

rationalizations might stretch credulity beyond the breaking point for most of us, they would be quite acceptable to certain guilty minds. And I have little doubt that though many members of the Biddulph Peace Society lived to a ripe old age, in their final moments many of them may have died tightly clutching their rosaries.

61

Chapter 10

Tipperary At Last

In pursuit of my searching, my wife and I twice travelled to Ireland, first in 1978 and then ten years later. The so-called Outrage Reports were stored in the Record Tower on the grounds of Dublin Castle.[1] There I perused not only the Outrage Papers—reports to the royal officials in Dublin from local magistrates and police of any supposed crime or disturbance—but Convict Records and many other documents.

While in Dublin, I looked in other depositories of information. Entering the National Library was like walking into a Dickens novel. Behind the front desk sat a sternly officious man in charge who pontifically decided the fate of each request. It was handed to him in writing. Behind him two callow youths wearing over-sized green jackets slouched at attention. I had perused some papers and decided to ask for

From this small area with a diameter of about twenty miles came many of the pioneers who settled in Biddulph, Canada. The barony of Lower Ormond is on the left and the barony of Ikerrin on the lower right. Both are in North Tipperary. In between, with dotted outline, is the panhandle of Kings County which juts into Tipperary. Note the village of Moneygall where President Barack Obama's great great great grandfather was born. A short distance to its east lies Rathnaveoge where Mrs. Donnelly was born.

62

photocopies of a few pages. "Excuse me, sir," I asked the Captain of the Guard, "I wonder if I could have a few copies made."

For a moment, the Captain seemed dumbfounded. Either he was taken aback at being addressed orally or could not comprehend the enormity of my request. Then he suddenly sat upright and called out to the Clerks behind. "An order! An order!" he cried.

Immediately the two youths bolted upright, looked at each other and cried, "An order!"

For a moment they too hesitated as if not knowing which of them must do what. Then one quickly turned and disappeared into the back recesses. The other came forward and opening a swinging pass-gate, ushered me through.

"Please follow," he said solemnly. We went through the door, which the other had

The Record Tower on the grounds of Dublin Castle where the Outrage Reports were kept.

taken and passed into a marbled foyer and then into a private office.

"Please be seated," he said, "the Director will be with you in a moment."

"The Director?" thought I. Surely there has been a mistake. All I wanted was a few pages to be photocopied.

After the lapse of several minutes, a well-dressed gentleman bearing an air of importance came in, nodded a silent greeting and sat himself at the desk in front of me.

"Now, then," he said, "you wish to place an order?"

"Yes," I mumbled, a little stunned at the train of events my innocent little request had started.

"I shall require full particulars," said the Director, picking up a pen and pulling in front of him a sheet or two of paper.

I felt like telling him there must be a misunderstanding and all I really wanted were copies of a few pages. The thing, however, had got started and I must see it through. There was a long form which he slowly completed from my answers, with full name, address, particulars of request and the reasons therefor. He went into lengthy explanations as to the form of invoicing, the method of payment expected and how delivery was to take place. The amount of manpower to produce a few cents' worth of paper was awesomely astonishing. Nevertheless, the copies were received in due course.

In my imaginings, Ireland was a mythical, magical and mystical land. Inevitably, going there dispelled some of these feelings although not all. In the town of Roscrea we asked a young man at the side of the road for directions to Cloughjordan. Many of the pioneers of Biddulph had come from that place and it was on the way to Borrisokane.

"Ye want to go to Cluckjordan thin?" the young man answered with a twinkle in his eye. "Weel, ye jist take dat rhoad over dere," he said pointing and then added, "Mind, it's a crhooked rhoad but it's a straight jo'rny, if ye know what I mane."

On the way to Cloughjordan we picked up a broad-shouldered, red-haired youth who proudly told us, "I am a Kennedy and my people once owned all of this country hereabouts." And, of course, he was right. The past he referred to, however, was six to eight hundred years before the present. Long before that in even more remote and legendary times the Celts had divided Ireland into four provinces, each with its great royal families who only sometimes held sway in their respective spheres: O'Neils in Ulster, McMurroughs in Leinster, O'Briens in Munster and O'Connors in Connaught. Occasionally a high king of the whole country was nominally recognized by the other royal families but his sovereignty was more fanciful than real.

The English eventually divided each province into several counties. The thirty-two counties of the country were formed for the most part by the gradual bringing of the Irish under English rule over the hundreds of years following the first arrival of the Normans in the twelfth century. Each county in turn was divided into baronies. Below the baronies came the parishes, the enduring territorial and originally ecclesiastical units. Within the parishes were the basic and most ancient of all the territorial units, the townlands.[2]

In the medieval times referred to by our youthful red-haired passenger, the fertile plains of Upper and Lower Ormond usually formed the tribal territories of the local princes of the O'Kennedys. To the east lay the lands of the O'Carrolls later designated as the baronies of Clonlisk and Ballybritt.[3] Still further to the east the barony of Ikerrin, the ancient heartland of the O'Mahers, straddled the mountain range that in its greater length separates Tipperary into north and south. The other baronies of North Tipperary do not much concern us: Kilnamanagh, the land of the O'Dwyers and Owney and Arra, the land of the O'Ryans.

Thus was North Tipperary occupied in ancient times. Within their respective territories the powerful paramount families held sway by tradition and by exerting their wealth over many of their lesser branches. The Celts were farmers; in their world, wealth was counted in cows and grazing land. Their houses were of wattled walls of sticks and mud with thatched roofs; those of the wealthy were simply larger and more elaborate. Circular mounds of earth, called raths, surmounted by wooden palisades surrounded the house and outbuildings of an important farmer. By some of the people we met, the remains of these raths were called fairy-rings.

At Killavalla House, a short distance by foot from the town of Borrisokane, a little bed-and-breakfast enterprise was operated by the Hogan family. This is where we set up our headquarters. With Killavalla House as our base, we toured at our leisure the landscape which had been well over a century before the world

Killavalla House, where we lodged in 1978, had a greater connection to the Donnelly story than we ever imagined, as we later learned.

of James Donnelly and Judith Magee. How

surprised they would have been, we thought, if they could have known that strangers from Canada who had no family connection with them whatever would come to their native place poking around for their haunts in the hope of finding any faint trace of their probably commonplace lives. What I did not realize until a few years later, however, was that Killavalla House had an even closer connection to the Donnelly story than I would ever have imagined.

Not surprisingly, Killavalla House sits in the townland of Killavalla. Upon my first introduction to Irish landscape names, I was struck by the frequent occurrence of what I thought was the English word "kill" as part of the name. In my naivety, I thought that such names as Kilcommon, Killeen, Kilkenny, Killavalla and Kilodiernan referred to a battle or murder. This nomenclature would surely suit the so-called fighting Irish of legend who must have been a bloodthirsty lot indeed. I soon learned that nothing could have been further from the truth. "Kill" or "kil" in these names derives from either of two Gaelic words meaning "grove" or "wood" in one case or "church" or "cell" in the monastic sense in the other. Far from importing violence into a name, they bring into it either the bucolic serenity of the countryside or of a place of contemplation and worship.

Some of the most striking man-made features of the Irish landscape were the round towers. At Roscrea we stood amazed as ponderous transport trucks thundered by on the main road that had been squeezed between the round tower on the one hand and the ancient ruins of St. Cronan's church and monastery on the other. The latter had been founded some time between the years 600 to 620 A.D. Yet vehicles sped by within inches of the ruins, their drivers seemingly oblivious to the hundred of years of history that might at any moment be toppled by an errant swipe.

On our way to view another round tower standing on the famous Rock of Cashel in South Tipperary, we made a stop at a fuel station. Looking at a map, we casually wondered out loud whether we should call in at a place called Holycross.

The young man filling the tank was incredulous. "Of course ye should," he said.

"Why?" I asked innocently, "What's at Holycross?"

The young man could hardly suppress a sneer at our gross ignorance. "There's a pace of the thrue cross," he said curtly, as if further elaboration on the subject of the holy artifact would be a sacrilege.

It turned out that at Holycross were the ruins of a monastery whose monks had for centuries claimed to possess a relic which was said to be part of the cross upon which Jesus Christ had been crucified. Traditions like this were common in the Irish countryside. Upon the Rock of Cashel which we finally reached, tradition again has it that when Saint Patrick was converting King Aengus to Christianity, he inadvertently thrust the end of his crozier into the king's foot. Believing the pain to be part of the new religion, the latter suffered in silence.

North Tipperary was once known as Muscraighe Thire. Here the parish of Dunkerrin straddles the boundaries of Counties Tipperary and Offaly, formerly part of the ancient land of Ely O'Carroll. Dunkerrin is sometimes claimed to be the centre of Ireland.[4] It was here in Dunkerrin parish where Judy Magee was born and where she married James Donnelly.

In search of a possible feud which may have been exported from Tipperary to Canada, I have already mentioned that few counties in Ireland had as bloody a history as Tipperary. "Bluidy Tipperary" was so engulfed in crime in the first half of the nineteenth century that it was said its very name was "a bye word of reproach amongst the nations of the earth".[5] Robert Peel, when Home Secretary of the British cabinet and therefore in charge of the governing of Ireland, said of Tipperary:[6]

That county is by far the most troublesome county in Ireland . . . For the last thirty years and probably for the last three hundred—this same county of Tipperary has been conspicuous even in the Irish annals of violence and barbarity . . . .

During the time that Jim Donnelly lived his early years there, the murder rate of the county was about three times the national average. Prominent victims of assassinations in the county during that time or shortly after were Richard Chadwick, a land agent near Holycross for whose murder Patrick Grace was hanged in 1827; magistrates Austin Cooper and Weyland near Cashel in 1838; Charles O'Keeffe—a prominent and prosperous Catholic—in 1838; James Scully near Kilfeacle in 1842; Thomas Waller at Finnoe near Borrisokane in 1844; Maxwell and Cleary, the stewards of Baronet Robert Carden in 1844, and many others.

Concerning the last two named victims, the editor of the Nenagh *Guardian* wrote:[7]

> In our publication of Saturday last, it became our melancholy duty to record the particulars of two of those fearful cases of deliberate homicide which had affixed the terrible epithet of "blood-stained" to a lovely portion of our island. Tipperary, indeed, has long been prominent in the infamous annals of crime; and yet we question if any murders more cruel or atrocious than those of Maxwell and Cleary ever disgraced even that lawless district.

And yet there were many other such murders equally cruel and atrocious. One of the most infamous of Tipperary crimes was the murder in 1841 of Robert Hall of Merton Hall near Borrisokane. One William Kent, with others, was charged with the murder but was found not guilty. Following his liberation, a report was sent to Dublin Castle which read:[8]

> Lower Ormond . . . 17 day of July 1842 . . . Mr. Rich Armitage's house robbed of a Gun. This Gentleman is uncle to Kent the man who was acquitted of the murder of Mr. Hall it appearing the people believe he was the principal and have an ill feeling towards all his connection.

The gun mentioned in this report was later restored to its owner by the parish priest, Father Anthony Nolan, after one of his parishioners had surrendered it to him. Later we shall see that a man named Donnelly was brought to the North Tipperary Assizes on a charge of stealing a gun from Richard Armitage's property and that later still, in Canada, James Donnelly of Biddulph was said to have saved two young Armitage boys from the wrath of a mob of Catholics. On that occasion the reason given for the rescue was to pay back a favor arising out of an incident in Ireland in which the boys' father had got Jim Donnelly's father out of a scrape. The rescue in Biddulph, as we shall see, may well have been connected to the theft of this gun near Borrisokane in Ireland.

My interest in the local history of North Tipperary focused on the years from 1835 to 1845. Land in almost every case was the basis of all wealth at that time. From the time of Elizabeth I of England to the French Revolution in 1789, Tipperary was for the most part laid out in pasture. In 1836 Lord Glengall, lord lieutenant of the county, described the change which took place during the revolutionary turmoil in France when he stated:[9]

> The subdivision of lands took place in this country during the French revolutionary war; before that time the country was laid out in pasture—then it was that the high price of corn induced tenants to sublet and divide their lands—thence arose the present surplus population . . . .

It was at about this time or shortly before—during the rise of Napoleon and the war between England and France—that the Donnellys came to settle in North Tipperary. They came either from Tyrone in Ulster or from the barony of Longford in County Galway just across the Shannon River. They set down roots in North Tipperary in the area east of Lough Derg in the vicinity of the towns of Borrisokane, Roscrea, Nenagh and Birr. Those Donnellys who came in were

Catholics and they soon became some of the largest landholding tenants in the area.[10]

These large tenant farmers lived in comfortably roomy cabins with glazed windows and slated roofs and often acted as stewards or managers of the farms of the Protestant gentry. The latter lived in the Big Houses and were in this part of Ireland of the minor Protestant Ascendancy class rather than great lords who sat in the House of Lords. Largely on this account those large landholding tenants, even though Catholic, had more in common with their landlords than with the small farmers or landless peasants of their own religion. The latter called their large landholding Catholic neighbors "land grabbers".[11]

By contrast to their land grabbing compatriots, a small farmer would hold a plot of ten to twenty acres. His tiny sod house was thatched with straw and had one or at the most two windows—and that without glass. The floor was the bare earth shared in inclement weather with the cow or pig— should the family be fortunate enough to possess those animals. Even with a small farm, a family could manage to survive for a few generations but the economic trend of its fortunes was downwards.

Thus it was that the lower orders often came into conflict with those who owned the land outright or their agents, the large landholding tenants who acted as their stewards and go-betweens. To all classes of the Irish, but especially the lower, attachment to the land was crucial. To be without it usually meant dependence upon seasonal day labor, which was notoriously unreliable. Possession of land then was the cause of most of the violence in the county where James Donnelly and his neighbors were reaching manhood and about which it has been said:[12]

> Living on the margins of danger, less than perfect health, or creeping malnutrition, could mean an early death. The possession of land, either to obtain it or keep it coupled with the lack of mutual confidence in landlord-tenant relations was the critical quintessence of agrarian turmoil in pre-famine Ireland.

The Irish priest, Nicholas O'Connor, in a statement to a parliamentary committee described the attachment of the Irishman to his land thus:[13]

> . . . every string of their heart is twined round every twig upon them . . . it is impossible to induce the people to forgive turning them out of a place where their father and grandfather lived.

It is little wonder then that the possession of land also became the focus in Biddulph of so much of the early troubles and was the root cause of the enmity between the Donnellys and those who killed them. Scott Garrett was referring to the granddaughter of Jim Donnelly, Sr., when he wrote: "Mrs. Clay used to say that the scrapping over the south 50 acres had a lot to do with the later troubles in Biddulph."[14]

It was the security they saw in land which drew the Irish "land-grabbers" of North Tipperary to America. Besides the Donnellys they were such families as those bearing the names Maher, Toohey, Lamphier, Cain, Breen, Carroll, Ryder, Quigley and many others who ultimately became their most bitter enemies in Biddulph.

Ballycasey Cottage, typical of the home of a substantial farmer with a large landholding, was associated with the Donnelly family for most of the nineteenth century

Chapter 11

Borrisokane

We had gone to the town of Borrisokane in North Tipperary looking for Donnellys past or present. From our bed and breakfast base at Killavalla House we drove into town. At the post office I noticed an election poster on the wall listing the names of residents entitled to vote. The name Donnelly immediately jumped out at me. I asked the attendant if that person shown on the list as "J. Donnelly" lived nearby.

The quick reply surprised me. "Oh, is it Mrs. Johannah Donnelly you're looking for? Yes, she lives down the little street off the road to Cloughjordan. Just go up to the corner there, turn left and it's the first little street on the right. There are only two or three houses there so you can't miss it."

The coincidence seemed uncanny. Finding a Johannah Donnelly in Borrisokane with hardly a search seemed too good to be true. The little street on the outskirts of town was indeed a short one with only two houses—both yards fenced by stone walls. As I approached the gate of the first house, the air had a heavy stillness about it and even the ravens in the treetops had ceased their almost constant cawing as if in silent anticipation of what was about to happen. The building itself was large and substantial with huge uncurtained windows and a tall slated roof, but the whole gave the appearance of having seen better days. From its unkempt stone walls the once bright yellow paint had been almost washed off leaving weathered leach marks streaking from every window down to the ground.

Had I caught a movement out of the corner of my eye behind one of the windows? I was not sure but with a feeling of gloomy misapprehension I gingerly lifted the latch and swung open the iron gate. Before I had barely taken a step into the yard the front door of the house was flung open and out of it hurtled a low, snarling, spitting beast. Barely a fraction of a second seemed to elapse before the creature flung itself at me. My mind hardly had time to register the sudden stabbing pain in my ankle when a blood-curdling shriek burst forth from the cavity of the house and nearly made my heart stop. Out flew a toothless, wild-eyed hag, her arms and long grey hair flying frantically in all directions. She was shrieking at the top of her voice. From a great mug in one hand huge splatters of witch's brew splashed hither and

Top: The western entrance to Borrisokane. Bottom: Except for the donkey cart, Main Street resembled Lucan, Ontario.

yon as she lunged straight at me. Before I knew it she had thrown her arms around me and clutched me with a desperate grip. I almost fainted.

"God in heaven," raced the thought through my mind. "It's Johannah Donnelly come back from the dead to wreak vengeance on me for trying to track her down in Borrisokane."

With her bulldog still gripping my ankle and the hag clutching the breath out of me, I

Top: Near the site of the 1829 riot in Borrisokane.
Bottom: James Hodgins shot and killed Thomas
Smith during the 1829 riot not far from this spot.

tottered and almost fell. Regaining my senses in a moment, I realized the old woman was screeching at the dog and trying to kick it away.

"Go on, begone wid ye!" she screamed, and the beast of foaming mouth and gnashing teeth finally let go my ankle and, although still snarling and spitting, backed off.

The toothless mouth of the hag turned its attention to me. "Oh, me darlin', me sweet," she breathed into my face. "Are ye hurt at all, me darlin'?"

Unwrapping her arms but still clutching at my jacket she smoothed my clothing, my arms, my hair, all the while alternating dire curses at the dog with expressions of utmost solicitude and care towards me.

Through my torn sock I could see the beast had sunk its teeth well into my flesh. If not infected with rabies, I thought, I would probably survive, and regaining composure I assured the hag I would be all right. In the

meantime, my wife had got out of the car and seeing that the miserable cur had retreated, approached us. As the woman finally began to release her grip on me, I happened to glance at the mug, which she still held in one hand. She must have seen my look for she quickly flung the rest of its contents to the ground and with a deft swipe of the large dirty apron around her waist she slipped it into one of its ample pockets. Turning to my wife but still clutching me, she apologized profusely.

Finally when we had all calmed down, I asked her, "Are you Mrs. Donnelly?"

"Oh, no, me darlin's," she said. "Mrs. Donnelly lives next door here. She's not to home right now. But come, we'll go and find her."

In the twinkle of an eye and without waiting for an invitation, she hopped into the car and perched herself in the back seat ready for the treat of a ride through town in an automobile. Just a little chagrined at the brashness of our new-found friend, we began to drive up and down the streets of Borrisokane all the while being cajoled this way and that by our erstwhile guide.

"Now just drive op here a bit, me darlin'" she'd say, "She jist moight be op here."

Surprisingly, after traveling along the streets for a bit, we did find Mrs. Donnelly walking on the roadway. She was a complete contrast to her next-door neighbor.

"I see ye've found yerself a ride, Babs," she said knowingly as she instantly sized up the situation.

"These people are from Canada," Babs told her. "They've come all the way here to find ye." Then she added wistfully, "Oh, I would like to go to Canada."

Johannah Donnelly was very friendly and gave us as much information as she could about her late husband though she knew little of his family background. She suggested that his brother, who lived nearby in Conger could help us. Babs—I later learned her name was Lawlor—was all in favor of accompanying us to Conger then and there.

Still perched on the back seat of the car, she began to chant, "Conger, Conger, Conger." Thinking we might never be rid of her, we decided politely but firmly to take her home instead.

At Conger we met James Donnelly whose father was the last caretaker of the derelict but still beautiful little Church of Ireland building across the road from his house.[1] He confirmed what I had learned as early as 1967 when I first got in touch with the Donnellys of Borrisokane, that there was some inter-family jostling among those bearing the name in that vicinity. Some claimed the others were not really Donnellys at all but Donnellans from County Galway. Others claimed the Donnellys of North Tipperary were originally from County Tyrone who had been dispersed to Connaught and found their way across the Shannon to North Tipperary. Still others said that all of the Donnellys of the Borrisokane area had indeed come from County Galway and were not Donnellans at all but genuine Donnellys.[2]

It is true that in the first half of the nineteenth century, references in and around Borrisokane to the names Donnelly and Donnellan were often interchangeable. This was done, in my opinion, out of sheer carelessness of the transcriber such as in the entries in the Catholic parish register. Again, the small townland of Greyfort[3] is but a short walk out of Borrisokane. In 1805 a John Donnelly, described as a laborer of the townland of "Grayford", was witness to a deed of Mitchell Haskett's grandfather, Samuel Haskett, Sr. In 1838 the house of a Harry Donnelly acting as steward to Henry Saunders of "Greyforth" was broken in with stones, one of which cut Donnelly on the leg. When the chief constable of police at Borrisokane made a report of this incident to Dublin Castle, he referred to the injured man as Henry Donnellan.

The position of Henry Donnellan, alias Harry Donnelly, in the local hierarchy of Borrisokane is instructive. When a gun was stolen from his house—and again the following year—it was reported in the local newspaper:[4]

> Some night last week a number of men went to the house of a caretaker of Henry Saunders, Esq., of Greyforth, but being unable to effect an entrance, they made a grave near his door, and left a notice threatening him with immediate death if he did not quit his employment.

This Donnelly, then, was not quite of the landless peasantry of North Tipperary nor even a small tenant farmer but a steward of the local landed gentry. As such, he was in all likelihood a large landholding tenant farmer in his own right. And he was authorized to possess firearms—unusual for a Catholic and a sign of some local standing—and was the object of the hostility of lawless gangs of the poor with grievances. At the same period of time, others of the family bearing the names Michael, John and William Donnelly occupied large parcels in the townlands of Tumbrikane, Ballycasey and Liskanlahan just outside the town of Borrisokane. The Donnellys of the Borrisokane area, therefore,

Greyfort House, on the outskirts of Borrisokane.

70

were large tenant farmers or tradesmen of some standing in the community.

Through a contact in Dublin I was put in touch with the venerable Irish genealogist Edward McLysaght.[5] In his great work, *Irish Families*, he wrote at page 121:[6]

> According to the latest available statistics there are not far short of ten thousand persons of the name of Donnelly in Ireland today, which places this name among the sixty-five most numerous in the country. Practically all these may be regarded as belonging to the Ulster Donnelly sept—O Donnghaile of Cinel Eoghan. This is of the same stock as the O'Neills, the eponymous ancestor of the sept being Donnghaile O'Neill, seventeenth in descent from Niall the Great, ancestor of the royal house of O'Neill.

If the Donnellys of Borrisokane originated in Tyrone, they had a long and proud history. The chief of Tyrone was the O'Neill. The O'Neills emerged from obscurity about the time of Saint Patrick and from their fortress in Dungannon retained their paramountcy for well over a thousand years. By ancient tradition, the marshal or head of the warriors of the O'Neills was the chief of the clan O'Donnelly. By virtue of their importance as swordsmen to the ruling family, the O'Donnellys were intimately involved in the bloody internecine intrigues of the O'Neills.

Of the ruling O'Neills, Shane the Proud was one of the most colorful. Pursuant to ancient Celtic custom, the O'Donnellys had fostered Shane and as a result he was sometimes referred to as Shane O'Donnelly. He grew up into a warlike, fierce and bloody combatant. Even before the death of his ruling father, he imprisoned him and claimed the lordship over his head. Hunting down and hanging his chief rival, a half-brother, one by one he had the latter's sons assassinated. Only one of them, Hugh, escaped. As well as fighting his own family, Shane fought not only his other arch enemies, the O'Donnells, but the forces of Queen Elizabeth as well. Totally unscrupulous in all his dealings, Shane O'Neill had an eye for drama. Once, when hard pressed, he took to the English Queen's court in London six hundred of his warriors carrying their battle-axes and adorned in their barbaric furs. Before Elizabeth herself Shane

This oft-reproduced image showing the impaled heads of the enemies of the English crown over the gate of Dublin Castle is from a book published in 1581 during the reign of Queen Elizabeth I. The head of Shane O'Neil, also known as Shane O'Donnelly, was so displayed.

71

prostrated himself to beg for, and was granted, the royal pardon.

No sooner had he again set foot on Irish soil, however, Shane O'Neill rebelled once more, destroying Armagh and Derry. One writer contends most aptly that Shane was nothing more than an Irish warlord very energetic both in warfare and in sexual exploits. He wrote:[7]

> Insatiable, inexhaustible, he was a leader of immense physical energy. His weeklong bouts with *uisce beathadh* (whiskey) and the daughters of Armagh were legendary, and the tale survives of Shane buried to his neck in cool, moist sand, a fabled cure for hangover and sexual exhaustion.

Finally, in 1567 he was betrayed and hacked to death by his old foes, the O'Donnells, who sent his head to Dublin. There, covered with pitch, it was set out on a long pole over the northwest gate of Dublin Castle as a warning to others who contemplated treason against the English queen.

After Shane's death, his nephew Hugh became the Earl of Tyrone. He, too, rebelled against Elizabeth, won some notable victories, and almost united the entire country against the aging queen. Clashes occurred everywhere in Ireland. One of these was a bloody engagement at the little castle or keep called Tumbrikane in what later became North Tipperary. Here at Tumbrikane, later to be associated with the Donnellys who I believe bore kinship to the Biddulph family, Owen O'Kennedy was slain as a rebel. And in the end, Hugh O'Neill too met defeat in a great battle at Kinsale where Donnell O'Donnelly and one hundred of his warriors were slain. Tradition persists that on the retreat from Kinsale, members of the Ulster nobility such as the O'Donnellys dropped off to begin life in a new county. This it is sometimes suggested is how some of the Donnellys of Ulster settled in the lands of the O'Kennedys and O'Carrolls in what later became North Tipperary. If the story is indeed true, two hundred years later the Donnellys of North Tipperary returned to their ancient patrimony in Tyrone, for it was there in Dungannon itself that I discovered one of them, Michael Menon Donnelly, then a very elderly man.[8]

The quotation about the Donnelly families from Edward McLysaght's book, *Irish Families*, which I set out on a previous page goes on as follows:[9]

> . . . Another sept called in English O'Donnelly, but in Irish O Donnghalaigh, belonged to Lower Ormond in Co. Tipperary, but as there appear to be few survivors of it today it can be dismissed with a bare mention.

This sentence haunts all who attempt to investigate the Irish origins of the Donnellys of Biddulph Township in Canada.

Lower Ormond—some authorities say both Upper and Lower Ormond—was known in ancient times as Muscraighe-Thire. From McLysaght's statement above quoted, it seems a simple matter to assume that the Donnellys or O Donnghalaighs of Muscraighe-Thire may have been the ancestors of James Donnelly who settled in Biddulph, Canada. His niece had, after all, come out from Borrisokane in Lower Ormond in 1878 leaving her parents still residing there. But matters are not so simple.

The Donnellys of Muscraighe-Thire disappeared from the recorded history of Ireland about the year 1100. This is the last reference to the clan by the Four Masters in their famous Annals. In an unpublished paper in 1976, John J. W. Donnelly, then an undergraduate student at McMaster University, cogently argued that the Donnellys of Muscraighe-Thire were but temporary inhabitants of that area and that they were there for only about a hundred years. He contended that these O Donnghalaighs were really of the Siol Anmchadha of Longford Barony in County Galway. The Siol Anmchadha—meaning the seed or race of Ambrose—were a branch of the tribes of Hy-many of Galway who for centuries made incursions across the Shannon into the territory variously known

The ancient territories of the Siol Anmchadha (light) and Muscraighe Thire (dark) superimposed over the modern counties of Ireland.

distinguished from the O'Donnellys of the province of Ulster, who are of a different race.

These Donnellys, according to O'Donovan, who based his conclusions upon an ancient Irish tract known as the Book of Lecan, were descended from Anmchadh—anglicized as Ambrose—whose son Donnghallach gave his name to the family. It is quite clear, too, that the O'Donnellans are again a quite distinct family even though they also are one of the Siol Anmchadha of Hy-Many.

The student, John J. W. Donnelly, contended that the O'Donnellys of Longford barony in county Galway had raided Muscraighe-Thire, set up a lordship there for three or four generations, and about the year 1100 were driven back across the Shannon by the original inhabitants of the territory. A small confirmation of this view is found in a map of Ancient Thomond in approximately the year 1300 A.D. showing a clan of O'Donnelly (Ui Donaile) across the Shannon opposite North Tipperary.[11]

Whatever their origin—whether Donnellys of Longford barony in Galway or O'Donnellys of County Tyrone—the name Donnelly was associated during almost the entire nineteenth century with townlands clustered around the town of Borrisokane. One of these townlands was Tumbrikane.

throughout the centuries by the names Muscraighe-Thire, then Ormond and finally North Tipperary.

James Donnelly of Conger near Borrisokane had indeed told me that "all the Donnellys from around here came from a place in County Galway outside Portumna called Killimer on the road to Galway city." He pronounced the name ki-LYE-mur. Indeed, in the ancient territory of Siol Anmchadha now the barony of Longford is a place called Killimer. And the illustrious early Irish antiquarian, John O'Donovan, wrote:[10]

Ui Donnghalaigh—O'Donnellys, now written Donnelly without the O'. This family is to be

Chapter 12

Tumbrikane

The name Tumbrikane will always conjure up in my mind the looming and derelict stone pile which arose abruptly out of the landscape upon our turning a corner on the Portumna road about a mile outside Borrisokane. When Jim Donnelly trod this road towards the bridge at Terryglass, Meara's forge stood at the crossroads near Tumbrikane Castle, as it is often referred to locally. It is more properly a keep or fortified towerhouse around which, when it was inhabited in medieval times, stood substantial wooden outbuildings, yards and houses of servants and farm laborers.

Tumbrikane was erected by one of the O'Kennedy overlords in about the fourteenth century. Three centuries later, to crush a fresh rebellion in Ireland, Oliver Cromwell and his forces invaded with a ferocity that still burns in the Irish memory. As stone castle walls could not resist their cannon balls, his soldiers easily captured Tumbrikane castle. To make the towerhouse uninhabitable, they lay on the dynamite and blasted to smithereens the spiral staircase in the southeast corner. Ever since then it has remained derelict and forlorn sticking 80 feet into the quiet countryside.

When we first saw the little castle it had been lying derelict for more than three hundred years. Throughout much of the nineteenth century it and its townland of the same name had been associated with Donnellys. By 1901 a couple of elderly bachelors of the name, Christopher aged 61, and Charles aged 60, occupied the farm which was owned by their first cousin, Michael Donnelly, of Limerick.[1]

Michael Donnelly had been born in Borrisokane and was Lord Mayor of Limerick in 1904 and 1905. He was the son of John Donnelly who in 1852 held 72 acres of land and fifteen of bog in the townland of Tumbrikane in the parish of Borrisokane. This was the largest holding in the parish. Another Donnelly, also named Michael, held another 125 acres in Ballycasey townland in the adjoining parish of Uskane and this, too, was the largest holding in that parish. The remains of his home, the substantial-sized house with slated roof and glazed windows of a large tenant farmer, were still in existence when we visited the area. Other families of the name headed by Robert and Patrick lived in the nearby parishes of Terryglass and Kilbarron.

I believe there is a direct link between these families of the Borrisokane area and James Donnelly who settled in Biddulph Township in Canada.[2] My best guess is that John Donnelly of Tumbrikane and Michael Donnelly of Ballycasey in 1852 were brothers of James Donnelly of Biddulph. They had at least one other brother named Robert and at least one sister named Bridget. All were the children of an older John Donnelly of

Michael Donnelly, Lord Mayor of Limerick in 1904-1905, was born at Borrisokane and was, the author believes, a first cousin of James Donnelly, Sr., of Biddulph Township, Canada.

Tumbrikane, the medieval towerhouse sitting on the townland of the same name outside Borrisokane, was for most of the nineteenth century associated with the Donnellys.

Tumbrikane who lived from about 1775 to 1855.

From Borrisokane we travelled to Dunkerrin looking for the birthplace of Judy Magee. The parish is about ten miles from Borrisokane as the crow flies with only one other parish lying between them. We knew that within Dunkerrin the Magees lived at a place called Castletown. This is a name which recurs again and again in the Irish landscape. It was not, however, listed as a townland in

The Moat of Castletown, as it is known locally, from the top of which one can see the birthplace of Judith Magee as well as the spot where she married James Donnelly in 1840.

the parish of Dunkerrin, and our task was to find that place called Castletown.

At the time of Judy Magee's marriage to James Donnelly there were three Roman Catholic chapels in the parish. They were not the proud stone edifices of the Normans—many now lying in ruins since the Dissolution of the Monasteries in Tudor times—nor the commanding great churches of the later nineteenth century. They were humble little chapels of wattled walls made of sticks and mud with earthen floors and roofs thatched with straw. Moreover, a Catholic parish would not normally be co-extensive with a civil parish of the same name but would more likely encompass several of the latter. The Catholic parish of Dunkerrin fit this pattern for its full name was the United Parishes of Dunkerrin, Moneygall and Barna. As its name indicated, it was the consolidation of three medieval Catholic parishes of the thirteenth century and its territory covered the civil parishes of

Cullenwaine, Templeharry, Dunkerrin, Rathnaveoge and Castletown-Ely. Despite the similarity of the name of the last-mentioned place, it could not be the Castletown of the Magees as it in itself consisted of three disjointed townlands. Where then could Castletown be?

A clue came from the so-called Griffith's Valuation[3]—compiled for this part of Ireland in 1851—in which a James Magee is shown as the occupant of a small acreage in the townland of Moatquarter in Dunkerrin parish. Could Moatquarter be the elusive Castletown? A small reference to a road repair contract in the newspaper provided another clue. It read:[4]

BARONY OF IKERRIN. The Adjourned Road Sessions . . . 20—To repair 699 perches of the road from Nenagh to Templemore, between the King's County bounds at Castletown and Longford wood....

The Ordnance Survey map of this area provided the answer and it was unequivocal.

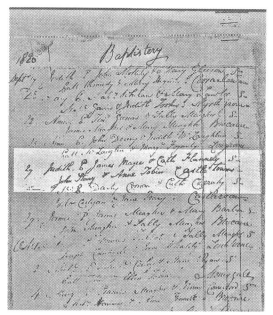

The 1820 baptismal record of Judith Magee puts the lie to her date of birth shown on the tombstone.

Castletown, it now seemed clear, was the townland known officially as Moatquarter, or at least a part of it, as it was the only place, which could possibly fit this location. It turned out that Castletown was the name of a small medieval townland, which the Ordnance Surveyors of the mid-nineteenth century incorporated into a larger one. As so often happened, the surveyors "generally selected the name of the central townland area and consigned the subdivision to oblivion."[5]

When we stopped at Dunkerrin crossroads and inquired about any Magees or Donnellys living in the area, we were told that Pat Donnelly lived "below the moat" and were directed in the direction of where it stood. Now for me, a "moat" had always meant a ditch filled with water surrounding a castle. On the one-inch to the mile Ordnance Survey maps at this location, the word "Moat" appeared in old English lettering signifying an ancient structure or ruin. No sign of a castle, however, was shown on the map. On the larger scale six-inch to the mile Ordnance Survey map, there appeared a rectangular mound which I surmised could

have been the remnant of the moat of a castle which, I thought, had disappeared into the mists of time so long ago that even its name was forgotten.[6]

What I did find on visiting the site for the first time, however, was a complete surprise. For a change, the day was bright and clear. At eleven o'clock in the morning I had left Beverley doing domestic chores in the town of Roscrea and drove alone past the crossroads or hamlet of Dunkerrin to the little village of Moneygall and then doubled back on the uphill road. Coming over a hill, I came upon—wonder of wonders—the Moat of Castletown! It rose up in the distance—an eerie sight—directly in front of me. It caught me so by surprise that I stopped the car and stared. The Moat, it turned out, was not a moat in its proper sense at all but a *motte*. That is to say, it was a huge spherical mound of earth so round that it seemed unnatural. And indeed it was, for it had been thrown up on top of a hill by the early Norman invaders apparently as part of their fortification. The psychological impact on the native Irish of such a huge and unnatural earthwork rising out of the landscape was not lost on the Normans who were ever masters of such intimidation. With a *motte* there was usually a bailey, which was a palisaded courtyard, but it had apparently long since disappeared even though the outline of its remnant was still shown on the six-inches to the mile Ordnance map with its label in old English lettering.

When I had got over my astonishment, I happened to spot some little distance off a young lad of about thirteen or fourteen silently watching me from the side of the road. I drove up and spoke to him.

"What is that strange looking hill?" I asked the lad.

"That's the Moat."

"What is it?"

"I dunno. But I think it was something like a lookout. They signaled from the top of it to the tower over there."

He pointed, and for the first time I saw a little distance off to my left a small stone tower sticking up over the crest of a hill.[7]

"That's Busherstown," he added. That was interesting, I thought, as Judy Magee may have been for a time employed there as a servant.

"Is there a graveyard around here?" I asked.

"Yes, right there up on the hill."

He pointed towards the crest of the hill to my right.

"Is it old?" I asked.

"Yes, but there are still people being buried there."

I then directed his attention back to the curious round structure at the top of the hill in front of us that he had called the Moat.

"Have you ever climbed it?" I asked.

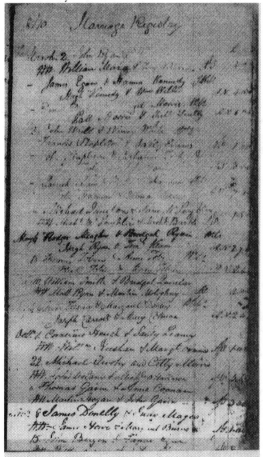

Marriage record of James Donnelly and Judy Magee on November 8, 1840.

"Oh, yes, lots of times."

"And whose house is that at the bottom of it?"

"Mr. Donnelly's."

"What's his first name?"

"Pat," he answered, and then added ominously, "but you can't go there."

"Why not?" I asked.

"The dog," he answered with foreboding in his youthful voice.

On my way back to Roscrea, I puzzled over the reference to the dog, for in my excitement at the anticipation of meeting the Donnellys below the Moat I had forgotten to inquire further about it. After picking Beverley up in Roscrea, I retraced the route back through Dunkerrin and Moneygall to call on them.

Pat Donnelly of the Moat was to my mind the spitting image of Bob Donnelly of Biddulph. He was the same height and build, spoke with a dry sardonic humor and greeted you with the same hail-fellow-well-met manner which I always imagined Bob to have affected. As we chatted in the yard, Pat's brother John happened drive into the yard atop a huge tractor. Again, as he alighted, I could hardly believe my eyes.

John was again what I imagined Tom Donnelly to have been. He was the same height and build as Tom—taller and more angular than his brother—with beetling brows and an intense piercing glare in his eyes. When I introduced Beverley to him, he stuck out a big ham-sized fist. His face suddenly and unexpectedly—because of his previous black frown—broke into a wide grin.

"I know that name," he said, "It's like Beverly Hills in Hollywood."

As I looked at the two brothers, I could not suppress the thought that these two men standing before me could have walked right off the dust jacket of *The Donnelly Album*.

Pat and his wife Maureen invited us inside. And, yes, they had a dog—a black Labrador Retriever. He would let you come in and sit, they said, but don't ever try to get up and leave without warning. Before we did, in fact, Maureen quickly got up and locked him in the other room. Prior to that, however, Pat pulled out his maps and on one of them laid down a finger to point out the exact location of the ancient townland known as Castletown. It was indeed now a part of the modern townland of Moatquarter. But while Moatquarter was within the Catholic parish of Dunkerrin, for civil purposes it was part of the civil parish of Rathnaveoge in North Tipperary. We discussed the history of Pat's family for they had not heard of the so-called Black Donnellys of Canada. I asked him if he knew of the Donnellys of Irishtown, a townland also within the parish of Dunkerrin where I knew from my previous research a family of the name had lived for generations.

"We are the Donnellys of Irishtown," Pat declared. "Come and I'll show you where Irishtown is from here."

We went out and clambered to the top of the *motte*. Here a magnificent view of the countryside presented itself. From the summit one could see not only the townland of Irishtown two or three miles distant but also the tower of Busherstown, Knockshegowna (the fairy hill of the O'Carrolls), Lisduff House (one of the Big Houses of the parish) and Benduff Mountain looming in the distance. Borrisokane itself was just beyond one of the hills on the horizon. Pat Donnelly also pointed out where the Magee home had in all likelihood stood. This was the birthplace of Judith Magee whom we know as Johannah Donnelly. And it was here that she first rolled down the grassy slope of the ancient *motte* itself, romped through the very green meadow, walked the narrow tree-lined laneway, crossed the bubbling stream over the little arched stone bridge which led to the cluster of cabins which once stood beside the hedge, and viewed from the doorway of her father's probably humble house Benduff Mountain brooding in the distance.

On the hill directly opposite from our viewpoint, not quite as high as that of the *motte*, lay the ivy-covered ruins of an ancient abbey church which in all likelihood was abandoned at the time of the Dissolution of the Monasteries during the reign of Henry VIII. Local tradition has it that the humble thatched Catholic chapel with earthen floor stood within the walls of the ruins of that abbey church. And it was here at the chapel of Castletown where James Donnelly married Judy Magee. That very ground was now littered with graves—none, however, bearing the inscription of a Magee. But there was one which bore the name Donnelly.

The priest who married James and Judy signed himself "AJS" and he would therefore have been Andrew J. Scanlan who served as curate under the parish priest, Father Anthony Nolan. From the Dunkerrin Catholic parish register, we learn that the civil parish of Rathnaveoge was the home not only of the Magees but also of the Farrells, Tooheys, Flannerys and Heenans, names all

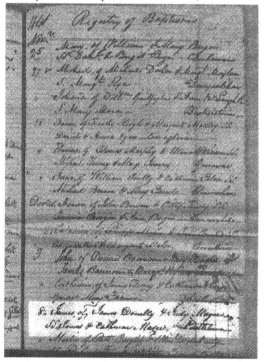

James Donnelly, Jr.'s record of baptism.

79

later found in Biddulph, Canada. Also associated with the parish are the names of Roger Carroll, William Thompson and Michael Maher which crop up again in the Donnelly story in Canada.[8] Griffith's Valuation shows Moatquarter occupied in 1851 by six small farmers among whom was James Magee, the father of Mrs. James Donnelly. Only two of the farms were smaller than James Magee's six acres.[9]

As we walked up and down the townland where Judith Magee had been born and raised, I pondered the question, which has haunted followers of the Donnelly story. More often than I care to remember, I have heard it said that the feud between the Donnellys and their neighbors had been

£30 Reward.

WHEREAS on the night of the 13th instant, the Dwelling-house of Widow *Nolan*, of *Tumbricane*, in the County *Tipperary*, was attacked and forcibly entered by a party of Persons unknown, who broke every article of Delf in said House, set fire to her bed, and subsequently set fire to the house of her father, *John Donnelly*, of said place.

I HEREBY Offer a REWARD of

THIRTY POUNDS

To any Person who shall, within Six Months from the date hereof, give me such information as may enable me to discover and bring to Justice all or any of the Persons who were concerned in these Outrages.

J. H. BRACKEN,

Sub-Inspector.

Borrisokane, 18th February, 1840.

The Widow Nolan, alias Bridget Donnelly, and John Donnelly—mentioned in this notice—are, the author believes, the sister and father respectively of James Donnelly who emigrated to Canada.
(Copied by permission of the Irish National Archives)

imported from turbulent Tipperary. What evidence was there of such a feud in Tipperary? If not a feud, was it possible to discover what great troubles the Donnellys had become involved in back here in Ireland?

We could uncover none in Dunkerrin, but back in Borrisokane there came to light a little episode involving one of the Donnelly families of that parish. The trouble appears to have arisen not so much out of an alleged rape but the common lovers' triangle.

I have already referred to John Donnelly who lived from about 1775 to 1855, the tenant farmer in the nineteenth century holding a large farm in the townland of Tumbrikane in the parish of Borrisokane. He was, I now believe, the father of James Donnelly who settled on the Roman Line of Biddulph. Others of his children were John, Michael, Robert, Bridget and perhaps others. His daughter Bridget lived from about 1820 to about 1910. Bridget Donnelly first married a man named Nolan but soon became the Widow Nolan. What caused the death of her husband is unknown. In any event, the young widow was by the year 1839 living as a tenant in a small house in the townland of Tumbrikane. Her landlord was her own father, John Donnelly, possessor of the largest acreage in the immediate vicinity. As a Catholic, however, he was still only a tenant himself albeit with a large landholding.

In the nearby townland of Kylepark, the seat of John Donnelly's landlord who was Thomas George Stoney, lived a young farmer named Darby Slevin. Darby began paying his respects to the young widow Nolan and it soon became evident that the couple had marital vows in mind. This did not come without repercussions within the community. It seemed that another young woman named Jane Coonan had also "put her comether an" Slevin, and when it became obvious he was going to throw her over for the young widow, Jane Coonan brought a charge of rape against him. Talk in the community, however, was that this was simply a common lovers' triangle in which Jane had come out the loser. Towards the end of July in 1839, the charge of rape was laid before the Grand Jury. They dealt with it on a Friday by throwing it out.

By Monday there was a reaction occasioning the Chief Constable of Police at Borrisokane, John H. Bracken, to write to Dublin Castle.[10] He reported that on the

> 27th instant the dwelling house of a farmer named Darby Slevin of Kylepark was discovered to have been maliciously set on fire . . .

As the thatch had just started to blaze, the fire was got under control and the house saved. The chief constable added, however, that

> There can be little doubt as to its having been caused by some friends of a young woman named Jain Coonan.

A poster was printed up in the matter, which reads:[11]

£20 Reward
I hereby offer a Reward of Twenty Pounds To any Person who shall, within Six Months from the date hereof, give me such information as may enable me to discover and bring to Justice the Person or Persons who, early on the morning of the 27th instant, set fire to Darby Slevin's Dwelling-House, at Kylepark, in the Parish of Borrisokane, and County Tipperary.
J.H. Bracken
Chief Constable, Borrisokane
31st July 1839.

Darby Slevin continued to court the young widow Nolan for the next few months. When in February of the following year the wedding seemed imminent, Jane Coonan herself confronted Bridget Donnelly Nolan and threatened to burn her house over her head should she persist in going ahead with the marriage to Slevin.

On February 13, 1840, even as the young couple were exchanging their vows, Bridget's house was broken into and her bed set ablaze. Some of her furniture and clothing were consumed. The wedding nevertheless went ahead, but on the evening of the same day while the Donnellys and their friends

were celebrating the nuptials with a dance at a neighbor's, the house of the bride's father was also discovered to be on fire. The celebrants immediately rushed forth, however, and saved the home of John Donnelly.

This time Bracken of the Borrisokane police took immediate action. He reported to Dublin Castle:[12]

> I concluded this is a continuation of the same intimidation [and] therefore had Jane Coonan arrested . . . .

Again, a reward poster was printed up and posted throughout the district referring not only to the breaking into of the house of Bridget but also the setting on fire of her father's house. As there appeared, however, to be suspicion alone and no hard evidence, the magistrate committed Jane Coonan for further examination. At the ensuing assizes, it appears that no evidence at all was forthcoming and the authorities had no option but to drop the charges against her.

At the same assizes, the Grand Jury awarded to Bridget Donnelly, now Mrs. Darby Slevin, damages of eight pounds to be paid out of the county treasury for "furniture and clothing maliciously burned in the parish of Borrisokane."[13] This appears to have been the end of the affair. In the years following, Darby Slevin and his wife Bridget had several children who were baptized in the Catholic Church in the town of Borrisokane. And when the 1901 census of Ireland was made available on the internet, in the year 2010 I looked up and found Bridget Slevin, nee Donnelly, still living at Tumbrikane with two grown sons and a daughter. She was then stated to be 85 years old and a widow.

Chapter 13

What About Sheehy?

On their arrival in North Tipperary, the Normans and later the English found the O'Kennedys, O'Carrolls, O'Mahers, O'Dwyers and O'Ryans in possession of the land. Over the centuries the newcomers knocked the native princes hither and yon and although they fought back and for a time regained their hegemony, the native Irish were eventually—particularly during the time of Elizabeth I of England and again fifty years after her death by Cromwell and his mercenary armies—banished from all power and influence.

After that final invasion, North Tipperary was parceled out to the Cromwellian soldiers. Their progeny and the wealthy English merchants and tradespeople who followed in their wake acquired ownership of the former tribal lands of the O'Kennedys, O'Carrolls, O'Mahers and the others. From the stone castles originally built for the most part by the Normans, the new owners of the land soon cowed into submission all orders of the native Irish. In a generation or two the new proprietors of the soil who were descended from the officers of Cromwell—the common soldiers quickly sold their small allotments to their superiors—were able to abandon their dank and draughty stone piles and move into snug new Big Houses which they built throughout the baronies of North Tipperary. With the cheap labor of the Irish working classes, they erected huge stone walls around their estates. For over the next two hundred years this so-called Anglo-Irish Ascendancy class held almost all the political power and influence in the country.

In *The Donnellys Must Die*, Orlo Miller puts a great emphasis upon Sheehy's Day claiming that the feud between the Donnellys—called by him Blackfeet—and their enemies, who he says were Whiteboys, had been imported from Ireland. This misreading of Irish history aside, who was Sheehy and what did he have to do with the Whiteboys? An old Biddulphite had a ready answer for me one day when he told me that the origin of the feud was quite simple, namely, that Father Sheehy's hangman was a Donnelly!

If only things were that easy. The truth is that in 1739, because of an outbreak of hoof and mouth disease in mainland Europe, Irish landlords began not only to convert small tenant holdings to pasture but also to enclose what had been up to then common lands. For the downtrodden Irish peasant this was the last straw.

Dispossessed in their own land and estranged from the framework of law and order by an alien people with an alien culture, religion, language and laws, the Irish Catholic peasants turned to the only form of redress they could trust. Coming together at night, they formed themselves into secret bands and pulled down the newly erected fences enclosing the former commonages. From this circumstance, they were at first called Levellers. The Levellers, however, soon came to be known by another name, which persisted for a hundred years and more—Whiteboys. The name originated from their habit of disguising themselves during their maraudings by pulling white shirts over their outer clothing. As the Irish peasant of this period owned perhaps but one coat or one pair of trousers at any one time—and that not often renewed—a particular peasant's attire was readily recognized. A white shirt over it would hide the appearance of his outer coat and hence his identity.

From leveling fences, the Whiteboys quickly progressed to other intimidations—burning farm outbuildings or haggards, raiding for firearms the houses of the more affluent Protestant tenants (Catholics were not generally allowed to bear arms) and giving warnings to particularly obnoxious landlords or tenants by cutting off the ears of their horses.

Typical of the way their form of justice often struck the wrong mark was the case of John Bridge. He was named from having been found as a baby abandoned on a bridge in a small town called Ballyporeen[1] in the south part of the county of Tipperary in the parish of Clogheen. He grew up and came to be known by his large white frieze overcoat with its distinctive shell buttons.

In 1755 when the incumbent of the Catholic parish of Clogheen died, the bishop of the diocese, a man named Creagh, appointed to that parish one Nicholas Sheehy.[2] Father Sheehy, born in 1728 and educated to the priesthood in France, soon began to ruffle the feathers of the local authorities. Virtually all local government authority of the day was reposed in the Protestant landed gentry. These men, "a body of country gentlemen, prosperous, contented, given to the pleasures of chase and table,"[3] were descended from officers of the Cromwellian conquest some five generations before. The remnants of the Old English and Irish princes and chieftains of the time before that—those not dispersed to the continent—were relegated to the ranks of the common Irish.

By the mid-eighteenth century, however, some Catholic families had begun to prosper despite the Penal Laws aimed for the most part against Catholics and their religion. When in 1761 a general election was held following the death of George II, Thomas Mathew, a Catholic, defeated for a seat in Parliament Sir Thomas Maude of Dundrum who was descended from a Cromwellian. The squires and parsons of the Protestant ascendancy of South Tipperary panicked. They decided to go on a rampage to put down the growing influence of the wealthy Catholics. They concocted a theory that those same Catholic families had worked up a Popish plot whereby they would assist the French in landing an invasionary force to usurp power in Ireland.

Maude brought a petition against Mathew and unseated him. Mathew's agent was challenged to a duel on the grounds that his wife was a Papist, and had been seen praying with a priest. In the resulting duel, the agent was killed. Led by Maude, the Protestant gentry began prosecutions against the younger members of those prospering Catholic families.

When the Whiteboys began to level fences in the winter of 1761 in the vicinity of the parish in which Nicholas Sheehy was ministering as the parish priest of Clogheen, the gentry immediately focused on him. He had already incurred their wrath by encouraging Catholics to pay no tithes to the Protestant church. After all, Sheehy had declared, there were no Protestants in the parish. Soldiers commanded by the Earl of

Father Nicholas Sheehy 1728-1766
(Copy permission Tipperary S.R. Museum)

Drogheda—a name peculiarly suited to dredge up the long Irish memory of the butcher Cromwell—were dispatched to Clogheen. Reports stated that the troops killed many "insurgents" and captured many more. Before long, the jails of the nearby county towns of Clonmel and Kilkenny were filled with Whiteboys.

In June 1762 Nicholas Sheehy was charged with failing to register as a Catholic priest. Presumably he was acquitted for he went on ministering. As the Whiteboys continued their nocturnal violence, however, the landlords grew certain it was Sheehy who was encouraging them.

In the winter of 1763 John Bridge, he of the white frieze overcoat with distinctive shell buttons, was staying with a farmer named William Cremins of Shanbally. Bridge was known as not the best of Catholics and while he himself did not attend midnight mass at the chapel that Christmas Eve, Cremins did. For the occasion, he borrowed Bridge's overcoat.

Shortly after Christmas, it was discovered that the chalice belonging to the church was missing. From the known fact that Bridge did not frequently attend services at the chapel but that he was allegedly seen there for midnight mass, suspicion of the theft immediately fell upon him. Bridge went to the authorities and complained that he was confronted by a group of parishioners headed by the parish priest, Father Nicholas Sheehy. When he denied stealing the chalice, Sheehy struck him.

In January 1764 more serious charges were laid against the priest. He was accused of treason for raising Whiteboys and inciting his parishioners to rebellion. Sir Thomas Maude, who was soon to assume the office of High Sheriff of Tipperary, found John Bridge and persuaded him to lay an additional charge of assault against the priest. Sheehy kept out of the way but continued to minister among his people.

When John Bridge disappeared and a large reward was offered for Sheehy's capture, the priest decided to take the bold step of surrendering to the authorities in the capital city of Dublin where he hoped his trial would then be held. There he could expect a fair hearing, as opposed to one in the Tipperary county town of Clonmel where his enemies were in complete command.

On March 16th, 1765 the Dublin *Gazette* reported:[4]

> About 8 o'clock on Wednesday night, Nicholas Sheehy, a popish priest, charged with being concerned in several treasonable practices to raise rebellion in this kingdom, for the apprehending of whom Government offered a reward of £300, was brought to town guarded by a party of light horse and lodged by the Provost in the Lower Castle Yard.

On February 10th, 1766 Sheehy stood before the bar of the Court of King's Bench in Dublin and heard the charge of treason read out against him. The trial lasted eleven hours. The court found a verdict of Not Guilty.

There now took place the betrayal of Father Sheehy, the memory of which has rumbled down through the ages in the Irish Catholic memory of the county of Tipperary. Instead of being released, Sheehy saw the prosecutor stand up and move to have him committed to prison and thence sent back to Clonmel to be tried—not for treason this time but for the murder of John Bridge. Much to the astonishment of Sheehy and his friends, the motion was granted.

Gleefully, the Tipperary squires paraded Sheehy back. He was put on horseback with hands strapped behind his back and legs pinioned beneath his mount. A heavy military escort accompanied the prisoner back to Clonmel. There in the old jail on Lough Street, he was chained to his cell with double bolts to await his trial.

Three weeks later, when the Clonmel Spring Assizes came on, the town was in a frenzy of excitement. Soldiers were everywhere. Rumors abounded that the priest had tried to escape. Everyone who came into Clonmel was under suspicion. Known friends of the prisoner were intimidated. One contemporary account states:[5]

> On the day of the trial a party of horse surrounded the court, admitting and excluding whom they thought proper, while others of them with a certain Baronet at their head, scampered the streets in a formidable manner; forcing into inns and private lodgings in the town; challenging and questioning all new comers; menacing his friends and encouraging his enemies.

The Baronet referred to was, of course, Sir Thomas Maude.

The priest was marched down Lough Street in chains to the Main Guard where the trial took place in a room at the rear. It lasted four hours. The gist of the Crown's evidence as reported, was that on the night Bridge was murdered in a field in Shanbally, the following occurred:[6]

> Nicholas Sheehy tendered an oath to John Bridge to deny his examination; who refused to take it; on his refusal Pierce Byrn struck at him with a slane which he defended with his left hand; then [Edward Meehan] drew a bill-hook from under a belt, and struck Bridge on the head which to his recollection clove the skull; Bridge fell down instantly.

The prisoner was defended by Mr. Sparrow. His defense was to attack the credibility of the prosecution witnesses and to set up an alibi. Sheehy, it was claimed, had spent the night in question nine Irish miles from the scene of the murder. When he attempted to call the witnesses to establish this alibi, however, they were arrested. The verdict was Guilty and the sentence was death.

Sheehy's enemies were jubilant but continued to press their intimidations. A contemporary account states:[7]

> Mr. Sparrow, his attorney, declares that he found it necessary for his safety to steal out of town by night, and with all possible speed to escape to Dublin.

The next morning, back in his cell at the jail, the priest wrote the following letter to one of the jail officials in Dublin who had been particularly kind to him during his imprisonment there:[8]

> To Joseph Sirr, Esq., Dublin.
> Clonmel, Friday morning, March 14, 1766
> Dear Sir,
> To morrow I am to be executed, thanks be to the Almighty God, with whom I hope to be for evermore; I would not change my lot with the highest now in the kingdom. I die innocent of the facts for which I am sentenced. The Lord have mercy on my soul . . . the prosecutors swore wrongfully and falsely. God forgive them. The accusers and the accused are equally ignorant of the fact, as I have been informed, but after such a manner I received the information that I cannot make use of it for my own preservation. The fact is that John Bridge was destroyed by two alone, who strangled him on Wednesday, the 24th October, 1764. I was then from home and only returned home the 28th and heard that he had disappeared. Various were the reports which to believe I could not pretend to, until in the discharge of my duty one accused himself of the said fact. May God grant the guilty true repentance and preserve the innocent . . .
> Your most obliged and humble servant,
> NICHOLAS SHEEHY.

On the morning of Saturday, March 15th, 1766 Father Nicholas Sheehy was hanged on a gallows erected in the street in front of the jail on Lough Street in Clonmel. The executioner, as it turned out, was not a person named Donnelly but a man named Darby Brahan.

For rebels, hanging was not punishment enough. The body was cut down, drawn and quartered. The head was severed and affixed to the turret of the Main Guard. Only then were the rest of the remains delivered to the family for burial. The head of Nicholas Sheehy remained on the turret of the Main Guard for twenty years.

The remains of the priest's mangled body were taken by his sister and other members of the family to be buried at the cemetery beside the ruins of the ancient church of St. Mary's in Shanrahan near his home.

Judging from almost every account of the trial and execution of Nicholas Sheehy, both contemporary to it and from successive generations, his death was a judicial murder. The Irish people had no doubt of it from the beginning. In their eyes, he was a saint and his sainthood only lacked official canonization from Rome.

"By March 1769, Fr Sheehy was already 'the blessed Martyr'; 'the cause he died by sanctified his Remains, his Ashes were pronounced holy' and his grave in Shanrahan and its supposed healing powers became the attraction for multitudes of the Lame, the Blind and the Diseased."[9]

Almost every account of the priest's trial and execution bristles with indignation at his false betrayal. The Tipperary landlords, it is said, scoured the jails of Clonmel and Kilkenny cajoling and bribing hardened criminals and other dissolute persons to testify against him. Among these were a man named Toohey, a prostitute named Dunlea and a young lad named Lonergan. Sheehy's defense witnesses were intimidated or hauled off to jail on false charges.

All who have written about Sheehy disparage the witnesses who appeared against him. Almost gleefully, most writers recount the miserable fates of all individuals connected with Sheehy's prosecution— victims of a divine retribution. All, whether judges, witnesses or members of the jury, were said to have died miserable deaths within a few years. Only one died naturally, it is asserted. The executioner of Sheehy, Darby Brahan, was stoned to death four years later in County Kilkenny.

The Protestant gentry had targeted forty other Catholics of the wealthy middle class. Their campaign collapsed, however, when Edmund Burke, the political philosopher in London, took up the cause of the victims and

The Main Guard in Clonmel atop the turret of which the head of the executed priest Sheehy was placed for public view and remained for twenty years.

rallied a powerful defense at Westminster in their favor. Burke was almost the same age as Nicholas Sheehy and, though born in Dublin, his roots were in the same region of the province of Munster as the priest's. Furthermore, although Burke was a Protestant like his father, his mother and her relations were of the same Catholic gentry stock as Sheehy's family.

While in Ireland, we went to visit the grave of Nicholas Sheehy in Shanrahan, South Tipperary. I find it curious that Samuel Lewis, writing presumably shortly before the publication of his *Topographical Dictionary of*

Edmund Burke

Ireland in 1837, made no reference to Sheehy's grave when he mentioned the ruins of St. Mary's church at Shanrahan. The omission may have indicated that after about three generations the memory of the martyred priest—though not completely absent in the minds of the people—was nonetheless slumbering. It was suddenly revived, however, in an emotionally charged election campaign, which took place in Tipperary in 1841.

That memorable contest on the hustings in Tipperary which occurred during the general election that year, was seared into the memory of those Irish Catholics who, like Jim Donnelly and many of his neighbors, emigrated to Canada shortly thereafter. Those emigrants were not for the most part fleeing famine but were the sons and daughters of the rising middle class of Catholic farmers who were at this time gradually wresting political power from the waning Protestant ascendancy, the class which had ruled unchallenged since Cromwell.

Only a few years before that election of 1841, Daniel O'Connell had achieved Catholic Emancipation allowing his co-religionists to sit in the British House of Commons at Westminster. When Parliament was forced to give, however, it also took away. The qualification to vote of the forty shilling freeholders was abolished. In some estates the forty shillingers had been driven to the polls almost like cattle to vote at the landlord's behest. To offset the admission of Catholics and to replace the forty-shilling voters, the bar was raised from forty shillings to ten-pounds. And it was the ten pound freeholders, many of them Catholics (in Tipperary at least) who were becoming the new political power in Ireland. Their numbers were far fewer than the old forty-shillingers—there were only about three thousand of the new class of voters in the entire county of Tipperary—but they were much more independent. The rise of this class made itself evident in the 1841 election contest of Tipperary and it was from the younger members of this class that the emigrants bound for Canada came.

Curiously, the political parties active in Tipperary at this time bore the same names as they did in Biddulph Township in Canada about forty years later. There were Conservatives or Tories on the one hand and Liberals—otherwise known as Radicals or Whigs—on the other. In this 1841 election the ghost of Father Nicholas Sheehy was dredged up from the past and his name once more became a household word in the Catholic homes of the county. The cause of

Shanrahan Graveyard

such revival was one of the candidates. His name was Cornwallis Maude, and he was descended from the notorious Thomas Maude, the nemesis of the martyred priest, Nicholas Sheehy.

When the canvas of voters by the candidates began, the Nenagh *Guardian*, as usual, was totally behind the Conservative choices. On June 12th the newspaper stated:

> We have to apologize to our readers for not introducing more early to their notice two candidates of sound constitutional principles— men too independent in property and station to barter their country's birth right, Shiel-like, for a government "mess of potage." One is the Hon. Cornwallis Maude, only son of Viscount Hawarden, nephew to the Lady Dunalley, and closely allied to the most influential families in this county—the Pritties, Bagwells, Perrys, &c. The Hon. Maude's ancestors represented the county of Tipperary in the Irish Parliament for many generations; his claim of family is, therefore, not one of yesterday.

What the *Guardian* did not state, however, was a fact, which certainly the Catholic bishops knew well. This was that it was the ancestor of this candidate, Thomas Maude, who had led the persecution of Nicholas Sheehy some three generations before. When the name of Cornwallis Maude was put

forward as a candidate for one of the two seats in Tipperary, the Catholic bishops were determined to see him routed in the polls. Feeling ever more confident in the increasing political power of not only their church but also their principal financial supporters, the large Catholic farmers, they fueled the opposition against the old Tory family. Through the Sunday sermons of their parish priests, they recalled to their people the judicial murder of Nicholas Sheehy those many years before. The flame once kindled among the Catholic people of Tipperary grew into a bonfire of outrage.

The *Guardian*'s reference to a "mess of potage" was to the former member for Tipperary, Richard Lalor Shiel, a colleague of Daniel O'Connell. The Whigs whom O'Connell had supported in Parliament had appointed Shiel to a junior government office. And the Pritties, Bagwells and Perrys were families come to Ireland with the hated Cromwell almost two centuries before.

The other candidate for the Conservative side was William Ponsonby Barker. It was said that in his dotage this same man had made it his custom each evening after prayers to pick out a maid servant to accompany him to his bed ostensibly as a "human hot water bottle" to warm his aging bones.[10]

The *Guardian* noted the two Conservative

Sheehy's grave, Shanrahan, Tipperary

88

candidates' campaign progress on the last day of June:

Haut Ton—County Tipperary Candidates.

The Hon. Cornwallis Maude, and R. U. Bayly, Esq., proceeded on Monday morning in their canvas for the former gentleman and Mr. Barker, from Roscrea through Shinrone, Borrisokane, and Cloughjordan, and in the evening were hospitably entertained at Modreeny, by Thomas B. Dancer, Esq.

The infamous ancestry of Maude, however, soon began to dog the young candidate. The

Scene at Newport during the 1841 election

opposition posted placards—with language not always the most temperate—in every town and village of the county. One read as follows:[11]

Notice, Hurrah! Ireland for ever, down with the hell-hounds, the Orange Barker and bloody Maude. Revenge Father Sheehy, the murdered Priest. To the poll man and woman and child that hate taxes, tithes, tyranny and taxation, torture and threachery; hell-begotten, blood-stained Priest-and-People murdering Tories. — Now's the day, now's the hour, down for ever with Orange power, to the poll, Ireland for ever!

As expected, the *Guardian* assiduously reported the delivery of threatening notices

by Captain Rock "in favor of his friends the Liberal candidates". For example, it found one served on Mr. John Martin of Dangansallagh which read:[12]

If you vote for Barker or bloody Maud[e] who hung the priest, mark what HALL got.

The reference to Hall was to the unpopular landlord of Merton Hall near Borrisokane in whose murder one, William Kent, was alleged to have been implicated, as already noted. With provocations like this, it was not long into the election campaign before the people became inflamed with passion. In Roscrea a mob of 350 strong assembled in the market square. The Nenagh *Guardian* blamed "some Roman Catholic Clergymen" for what followed because they had "Frankenstein-like, wantonly called into existence the monster of outrage"[13] The mob, accompanied by fife and drum, bellowed offensive tunes. They paraded about the streets a wretched dog decorated with orange lilies. In the evening they burned an effigy of Cornwallis Maude. Some of the more boisterous went about shattering the windows of Protestants whom they knew would be sure to vote for the Conservative candidates.

The crowning incident in Maude's ill-fated campaign took place on Sunday, July 4th at Newport, a town about 25 miles from Borrisokane. That morning the Newport priests had harangued their congregations on the subject of Father Nicholas Sheehy. Shortly after church was out, a blacksmith named Thomas Mulcahy hung a sign on Maude's carriage which read: "WHO HUNG THE PRIEST?"

When a crowd of about a hundred emerging from Sunday Mass spotted his carriage, they seized it, dragged it to a nearby bridge and flung it over. It landed on the rocks below with its wheels spinning in the air. Split asunder by the boulders, the carriage "disgorged champagne, cheroots and cold meats" while the crowd on the bridge jeered. Though Maude himself was elsewhere at the time, his servants and attendants were attacked. The crowd threw mud and dirt at them and the police eventually came and tried to rescue them. All the while, the Newport Temperance Band bellowed away on their instruments "in support of the tumult".

For the remainder of the contest, the jeering phrase "Who hung the priest?" followed poor Maude relentlessly. When he rose to speak at the county town of Clonmel, it was jeeringly shouted at him from the crowd. In those days an elector was required to attend in person in the county town on the appointed day and proclaim his choice in public. From Nenagh, a small group of Conservatives banded together and set out for Clonmel. At Hollyford Wood they narrowly escaped an ambush by an unruly mob. Another group headed for Clonmel by way of Upperchurch. There a large mob blocked the road and prevented further passage.

The 1841 contest reminded the Irish people who their enemies were. The most virulent hatred was reserved for those whom the people called Orange Catholics—Catholics who voted for or otherwise supported the Conservative candidates. Such "black sheep", as they were called, were ostracized. Shortly after the general election which, needless to say, the Conservative candidates lost, a crowd in County Carlow followed James Nash and his daughter jeering them with shouts of "Stone the damned Orange Catholics to death." The crime of Nash was that he had dared to buy turf from a "black sheep" of the community.

Three years later when one of the successful candidates who had been elected in 1841 died, a by-election was called in Tipperary. Maude did not run again and Barker, when he was approached, wrote bitterly:[14]

> I . . . have recalled . . . the last Election . . . I should have been returned to parliament, had not an organized insurrection, extending from the north to the south of this great county,

have been brought to bear . . . [my supporters suffered] intimidation . . . [were] attacked on the highways, and driven away from the County Town . . . I decline coming forward . . .

The Tipperary general election contest of 1841 foreshadowed one more great campaign of Daniel O'Connell's—for Repeal of the Union between England and Ireland. It held so-called monster repeal meetings all over the country—some of the largest in Tipperary—and reached its climax in 1843. It collapsed when O'Connell was imprisoned the following year.

Jim Donnelly and Judy Magee were not around to experience O'Connell's joyful liberation a few months later. Like so many of the younger set of their fellow Catholics of North Tipperary, they had emigrated to Canada. But they and their fellow emigrants took with them the memory of that exciting election in their county of 1841 in which the name of Nicholas Sheehy had been resurrected and whose martyrdom lived on in the hearts and minds of those who settled in Biddulph, albeit in a vague and garbled fashion.

It must be stated here, however, that although Sheehy's Day was remembered by the older generation of Irish who came to the Catholic Settlement of Biddulph, it had very little reference to the later troubles in that community. It is true that hatred of Orangeism was alive and well in the hearts of many of the Catholics of Biddulph even in the later nineteenth century. And it is true the Donnellys were tainted with that brush because of their ancestry. The memory of Nicholas Sheehy, however, was in my opinion not a major factor in the falling into line against them of many of their neighbors behind the small knot of their most bitter enemies in the two or three years before their murders. There were other more local reasons for such an alignment.

Chapter 14

Faction Fighting

In June 1880 a notice was placed on a pump referring to the Donnellys, or those who sympathized with them, as Blackfeet.[1] Largely because of this incident, it is sometimes contended that the enemies of the Donnellys in Ireland belonged to a faction called Whiteboys and that the Donnellys themselves belonged to an opposing faction called Blackfeet. These factions, it is argued, were brought from the Old Country to Biddulph where the fighting between them continued. This, in my opinion, is a misreading of Irish history.

When James Donnelly was growing up in the nineteenth century before the Great Famine of 1845-1849, it is true that County Tipperary had more than its fair share of factions. Their labels are numerous and bewildering: Dwyers and Ryans, Ruskavellas and Coffees, Blackhens and Magpies, Poleens and Gows, Dingers and Dowsers, Gleesons and Stapletons, Maddens and Graces, Rasoulters and Gurtaloughs, Shanavests and Caravats, Three Year Olds and Four Year Olds, Darrigs and Cumminses and yes, Blackfeet and—not Whiteboys, but—Whitefeet. Finding references to these factions is easy; trying to make sense out of them is another matter.

Irish historian Paul E. W. Roberts distinguishes between the Whiteboys movement on the one hand and faction fighting on the other. The latter, he states[2]

> refers to pitched battles between feuding bands at fairs and other public gatherings. The older feuds were largely territorial, but the new fighting often reflected more modern tensions, such as power conflicts between kinship-based mafias led by ambitious members of the middle class . . . .

Although the Whiteboys were a widespread movement of agrarian protest

A couple of Whiteboys

rather than a faction because, in the Irish context by definition one faction always opposed another, factionists nevertheless would sometimes act as Whiteboys in the sense that the same individuals who belonged to a faction might be Whiteboys on any particular night. But they were not then acting as factionists.

On the subject of the Whiteboys Roberts states:[3]

> Small farmers and rural laborers in prefamine Ireland thought of themselves as one distinct class—as 'the poor' . . . Their most direct economic relationships tended to be with the rural middle class, by which I mean the medium and larger farmers, and such people as publicans, millers and shopkeepers . . . For most laborers and many small farmers they were also their immediate landlords as a result of various forms of subletting . . . Beginning in the mideighteenth century, relations between these two classes became increasingly strained under the pressure of rapid economic and demographic growth. The most spectacular manifestation of this conflict was

91

Whiteboyism—outbreaks of agrarian terrorism that repeatedly swept parts of Ireland between 1760 and 1845, primarily aimed at redressing the economic grievances of the poor and thus mainly directed against the middle class.

Roberts goes on to explain that in the small watershed of the River Moyle in South Tipperary in the 1790s, were spawned the Moyle Rangers led by the notorious Nicholas Hanley. Little is known of Hanley except that he was charismatic, bold and audacious. As head of a small local gang, he soon organized a larger federation of several other gangs who had been feuding among themselves for generations. Acting as Whiteboys in the tradition of the district since the time of Father Sheehy, the Moyle Rangers terrorized their locality in small groups of about a dozen men with faces blackened by soot and wearing women's clothing.

Hanley's followers were poor and ragged young men, exclusively laborers or small subsistent farmers. Hanley himself, however, dressed in conspicuous contrast to his followers, sporting the finest clothes his illegal booty could buy. At a time when an ordinary Irishman could not even possess a firearm on pain of severe penalty, he often pranced about in open daylight bearing a blunderbuss and a brace of fine pistols. On his breast he wore a conspicuous red cravat.

Chief victims of the Moyle Rangers were the wealthier farmers of the rising Catholic middle class. It was they who were most resented by the poor on account of their "land grabbing". They would not hesitate to take land from the poorer farmers whose leases had run out or who were evicted for failure to pay the rent. Thus, says Roberts, at the same time that the agricultural boom of the Napoleonic Wars produced higher prices for farm produce and higher profits for the large middle class farmers, the rising land values forced many small subsistence farmers off the land. Many of them joined Hanley. The Whiteboys, then, were not a faction at all but more akin to a terrorist organization of the poor. Moreover, they were not confined

to the small area we now speak of but were widespread throughout the entire south of Ireland.

Out of the Whiteboys of the Moyle watershed arose factions when the large land-grabbing farmers formed their own group. They fought back under the leadership of one, Patrick Connors, who bore the nickname Paudeen Gar, meaning Sharp Paddy. He stood for the middle class values of shrewdness, thrift and hard work. He took pride in and was noted for his battered old waistcoat—his shanavest. Thus formed into opposing factions, the two groups fought not only at night but openly by day at the numerous fairs.

The fighting soon escalated into murders including the death of one of the chief land-grabbers at the hands of Hanley himself. Being less numerous than their enemies and feeling the tide of the warfare turning against them, the large farmers resorted to informing and began to instigate official prosecutions against Hanley and his followers.

On informations laid with the authorities by Paudeen Gar and his followers, Nicholas Hanley and several of his gang were eventually captured. In the winter of 1805-06 at a special commission held at Clonmel, Hanley and five of his cohorts were convicted and sentenced to hang. A huge crowd gathered in Clonmel for the executions. Tradition has it that as Hanley was brought out to the gallows, Paudeen Gar sneeringly called out that Hanley's colorful

A street in Clonmel

92

red cravat would soon be replaced around his neck by the hangman's noose. Hanley, uncowed to the end, retorted with a cutting remark about Connors' old waistcoat or shanavest. Then, still according to tradition, Hanley removed his bold red cravat from around his neck and ostentatiously tossed it to his followers among the crowd. With that, he stepped to his doom.

The two factions resumed hostilities in the fall of 1806. Hanley's followers now reveled in the name Caravats, while their opponents just as eagerly took up the name Shanavests. Both factions recruited adherents like wildfire and soon the fighting spread from its original heartland in the watershed of the little Moyle River to much of Tipperary and adjoining counties. Poor farmers, laborers, leaseless tenants, shoemakers and small tradesmen in the towns joined the Caravats. Large farmers of the middle class, wealthy traders, millers, publicans and master craftsmen, who employed others, joined the Shanavests. A persistent theme of the threatening notices served by the Caravats was their disgust at middle class greed.

Roberts concludes that almost all the major factions of the province of Munster, which includes Tipperary, were absorbed by the Caravat-Shanavest feud under different names. And names there were aplenty.

The government authorities of the day little understood nor could they penetrate the shadowy underworld in which the agrarian movements and the factions rose into being, melded with others, flared up, melted away or sputtered fitfully among individuals, families or groupings. Truly it has been said:[4]

> Caught in an oral world, and to that extent opaque to observers who place their reliance on literary sources, this group is often seen as a faceless, seething, turbulent, even brutal mass . . . Whiteboys, Rightboys, Caravats, Shanavests, Three Year Olds, Four Year Olds, Magpies, Blackhens flit in and out of Tipperary history as marginal men assert themselves in closely structured anarchy.

It is therefore understandable that the terms and labels have been misunderstood by some writers. Orlo Miller in his *The Donnellys Must Die*, for example, misreads the historical record when he sets the supposed Whiteboys—by which he means the Vigilance Committee of Biddulph—against the Donnelly family who are supposed Blackfeet. While the analogy is not totally apt, it would be something like saying that in Chicago in the twentieth century the Gangsters were in opposition to the Capone Gang.

By 1809-10 the Caravat-Shanavest factions had reached North Tipperary where they drew in a traditional old feud between two factions known as the Dingers and Dowsers. The Dowsers became Caravats and the Dingers became Shanavests. The latter also fought as Ryans, Cumminses, Bootashees, Coffees, Blackfeet, Magpies or Four-Year-Olds while the Dingers were also known as Dwyers, Bogboys, Darrigs, Blackhens, Whitefeet, Ruskavellas or Three-Year-Olds.

In North Tipperary, the factions often met on the fair day of Toomyvara.[5] On one such day, July 27th, 1838, Patrick Shea was killed in a faction fight. One of the participants, John Kilmartin, admitted he was a Blackhen. He was apparently an opponent of Shea, the fatal victim, who was therefore a Blackfoot, Magpie or Cummins for the respective opponents of these factions were Whitefeet, Blackhens and Darrigs. In the police and newspaper reports of the day, however, the fine distinctions were not always kept and the references to the factions often inaccurate.

The incident typifies how even to experts in the field, the Munster factions formed a bewildering array. One writer has aptly stated:[6]

> It is difficult, probably impossible, to separate and identify the many peasant organizations—Whiteboys, Carders, Rockites, Caravats, and others—which helped to create the rural chaos of this period. Different local officials in the

same area might designate a single organization by several names.

Perhaps because of the uncertainties regarding the names of factions, it is possible that Orlo Miller has confused the term Whiteboys with Whitefeet.

The names of the Whitefeet and Blackfeet factions may have originated as a form of labor dispute with the spread of the Caravat and Shanavest feuding into the coalfields of the so-called colliery district in Kilkenny and Queen's Counties, which lie adjacent to Tipperary. The area was roughly fifteen miles in length and about ten miles in breadth covering the southeast leg of Queen's County (now Leix) and the northern tip of County Kilkenny.

On our motor trips in 1988 from Dublin to Borrisokane, a half hour detour would take us there. The coalfields, discovered in 1728, apparently produced a high-grade coal from shallow surface bellpits. They were worked so extensively that within a hundred years the colliery district was said to be—save for the cities of Dublin and Cork—the most thickly settled area in Ireland.[7] By the late1820s and early 1830s, however, some of the coal pits were closing. Before a select committee of the House of Commons, it was stated that six hundred colliers were thrown out of work from one mine alone. One hundred more came from another and seventy more from a third. The reason given was that the mining operation "struck a stone fault, and the ground became convulsed, and the coal was lost and disappeared."[8]

When mining work grew scarce, competition for the few remaining jobs became fierce. Those who did find work did so at less than what had been the going wage rate when all the mines were operating. At day's end, those who collaborated with the mine owners and had taken work at the low rate had feet blackened with coal dust. Today they would be called scabs or strikebreakers. In the colliery district they were called Blackfeet.

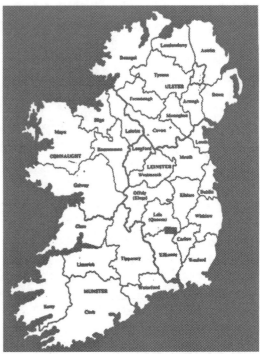

The colliery district is the small shaded rectangle covering parts of the counties of Kilkenny and Queens (now Leix) Counties.

At about the same time many small tenants near the colliery district were evicted from their farms. These individuals "remained for the most part as strollers in the place ever since,"[9] it was said, joining the idle colliers in throngs of over one thousand strong. It was a simple matter to transfer the epithet "Blackfeet" from scabs or collaborators to the more prosperous big and medium farmers outside the colliery district who took over the farms of the evicted small tenants. Those of the lower orders who opposed the Blackfeet would automatically be Whitefeet. The names soon spread outside the colliery district to North Tipperary and its adjacent territories.

There was still another reason for the rise of the Whitefeet. After the excitement of the so-called Emancipation agitation in Ireland culminating in Daniel O'Connell's victory in the opening up of Parliament to Catholics in 1829, a great disenchantment set in among the peasantry. Little wonder, for their expectations had been vastly unrealistic. Wrote one observer:[10]

On the night when the news that the [emancipation] bill had become law reached our part of the country, we were all assembled to see the bonfires which blazed on all the mountains and hills around us, and I well remember the shoutings and rejoicings on the road that passed our gate, and the hearty cheers given for us. I specially recollect one man, a farmer named James Fleming, generally known as Shamus Oge (Young James) being asked by someone in the crowd what emancipation meant. "It means," said he, "a shilling a day for every man as long as he lives, whatever he does." The ordinary wages of the laborers were then sixpence a day.

Following emancipation there grew up then a vague feeling among the poorer peasants that they had been cheated—for with emancipation came new election laws. The forty-shilling men lost their right to vote. The resentment of many of these poorer classes motivated them to become Whitefeet. The better-off middle class and large farmers, on the other hand, who could continue to participate in political life as ten-pound freeholders, were content for they retained the vote. They were more or less secure in their large farms and were relatively content with O'Connell's progress. They, too, awaited a millennium of sorts when their government would be restored to them. But this was not a pressing, everyday concern. They could afford to bide their time, augment their private fortunes and in the meantime send their children to seats of higher learning or to cheap land in North America.

And those who came to North America were of this class. In June of 1880 a journalist asked William Donnelly about factions in Biddulph and reported the interview thus:[11]

"What are the latest developments up there?" was the next question thrown at Bill by the reporter.

"There are two parties up in Biddulph now, more so than ever there were before."

"In what respect, Bill?"

"Well, I'll tell you. Pat Grace had a bee not long since, and quite a large number of the farmers around about were there. They were hauling manure, and the day being hot, a good deal of cold water was used for drinking purposes by the men. The well on Grace's farm is not a very good one, and so some of the persons who were at the bee knowing that Pat Darcy had a good well, went over and got a few pails full of water. I suppose they repeated this two or three times during the forenoon, and after dinner, one of the men was sent over again for a similar purpose. When he reached the pump, he noticed a piece of paper posted on it, and looking closer at it, observed some writing. It read:- No water for the Blackfeets out of this well. Go up to old Donnellys and get your water.

"What is meant by the Blackfeets, Bill?"

"I don't know, unless it is to distinguish those who belong to the Vigilance Committee from those who don't, and whose sympathies and feelings are with us and on the side of law and order. I got the paper anyway, and am going to keep it . . . .

There is no mention here of a feud being imported from Ireland. The newspaper, however, followed up the interview on Tuesday, June 29th, 1880, in which the journalist wrote:[12]

In order to arrive at the true state of affairs in the Township of Biddulph, I carefully interviewed several of the most respectable inhabitants, on whose statements implicit reliance can be placed, and who take an impartial view of the whole affair.

There were two factions in Tipperary, the Cummins and the Darraghs, who for half a generation maintained perpetual warfare on every occasion. They adopted or had given to them the names 'Blackfeet' and 'Whitefeet'. The old man belonged to the Blackfeet in his younger days, and Will must have known by tradition the origin of the term . . . .

Even in this strongly held view of the matter, it is not alleged that Blackfeet and Whitefeet factions were openly named or even existed in Biddulph. It is only "by tradition" Bill Donnelly is charged with knowledge of the term.

Whether James Donnelly, prior to his emigration to Canada, belonged to any faction at all is a moot point. It is true his son, William, in his bachelor days and perhaps harking back to the days of Nicholas Hanley, would sometimes assume the role of a well-dressed and charismatic leader who

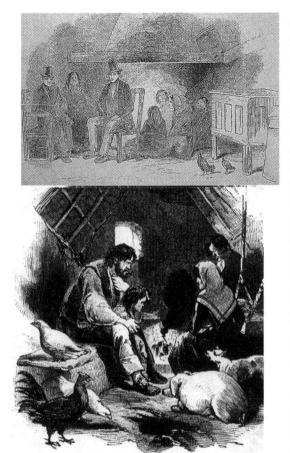

Interior of Donnelly's Cabin (above) from *The Pictorial Times, 1846*, shows the better sort of Irish cottage, in contrast to that of the small farmer (below) entitled *Cabin of J. Donoghue.*

economic betters, usually the farmers of the middle or large class. On the other hand, it could be argued that despite the thesis of Paul E. W. Roberts, the Blackfeet versus Whitefeet factional antagonism may also have had a class basis in that the Whitefeet were composed of the poorer members of society and the Blackfeet were the better off middle class. The problem with this formulation of the matter is that, in my opinion, all of the immigrants to Biddulph came from families of relatively well off medium or large farmers in Ireland. In other words, all would have been Blackfeet. The poor could not even hope to emigrate. Attempting to divide the society in the Catholic Settlement of Biddulph into factions of Blackfeet and Whitefeet harking back to the faction feuding in Ireland is therefore, in my opinion, a futile exercise.

One should also not forget that the words "blacklegs" and "blackfeet" were often used to designate felons, which would certainly have been appropriate to use in connection with some members of the Donnelly family. It may well have been to this meaning, rather than to factions in Tipperary, that the notice on the pump was referring.

drew around him a gang of his brothers and other young men resembling a faction and inspired them to go to great lengths to assist him in dubious enterprises. One such, for example, was the raid on old William Thompson's house in the neighboring township of McGillivray in February 1874 in an attempt to abduct his daughter Maggie, who had more or less invited him to try. But to stretch these kinds of incidents into faction fighting in Biddulph is to my mind questionable.

In conclusion then, one cannot logically pit Whiteboys against Blackfeet, as Miller attempts to do, in that Whiteboyism was a widespread movement of the poorer classes committing acts of terrorism against their

Chapter 15

The Nature of an Oath

It is doubtful whether Will's gang could be called a faction akin to the Irish factions. In Biddulph, it was almost always called the Donnelly Gang, though Will was usually acknowledged as its leader. But of the existence of factions of Blackfeet and Whitefeet in North Tipperary in the nineteenth century there is no doubt. A song written in the middle of that century by John O'Shea of Nenagh refers to them:[1]

Barrister Howley
Och, Barrister Howley, my jewel, what ails you?
    'Tis said you'll be after transportin' us all;
That in charging the gang, your tongue never
        fails you;
    That in preaching a sarmint you'd flummox
St.   Paul.

Chorus
Och, Barrister Howley, Howley, Howley!
    Barrister Howley, agragal, I vow
You'll not leave amongst us a Darrig or Cummins
    A Blackfoot or Whitefoot to kick up a row.

Who was Barrister Howley? John Howley was a Roman Catholic born in Limerick in 1789 and fourteen years younger that his much more famous compatriot, Daniel O'Connell. Like the latter, he became a lawyer and for thirteen years practiced in the Munster Circuit. In about 1835 Howley was appointed to the chairmanship of County Tipperary. This was a prestigious position for, as such, under the title of Assistant Barrister, he presided over the Court of Quarter Sessions. Among other things, the Quarter Sessions was a court, which was second only in jurisdiction to the assizes of the high courts for the trial of serious criminal cases.

The Tipperary Quarter Sessions court presided over by John Howley soon became the dread of the Tipperary faction fighters. It so happened that one of the first cases which came before him arose out of a faction fight. The defendant, a respectable and therefore in all probability a large farmer of the middle class, was a faction leader—probably a Blackfoot—who was charged with inflicting grievous bodily harm on an opponent. Howley convicted the man and sentenced him to transportation. The result of the case, as Howley himself explained later, left the impression among the Irish peasantry that one could be transported merely for faction fighting. Although contrary to the facts of the case, Howley did not attempt to rectify the misapprehension among the people. Moreover, he followed up this early case with many harsh sentences against faction fighters. Word quickly got around the countryside. For example, at the Thurles Quarter Sessions in April 1842, John Fogarty stated in the witness box under cross-examination: "Am not a Darrig now, Barrister Howley cured me of that!"[2]

When Howley first took his seat on the bench, he was not favorably viewed by John Kempston, the arch conservative and highly partisan proprietor of the Clonmel *Advertiser*. The new appointee was, after all, a Catholic and a nominee of the hated Whigs. Moreover, he was fresh from the despised Catholic Association of Daniel O'Connell. But by his stern sentences against malefactors, Howley quickly changed the minds of Tories like Kempston. And the latter, now editor of the same newspaper under the new name of the Nenagh *Guardian*, stated in 1842:[3]

It is a notorious fact, that offenders considered it heretofore a lucky chance in their favor, to have their cases sent for trial to Assizes instead of Quarter Sessions. For Mr. Howley's name had a more powerful effect upon their nerves, than that of all the Judges that ever adjudicated in North Tipperary . . . .

And the Earl of Donoughmore, when Lord Lieutenant of the County of Tipperary, gave the following testimony before a

Newspaper report of the testimony of James Donnelly
at the Borrisokane Petty Sessions Court in 1838.

committee of the House of Lords inquiring
into Crimes in Ireland in 1839:[4]

—Have factions diminished in Tipperary?
—Very much I should think.
—Since when?
—I should say since the appointment of the
crown prosecutor, since Mr. Howley became
chairman of the county of Tipperary.
—He directed his attention particularly to that
point?
—Yes.

The government was in fact so delighted
with Howley's actions in putting down the
factions in Tipperary that in 1843 it conferred
on him the prestigious title of Third
Sergeant–at-Law. In the House of Lords in
England, at the mere mention of his name
both sides lauded him. At that time, praise of
this kind for a Catholic was almost
unprecedented. Howley remained in the
position for thirty years and on his retirement
was knighted by the Lord Lieutenant of
Ireland. He died in 1866.

There is no record of James Donnelly ever
appearing before Barrister Howley. He may,
however, have come close. In August 1838,
when Jim Donnelly would have been about
22 years old, a case came up before the
Borrisokane Petty Sessions of the Peace.
Captain Duff, the Stipendiary Magistrate
stationed at Borrisokane, sat on the bench

along with magistrates Jonathon Willington
Walsh, Esq., Thomas G. Stoney, Esq.,
Charles Atkinson, Esq., Thomas Hemsworth,
Esq., and William Smith, Esq. One more
magistrate, Thomas Waller, Esq., acted as
chairman. This is the newspaper report of the
case:[5]

Outrage.

A man, named Noonan, was summoned
for breaking Major Bloomfield's gate, and for
riotously calling out for Ryan, Callanan, or any
informer.

In consequence of an unwillingness on the
part of witnesses to give evidence, the
defendants were acquitted—but the
magistrates said they had no doubt of his guilt.
They should, however, with regret, allow such
a character to go abroad unpunished for an
offence which they were sure he had
committed, but could not convict him for want
of sufficient evidence.

The nature of an oath.

James Donnelly, a fellow about twenty-
three years of age, on being sworn in the
foregoing case, manifested such ignorance that
the magistrates cautioned him to tell the truth,
and at the same time asked him was he aware
of the nature of an oath.

He replied—He supposed it was parjury.

Bench—Do you know what would be your
punishment if you perjured yourself?

Witness—I suppose I'd be transported for
seven years!

Bench—Did your priest ever tell you what
would become of you if you took a false oath?

Witness—Nothing, if I'd repint; for his
Riverence would forgive me!

This sounds very much like our Jim
Donnelly. Brash, outspoken and colorful
enough to have made an impression on the
magistrates, to say nothing of the news
reporter, he also displayed the all too
common attitude of the Irish Catholic who
could endure evil action with the comforting
thought that a trip to the confessional would
absolve all.

What was this minor case all about? At the
previous court session at Borrisokane, a man
named Daniel Ryan stood as prosecutor
against James Noonan. Again, we must rely
on the newspaper to learn what happened on
that day.[6]

98

Denis Callanan deposed, that he saw James Noonan at the Lodgegate of Redwood, Major Bloomfield's residence, and heard three knocks against the gate.

One of the presiding magistrates George Walsh took exception to Callanan's evidence.

Mr. Walsh—Did you not swear before me, that you saw Noonan break the gate, and heard him call out for Ryan, or any one that would harbour informers?

Callanan—I saw him at the gate, and heard the knocks.

Mr. Walsh—You have altered your evidence—you swore against him before me at Walsh Park.

The case was then adjourned to the next court a week later when, as we have seen, James Donnelly was called as a witness against Noonan. It is worth noting that the Ryan referred to here was very likely the same Daniel (who was better known as Dandy) Ryan—a noted faction fighter—who was accused, along with others, of the murder of Patrick Shea, a Blackfoot or Cummins, in the faction fight at the fair of Toomyvara in 1838 already mentioned.

On that occasion, the police chief of Nenagh reported to Dublin Castle:[7]

On the 27th instant I attended the Fair of Toomyvara . . . a man named Patrick Shea of Currinheen Parish of Aghnameadle and Barony of Upper Ormond was waylaid by Mathew, Daniel and Johnny Ryan of Allotram and Michael Maxwell of Glanaguile in said parish and barony aforesaid who struck him a blow of a stone on the forehead . . . .

Carpenter, C.C.

Nenagh 29th July 1838

This case is little more than a mere hint that Jim Donnelly may have belonged to a faction known as Blackfeet based on the reasoning that Shea was a known Blackfoot who had been killed at the Toomyvara Fair in the month before the petty sessions court hearing in Borrisokane referred to above. One of those who killed Shea in the faction fight at Toomyvara was Daniel Ryan who would then have been a Whitefoot. Donnelly had been called as a prosecution witness against Noonan, who was apparently in

opposition to Ryan (a Whitefoot) whom he called an informer. And apparently, rather than testify against Noonan (presumably, then, also a Blackfoot), Donnelly changed his testimony in order to side with a fellow Blackfoot. Scanty and convoluted as it is, this is the only evidence I have been able to find in Ireland of Jim Donnelly's belonging to the Blackfoot faction.

It has sometimes been hinted in some of the accounts that Jim Donnelly fled Ireland as a result of impending criminal charges. Once again, a faint suggestion of the truth of

An old smithy in Goatstown, also known as Killeen, outside Borrisokane.

this version of events is found in the newspaper report of a criminal trial at the Nenagh Spring Assizes in 1843.[8] The trial was that of John Hogan, charged with the murder of one, William Reid, at a place called Killeen, also known by the less euphonious name of Goatstown. Goatstown happened to be but a stone's throw from the town of Borrisokane.

The murder of William Reid took place in 1836. John Hogan was not put on trial for the crime until 1843, either because the evidence against him did not sooner come to light or he was not apprehended until then. One of the prosecution witnesses against Hogan was Patrick Toher. This man Toher was suspected of having knowledge of a great many crimes around the Borrisokane area, including the assassination of Robert Hall of Merton Hall although in his testimony he

Derrinvohill House near Borrisokane

denied coveting the enormous reward put on offer by the victim's family in that case.

On his examination, however, Toher made a statement, which I found interesting. He said:[9]

> I came here this assizes to prosecute Donnelly and Mara, but I do not know for what . . . It was for taking fire arms, I was with them myself . . . It is four years [ago] . . . from James Ralph's of Derrenvoohela that we got the gun . . . do not know the devil what they done with it . . . believes Ned was [Rody Mara's] brother . . . I [gave information] because Mara was taken, and for fear of myself I was charged with this murder . . . .

From the above extract of Toher's reported testimony, it seems evident that Donnelly was then in custody charged with the theft of a gun. Now the townland of Derrinvohill[10] outside Borrisokane was, as we have seen in Chapter 5, the home of the Donnelly family at least in 1823, and James Donnelly was presumably familiar with it even after the Donnellys had moved on. It was the object of raids for firearms on more than one occasion. For example, the newspaper in October 1838 stated:[11]

> ROBBERY OF FIRE ARMS. From our Borrisokane correspondent. On last Sunday between 11 and 12 o'clock, and while the keepers were at Mass, a party of armed men to the number of eight were observed to be prowling about the lands of Derenvohela, near Borrisokane, the property of Mr. Poe. One of the party having raised the latch, entered on the pretence of lighting his pipe, he then opened the door, and four of the persons

entered, while the remaining three stood as sentinels at the door and about the house. A minute search for fire-arms was then made; every corner was poked, every box opened, and drawers and chests ransacked, but without effect. Evidently much annoyed at their disappointment, they held a consultation, and recommenced searching. They at length succeeded in getting a beautiful rifle, and a bayonet which was affixed to a long pole, and then departed. Fortunately the keepers had concealed the remainder of the fire arms before they left the house for Mass.

The keeper of Mr. Poe at this time was James Ralph, which seems to accord with Patrick Toher's evidence, and the time is approximately correct. Curiously enough, however, the newspaper printed a correction of the original report in its next issue four days later, which read:[12]

> In the account given in our last, of the search for fire-arms made by a party of men in the house of Mr. Poe's shepherd on the lands of Derrinvohill, near Borrisokane, we misconstrued our correspondent's letter, when we stated that "a beautiful rifle was taken;" it should have been a beautiful rifle bayonet; we are happy to add, they did not succeed in getting any fire-arms.

About three years after this, in August 1841, another incident of much the same kind occurred at the same place. The newspaper report read:[13]

> State of the Country.
> Captain Rock After The Election.
> . . . Three armed men broke into the house of George Armstrong of Derravohela, and searched it for fire-arms.

Again, while the place is right the time does not correspond to Patrick Toher's testimony nor does the occupant of the house broken into.

The next incident may have involved Jim Donnelly. This is the *Guardian*'s report in July 1842 which reads:[14]

> On last Sunday . . . three armed men entered the house of Richard Armitage, of Derrinvohela, near Borrisokane, and succeeded in possessing themselves of a gun and pistol.

Mr. Armstrong and family were at Divine Service . . . .

Richard Armitage was related to William Kent who had been tried and acquitted of conspiring to murder Robert Hall of Merton Hall. There were suspicions abroad that this robbery had something to do with the

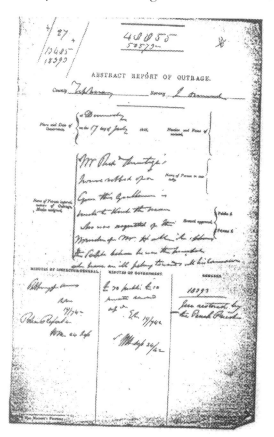

Report of the outrage in 1842 when the house of Richard Armitage was "robbed of a gun".
(Copy by permission of the Irish National Archives)

murder. Spencer Sceli, who later assumed the name Armitage-Stanley, was born in Lucan in 1899. He related to me the incident involving Jim Donnelly, Jr. and two of Spencer's great uncles named Armitage in the early days of the Catholic Settlement of Biddulph. Thomas and William Armitage were then youths when they attended a bee on the Roman Line. Before long, some of the Catholics picked a fight with the Armitage boys. The Armitages were a family, after all,

of known Orangemen. Young Jim Donnelly at once sprang to their rescue.

"These boys' father helped my father out of a scrape back in Ireland," he declared, "and I'll not let them be harmed."

If true, this story may relate back to the taking of the gun or pistol of Richard Armitage's keeper at Derrinvohill in 1842. How Armitage saved Donnelly is sheer speculation, but it may have been Armitage who in October 1838 had prevailed upon the Nenagh *Guardian* reporter to correct the first report about the robbery at Derrinvohill house to say that the item stolen was a rifle bayonet and not fire-arms, a much less serious offence. Or, referring to the August 1841 incident of robbery of fire-arms from the same place, Armitage may have had his guns returned to him by Father Anthony Nolan, the parish priest of Dunkerrin. Nolan had induced his flock not long after to turn in several stands of arms.[15] Armitage may then have refrained from pressing legal action perhaps because Donnelly's father, John, and uncles were, like himself, respectable farmers with large landholdings nearby at Tumbrikane, Ballycasey and Liskanlahan. Not only did John Donnelly hold a large acreage but had been residing at Derrinvohill in 1823. The Protestant landlord of the Donnellys at Tumbrikane and Ballycasey was Thomas George Stoney of Kylepark, one of the presiding JPs in the case in which James Donnelly was called as a witness, and another Stoney, Captain Robert Johnston, occupied Killavalla House. All these families, being of the same social standing in the society of that time and place, were in all probability on friendly terms with each other notwithstanding that some were Catholic while others were Protestant. We will find a small confirmation of this in the next chapter dealing with Bridget Donnelly who came out to Canada and was murdered along with the family of her uncle in the Donnelly tragedy.

There remains one last question about Toher's testimony. If Patrick Toher went to the Nenagh Assizes in 1843 to prosecute

The Governor's House at the hub of the radiating wings of Nenagh Jail

Donnelly and Mara, why was there no trial involving these men? The answer may lie in a short newspaper report of March 25th, 1843 which reads:[16]

> Tipperary North Riding Assizes . . . His Lordship closed the assizes by discharging a number of prisoners by proclamation.

If James Donnelly was among the prisoners in Nenagh Jail whose trial had not yet come off, as a result of this amnesty he would never have been tried for his escapade at Derrinvohill but released by mercy of the Crown. And shortly after this event, he took ship to Canada.[17]

Chapter 16

Bridget's Secret

Bridget Donnelly came to Canada from Ireland in 1878 on the Polynesian that steamed out of Liverpool on September 26th that year and docked at Quebec City on October 5th. Listed in the ship's manifest among the passengers in cabin class is "Miss Donnelly" who is described as "Lady" and "Adult". While the ages of the steerage class passengers are meticulously noted,[1] the ages of the cabin class are not. Here all were simply noted as either "Gentleman" or "Lady". Since the ages of the cabin passengers were not given, I must set out my arguments concerning Bridget's true age in greater detail than I would have otherwise.

Following the Donnelly tragedy and the publication of the event in the Dublin newspapers in Ireland, her brother wrote to William Donnelly. The letter was published in the newspaper and it reads:[2]

Dublin
March 18th, 1880
Dear William,

Would you be kind enough to let me know if it is true that your father and mother and two brothers and my poor sister Bridget were murdered? We saw a long account of it, but cannot believe it is true. I do not know whether my father wrote to you yet or not, but I am sure if the account we saw of the murder is true, it will be the breaking of my father's and mother's heart. As for myself, I cannot give you any idea of my feelings. When I think of the pleasure it gave me to hear Bridget going to my uncle, and he so many years away without hearing from him, and compare that pleasure with the sorrowful tidings I have now, it almost drives me crazy. Dear William, during the last year I have often thought I would some day have the pleasure of seeing ye all, but the sad news of the wholesale murder has disheartened me, and I know my comforts in this world are blasted forever. If the account be true, we have only to pray that their souls may be happy. The murderers may escape punishment in this world, but they cannot accuse themselves of the crime and expect to escape punishment in the world to come. I thought you were a bird alone, until my mother wrote to me telling me you had two more brothers alive (Robert and Patrick) and also a sister. Had I seen poor Bridget before she went to America I would not feel so bad, but I am now living in Dublin 11 years, and had not the pleasure of seeing her before she went. She wrote me a letter after arriving at your father's, telling me of all your kindness to her. That was the last I heard of her, or ever will again on earth, if what we hear is true, and if so, may the Lord have mercy on all their souls. Dear William, you will please write soon, and let me know all the particulars.

Your loving cousin,
Michael Donnelly
Address:
#47 Belview Buildings
Dublin City, Ireland.

Later that year, the father of Michael and Bridget Donnelly also wrote.[3] He stated that the sorrow borne by him and his wife on learning of the death of their daughter in such a cruel manner was increased by the fact that they were without even a photograph by

Front entrance to Belview Buildings in Dublin

which they might remember her.

Although for many years through correspondence to Ireland I had tried to locate and find out about this Michael Donnelly, the brother of Bridget, such efforts were unsuccessful. I also tried to locate Bridget's birth in the area of Borrisokane in North Tipperary but it, too, failed—or so I

One of the last inner courts of the Belview Buildings

thought.[4] Then when we visited Dublin about a hundred years after those letters to William Donnelly were written, we of course looked for the Belview Buildings address. Our map told us it was located in a very old part of Dublin which then happened to be celebrating its one thousandth year anniversary. In that ancient part of the city, not far from the remains of its medieval wall, was a short street called Belview which ran off Thomas Street West as did another short street called Thomas Court. At the corner of the latter stood the ancient Church of St. Catherines.[5]

From the National Library in Dublin, I learned that the Belview Buildings had stood between Belview Street and Thomas Court. I also understood that the area had been a district of tenement houses but by about the late 1870s a new development had cleared the old tenements. In their place there were then erected row upon row of small and attached but elegant middle class houses. When we arrived on the scene a hundred years later, however, the new development of a century before had itself become rundown, and when we saw it most of the row houses had been razed leaving only a small part of the Belview Buildings still standing. We soon found out why. On the other side of St. Thomas Street West is the huge St. James's Gate Brewery of the well-known Guinness beer family. Over the years, the brewery had expanded into the area across the street and would soon, it appeared, occupy the entire former site of the Belview Buildings.

Although we could not find his 1880 residence in the remnant of Belview Buildings still standing, we continued to search for traces of Michael Donnelly in Dublin. We returned from our trip, however, having found nothing further about the elusive brother of Bridget.

Then one day in the summer of 2003, I received the following e-mail message from Ireland. It read:

> I live in County Dublin and I believe I am a distant descendant of the Donnelly family. Papa Donnelly, as I believe him to be called, lived in Dublin or Tipperary and would be my great great grandfather on the maiden side. I would estimate he was born about 1840/50. I have in my possession a picture of William Donnelly which I see on the website. I am astonished at the likeness. According to the note on the rear of this old photo William Donnelly was born on the 13th day of August 1846 in the city of London, Canada West.

Needless to say, I was thunderstruck. After so many years of searching, I knew immediately that Papa Donnelly, as my correspondent referred to him, must be the long-lost Michael Donnelly, brother of Bridget, and first cousin to the Donnelly boys of Biddulph.

My correspondent, Desmond Murray, not only confirmed that his great grandfather—in his haste he had put one too many "greats" in his e-mail—was indeed Michael Donnelly, but he also sent me copies of both front and back of the photograph he referred to. He also sent me a copy of a photograph of Michael Donnelly, who had written to Will in 1880. Finally, after so much speculation and guesswork over the years, not only did we locate the writer of the 1880 letter but we knew what he looked like. And as a bonus, after so much speculation and guesswork both by myself and others over the years, we discovered the exact date and place of William Donnelly's birth.

104

Des Murray also told me that his great grandfather Michael Donnelly was a brewery worker. He had been born in 1842 and in his later years, following the death of his wife and retirement from employment at the brewery, he lived in Dublin with his only daughter, Mary, grandmother of Des. Mary had, of course, inherited the photograph of William Donnelly from her father and in turn had passed it on to her son, Des's father. Now in this family's possession, Des said it had lain in a drawer for about a hundred years or more. He also said that Michael Donnelly, who died about the year 1918, did indeed have connections in North Tipperary and almost all the few small details they were able to glean from memory or from older members of the family seemed to confirm that the family had resided in Borrisokane or vicinity in the latter part of the nineteenth century.

"Thank you for the wonderful surprise to discover that we have an interesting historical past in the new world and not the other way around," wrote Des after reading my two books on the Donnelly story which I sent him.

But there was more. Almost from the beginning of our correspondence, the Murray family in Ireland was engrossed with the adventures not of Bridget but her younger sister Anne. Apparently the hand of Anne Donnelly had been promised, it seems more by her parents than their daughter, to a man named Jim Maxwell who had emigrated to New Zealand. When she was about twenty-three or twenty-four years of age, Anne Donnelly was sent off to New Zealand in order to make good on the promise. Accompanying her was a sister of her intended husband, whose other two sisters, Mrs. Middleton and Mrs. Haskett, were well off. The former had apparently married into a family of hotel owners in New Zealand. On the long voyage over, however, Anne met another man and was determined to marry him instead. And she did.

William Donnelly sent this photograph of himself to his cousin in Ireland in 1880.

Upon her landing in New Zealand, Anne was married to James Henry Fowler at Christchurch on September 9th, 1875. The marriage proved to be long, happy and fruitful and, notwithstanding her surprise nuptials, Anne remained on good terms with her family back in Ireland. She exchanged letters with them until she died in 1935, just short of her diamond wedding anniversary. After her death her daughters continued exchanging letters with the family in Ireland and the descendants on both sides have kept in touch with each other to the present day.

Not long ago Desmond Murray's sister, Patricia, went to New Zealand to visit her cousins. Two of the granddaughters of Bridget's sister Anne, aged eighty and ninety, were still living. On that trip she obtained the birth certificate of Anne, which she brought

105

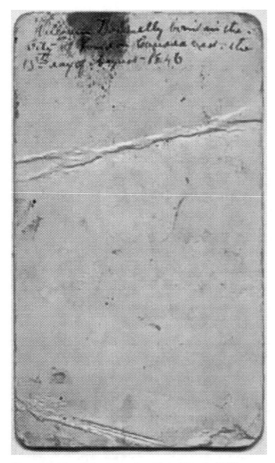

**Reverse side of photograph with writing in Will's own
hand: "William Donnelly born in the City of London
Canada West the 13th day of August 1846."**

back with her to Ireland and placed it among
the family papers. With the new information
that I sent her brother from Canada,
however, they dug it out and were now able
to go back to the parish where Anne had
been baptized to turn up information on
Michael. Sure enough, they told me, the
current parish priest replied that Anne was
shown in the parish register along with her
brother Michael, their great grandfather. And
Anne had another brother Patrick, to whom
some of Anne's letters were addressed over
the years as well as two other brothers. And,
yes, there was a Bridget in the family. They
said, however, that this Bridget had been
born in July 1844 and therefore could not be
the Bridget who had gone to Canada in 1878
as the difference of fourteen years between

the birth date in this record and the grave
marker seemed too great.

As I mulled over this new information, I
decided to look back on my searches of Irish
records made many years before. Sure
enough, I did find the same family in a search
which I had made in 1982 of the microfilm
of the church registers of Terryglass and
Kilbarron parish, close to Borrisokane. The
parents were Robert Donnelly and Mary
Carroll who were married June 29th, 1838.
And yes, here was their first child, John, born
in November 1839, their second child,
Michael (who had written to his cousin
William Donnelly in 1880) born in 1842.
And then there was the next child, Bridget,
baptized on July 15th, 1844 and whose
sponsors were Michael Donnelly and Judith
Nolan. Although I had located this family
many years before, I too had at that time
dismissed this Bridget because of the year of
her birth. The tombstone in Canada, after all,
said that she had been born on May 1st,
1858. Could the tombstone date be in error?

The more I thought about it, the more I
realized that that was in fact the case. Bridget
Donnelly, the niece of James Donnelly, Sr.,
who came to Canada to live with her uncle's
family and was murdered with them, was
indeed thirty-five years old at her death and
not twenty-one.

I realize that this is a startling new fact
about the Donnelly story, but I will set out
my reasons and let the reader decide for
herself or himself. First, I went back to the
microfilm of the church register for the
parish of Terryglass and Kilbarron and found
that it also listed the baptisms of the other
children of Robert Donnelly and Mary
Carroll. After Bridget came Patrick, born in
1846; then James, born in 1848; and their
final child, Anne, born in 1850. And, of
course, it was this Anne Donnelly who had
gone to New Zealand to be married.

At the times of all these births, with one
exception, the residence of the parents was
the very small townland of Stonepark. In the
case of Bridget, the place of residence of the

106

Bridget's sister, Anne Donnelly, in later life

She would not have attained this age for seven or eight more months. It seems to me that in that case the designation "spinster" may have been more appropriate. I admit this is a small point.

The New Zealand story of Anne Donnelly has yet more of a bearing on the identity of Bridget. After the death in 1935 of Anne Donnelly, then Mrs. James Henry Fowler, her daughters and granddaughters in New Zealand continued writing to their cousins in Ireland, one of whom was Mary, daughter of Michael Donnelly. A bag of these letters dated from 1916 to 1949 was handed down to Desmond Murray when his Aunt Vera died about 1978 aged about 70 years. In one of these letters dated in 1939, Anne's daughter wrote to her cousin Mary in Ireland and mentioned her Aunt Bridget, as follows:[6]

> About Aunt Brigit, I was like you very tiny and I just knew something happened to mother's sister as she was so upset—she was the one that saved two children from being killed by a snake, it was seen by her creeping up to the children's cot and Brigit got an axe and killed it, and then screamed and collapsed and the parents of the children would not let her go, and they kept her with them for saving the children . . . .

The writer of this letter would only have been about three or four years of age in 1880. The story of the snake is peculiar and in my opinion has obviously been changed in the retelling. There were, after all, no snakes in Ireland and, I underdtand, few in New Zealand, but plenty in nearby Australia.

In another letter sent by Anne's daughter back to the relatives in Ireland, there was again a brief reference to Bridget. It read:[7]

> Anne Donnelly and her sister Brigid left Ireland around the same time with Anne going to New Zealand and her sister going to America where she was murdered by a negro.

Again, as bizarre as this sounds, the gist of the story which has obviously been reworked in its repeated telling is that Bridget had suffered a tragic death overseas.

parents was the larger townland of Ballinderry, which is immediately adjacent to Stonepark. The parents, therefore, appear to have lived in almost the same spot their entire married life, about a mile or two from Borrisokane. And although I continued searching the registers for over two decades after Anne's baptism, there were no other children born to this couple.

My mind then went back to the passengers listed in the ship's manifest of the steamer Polynesian. Here, the passenger who we are quite sure was our Bridget Donnelly was listed as "Miss Donnelly", "Lady" and "Adult" in the ship's entries at the time of her embarking in September 1878. The entries would have been perfectly appropriate to designate a young woman of thirty-four. If she were indeed born May 1st, 1858 as stated on the grave marker, however, she would not technically be an adult at all as the age of majority at the time was twenty-one.

107

Regarding Bridget's date of birth on the tombstone, we have to consider that a baptismal record, especially for Irish Catholics of the nineteenth century, is a far more reliable record than a record of death. This proved to be the case with Judith Magee who became Mrs. James Donnelly, where her birth year turned out to be 1820, as shown on her baptismal record, and not 1823 as shown on the grave marker. Then we must consider that the Donnelly survivors of the tragedy, namely, William, Patrick, Robert and Jenny, were those members of the family who were least familiar with Bridget. At the time of her arrival in early October 1878 and for the fifteen or so months thereafter, those survivors had all been living away from the homestead for some years. They were the ones least likely to know Bridget at all, let alone her true age. My guess is that May 1st, 1858 was simply pulled out of a hat, especially as it seems that Bridget's true age was not known by them in any event. Newspaper accounts shortly after the massacre variously noted her age as 19, 20, 21 and 22.

In her official death return in which William Donnelly was the informant, she was stated to be 24. Will would have been well aware that the younger one of the victims could be made out to be, the more heinous the crime would appear. In circumstances in which Bridget's age was not really known, Will would therefore not have hesitated, in my opinion, to paint his cousin newly arrived from Ireland as a young woman in her early twenties.

Because a daughter of Robert Donnelly and Mary Carroll was sent to New Zealand in about the year 1874 or 1875 to a prospective husband, but was able to find not one but two such candidates for spouse, it would be not unnatural for the same parents to send out another daughter, this time to America, in the hopes that she, too, could find a husband. And it would be quite understandable for a young woman going out to a far-off country to subtract a few years

from her age in order to make herself more eligible for marriage. There would be, after all, no girlhood chums, family members or neighbors familiar with her true age to contradict her. And Mrs. Donnelly, even if she were aware or had suspicions of the little deception, would likely have gone along with it. Or, she may have considered it indiscreet to inquire in the circumstances. Fourteen years is admittedly a large difference, but we have all known women who in their thirties looked like teenagers.

We know that Bridget was summoned to give evidence in Grouchy Ryder's case against the senior Donnellys and that she attended in Granton and did testify. This is the only instance of which we have certain proof that she left the homestead. She did not even, for example, accompany her cousins to attend the wedding celebration on January 14th, 1880 of Michael Quigley and Martha Keefe at the home of the bride's father about a mile or so up the road from the Donnelly place. When she was in the witness box at the arson trial in Granton and was asked why she did not go to the wedding celebration at Keefe's, she said, "The reason I

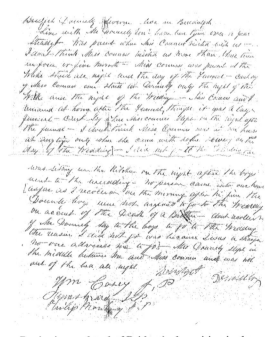

Beginning and end of Bridget's deposition in the Ryder arson case at Granton, including her signature.

did not go was because I was a stranger—no one advised me to go." The reason seems, in my opinion, a little lame. The fact is she kept very close to the homestead, and if she were shy and retiring, it was probably not without good reason in view of the possible deception that she was attempting to carry off regarding her true age.

It is possible, on the other hand, that there was no deception at all but that the subject of her age just never came up. The fact is we know very little about Bridget in Canada. After landing at Quebec, for example, how did she get to Biddulph? Did someone travel there to fetch her or did she take the train to Lucan? The latter seems more likely. Was she at the homestead on October 14th, 1878 when the confrontation took place between James Carroll on the one hand and the four Donnellys—John, Thomas, William and Judith—on the other? If she were present, did she mention this incident in her letters to her parents near Borrisokane or her brother in Dublin, Ireland? We know she met Father

Bridget's brother, Michael Donnelly

John Connolly and attended church services at the Donnelly Schoolhouse with her uncle and his wife, but did she go down to the church with them during her brief sojourn in Biddulph?

The descendants of Bridget's brother back in Ireland told me that their great grandfather, Michael Donnelly, had been employed in a brewery. This was confirmed when the 1911 Dublin census was released on the internet[8] and we were able to look him up. Sure enough, by that date he was found living with his married daughter Mary and her family and was shown as a "brewer pensioner". It appears that Michael Donnelly went from the Borrisokane area to Dublin originally in about 1869. He obtained employment in the stables of the St. James's Gate Brewery of the Guinness family, eventually rising to the position of foreman. About the time that his sister Anne left for New Zealand, he himself married. His daughter Mary was born about 1876. In 1880 he was living with his family at Belview Buildings, close by the brewery. From here he wrote the letter to his cousin in Canada in 1880 after the news of the massacre was reported in that city. And in his later years, as related by his descendants, he lived with his only daughter and her family in the city of Dublin. He died in 1918 and is buried there in Glasnevin Cemetery.

Earlier in this chapter I mentioned that the first child of Robert Donnelly and Mary Carroll was John, Bridget's oldest brother, baptized in November 1839. The baptismal sponsors were Bridget Nowlan and Patt Nowlan. The Nowlans may have been husband and wife and it would not have been unusual for Bridget Nowlan to have been a sister of the father of the child being baptized. A little later on, this Bridget Nowlan may well have become the Widow Nolan whom we have met in connection with the burning of her clothes and bedding as well as the house of her father, John Donnelly, of Tumbrikane, upon her marriage to Darby Slevin. This John Donnelly of

Tumbrikane would then also have been the father not only of the Bridget who was caught in the lovers' triangle of 1839-40 but also of Robert Donnelly, of Stonepark in Terryglass parish, and of James Donnelly who married Judy Magee and emigrated to Canada.

Further evidence of the relationship is that the given name Robert tends to be more of a Protestant name than a Catholic name. The mother of Robert and James, after all, was reputed to have been a Protestant woman named Ashbury. That Robert is a Protestant given name is suggested by the fact that out of some 105 Catholic families in Biddulph Township in 1881, there were only three with the name Robert. By way of contrast, the name James appeared in 52 of those same families.

In a letter sent from New Zealand in 1937 by the daughter of Bridget's sister, Anne, she recalled her mother's memories of her earlier days in Ireland. One of the things she said was, "I always remember my mother talking about a Captain Stoney's place." Captain Stoney was Robert Johnston Stoney, one of the Protestant gentry of the Borrisokane area.[9] In the 1830s and 1840s he lived at Killavalla House, a short walk out from Borrisokane.

The Stoneys were descended from Cromwellian officers. Other members of the family included Thomas George Stoney, whose seat was at Kylepark—the townland where Darby Slevin lived when he was courting the young widow, Bridget Donnelly—near Tumbrikane towerhouse. The Stoneys were the absolute proprietors of much of the land in the district, including nearby Emmel Castle.

It made sense that Anne Donnelly, and probably her sister Bridget, the daughters of Robert Donnelly of Stonepark, would socialize in the house of Captain Stoney which was Killavalla House. As I attempt to explain in another chapter, the minor Protestant gentry of the Borrisokane area, like the Stoneys, had more in common with their large landholding tenants like the Donnellys, than with their small tenant farmers or landless peasants. They socialized together and occasionally one of the Protestants would marry a Catholic. This happened in the Donnelly family and in the McLaughlin family. In the latter, a Catholic, Martin McLaughlin,[10] married Temperance Kyte (sometimes spelled Kite), a Protestant, and their descendants were close neighbors to the Donnellys in Biddulph.

Killavalla House, the home in the mid-nineteenth century of Captain Stoney, is where we stayed on our first trip to Ireland in 1978 and visited again in 1988. How curious that Bridget, in all probability in company with her sister Anne, spent many a social hour in this very house in her earlier and happier days.

Killavalla House in the latter part of the nineteenth century

Chapter 17

Affairs of the Heart

The first of the Donnelly brothers to marry was John. Early in the year 1871 the citizens of Lucan village carrying on their usual mundane affairs were startled by the sudden revelation that John Donnelly had eloped. His partner in the affair, it turned out, was a sprightly young lass of eighteen years named Fanny Durham (often spelled Derham), the daughter of a prosperous Protestant farmer on the fifth concession of Biddulph.

The newspaper reported:[1]

> Efforts to overtake the fugitives were fruitless, and the friends had to wait patiently and allow the affair to develop. They were soon rewarded, for the happy pair returned in a week and will, in all probability, with the exception of this little romantic episode, live an ordinary humdrum life in Biddulph.

Shortly after their return, the two were married in St. Patrick's Church on February 11th by Father Joseph Gerard. The groom's sister, Janey Donnelly, was one of the witnesses along with Samuel Hodgins.

Not only did John and Fanny form a new family in Lucan, they also went into business together. Next to the Royal Hotel on Main Street, Hugh Murphy had been operating a little saloon called "The Mechanics Home" catering to the taste of the many carpenters, bricklayers, masons, foundry workers, laborers and other employees of the several turning shops, planning mills and building trade shops then operating in the prosperously bustling little place.

Murphy agreed to sell his goodwill in the saloon to the newly wed couple and John had a new sign erected, proclaiming the new business to be the "Dew Drop Inn". From a couple of the local merchants, a new stove and furniture along with a line of liqueurs and other spirits were obtained, almost all on

John Donnelly as sketched by author

credit, and the new business appeared to flourish.

Suddenly on the morning of Monday, April 17th, however, the new enterprise came to a crash—along with the marriage. The cause of it all was debated, but the newspaper reported as follows:[2]

> . . . the news was circulated that the demon of jealousy, or some other potent motive, had caused the bridegroom to rise in his wrath 'And in despair to tear his hair', after which operation he left, and, it is supposed, letters to him must now be addressed to the United States.

The reason for the strife may well have been business capital, or rather the lack of it. Alluding to John's marriage, the Toronto *Globe* stated shortly after the murder of the Donnellys—no doubt relying on word picked up from around the village—that the cause of the breakup was that "her family would not give him money."

111

Needless to say, the creditors of the new business were alarmed at hearing of the marriage breakdown:[3]

> [T]hey determined to recover as much of their property as they could and accordingly made a rush for the Dew Drop. One laid hands on the stove and belonging, while the other went for the brandies, wines, cigars, &c., all of which were speedily removed, and put back amongst the original stocks.

Not to let an opportunity go by, however, Will Donnelly took possession of the sign, Dew Drop Inn, and moved it to premises on William Street where he carried on the business of saloon for a few months. The village became incorporated not long after and took over the granting of saloon licenses. The new village council declined to grant one to him. Will then began looking around for another enterprise and before long he went into the stagecoaching business.

Fanny, in the meantime, went home to her parents on the fifth concession of Biddulph. She soon after left for St. Thomas where she met Harry John Heard, a tinsmith. She and Heard went off to Detroit and there got married more or less in secrecy for, truth be told, the marriage was bigamous as she was

This little building on the Main Street of Lucan is believed to have been the Dew Drop Inn.

still married to John Donnelly. But when Fanny heard of the tragedy in Biddulph, she was suddenly free to re-marry Heard legitimately—she was pregnant at the time with her first child—and they were united in wedlock at St. Paul's rectory in London on March 20th, 1880. The witnesses to the ceremony were Fanny's parents, Michael and Ellen[4] Durham.

Many years later, a young man from Chicago told me:[5]

> Fanny Durham and Harry John Heard were my great grandparents. My father was the oldest of their seven children. From St. Thomas they moved to Croswell, Michigan, and there are old-timers there who still remember them. My mother who is still alive also remembers visiting them in Croswell in 1919 and again in 1929.

Croswell is a little town fifteen or twenty miles north of Port Huron in Michigan. Fanny died there in 1930 at the age of seventy-five.

If John Donnelly had indeed cleared out to the States after abandoning the Dew Drop Inn, there is no doubt he was back in the area soon after. In August of 1874 we find he is convicted by the London Police Magistrate, Lawrence Lawrason, for being drunk and fined one dollar. The cause of the apparent celebration may have been the reunion with

Fanny Durham

The Mansion House in Thorold

his brothers, for on the same day for the same offence by the same magistrate, we find Patrick Donnelly also fined one dollar. Both had been picked up by Constable Templar. What seems a little peculiar about this incident is that his brother Will Donnelly later declared, as reported in the Toronto *Globe* of March 3, 1880, that John "never tasted liquor".

Shortly before Christmas in 1874, John Donnelly was again arrested in London, this time by Detectives Murphy and Phair. The charge on this occasion was that of having committed an indecent assault and the complainant in the case was Susan Pepper of the Township of Stephen. She had laid the charge in Exeter. The newspaper reporting the case spelled her name as Pebber. When the case came on for hearing before a couple of the Exeter magistrates, however, Miss Pepper failed to put in an appearance and Donnelly was discharged. The Exeter *Times*

remarked that "it is supposed the woman was enticed away". Susan Pepper is found in the 1881 census for Paisley in Bruce North, aged 24, dressmaker, living with the family of a solicitor in the town. If this is the same person, which is likely, she would have been a mere seventeen years of age at the time of her encounter with John Donnelly.

Patrick Donnelly was the second of the brothers to marry. On October 6th, 1871 at the age of 21 he was wed to Mary Ryan in the Church of England parsonage in Biddulph by the popular Anglican minister, Reverend William Logan. On that occasion, Pat gave his full name as Patrick Kelley Donnelly. The bride, only nineteen years of age, was the daughter of Thomas and Mary Ryan of London Township and the witnesses to the ceremony were Patrick Quigley and, again, Janey Donnelly. Sadly, this marriage did not last long either for in July of 1873 Mary Ryan died. Sources differ as to the cause. It may

113

have been typhoid fever or childbirth. Their little child also died not long after on September 20th.

At the time of the murder of his parents, Pat was in partnership with a man named Franklin Becker in St. Catharines in the trade of carriage-building. Pat was the blacksmith

This 1969 picture shows what was once Patrick Donnelly's Geneva House in St. Catharines.

in the business. After the murders, Pat remained temporarily in Lucan until things had settled down and then located for short periods in different parts of the province such as London, Glencoe, Aylmer and Niagara-on-the-Lake, where he worked at his trade of blacksmithing. For a short time he even worked in East Aurora, New York. Eventually, however, he settled down back in the Niagara Peninsula.

His later years were for the most part uneventful except that he gave up blacksmithing and went into the hotel business. In Thorold he purchased the Mansion House and ran it for a while, but he also operated hotels in Niagara-on-the-Lake and St. Catharines. For a time he also ran the City House or Thorold Inn in Thorold, and eventually ended up operating the Geneva House in St. Catharines.

And he married again. His second wife was twenty-five year old Mary Donnelly, born in St. Catharines to Patrick Donnelly and Margaret Murphy. Patrick and Mary were blessed with the following children: Mary Agnes (Mayme) who lived from 1886 to 1970; John Michael who lived from 1887 to 1945; Margaret Anne who lived from 1889 to 1951; Edith Jane (Jenny) who lived from 1891 to 1919, when she died from an ear abscess; and Matthew Patrick who lived from 1899 to 1968. Other children born to the couple were named James Thomas (1872), Johanna (1884), Thomas (1889) and William (1894) but all these died shortly after birth.

As for Pat's memories of those terrible days in February 1880, his daughter once wrote:[6]

> My father never fully recovered from the effect of his terrible sorrow over the deaths of his people.

And stories were passed down in Patrick's family by his children that each year as the anniversary of the massacre was approaching, he sat them down "and made them write out cards to mail off to each member of the murdering gang."[7]

Patrick Donnelly died of pneumonia at his home on Russell Avenue in St. Catharines on May 18, 1914 and was buried in Lake View Cemetery in Thorold, a mere stone's throw from the old Welland Canal.

A curious relic of Patrick still exists in the form of a small wisp of his hair. Thomas P. Kelley, author of *The Black Donnellys*, explains the matter in a letter:[8]

> I wrote how I had been given a lock of Pat Donnelly's hair by an elderly Toronto lady, a Mrs. Millage and formerly Sadie Frank, the daughter of John Craven Frank of Lucan, Ont. She told that her people had been on good terms with the Donnellys, then mentioned an amusing story of how, as a youngster and on an impulse, she had snipped off a lock of Pat Donnelly's hair with a pair of scissors as he passed her house . . . .

Thomas P. Kelley had great expectations of making his fortune with this relic, proposing to put it on exhibition at the Western Fair in London. In a subsequent letter he elaborated on his scheme:[9]

> I visualize our display with a large and colorful canvas painting, which shows the Donnellys being clubbed to death by their enemies, underneath which is emblazoned: "Last Moment of The Black Donnellys"
>
> Then on drawing closer, the curious—and all of them will be curious—they will see the worded invite: "Come In And See The Greatest Curio In Donnelliana. A Lock Of Pat Donnelly's Hair."
>
> Inside, with someone there to watch it at all hours, and behind a glass case, we would display the lock of hair. I believe we could get a dollar a throw to see it.
>
> And there also would be the pamphlets, which would cost us practically nothing but which we could sell for fifty cents. The pamphlets would tell how the lock of hair got into my possession.

Nothing ever came of the scheme, but I have a feeling that this lock of hair, like the original Donnelly tombstone erected in 1889, will one day end up in the Donnelly Museum in Lucan.[10]

By the beginning of 1875 William Donnelly

Norah Kennedy, who married William Donnelly

had recovered from the notoriety of the Maggie Thompson affair the year previous. At that time Maggie's father and brother had laid charges against him and his brothers. In his defense, Will had produced Maggie's love letters in court. In one of the letters Maggie accepted his offer of marriage and begged him to come and take her away by force if necessary. Naturally, the newspapers gleefully printed the letters and the public eagerly devoured them.

On January 28th, 1875 William Donnelly eloped with Norah Kennedy. Pointing to a possible *modus operandi* when it came to the Donnelly boys and local girls, it was reported that William had been advised by friends not to marry the girl until he had obtained some property from her parents. But the girl was the daughter of an old friend of Will's, John Kennedy, Sr., over on the eleventh concession of Biddulph. Will had always been a favorite of the older man and upon their return they were married without further ado and much to the joy of both sets of parents. The wife of Jack Donnelly, Will's son, told me that all of the groom's brothers stood up with him at the church. The bride herself had told her this and added that the parish priest had never seen such a fine group of young men.

Meanwhile, the brothers of the bride, John Kennedy, Jr., and his brother Rhody, had been in years past close chums of the Donnelly boys. The unexpected union between Will and their sister came as a shock to them. They immediately quarreled with Will and his brothers. A row between Bob and Tom Donnelly on the one hand and Rhody Kennedy on the other at the Fitzhenry House included fisticuffs. A bitter enmity rose between the two sets of brothers.

With Will's marriage to Norah Kennedy, Maggie Thompson was thrown over. There has always been a lot of speculation as to her eventual fate. One version had her father marrying her off to a disagreeable old man. Another had her drifting off into old age as a

Maggie Thompson's grave marker, along with that of her husband, Edward Ryan, in Bay City, Michigan.

pining spinster who occasionally dreamed of the life she might have had with her old beau.

Such speculation can now stop, for the eventual fate of Maggie Thompson has finally come to light. When Maggie's affair with William Donnelly came to an abrupt end, she returned to her parents' home in McGillivray Township. There she spent the next decade and a half of her life working in her own home or in those of relatives or near neighbors as a seamstress, dressmaker and milliner. By the year 1890 she was forty years of age and her marriage prospects seemed dim indeed.

In McGillivray Township about three miles from the home of her father, however, was a large Catholic family named Ryan whose members she had known most of her life. Some of the Ryan girls, Sarah, Eliza, Mary Ellen and Annie, were about her own age. The head of the family was Patrick Ryan who farmed at Lot 16 in the second concession of McGillivray not far from Clandeboye. The Ryans and Thompsons would see each other regularly as both attended St. Peter's Church on the Exeter Road in Biddulph. Mixed in among the Ryan girls were a number of Ryan boys. Among them was young Edward Ryan, about four years Maggie's junior. The two had many years to get to know and become fond of each other but it is quite likely that the notoriety of Maggie's past connection with

William Donnelly prevented their contemplating any kind of union between them.

Then in 1890 Edward Ryan left home and went to live in Bay City, Michigan. Not long after, and perhaps by secret design, Maggie followed him there. Within a matter of weeks after her arrival, Edward Ryan and Maggie Thompson were quietly married on November 4th, 1891. They settled down to a long and happy life together, he working as a drayman, which usually meant a deliveryman for a brewery, and she continuing her work as seamstress, dressmaker and milliner.

Edward Ryan was a nephew of Edward (Ned) Ryan who on March 5th, 1878 claimed to have been robbed on the streets of Lucan by Tom Donnelly and James Feeheley. Patrick Ryan, the father of Maggie's husband, was an older brother of this Ned Ryan who pursued Donnelly and Feeheley in the courts for two years.

The union of Edward and Maggie produced two children. The first, born in 1893, died soon after birth but the second, named Anna Ethel, was born to the couple on August 3rd, 1894. Anna became a registered nurse and lived with her parents for many years, at first on Blend Street in Bay City and later in their home at 608 North Walnut Street. When her uncle, William Thompson of the Thompson cow incident, died in 1929, he included his sister Maggie as well as Anna in his will with a generous bequest to each of them.

Although raised as a farmer, Maggie's husband Edward Ryan worked at laboring jobs in Bay City, usually carting heavy loads with a low-bed wagon. The work must have taken its toll for by 1930 he was an invalid. Edward died in 1933 and Maggie herself continued to live into her nineties and died in 1942. Before that, however, she told her daughter Anna about her early days in Biddulph. Years later, Anna wrote to Orlo Miller a letter dated October 2, 1964, not long after the publication of his book, *The Donnellys Must Die*. It was no doubt prompted by the furor caused upon the removal by the church authorities, represented by lawyer Francis Carter, of the Donnelly grave marker. The letter reads:[11]

> The story of the Donnellys has been of great interest to me. It was given to me direct from my mother Maggie Thompson. She was not the type indicated in the book. As for the monument I would prefer to see it stay in Lucan. I do not want to be identified at present. But any mail will be appreciated. You may send it to my address below. A copy of this letter is being sent to Mr. Francis Carter attorney.
>   Yours sincerely
>   Maggie Thompson's daughter
>   Address: Maggie Thompson
>   Bay City, Sta A 48707
>   Michigan
>   (Correct name Anna Ryan)

After the deaths of her parents, Anna continued to live in their home at 608 North Walnut Street in Bay City. She did not marry and died at the age of 96 years in Bay City on January 29th, 1991.

Ellen (Nellie) Hines in her later years

Michael Donnelly in his early twenties

And so has been finally put to rest another of the strange fairy tales which have followed the Donnelly story for well over a century.

Nellie Hines was very young when she married her handsome husband, Michael Donnelly. They were quite happy as a couple despite having been burned out while living on Alice Street in Lucan during the stagecoach troubles. By the end of 1878 Mike Donnelly had given up the coaching trade and had obtained employment with the Canada Southern Railway which had a large terminus in St. Thomas. Working out-of-town for days at a time on the railway, Mike took a house on Fifth Avenue and moved his little family there to make it much easier to get home. Shortly after the birth of their second child, Nellie was devastated when on December 9th, 1879 she received word that her husband had been killed in a bar-room fight in Slaght's Hotel in Waterford. Her sister-in-law Jenny left her own young family in Mosa Township and rushed over to St.

117

Slaght's Hotel in Waterford was sold by Freeman Slaght to Henry F. Teeter soon after Mike Donnelly was stabbed to death in its bar-room and was renamed after the new owner. The house of Dr. Duncombe in the background still stands.

Thomas to help Nellie get over the shock of her loss. Shortly after, however, came the other blow to both of them with the news of the murders of several members of the Donnelly family in Biddulph. Nellie's life fell apart.

After the second trial of James Carroll for those murders, Nellie was found living in the village of Lucan with the family of Will. For a short time, Patrick, then a widower, also lived with them. But the ménage proved too uncomfortable and could not continue. The young widow subsequently moved to London to be near her sisters. One of them, Mary, had married a Lucan man named William Bernard Hodgins and moved with him to Toledo where Hodgins operated a wagon works and later a motor garage. When Nellie went to visit her sister in that city, she met an Englishman named James Clarke. They were soon married. Clarke was or later became an electrician and with her new husband Nellie made a fresh start and

tried to forget the past. They moved to Cleveland, Ohio where they spent the rest of their lives. Here Nellie had several more children, half-siblings to Catherine and James Michael Donnelly.

When I contacted the second family of Nellie Hines in Cleveland, they were astonished to learn of her connection to the Donnelly story. They knew their mother had been married before—they were well acquainted with the two children from the first marriage—but they had always believed that the first husband had died in a railway accident.[12]

Nellie's son from her first marriage, James Michael Donnelly, was informally adopted by his uncle Robert Donnelly and his wife, Annie Currie. While they were alive he spent most of his life with them in Glencoe and later in Biddulph and Lucan. He and his uncle Robert purchased the Western or West End Hotel in Lucan in 1901 and after its sale in 1905 he settled down with them in Lucan.

118

He did, on occasion, live for short periods with his mother in Cleveland and got to know his half-siblings. Having obtained experience in the hotel business in Lucan, upon the death of his uncle Bob and his wife Annie young Jim Donnelly spent the rest of his life working in that line, sometimes as manager but often as a desk clerk in various hotels and particularly in London.

In Kincardine, Ontario where his mother had family connections, he worked for a young widow named Catherine McDonald whose husband, Angus, died while proprietor of the Queen's Hotel in that town. Prior to her marriage, Catherine had acted as a nurse and had met young Jim Donnelly in the London Insane Asylum, as it was then called, where his uncle Robert had been a patient from June 15, 1908 until October 30, 1909. Catherine and young Jim were about the same age.

Fate threw the two of them together again when Catherine was left a young widow with three small children and the owner of a hotel in Kincardine. She could not operate the hotel herself, her son told me, because the Presbyterians and Baptists of the town were then all-powerful and would not countenance a woman acting in business under a liquor license. According to her son, Jim Donnelly had just returned from Cleveland at the time and was working part time at the Drake House in London and also at the Belvedere Hotel there. When Catherine turned for help to the Commercial Travellers' Association, that group recommended Jim Donnelly as someone who could operate the hotel for her. Catherine McDonald thereupon offered the position of manager to him and he accepted. She sold to him the stock of cigars, cigarettes, soft drinks, furniture, tables, glass and furnishings and he operated the business for her for five years from 1915. Catherine remained the owner of the hotel itself.

"He was like a father to us kids," her son John H. McDonald told me. "When he arrived, however, a great pall fell over the town for he was the first Roman Catholic to come to Kincardine. Jim was a well-built stocky man of about five foot and eight or nine inches and about 185 or 190 pounds. He was very close-mouthed and would answer a question put to him but he was not a braggart or one who would push himself forward. As a result, no one in Kincardine knew much about him. But he was very intelligent and even though he was soft-spoken and unassuming, he could engage in wonderful conversation. By the time he left Kincardine, he had been accepted by everyone and was held in the highest esteem by the townfolk."

Jim Donnelly left Kincardine in 1920 when Local Option came in and the town went dry.

"And they would have married," Catherine's son told me, "except for religion."

Jim Donnelly, however, was not the marrying kind as he apparently had other lady-friends. One was another widow in Biddulph named Katey Barry, who had been born Catherine McLaughlin. He visited her often and even went so far as to mention her in his last will, leaving her certain "goods . . . in boxes and a trunk and stored with Harold Hodgins, Hardware Merchant, of Lucan." I have a suspicion that Katey was never told of this little legacy or, if she were told, she did not take up the gift for the boxes and trunk were apparently left in the possession of the merchant mentioned. Among the personal possessions in the boxes and trunk were photographs.

Young Jim returned to Cleveland after leaving Kincardine but came back to London following the financial crash of 1929 because "he kind of got wiped out over there." As for what he thought about the history of his family, this is what young Jim Donnelly said, according to John H. McDonald:

My family took a back seat to no one. They would, however, give concessions if they felt they were in the wrong because, you know, they weren't always in the right. They were accused of a lot of things they weren't actually guilty of. Then again, they may have done a lot of things that they weren't charged with, and maybe people were sometimes afraid to come forward. But it's human nature that when once a person is down, everyone wants to trod on him.

Another curious fact about young Jim Donnelly was that on the very rare occasion when he would talk about the murder of his uncles and grandparents, he would tell the story as if he himself were the little boy who scrambled out from under the bed and hid in the long grass behind the house which the vigilantes then burned to the ground.

The oldest and the youngest of the Donnelly boys, James, Jr., and Thomas never married. That is not to say they did not have their dalliances, both local and further afield. A sometime member of the Ontario Legislature, C. M. Macfie of Appin, wrote on April 8th, 1954:[13]

> An illegitimate son of Tom Donnelly who was killed in the Biddulph affair was mothered by a young woman who went from Ekfrid Township to Biddulph to work   was raised by her and after her death lived in a farm home north of Glencoe. He died in his later teens as a result of a kick in the abdomen by a horse.

I was unable to confirm the fact of a young woman going to work from Ekfrid to Biddulph, but I did find a girl named Flora McKinnon who lived just outside Appin on a farm with her siblings and widowed father. Flora was about seventeen years of age in the spring of 1879. She seemed to have a penchant for casual relationships with the opposite sex. By late summer she was obviously bearing child and on December 7th she gave birth to a boy. Two days later, Mike Donnelly was killed in Waterford and within a few weeks the news of the terrible tragedy on the Roman Line of Biddulph was splashed all over the area newspapers. It was after these events that Flora's father registered the birth of his daughter's child naming him in the record as Thomas Donnelly, Jr., born out of wedlock to his daughter Flora and to Thomas Donnelly, farmer, of Biddulph.

Tom Donnelly as sketched by author

Now Tom Donnelly may well have spent time in the area of Flora's residence in 1879 with his sister Jenny Currie and her family for the Curries had not long before moved into their new house in Mosa Township not far away. And Flora seems to have had other amorous adventures with young local swains. Once a group of them came at night to her father's house, banged on the doors and windows and called out for her to come join them. This may seem like strange conduct to us today, but it was the kind of treatment perpetrated by gangs of young men upon a girl with a bad reputation in those days, especially where they knew that the girl's only protection was an aged father. Nevertheless, Flora's father finally convinced the gang they should leave.

On another occasion a young man met her in open day and apparently suggested some interplay. When she fled towards the farm of a neighbor whom she referred to as "Uncle Thomson," he followed her. She may or may not have escaped, but in any event

Tom Donnelly, Jr., was given the fatal kick by a horse on the McGregor farm at or near this spot.

not long after laid a charge of indecent assault against him. He was convicted. And curiously, Flora's sister Anne also gave birth to a child born out wedlock not long after Tom Donnelly, Jr., was born. Moreover, Flora herself in the years following bore several other such children out of wedlock. They were registered as the children of a near neighbor named Alex Thomson with whom Flora went to live after the death of her father in 1890. He may have been the same "Uncle Thomson" to whose farm she had fled when accosted a year or two before.

Tom Donnelly, Jr., went by the name Donnelly for a time but later adopted the surname Thomson. His mother apparently died before 1895. In that year, young Tom was a lad of fifteen working on the farm of Duncan McGregor when he was kicked in the belly by an unruly horse. He suffered for two days, likely without any medical attention, and then died. He was buried as an indigent at the expense of the township and his remains lie in an unmarked grave in the Eddie Cemetery between Appin and Glencoe.

Robert Donnelly's marriage to Jenny's sister-in-law, Annie Currie, was more or less successful except that the odd story is told of Bob's female friends or admirers. One was apparently Kate Waun, or Johnson, who the reader will recall was spending the night with Bob and his wife in the second house of the O'Connors in Lucan the night the first house was burned. We may find it strange today that all three slept in the same bed but it was not that unusual in those times. Nevertheless, the enemies of the family claimed that Kate was a woman of loose morals. She may have been, in fact, separated from her husband.

Bob was also rumoured to have had a female friend in Waterford, Ontario with whom he was supposed to have had a child but I have found no evidence of support for such an allegation. Another story has a little more credence. It seems that Bob received a letter from a female admirer. Annie found it. The story goes that in her anger she threw it down the hole in the outhouse and then told Bob that if he wanted to read it again he would have to fetch it from there. Bob in his turn became so annoyed at her that he picked up his horsewhip and herded her out to the railway tracks just outside Glencoe where he threatened her with a whipping for what she had done. It was not long after this that one-time Glencoe constable Archibald Riddell taunted the new constable, William Donnelly, that if Bob "had been handcuffed he would not have made such an indiscriminate use of the horsewhip on his wife not long ago."[14] Perhaps as he got older, Bob became less vain about his appearance for the couple settled down into a more or less harmonious life together and seemed in the end to genuinely care for each other.

Tom Donnelly's fifteen-year-old son lies in this cemetery near Appin.

Chapter 18

Village of Saints

William Donnelly's many scrapes with the law began early. When he was a boy, Big Bernard Stanley accused him of stealing a bottle of whiskey. Again, while still a youth Will was accused of theft of a sheepskin and, at the age of eighteen, he came up on a charge of stealing wood. Then in the spring of 1868 he was charged with theft of a pistol from a house in London.

In the last case, the complainant said he saw William Donnelly holding and examining the gun. By the time it was discovered that it was missing, Donnelly had departed for the States. Upon his return a year later, however,

William Donnelly's booking in 1864 on a charge of stealing wood.

he was taken up on the charge and put on trial at the Middlesex Fall Assizes. Then in 1871 Robert Burns Orme of Lucan woke up in the night and chased from his bedroom a couple of burglars he thought had stolen his cash box containing $400. Even though the following day he found the cash box and its contents secreted in a granary, Orme laid a formal charge against Will Donnelly[1] and an accomplice named Tom Gray.

As far as I am aware, William Donnelly was convicted of none of these charges. In the gun case, from the testimony given in court it appears that by that time—when he was about twenty-three—Donnelly liked to portray himself as a man of the world traveling easily to the United States and back and cultivating the airs of a well-dressed, sophisticated and cosmopolitan gentleman.

After eloping with Norah Kennedy, he soon settled down with his wife on the Swamp Line next to the farm of William Ryder near the Cedar Swamp Schoolhouse. Here a son, James, was born to the couple but the baby died. William Ryder fashioned a little coffin for the child and Donnelly never forgot the kindness of his neighbor.

Once Will recovered from the shock of the murders of his family—he was sick in bed for three weeks following the funerals—he set about trying to bring the guilty parties to justice.

On April 1, 1880, for example, the county crown attorney of Middlesex, Charles Hutchinson wrote:[2]

> I find great difficulty in restraining William Donnelly from hunting with Phair.

Henry Phair was the veteran London detective. Will Donnelly tracked down the Whalen's Corners blacksmith, Edward Sutherby, who had departed for the States immediately after the tragedy. And he sent to Hutchinson his friend and one-time neighbor, William Ryder, to report possible prosecution testimony against his own brothers, Grouchy Pat and Sideroad Jim

Ryder. Donnelly was all in favor of arresting many others of the vigilants[3]

> and summoning the rest of them to get their story. Mr. Irving said it was a wild idea but he must not attempt to handle those lambs with kid gloves.

Hutchinson, however, warned him again and again not to speak to potential witnesses. At one point the crown attorney wrote to Æmilius Irving who had been retained to lead the prosecution:[4]

> I merely write to say I have been careful not to let Wm Donnelly know any thing of the inquiries we are making.

In the meantime, Donnelly's friends were advising him to quit Biddulph, but he refused to give such satisfaction to his enemies. "I'll show them that there's some backbone in me yet," he is reported to have said,[5] "that Bill Donnelly did not die with the others."

Once, he and his brother Patrick considered accepting the offer of a theatrical promoter to appear on stage. The London *Advertiser* referred to the anticipated event:[6]

> . . . They will both give a graphic account of

that terrible murder and holocaust, and will exhibit some very interesting relics from the ruins of the Donnelly home. William Donnelly is a man of more than ordinary ability, and can interest his hearers with an account of this tragedy as no other man is capable of doing . . . interspersed with first class musical talent.
> "Tickets are only 25 cents."

The Biddulph vigilants heaped scorn on them for even contemplating such a course of action. Pat Breen contrasted those who had been charged and freed with William Donnelly, saying[7] that they were not of

> a class of men to make a figure on the stage or travel round with a panorama in order to make a livelihood.

When Charles Hutchinson heard rumors of the proposed enterprise, he immediately wrote to Donnelly:[8]

> I must say I do not think it will do your cause (by which I mean the cause of justice) any good if you and Pat endeavour to make money out of the misfortune of your family . . . .

Quickly changing his mind, Will replied:[9]

> I received your last letter in due time and must say I got a good deal of feeling advice in it and [have] entirely given up the idea of going out in the lecturing business as it would be my meanest turn to do anything contrary to your wishes being as you were a father to the continuing members of the family for the last year.

The month of April 1881 found Will living in the village with his wife Norah, baby daughter Jo-Anna, brother Patrick and sister-in-law Nellie, the widow of Michael, with her two small children Catherine and James.

That spring, Will took up again the stud business and drove his buggy along the dusty roads of McGillivray, Stephen, Usborne and Blanshard Townships with his trotting stallion, Wild Irishman, tethered behind. Almost two years later, when the progeny from those unions were maturing, it was reported that they "cannot be excelled as general purpose stock".[10] Shortly after, however, Will sold Wild Irishman to Charles

Charles Hutchinson, the County Crown Attorney

Bean of McGillivray Township for $430. He was almost immediately sorry for having made the sale but failed to persuade the buyer to sell the horse back to him.

In May with money in his pocket, Will took a train trip with his brother Pat heading west to Parkhill and beyond, perhaps looking to buy a business such as a hotel. Later that month an old friend, Jack Kent, moved Will's possessions to London, reportedly to a two-storey frame home at the corner of Clarence and Horton Streets where he planned to run a boarding house. Mrs. Donnelly was an excellent housekeeper and the premises would be able to accommodate fifteen boarders.

Will could not, however, stay away from Biddulph. In July, it was reported that while sitting in a wagon on the Clandeboye road near Lucan, he had been fired at with the bullet "passing within a few inches of his breast".[11] What Will thought of this is not known, but the report continues that it was merely a young man shooting at squirrels from an apple tree.

On his return visits to Lucan, Will Donnelly heard of a newcomer to the village named Francis Morrison West. West had arrived in mid-November 1880 not to work as a detective, he said, but because he had "a curiosity to see the Donnelly homestead".[12] He was originally from Prescott, Wisconsin across the Mississippi River and not far from St. Paul, Minnesota. His father, John T. West, was a cattle dealer and for two years Frank West had operated the city meat market in Prescott. After the business failed, he left his parents, brother and creditors and began to roam about, first to Dakota and then to Canada.

West arrived in Lucan with $700 in the pockets of his slick city clothes. He was described[13] by a journalist of the day as

> . . . very shrewd and clever . . . a young man, well-dressed, smooth-faced, with a retreating forehead and a quiet manner . . . .

Despite his disclaimer, his first object was to work up a case against the Biddulph vigilants and thereby make his fame and fortune. He took a room at the Queen's Hotel. Years later, Ida Elizabeth, the daughter of the proprietor Alexander McFalls, wrote to Orlo Miller:[14]

> I was 7 years old and remember it quite well but what I couldn't understand how you heard of Frank West—he boarded with us and I took piano lessons from him but I don't remember any others taking lessons and he wasn't in town very long—& I wondered how you ever heard of him . . . .

During the Christmas festive season when there was more than the usual amount of gathering, drinking and discussing in the Lucan hotels, it was an easy matter to buy a round or two and strike up new friendships. The Catholics—now that Fitzhenry's was gone—usually frequented the bar-rooms of either the Queen's or the Royal hotels. Frank West soon became a fixture in both and began to associate with the young men from the Catholic Settlement. Back in his own room, now at the hotel, he made notes of information gleaned concerning the Donnelly affair. One such note, which ended up in the files of the crown attorney of Middlesex reads:[15]

> Information picked up regarding the Donnelly murder by the undersigned. February 14, 1881. Have been burning [around] nearly all day [with] Patrick Keefe, Wm. Feeheley, Thomas Purtell, James Kane—In the afternoon went to the Grand Trunk Station to see Kane off as he started for Michigan today. In going we passed the house where detective Everett used to live. I was walking a little apart from the rest with Feeheley—and he (feeheley) pointed to the door and said this is the house Everett was in when he was shot at. And asked me to notice the marks of the shot in the door and door facing—I asked who shot at Everett and he (Feeheley) said Bob Donnelly—I asked him why Bob shot at Everett. He said he did not know. I then remarked "The Donnellys are a hard lot," to which Feeheley said, "Yes, but there are not many of them left, God damn them."

That shooting was the beginning of the downfall of the Donnellys. Sam Everett was born in 1841 and raised in the town of Dundas, Ontario. He began his career in 1863 in partnership with a brother-in-law as a pumpmaker and undertaker, digging wells,

Sam Everett is named at the bottom of the family marker.

cisterns and septic systems on the side. Sam soon progressed to building and operating a billiard saloon at the corner of King and Sydenham Streets in Dundas where his father had his residence, lumberyard and chair factory.[16] In 1865 his father's lumberyard and adjoining buildings in Dundas burned to the ground, and the family moved to Kalamazoo, Michigan. Sam accompanied the family to the States, but soon returned for in 1874 we find him as the chief bartender at the St. Nicholas Hotel in Hamilton. By the following year he had joined the city's police force. His career there apparently came to an abrupt end as the result of an incident, which was reported in the newspaper on Thursday, March 1st, 1877 as follows:[17]

> Illicit Distilling.—On Wednesday morning Samuel Lount Everett, of Wentworth, was brought up on a charge of having distilled spirituous liquors without a licence. The evidence went to show that the defendant had

admitted the manufacture of the liquor, but beyond this no direct proof was offered. His Worship imposed a fine of $200, in accordance with the Act.

Everett then set himself up as a private detective and, as we now know, shortly thereafter became the village constable at Lucan. After a tumultuous year or two engaging with the Donnellys and their friends, Sam Everett was fired by the council but continued to hang on in the village until the year 1881. Then his bitter enemy, William Porte, noted in his diary under date of Saturday, April 2nd in that year:[18]

> Mr. Samuel Lount Everett of Village Constable renown, moved out bag and baggage today. I am led to understand that not one solitary individual called upon him to bid him good bye . . . And I am here yet.

As to his ultimate fate, William Donnelly was reported in the Toronto *Globe* of Monday, December 4th, 1883 to have said:

> There was a man named Everett, a constable in Lucan, who swore my brother Bob here into the penitentiary for two years on a charge of trying to shoot him. He acknowledged afterwards that it was a put-up job, and that some big men in Lucan had made him do it. He dropped dead in the streets of Chicago not long ago.

He apparently died of "heart disease" and was buried on June 10th, 1882. His burial notice did not appear in the Kalamazoo *Gazette* until July 18th. He lies with his parents in Riverside Cemetery in Kalamazoo.

Meanwhile, Francis West continued to fraternize with the Feeheleys. In March 1881, James Feeheley celebrated St. Patrick's Day in the village by meeting John Bawden in hand-to-hand combat. In another confidential note, West related:[19]

> . . . After the fight. Fifteen minutes after two o'clock a.m. March 18, 1881. A little before one o'clock I went up to my room . . . Alex McFalls (proprietor of the House) came up bringing James Feeheley up to bed . . . McFalls stayed with Feeheley a few minutes talking— then went downstairs and proceeded to close his house—I sat a few minutes thinking over

the fight [and then] concluded to go into Feeheley's room and have a talk with him as I wanted to appear friendly towards him—He sat down on the bed and began to cry and said he got no show in the fight [and] that he knew he would die a hard death—but would not give in to Old Christ himself. I asked what he meant. He replied, "Because both parties are against me." I asked, "What parties?" He said, "Both the Donnellys and the vigilants." He said that his backbone was gone now—I asked what he meant—He said his old man knew too much for the whole of them while he was alive. "I will have revenge on Bawden. One of the Donnellys nearly beat me dead once, but I have had good satisfaction since and I will get satisfaction out of Bawden. I helped put one son of a Bitch out of the way and I know who finished four more." I then asked him whom he had helped put out of the way. He then replied, "It don't make any difference to you." Furthermore, he said, "I could have made a few thousand out of it once" and that he was a damned fool that he did not.

West felt that on that occasion he had come close to obtaining a confession. He therefore continued associating with the brothers and his note dated April 14, 1881 relates:[20]

Today William and James Feeheley came to Lucan and were arrested for assault on James Carroll—were bailed out and I burned around with them. James Feeheley and I walked from the Queen's Hotel to Cain's Hotel then down past where Donnelly lives. William Donnelly saw us—came out and shook hands with Feeheley and had a short chat together—Then Feeheley and I went on to Walker's Hotel—Feeheley seemed a little nervous and he remarked, "It was too bad almost for anyone to help Carroll out of the murder, as he was worse than the Donnellys." I asked him how that was. Feeheley said, "After we helped swear him out of the murder, he and a few more of the vigilantes were robbing us out of our property, and if they don't whack up to us Will and I are going in for the reward." I asked, "Do you know enough about it to get a reward?" Feeheley said he knew all about it and that they could never have done the murder only for his help.

Two days later, West made another note, which reads:[21]

Apr. 16, 1881—Carroll withdrew complaint paying costs. I and the Feeheleys were together at the Queen's Hotel most of the time after court—After I had tea I started up the street towards the post office and I saw William Feeheley taking off his coat asking Carroll to fight him telling him if he would fight him five minutes he would give him six dollars more—called Carroll a murderer, saying he could prove it. Then in a few minutes James Feeheley and Martin Dorcey quarreled—Feeheley called Dorcey a murderer and said he could whip him and began taking off his coat—I interfered on Feeheley's part—Then Dorcey told Feeheley to come out of town—we started and went up the RR track back of Maguire's carriage works when we had to clear the track for a train—Feeheley was still calling Dorcey a murderer and told him he could produce the boy they sent to Whalens Corners the morning of the Murder to see if William Donnelly was dead. Dorcey cowered down and would not fight so we went back to Queen's Hotel and Dorcey treated—I then followed William Feeheley into the hall and said to him that James was a fool for talking so to these men if he knew nothing of the Murder. William replied, "We don't say anything but what we can prove. One of the men that helped carry Tom Donnelly into the house after he was killed was walking around the streets this afternoon—and long Jim Toohey is the man who broke his head with the spade." I then said, "It seems you do know all about it." Feeheley said, "Yes, and if they don't let us alone we will squeal and hang the whole of them."

Will Donnelly stated that during West's undercover work to obtain evidence against the Biddulph Peace Society, the erstwhile private detective had at least three personal interviews with the county crown attorney but "did not impress Mr. Hutchinson at all favourably".[22]

It is true that West obtained no further information from the Feeheleys as they, too, soon left for Saginaw. His efforts with others from the Catholic Settlement also went nowhere for as an outsider he was just not trusted. Then, from his entry through his piano teaching into the homes of the more affluent and respectable Lucanites such as the Stanleys, he soon realized that it would be more rewarding to work on the anti-

Donnelly side of the case, for the Donnellys were not exactly popular in those homes. He thereupon resolved to get to know the Donnellys well and to learn of their schemes for revenge. To that end, he soon claimed to be intimate with all three of the surviving brothers.

William Donnelly always remained suspicious of West and sarcastically referred to the would-be sleuth as "detective Pinkerton".[23] When West got himself hired as a farm hand with John Kent, to whom the brothers had rented the homestead, Donnelly told his tenant, "West is too good a music teacher to be working about a farm without sinister motives."[24]

It was not long before Frank West began to experience midnight escapades in and around Lucan. He claimed that on or about the first day of April in 1881, he and Pat Donnelly stole a couple of government rifles from the Lucan drill shed. When Kent refused to buy them, he hid them on the farm. Other thefts included a couple of hens of Sam McLean and a cow belonging to a man named Fogarty.

"I was laying for the Donnellys all summer," West later recalled, "but told no one about it. I was pretending to be their friend all the while."[25]

In the meantime, after giving up his attempts at opening a boarding house in London, Will Donnelly moved back to Lucan in the fall of 1881. Upon his return, the vigilantes grew uncomfortable and the London *Free Press* voiced their feelings:[26]

> In addition to hating William Donnelly, the Vigilants of Biddulph fear him. They cannot hide it. He has always been known to them as a shrewd, cunning man, who could govern his temper and keep his tongue quiet when he liked. They call him "the lawyer". His determination, too, was as marked as his cunning, and his fearless movements among them when danger seemed greatest, has given them an instinctive dread of him . . . It requires no wide stretch of the imagination to form some idea of the unrest and secret dread that must come to the homes of these people in the

dark hours of the night. If weird dreams have ever waked them, who knows but that the shadows of the room have not been to them the phantasm of the avenging William? That the creaking of some swinging gate has stirred them to the deepest alarm?

As for Francis Morrison West, Will soon got to know him better but came to regret it. The *cause célèbre* for which West reached the apex of his notoriety in and around Lucan was the alleged plot by William and Robert Donnelly to burn down the grist mill owned and operated by the Stanleys, William and Bernard, and Thomas Dight. West claimed to have been part of the plans. He went into painstaking detail to show how intimate he had become with the Donnellys to get them to confide in him.[27]

The plot began at John Kent's threshing on Saturday, October 1st of that year of 1881. That day Robert and William Donnelly drove up to the homestead. William went in to the stable or barn and called to him, "Come here, Frank, I want to talk to you." West went in and Donnelly disclosed the

Will Donnelly as sketched by author

plan to burn the mill. Young Simon Howe and Cornelius and Dennis Carty were in on the scheme. On one occasion when Bob left to go down to Judge's to get a brace and bit and some coal oil, Will said, "You know my baby is sick, and so unknown to my wife I am filling it with brandy. Everything is fair. The mill must go. It must be burned now because Saturday night is the only night it's shut down. That will happen at 12 o'clock and two o'clock would be the time for you and I to set it on fire. By that time I'll have the baby drunk and I will send Robert to the other end of town for an old lady. When he comes back, he will go to the mill and help put the fire out and thereby gain credit for the Donnellys. We want to get all the credit we can on account of the Feeheley case."

The Feeheleys were then being extradited from the United States and it appeared that the charges against the Biddulph suspects would be revived.

West, probably to give him an opportunity to warn the proprietors, wanted the fire postponed, and Will finally agreed to put off the burning. "But those Stanleys swore hard against us at the Carroll trial," he said, "and I want the mill burned."

West then sneaked over to William Stanley's place and informed him of the plot.

After one more postponement, on the final appointed day West went to the Queen's Hotel, rented a room, climbed out the window and went over to William Donnelly's.

After all the painstaking details of preparing for the job as elaborated by West, one wonders what it all amounted to. To find out, we will continue in West's own narrative:[28]

> We went behind Donnelly's barn, climbed the fence and went to the street which turns back of the mill. I went to the other street in front of the mill to see if anyone was around. I motioned for Howe to come and he followed me across the street. We went on the west side of the mill and I began boring under a window near the engine room. Howe asked me what I was doing there. He told me to come and bore

on the main building. I moved, bore a couple of holes and Howe poured the coal oil into them. I bored another hole and struck the studding, then bored a fourth hole and emptied my bottle into it. Howe was trying to light a match to ignite the oil but the wind kept blowing them out. He must have tried four or five matches when they pounced upon us from the inside. Howe ran off, up through the town, and got away.

As it turned out, the only one caught was West. And how did he manage to get caught? "Because," he said, "I ran the wrong way."

His captors took West to William Stanley who put him in a buggy the next day, Sunday, and drove with him twelve or fifteen miles up and down the Roman Line looking for Simon Howe. They failed to catch him, but William and Robert Donnelly were soon arrested along with Cornelius Carty.

On hearing of the arrests, the vigilants of Biddulph were jubilant. The journalists now had a new Lucan sensation to write about. Both groups flocked into the village and the latter reported on the former as follows:[29]

> . . . men like Patrick and Thomas Ryder, James Carroll, Patrick Breen, James Twohy, P. Heenan, M. [recte, J.] Harrigan, M. Blake . . . had heard of the arrests and came in . . . they settled down in knots of four or five on the streets and in the hotels . . . the general opinion [was], "We have caught them at last in the very act of trying to burn down the mill, and perhaps the village; they'll get their deserts now . . . ."

And they toasted Frank West as "the hero of the hour in Lucan." When the London *Free Press* reporter approached him for a statement standing in the midst of a group of admirers, the journalist had to be content with filing the following:[30]

> He would have nothing to say. He smiled crushingly on him, as much as to say, "Do you think I'm green?" and the crowd laughed and comforted the reporter by assuring him that West was too smart for him.

The following encounter between Grouchy Ryder and William Donnelly's wife Norah was also reported:[31]

Old William Street in Lucan looking east towards Main Street, with the Stanley and Dight flour and grist mill on the right.

Mr. Patrick Ryder, Sr., was standing with a number of others at the Central Hotel yesterday. When Mrs. William Donnelly came along, looking sad and downcast. "How are you, Mrs. Donnelly?" he asked. "Pretty well, thanks. You seem to be happy." "Yes, I'm well. How's Mr. Donnelly?" "He's all right." "Yes. He's where he ought to have been long ago."

Before Frank West agreed to turn crown evidence against his co-conspirators, however, he had to arrange with the crown attorney for immunity from his own prosecution for stealing the drill shed rifles, Sam McLean's chickens and Fogarty's cow. To assist him, he retained the known anti-Donnelly firm of lawyers in London, Messrs. Street and Becher. Probably on their advice, he quickly took the precaution of leaving the country to await word of the amnesty from the safety of Port Huron, Michigan. Crown Attorney Hutchinson referred the matter to the attorney general's office in Toronto and it

was eventually agreed not to prosecute West in return for his "turning Queen's evidence".

Hutchinson also wrote to Æmilius Irving as follows:[32]

> The new sensation in Lucan is I think a put up job. It may be that Bob Donnelly has got drawn into something foolish, but William is no doubt in this the temporary victim of a treacherous plot.

Saddened by the brothers having been consigned for three days and nights "to the horrors of the Lucan lock-up," he said that the magistrate who had committed them was "part owner of the mill which they allege was attempted to be set on fire, and a vigilant and boon of the vigilance faction."[33]

William Donnelly, on the other hand, was in good spirits. From his cell in the "Lucan Boarding House," as he called it, he wrote to the editor of the London *Free Press*:[34]

> As the readers of your valuable paper are no doubt anxious to hear how things are

progressing in this Village of Saints, I will now take the liberty of dropping you a few lines . . . . The only part of the village I can at present speak of is the inside of the hall over the lock-up, the pig-sties used for sleeping cells, down stairs, and the line of March from there to the Queen's Hotel where we receive our support for the inner man . . . but oh! Think of the nights locked up in a cattle car, listening to Bob snoring and Carty hollering for more fire . . . In about an hour and a half after our arrest Tom Ryder (whom Johnny O'Connor saw at the murder of our family) came into the lock-up with Barney Stanley, and told us he was sorry for our trouble. It seems strange to me that he was not at home playing cards.

The Stanley and Dight mill eventually burned down and was rebuilt as shown here.

Mention of cards was a sarcastic reference to Ryder's alibi that he was at home playing card-games with friends on the night of the massacre.

A preliminary hearing was held in the Town Hall at Lucan on Thursday, October 13th, 1881 before the magistrates William Stanley, J. D. McCosh and Patrick McIlhargey. Naturally the Lucan magistrates were disenchanted with the London journalists who again flocked to the village to report on the latest Lucan sensation. One of the reporters has preserved the reaction of Squire Patrick McIlhargey who said,[35] "Faix, I know a few of the byes about here who wouldn't mind working ye and the likes of ye off."

Attending the hearing, no doubt chortling at the discomfiture of their enemies, were members of the Peace Society including James Carroll, Michael Heenan and young James Maher. While crown attorney Hutchinson was present, it was merely as an observer. The Donnelly brothers were committed to trial in London.

The prisoners were then taken over to the Queen's Hotel to await the omnibus to take them to the train station at Clandeboye. At the Queen's, they met up with their old friend, Robert Keefe, but he and the Donnellys were soon confronted by a trio of the Peace Society. What followed is best told by Will Donnelly in his own words:[36]

A few minutes before we left the Queen's Hotel, Red Bill Stanley brought in old Patrick Ryder (better known as Grouchie), Jim Maher, and Side Road Jim Ryder. They all appeared to be in fighting trim. Stanley called my brother Robert and myself up to drink, and, of course, we responded nobly to the call. Ryder and Maher, on seeing us approach, were somewhat taken aback, but managed to say, "Good luck to ye, boys." We thanked them, as a matter of decency, and took our New England rum (as Artemas Ward used to say) with considerable relish. Old man Ryder then spied Robert Keefe, and in a sarcastic tone said, 'Good luck

Red Bill Stanley, the oldest son of Big Bernard

to you, Robert Keefe.' Bob thanked him and offered his hand. Ryder looked disdainfully at him, and replied, 'No, I wouldn't shake with no such man as you.' Keefe said in response, 'I'm an honest man, and that's more'n you can say.' He also told him he was a rogue, and that he murdered the Donnellys and Brinnigan on the Roman Line in '57. Jim Maher then jumped up for a fight, and as he has an impediment in his speech, his conversation ran something after this fashion. 'Be —, Keefe, ca-ca-can you swe-

Robert Keefe, Sr.

swe-swear that?' The answer and questions came fast and loud, and for a few minutes there was every appearance of a row. Peace was restored for a moment, however, and the 'bus for Clandeboye came along, and was filled with the most notable men of the county, including myself and Bob, Constables Shoebottom and Schram; Mr. H. Becher, Mr. Ed Meredith and the Crown Attorney, Mr. Hutchinson.

Then you were driven off without seeing the end of the diversion, were you? queried the reporter.

No, faith; we hadn't only got seated when a great noise as of glass being broke was heard, and we again repaired to the bar-room. On entering we saw Bob Keefe holding old Ryder's head through the window, and noticed an odd tuft of gray hair floating in the air. It looked to me at first as if Keefe was playing circus and trying to get the wild beast into the cage. Just then I heard, "Oh, merciful Heavens, am I going to be scalped; the constables are laughing instead of holding the prisoners." At this point quite a number of the notables interfered, including Mr. McFalls, the proprietor, Mr. Hutchinson, Constable Shoebottom, my brother Robert and myself.

So no particular damage was done to either of the parties?

Oh, no, nothing to speak of. Side Road Jim Ryder threatened to strike me for trying to make peace, but I drew myself up to my full height and told him his time for striking was four hours and a half away yet, and to keep his blood-stained hands off me. He wilted, and we again entered the bus and were driven to Clandeboye.

While Will awaited the trial in London, the *Free Press* reporter wrote:[37]

An interview with William Donnelly, albeit a visit to the County Jail is necessary to accomplish it, leaves the unprejudiced mind confirmed in the belief that a man of his sagacity, cunning and shrewdness, much of which has been acquired by him since the memorable 4th of February, 1880, would be the last one to confide his secrets or impart his thoughts to a comparative stranger like F. M. West, the amateur detective of Lucan. But time will tell!

Time did tell when West having been granted amnesty returned from Port Huron and finally gave his evidence against the Donnellys before the county judge, William Elliot, on November 8th and 9th, 1881. Edmund Meredith defended the brothers. Again, as Hutchinson could not bring himself to prosecute the men with whose cause he had been in so much sympathy for almost the previous two years, he arranged for the crown attorney from Stratford, J. Idington, to take his place.

The Exeter *Times* reported the outcome as follows:[38]

The trial in London of the Donnelly brothers ended with their acquittal. The judge ruled that it was a put up job by the man West whose testimony could not be believed.

Immediately after the verdict, Frank West was arrested on the charge of stealing the hens, cow and rifles already alluded to. As agreed, he was soon freed on his own recognizance of $500 which, in effect, was a dropping of all charges against him. He left the country. William Donnelly later claimed that he perished the following year in the great Newhall House hotel fire in Milwaukee.[39] While his name could not be found among those who perished in that conflagration, a great many of the victims could not be identified.

In retaliation for having been arrested on the arson charge, Will and his brother Patrick set about to find evidence against a known vigilante sympathizer named John Morkin on a charge of moonshining but the case dragged on for many weeks. More immediately, the three brothers began to rebuild the house on the homestead. The replacement was of frame. For a time, the brothers lived in the granary behind the house site near the old log stable and Bob continued to travel back and forth from Glencoe where he had left his wife, Annie.

Meanwhile, crown attorney Hutchinson succeeded in extraditing the Feeheley brothers back from Michigan and had them lodged in the London Gaol. He was now convinced that a successful prosecution of the murderers was imminent. Unfortunately for him, he did not reckon with the political interference emanating from the office of the highest power in the province, namely, that of the premier, Oliver Mowat, who also held the office of attorney general.[40] Keeping his nostrils in the air and perhaps figuratively holding them, Mowat eventually decided that he had had enough of the Donnelly troubles in that part of the province as the affair was obviously affecting his support politically. In a clear countermand of the wishes of Hutchinson, he ordered the Feeheleys to be freed on bail. The crown attorney complied but immediately thereafter threw up his hands, knowing full well that this was the end of the Donnelly case and that the lynchers had got away with murder.

Report of the Newhall House fire in Milwaukee

Chapter 19

The Feud A-Fizzle

On Wednesday, February 15, 1882 the Donnellys attended the funeral of their old neighbor, Patrick Whelan, who had lived across the road from their parents for many years. By April of that year Will had left Canada for Ohio with prospects of a well paying job in the coal mining district of that state. Pat remained in Biddulph for a time and continued trying to work up the case of moonshining against John Morkin, the vigilante sympathizer.

That summer and fall, the so-called feud on the Roman Line fizzled out in three little episodes in which Will's good friends, the Keefes, seemed always to be involved.

The first of these incidents took place in August. It seems that James Keefe, also known as Big Jim, and his brother Thomas were attempting to break in a colt which they were leading along the Roman Line. When they came to a little bridge on the road between the old Feeheley place and Mick Carroll's farm, who should be lounging there but Jim Carroll along with some of his youthful admirers, sons of his fellow members of the Biddulph Peace Society. Big Jim Keefe claimed that as they were crossing the bridge, "the rowdies" frightened the colt and Carroll seized its reins. Keefe was angered by this action and called Carroll "a damn murdering son of a bitch". His brother Thomas joined in with the insults. Both groups parted without further incident but Carroll immediately repaired to a justice of the peace and laid a charge of abusive language against the Keefe brothers. They were convicted and fined one dollar each. A London *Free Press* reporter got wind of the matter and interviewed Big Jim Keefe, who said, "The vigilantes would like to drive us out of there, but they can't do it."

The second incident occurred a few weeks later near the boundary between the farms of Buckshot Jim Ryder on the one hand and the 25 acres rented by Jim Carroll from his uncle James Maher on the other. As the Buckshot Ryder family continued to remain friendly with the Donnellys notwithstanding the alienation of the Grouchy Ryder branch—the two Ryder pioneers were first cousins—it was said that after Carroll's acquittal "there was not the best of feeling between the two." Les Bronson retold the story of the altercation in the column *Looking Over Western Ontario*.

> Carroll's horses, it was charged, broke through a fence on to Ryder's property; Ryder objected to Carroll taking a shortcut through his property and ordered him not to do so any more. Carroll apparently kept on crossing the Ryder farm.

Big Jim Keefe, longtime crony of the Donnelly boys.

The two then came to blows in hand-to-hand combat which

> terminated when Mrs. Ryder ran to a nearby farmhouse asking for help.

The farmhouse she ran to was the old place of her father, James Keefe, where she had been raised. Her brother, Thomas Keefe, came running but not before

> Ryder suffered a black eye in the brawl, also telling the court that Carroll put his hand to his pocket, as if to draw a pistol.

In the ensuing resolution of the charges laid by Ryder, Carroll was arrested and fined $10 for assault, $2 for trespass and was assessed $14.75 in court costs.

The third incident occurred on Sunday, September 3rd, 1882. That morning Father John Connolly had conducted church services at the Donnelly Schoolhouse. About seven o'clock in the evening, two parties were making their way along the Roman Line in opposite directions. John Kent, then tenant of the Donnelly homestead, was proceeding north from the schoolhouse in the direction of the Keefe farms in company with Thomas Keefe. Coming towards them was 26-year-old Hugh Toohey, son of Timothy, in company with Annie Carroll, the daughter of old Mick Carroll. About in front of Grouchy Ryder's farm and, again, not far from the little bridge between the old Feeheley place and near the Mick Carroll farm on the other side of the road, the two parties met.

What happened next depends on whose version of events one believes. According to John Kent, he turned out to let Toohey and his companion pass, but as he did so Toohey struck him with his fist on the side of the face and kicked him in the stomach. Kent fell down, then dragged himself up and drew a revolver to protect himself. According to Hugh Toohey, however, it was Kent who ran against him as he attempted to pass and thereupon Toohey struck back.

Toohey then pulled off his coat, took hold of Kent and began to drag him and at the same time crying out, "You Orange son of a bitch, I will kick the shit out of you."

Annie Carroll testified, probably more truthfully than the other two, that as Kent and Toohey met on the roadway they were each walking in the east wagon track. As they met, they jostled each other and that is how the row began. In any event, it was not long before reinforcements arrived on both sides. First, Patrick Sullivan, who ran up to defend Kent and Keefe, cried out, "What's going on here?"

"It is none of your business, you red son

Mary Quigley, above, married James Keefe, Sr., and their sons were James Jr., (Big Jim), P.J., and Thomas.

of a bitch," replied James Toohey, who also arrived to defend his older brother, Hugh. Behind him was a large crowd. Toohey struck at Keefe with a stone in hand and Keefe drew his own revolver.

Quickly coming to defend the trio of Kent, Sullivan and Tom Keefe were the latter's first cousins, Robert and P. J. Keefe, the sons of Robert Keefe, Sr. The Toohey

John Kent, holding horse, with his family on the Donnelly homestead.

faction, however, proved not only much more numerous but they had all come with stones in hand. Among them were William and Michael Carroll, younger brothers of the ex-constable; three of Grouchy Ryder's sons, Patrick, James and Michael; and two of old Jim Maher's sons, William and James, Jr. The Toohey faction also had a number of younger supporters who may have cheered them on but did not join in the stone-throwing which followed. Among this group were—besides Annie Carroll—John Bennett, Mary Toohey, Mary Ryder, Thomas Maher, Catherine Maher, Mary Casey and one of the younger sons of Grouchy Ryder.

The hurling of epithets quickly followed from each side. Then someone knocked the gun out of Kent's hands and there was a scuffle for the weapon, but Tom Keefe managed to grab hold of it. Then Jim Toohey and Pat Ryder ran up the lane to the Ryder house, nearly opposite the Feeheley place, and returned with guns of their own in their pockets. Soon Big Jim Keefe, brother of Thomas, also ran up and demanded to know

what was going on. Hugh Toohey replied by saying, "I can lick any son of a bitch in the crowd" and at the same time bent down to pick up a stone. "Come on, boys," he continued, " Why don't we use them stones and kill that son of a bitch."

The two groups then backed off from each other and began hurling stones.

In the meantime, old Grouchy Ryder himself came down to the roadway from his house and took a seat on his fence to watch the show. Thomas Keefe called out to him, "Call off your gang and let us pass."

"Oh, my gang is all right," Grouchy replied, and then called out to Jim Toohey, "Why don't you use that revolver?"

Kent turned to Sullivan and said, "They are going to kill us entirely. Let's fire off our revolvers."

When Kent and Sullivan shot their guns into the air, it had the desired effect. The stones stopped coming. The Keefes in the meantime had managed to hold their own in this department, for the only person much

Michael Ryder, son of Grouchy, one of the participants in the 1882 incident.

half-past ten in the morning, and ends about noon. So it would be impossible for Toohey & Co. to loiter on the road from the notorious house, as your special is pleased to call the school where divine service was held, until 7 in the evening—the time when Toohey & co. began the ruffianism that discharged pistols in the air and caused cowardly creatures to cease stone throwing. When I saw Toohey dragging John Kent and heard him call out, "You Orange son of a bitch, I will kick the shit out of you!" I immediately ran to Kent's rescue, James Keefe, Robert and J. T. Keefe arriving in a few minutes, caused the wretched set to retire. In conclusion, I will make the case plain. John kent and Thomas keefe were mobbed by Hugh Toohey, James Toohey, Pat Ryder, Jas. Ryder (Late of London prison), Michael Ryder, Michael Carroll and Wm. Carroll, brothers of the notorious James Carroll, James Maher and his brother Wm. Maher, headed by old Patrick Ryder (Grouchy) and his wife . . .
Patrick Sullivan
London, September 7, 1882.

William Porte also referred to the incident in his diary:[4]

Row on Carroll's bridge on the 6 & 7 Concession Biddulph between Kent—Tom Keefe & Pat Sullivan on one side—Hugh & Jim Toohey & Pat Ryder Jr. on the other. Stones thrown & Revolvers fired but no one much hurt. Warrants out by both parties about 20 in all.

In the end, the entire affair sputtered out as William Porte again noted in his diary a few weeks later:[5]

The riot on the Roman Line . . . for which 15 parties were committed to stand trial at the assizes . . . ended in smoke today – the Grand Jury not finding a true bill against any of the parties.

Thus ended the so-called feud on the Roman Line of Biddulph.

Sixty-four years later Alice McFarlane's presentation in 1946 of a paper on the Donnelly case to the London and Middlesex Historical Society was a reaction to magazine articles that Thomas P. Kelley was beginning to write for Canadian magazines. The articles gradually became longer and longer until they turned into his book, *The Black Donnellys*.

hurt in the affray was Hugh Toohey whose knee was badly damaged.

"Follow them up and give it to them. Kill them all," old Grouchy Ryder is reputed to have said. His wife, in the meantime, had joined him.

Each party skulked off frowning at the other side and took counsel amongst themselves. After parting, Hugh Toohey laid charges against Kent and the Keefes in Lucan before justice of the peace William Stanley. Kent and the Keefes, on the other hand, went to London and laid charges against the Toohey crowd. The constables went out and made wholesale arrests of everyone but Patrick Sullivan.

For his part, Sullivan took pen in hand and wrote a letter to the newspaper. Although not an unbiased account by any reckoning, it read:[3]

To the editor of the Free Press: Sir,—Your special from Lucan, September 4th, got systematically astray in point of facts—heading "Biddulph Again". The church services in this diocese commences as a general thing about

Twenty years after she had delivered her paper, Miss McFarlane wrote to me:[6]

> Well do I remember the evening in question. We had standing room only. I got through without interruptions but before I could sit down an old gentleman bore down on me brandishing a shillelagh and he said, "Well, I've listened to what you had to say and some of it was true but the Donnellys never cut the tongues out of horses!"

The news account of this meeting reads:[7]

> Donnelly Feud
> Tempers Rise As Murders Recalled
> London, Ont., Nov. 19 (CP)—The feuding that made Lucan a place of terror in the 1870's and led to the five Donnelly murders on Feb. 4, 1880 fired with fresh flame tonight when a man stalked from the meeting of the London and Middlesex Historical Society in protest against stories of atrocities committed by the Donnellys. The meeting was held here.
>
> The man's name was not revealed but he was identified by others who went to the meeting a dozen strong, from Lucan and Biddulph Township, as a friend of the Donnellys.
>
> . . . Referring to the stories of them cutting tongues of horses, he declared as he left the room, "The Donnellys might cut the tongues of people, but they would never cut the tongues of horses."

Typical of the Donnelly story, however, the first man's reaction did not go unchallenged for the report continued:

> . . . In reply to the protest of the aged friend of the Donnelly family, another resident of Biddulph township, who is the son of one of the men accused, but found innocent of the murder, said, "That man knows the Donnellys cut the tongues of horses and were guilty of many other crimes. He just won't admit the stories are true."

The man who confronted Alice McFarlane that night was John Francis Nangle, the son of Patrick Nangle and Frances Barry. He was known as Black Jack to distinguish him from another John Nangle, called Red Jack, who lived on the Swamp Line. Black Jack had inherited the farm of his father across the road from St. Patrick's Church in Biddulph. One of the most important events of his life occurred during the week of the Donnelly tragedy when Black Jack Nangle, then only ten years old, happened to be one of the two altar boys who assisted Father John Connolly at the funeral mass of the victims. He remained on the farm most of his life and died in 1948.

James Toohey, above, was a son of Timothy, and participated in the 1882 incident along with his brother, Hugh Toohey.

Chapter 20

Constabulary Duties

In 1882 when William Donnelly went to Ohio to take up his job with the Hocking Valley Coal Mine, he left his wife and child behind in London with the plan that they were to join him when he had settled in. In the meantime, Robert had moved back to Glencoe. As for Patrick, crown attorney Hutchinson was not at all satisfied with his investigative talents in the Morkin moonshining case.

"I could not get much assistance from your brother Patrick," he wrote Will, "as what he did tell me was under the pledge of secrecy, and did not amount to very much."[1] The pledge was intended to protect James Keefe, Jr., the one known as Big Jim, who

Norah Donnelly, in later years. *(By permission of The Donnelly Museum, Lucan, Ontario)*

was a close friend of the Donnellys. It turned out that the illegal distilling apparatus had been made for Big Jim himself, but he later changed his mind.

Because part of the apparatus had been found on premises of Morkin, Will was indignant at the news that the latter would not be punished. He threatened to write a letter to the *Free Press* exposing the entire affair. He also took umbrage with the testimony of William Stanley, then the reeve of Lucan, who had been called as a witness for the defense. Stanley had testified that he thought the apparatus was one used for distilling oil and only on being pressed in cross-examination did he admit that it could also be used to distill whiskey. "Bill Stanley knew very well what the worm and can were for," Donnelly asserted, "Why, he and his brother James ran an illegal distillery for many years in Biddulph."[2]

In the end, Will Donnelly refrained from complaining to the *Free Press* and the affair died. Patrick for a while worked at his trade of blacksmithing in various places throughout southwestern Ontario, but eventually drifted back to the Niagara Peninsula where he remained the rest of his life, returning to Lucan only on brief visits.

William Donnelly stayed in Ohio for a little over a year, employed by this time at The Ohio Central Coal Company as weighmaster in the coal-mining town of Rendville. Although his wife and child soon joined him, his old enemies were never far from his thoughts.

"Doctor Sutton of Clandeboye keeps me posted on the doings in Biddulph," he wrote Hutchinson, "and from him I learned that the Vigilants are still keeping up a warfare. But I supose [sic] they cannot help it and will continue so until the rope shuts off some of their breaths."[3]

When he had earned enough to pay off the debts he had left behind in Canada, William Donnelly returned. During their sojourn in Ohio, his wife Norah had broken a leg in an accident and suffered from the recurring pain of the fracture for a long time after. Years later, Will cautioned his friend Hutchinson about it: "Do not make Mrs. Donnelly's trouble known[n], as it would only please my Biddulph friends too well."[4]

The beginning of April in 1883 found him in Glencoe, the home now of his brother Robert and near the home of his sister Jenny. Here he again contemplated the purchase of a property appropriate for the operation of a boarding house. "He still has hopes of bringing the murderers of his family to justice," it was reported[5], "and whom he believes are now in Biddulph."

On June 30th, 1883 another son was born to Will and Norah. They took him back to St. Patrick's in Biddulph where Father John Connolly christened him John. The baby proved weak and sickly, however, and died on September 3rd that same year.

That summer Will learned that the municipal authorities of Glencoe were unhappy with their local constables and were looking for a new man. On the urging of one or two of the village officials, he decided to apply for the job. A petition to have him appointed was drawn up and circulated. Most of the influential citizens of Glencoe supported him: the petition was signed by three ministers of religion, a former member of parliament and forty-nine other respectable business and professional men including three physicians and the Division Court clerk. On Monday evening, October 1st, 1883, a Glencoe justice of the peace, Malcolm Leitch, swore him in as county constable. His appointment was shortly after confirmed at the next Sessions of the Peace.

Even though his health was not always the best, William Donnelly settled into the village and, in addition to performing his constabulary duties, took up the business of horse-breeding with his brother Bob. The latter soon gave him some business as constable when he charged Hugh McKay with theft of a goose. William executed the warrant for arrest but the charge was dismissed. In 1884 Will assisted in the closing

down of a notorious brothel in East London kept by Esther Ascott and once more arrested Hugh McKay, this time for aiding the escape of one, George Ghent. As village constable, he was called upon to make other routine arrests of tramps, drunks and the occasional thief all of which he capably accomplished.

Meanwhile, General William Booth's aggressive evangelism known as the Salvation Army had invaded Canada and its campaign of brass bands and street meetings soon reached southwestern Ontario. The Army's advance was not without dismay and resentment among many respectable circles of Ontario society, whose members considered such public displays of religious worship to be shameful and a disparagement of all true Christianity. In many places the Salvation Army was, if not persecuted by

The gold chain and horse-head fob worn by William Donnelly in this undated photograph are in 2011 on display along with the watch itself at the Donnelly Museum. *(By permission of Jim Cameron)*

public officials, at least frowned upon. Charges of disturbing the peace were frequently laid as a result of their street marches and meetings and county constables sent to make arrests.

Constable William Donnelly was soon called upon to deal with the Army in West Middlesex when in the summer of 1885 he arrested Captain Thomas of the Army in Wardsville. The local correspondent of the Glencoe newspaper sarcastically reported the arrest, comparing his valor to that of the troops then serving to put down the Riel Rebellion in the Canadian West. He wrote:[6]

> While the papers are sounding the valor of our troops at the front we feel we should not forget our heroes at home. Perhaps a more daring feat has not been recorded than that performed here on Friday evening last, when constable William Donnelly marched into the S.A. barracks and captured and "handcuffed" the captain, the soldiers meanwhile firing volley after volley. The captain is a quiet, unoffending man and was quite willing to go, which made the exhibition of courage more creditable.

William Donnelly did not take long in answering the sarcasm. His reply stated:[7]

> The law distinctly says a constable is to be guided by the circumstances as to whether he will handcuff a prisoner. Captain Thomas was a stranger to me, the charge against him was a serious one; he had no property to hold him in the country and could no doubt preach as well with Brigham Young in Salt Lake City as in Wardsville. It is not the duty of a constable to know if a prisoner is guilty, but simply to convey him safely to the JP. 'Tis but a short time since George Ghent escaped from a constable in Newbury; another distinguished gentleman, after nearly biting the nose off a man in this town, escaped from a constable, and Clarke, the notorious Glencoe bailiff, played the same trick. Now, if these three men had been handcuffed neither of them would have escaped. But if my worthy Wardsville friend would call on Captain Thomas he would learn from the latter that I did not use the handcuffs as an advertisement, nor in any way act ungentlemanly with the Captain. When I came to the conclusion he would not try to escape I took the handcuffs off. I went with him to four different places in Newbury to see

> some of his friends for the purpose of getting him bailed out. I did the same thing with him in Glencoe, and when I had to put him in the lock-up, I took the bedding from my own house to make him comfortable in his cell . . . I am a little tender in the front feet, and to prevent any chance of giving an exhibition of speed across the country in pursuit of a prisoner, I will in most all cases use the handcuffs . . . .

In concluding, Will Donnelly perhaps unwittingly showed his attitude towards the new Salvationists:

> . . . I have never given annoyance to the Salvation Army, either in Glencoe or in any other place, nor even ever being present at one of their meetings. If the young men of Glencoe have annoyed the Army in any way they were never encouraged to do so by me, and will in future be prevented from doing so if putting the law in force will accomplish it. And I wish the army to distinctly understand that I will put a stop to their can-can and war dances on Main Street, Glencoe, with which they endanger the lives of ladies who drive along the street attending to their business.

The last sentence did not augur well for the Army, as we shall see.

Will Donnelly's drawing attention to the mistakes of previous constables of Glencoe in allowing prisoners to escape quickly drew the wrath of one, Archibald Riddell, a one-time constable himself and a well-known character of Glencoe. He responded in the next issue of the newspaper[8] referring to the object of his hatred as the "justly celebrated and notorious Wm. Donnelly of Biddulph fame, now county constable." He wondered "in what way he can justify himself in handcuffing prisoners to his brother Robert and marching them through the streets of Glencoe" and said "that had his brother Bob been handcuffed on the 2nd of July last year he would not have sneaked up behind an unsuspecting man to brain him with an assassin's club, and if he had been handcuffed he would not have made such an indiscriminate use of the horsewhip on his wife not long ago." He could not resist a final jab by concluding, "He must remember he is not in Lucan now; that no one here craves his favor or fears his frowns . . . ."

The issue had been joined and William Donnelly quickly took up his pen to respond in the following issue of the paper[9] referring to Riddell as "the notorious whiskey destroyer and boarding house dead-beat".

"Judging from the way in which he took several drinks (at my expense) lately," Donnelly wrote, "[I] fancied he was my friend. But I find I was mistaken, and here again the words of General Douglas fit to the nicety—'Oh, Lord, protect me from my friends, my enemies I can watch.'"

As to Will handcuffing his brother Bob to a prisoner, he stated:

> In this case he is referring to the arrest of the notorious Joe Cram who robbed a number of the folks of Glencoe and vicinity last fall . . . Cram is a dangerous character and had made threats to shoot me. I had no person to help me lock him up, and my brother coming past Cram and I in the street, I slipped one handcuff on Cram and the other on my brother and marched both to the lockup.

And he answered Riddell's reference to Lucan as follows:

> No, I am not in Lucan. I lived there for thirty-five years, and left when I got ready, with all my boarding-bills paid up. But Mr. Riddell could not live in Lucan one year. The hotel men there compel boarders to pay up every Saturday night, hence the impossibility of him remaining the second week in that town . . . I defy Mr. Riddell to bring 5 cents worth of crime against me during my whole life . . . .

Donnelly ended by alluding to Archibald Riddell's shameful personal life in Glencoe, accusing him of allowing his wife "to die in an old shanty of hunger and ill-treatment" and of being "caught in a very questionable position with a grass widow in the stable of Hugh McKay" whom he had referred to previously as his "so-called stepson".

During his stay in Glencoe, he and his brother Bob purchased a thoroughbred stallion and racehorse named Lord Byron, well known throughout southern Ontario racing circles as one of the finest horses which had ever been raced in Canada.[10] In January 1886, Will and Robert purchased another trotting stallion named St. Nicholas which they successfully bred. Will was so pleased with this new stallion that in later years he named two of his hotels after the horse.

On October 28th, 1886, the house occupied by William Donnelly and owned by his brother Bob burned to the ground. No one was injured in the blaze but Will was obliged to move his little family to new premises.

Towards the end of the year 1887 on a dark Saturday night, Will and a companion were returning from Alvinston in a buggy. They overtook a team and rig on the road driven by two drunken men who refused to let their buggy pass. When the first team collided with a cow, Donnelly's buggy ran into the rig and he fell into the spokes of one of the vehicles, injuring his head, arm and leg. He was down a few weeks.[11]

It was not long after this that Will decided to leave Glencoe and move to Bothwell. Here he rented the Martin House,[12] which he renamed the St. Nicholas. Before his departure he was given a grand farewell complimentary supper.[13] The business in Bothwell did not go well. Three or four charges under the Scott Act were laid against him for selling liquor illegally resulting in fines of $50 and $100. In March 1888 he resigned the position of county constable[14]— likely he was forced to resign when caught selling whiskey to Indians from a nearby reservation. "I have been a constable for four years," he stated, "and I haven't murdered anybody yet. Let some other Biddulpher tackle the job now."

In July 1888 a fracas broke out on the sidewalk in front of the hotel. A man named Randolph Parker was creating what Will thought was a noisy disturbance among a crowd. Donnelly charged out and struck the man over the head with a sling-shot. He then pulled out a revolver and flourished it over his head defying anyone to interfere.[15]

Although his health remained poor, during the studding season he would make the countryside circuit with his stallion and otherwise engage in horse-trading. He even took up conducting sales as an auctioneer. He continued, however, to keep track of events in Biddulph and was especially gleeful when news arrived of misfortune to any of his enemies.

In the summer of 1888 he wrote to Hutchinson from the Revere House in Alvinston:[16]

> I am very seldom at home being away with my stallion for the last two months and am sick pretty near all the time. Mrs. Donnelly and Children are well. I sepose [sic] you heard of the very sudden death of John Kennedy's wife leaving six little children on his hands. This makes twenty seven that were directly or indirectly concerned in our tragedy, who were taken away without a moment's notice and none of the Donnellys have murdered any one yet.

Donnelly operated the hotel in Bothwell for a short time only, as he soon found a better opportunity as a result of what was reported in March of 1889 in the following news item:[17]

> Robert Donnelly has purchased the hotel at Appin, occupied by F. McNaughton, from McCallum & McPherson. We understand the hotel will be conducted by William Donnelly.

The Donnelly brothers made extensive renovations to the building and when the hotel opened under Will Donnelly he again called it the St. Nicholas.

In the fall of most years, Will Donnelly would often race his horses at the country fairs. In 1894 his Billy D. came second at the fair in Lucan.[18]

Three of William Donnelly's children grew up to adulthood. Jo-Anna, who sometimes used the name Josephine, lived from 1880 to 1951. She married Alva Clay and they had two children, Jack and Ione. Will and Norah's only son who grew to adulthood was John William who lived from 1884 to 1973 and whom I met in Detroit. He married Effie Ahara and they had no children. Will's youngest child was Nora who was born in 1887, married Charles Lord, had several children and died in 1975.

For about the last two years of his life,

The three children of William and Norah Donnelly: Jack, Norah and Jo-Anna. (By permission of Jim Cameron).

William Donnelly was for the most part confined to bed and finally died on Sunday morning March 7th, 1897. He was a few months over 50 years of age. Decades later, his daughter Nora wrote:[19]

> Strife and tragedy continued in Biddulph long after the Donnellys were murdered and, be it known, that my father, Bill Donnelly, died a natural death, in his bed, not with his boots on, as many of the murderers did, and I know them all.

Both his surviving brothers accompanied William's body on the train to Clandeboye and then on to St. Patrick's Cemetery in Biddulph for the burial.

Chapter 21

Courtship of Jenny

Jenny Donnelly[1] was christened Jane but she was always called Janey by the rest of her family, hence Jenny or Jennie. Upon her marriage at an early age to James Currie[2], Jenny went to live in the neighborhood of the village of Glencoe in the southwestern part of Middlesex County. Glencoe sits astride the townships of Mosa and Ekfrid and it was in either of these two places where she spent the remainder of her life with the exception of the few weeks she lived in a rented house in St. Thomas assisting her bereaved sister-in-law, Nellie, following the sudden death of her brother Michael.

Jenny's grave is in the little North American Martyrs Catholic cemetery in Wardsville in the same part of Middlesex. The monument over her last earthly remains is inscribed "Jennie/wife and Mother/1858-1917". I have not, however, found the record of her baptism and therein lies a small controversy about her true age. Notwithstanding the grave marker, her death was officially reported as occurring on September 3rd, 1916 when her age was given as 59 years and 11 months. This would put her date of birth in October 1856. And if she were indeed seventeen upon her marriage on February 7th, 1874, as stated in the record of that event, 1856 would be her birth year.[3]

Jenny was nine when her father returned from prison. At that endearing age she instantly became his darling and pet and for most of the rest of his life he spoiled her thoroughly. Jenny's playmates included Winnifred, Mary Anne and Julia Orange—she and Julia were the same age—daughters of Edward Orange, a near neighbor who taught at the Donnelly School. It was the Orange girls' young brother who had gone over to Sarah Farrell to give her the news that her husband had been hurt over at Maloney's logging bee on June 25th, 1857.

"Who done it?" she asked the boy.

"Oh," he replied, "who done it before."

Sarah Farrell knew immediately it was Jim Donnelly for he and her husband had been at loggerheads for months in their dispute over land.

Jenny Donnelly was a prepossessing girl and even at the age of twelve she had her male admirers, some from outside the Catholic Settlement. One was Fred Dobbs, two years her senior. Smitten by the young Donnelly girl, he would often be found at her father's homestead on the Roman Line, which was the next concession over from the Dobbs place. One incident from those days, improbable as it may seem today, stuck out in his mind. Near the house, he said, the Donnellys had a well that had been naturally at that time dug by hand. The hole was covered by thick boards through which the wooden pipe reached down to the water below to connect it to the hand pump above. Among Jenny's usual household tasks at age twelve was the fetching of pails of water from the well into the house. According to Dobbs, someone had surreptitiously removed the boards and had sawn them almost through from the underside before replacing them. The obvious intention was that the next time Jenny went to fetch a pail of water, the boards would give way and she would fall through into the well. Fred Dobbs could not understand why anyone would have done this. "The Donnellys were not bad people," he said, "but they had bad enemies."

By the beginning of the 1870s, Jenny had had all the formal education she was ever going to get. Now she was more interested in life and she led an active social one. She was only fourteen when on February 11th in 1871 she stood as bridesmaid at the wedding of her brother John. The bride was Fanny Durham. Although the marriage took place at St. Patrick's Church on the Roman Line and was performed by Father Joseph Gerard, Fanny was a Protestant—her mother was a

Jenny Donnelly, in the prime of her life.

"My mother met my father," the son went on to say, "through his sister Annie." James Currie and his sister Annie were the children of Robert Currie and Anne Stinson of Glencoe, the Curries being a prominent family in that area. Although the old man Robert had been himself born a Catholic in Londonderry, Ireland he did not practice the faith. And even though his children as a measure of safety were on one occasion all baptized into Catholicism, they were brought up Protestants. Besides James and Annie, the children of Robert Currie and Anne Stinson were Catherine, David and Robert, Jr.

By the time Jenny's father had returned from prison, the Orange family had moved away from Biddulph. Some of them settled in Glencoe, a village then starting up in southwestern Middlesex. Its first house was built only in 1853. Not surprisingly, most of the settlers of the town were Scottish, but the Orange family settled in amongst them purchasing land in what became the centre of the village and soon becoming prominent citizens of the place.

Hodgins—as was the best man, Sam Hodgins. Later that year, on October 6th, Jenny stood up for another brother, Patrick, upon his union to Mary Ryan. Although the bride this time was Catholic, the marriage was performed in the rectory of St. James *Anglican* Church in Biddulph. The best man in this case was Patrick Quigley. And almost a hundred years after Jenny's own marriage to James Currie, her son said: "My father was a Protestant, but a man can't help what he is."

Another member of the family moved to the Township of McGillivray adjacent to Biddulph on the west.[4] McGillivray and Stephen Township to its north had a thriving Catholic community with the parochial seat being the Church of Our Lady of Mount

144

James Currie, in his later years.

Catholics in the neighboring townships of McGillivray Stephen and Biddulph.

This is how in the early 1870s Jim Currie found himself staying with the John Orange family near Mount Carmel. His younger sister Annie had accompanied him from Glencoe in the capacity of nurse. The treatment chosen by Dr. Quarry, according to Currie's son, was to place around his infected neck a piece of cord which had been tied along its length with knots. This device the doctor positioned around Currie's neck and tightened it in just the right way as he pulled the cord to force out the accumulated infection. Whether or not this was a sound medical procedure or a correct description of the treatment, in the result Currie began to get better.

It was almost an Irish tradition for young people to seek a mate not in one's own but in an adjoining parish, and it was therefore natural to find among the young people a great deal of coming and going between the parishes of St. Patrick's in Biddulph and Mount Carmel in McGillivray and Stephen. Those of one parish would not think of missing a picnic, dance or wedding celebration in the other. Thus it was that as Jim Currie was recuperating, the younger set of Donnellys spent a great deal of time in Mount Carmel parish. They included Jenny, now about fifteen, and her brothers, Bob and Tom, who were twenty and nineteen respectively. Jenny soon became acquainted with eighteen-year-old Annie Currie, and through her, Annie met Jenny's brother Bob. These two began to spend a great deal of time together.

Carmel at a place known at different times as Limerick, Offa and finally Mount Carmel.

Young James Currie of Glencoe was a jack-of-all-trades who put his hand to many occupations, among them farming, collecting hides and moving buildings. One day when he was about twenty-one years old, he was working atop a barn when he slipped and fell to the ground. His fall was broken by a group of bushes and except for a fractured limb and a few cuts around his neck he first appeared to have suffered no major injuries. But it turned out that the bushes into which he had fallen were dogwoods. The poison from this plant prevented the cuts around his neck from healing. They became infected and the injury became so serious that it was thought his life was in danger.

As the physicians in Glencoe seemed unable to treat young Currie effectively, the Oranges of Glencoe suggested to the family that they send him up to McGillivray. Here near their Orange cousins lived a brilliant young physician named William Brown Quarry. The young Catholic doctor had begun to practice only in 1870 but already he was gaining a reputation in the district as a wonderful healer, especially among the

145

As for Jenny Donnelly and Jim Currie, many years later Jenny's son related the story of exactly how the ice was broken between his parents. A Sunday afternoon would find Bob Donnelly going over to the Oranges in McGillivray to visit his budding romantic partner, Annie. When the latter's brother learned that Bob had a younger sister, he was curious.

"What's her name?" he asked Bob.

"Janey," Bob said.

"Oh," Currie went on, "Is she as pretty as the song says?"

"What song?"

"You know—Jeannie with the light brown hair."[5]

"Well," Bob replied, "I'll let you see for yourself and bring her along next time."

And he did. Soon during those summer months a strong personal attachment developed between Jenny Donnelly and Jim Currie. On one occasion when Jim was able to get up and around comfortably, he secured a rig and horses and drove Jenny home to Biddulph. She proudly introduced her new beau to her parents. Jim Currie went around and boldly shook their hands. Jenny was obviously smitten but the older folks were not convinced that it should be a match. She had always been the darling of the family and they did not want to see her leave the homestead just yet. She was much too young, they said.

When Jim Currie was fully recovered and he and his sister returned home to Glencoe, they found every excuse they could in the next couple of years to visit their friends the Oranges up Lucan way. By the fall of 1873,

emotions between Jenny and Jim had run away with them and they became intimate.

The mid-1870s was a time of great turmoil within the Donnelly family. Will had got himself mixed up with Maggie Thompson, who was also from Mount Carmel parish but keeping house for her brother next to the Donnelly homestead. The attempted abduction of Maggie from her father's home in McGillivray had led to threats, counter-threats and physical confrontations in Lucan. Old chums from their boyhood days such as Long Jim Toohey helped thwart the abduction—on that night Toohey had hidden Maggie in his own home. Toohey had himself married Maggie's sister, Sarah, and, siding with his father-in-law and brother-in-law, he fell into a hard alignment against the Donnellys.

And there was another factor at work. The sons and daughters of the pioneers of the Catholic Settlement of Biddulph had by the late sixties and early seventies reached sexual maturity. Almost all of them were frantically scurrying around looking for life mates. Social and sexual tensions were at their height. While the younger Donnellys may not even have been conscious of it at the time, their efforts at making respectable unions with members of the opposite sex were faced with a tremendous unspoken hurdle. Their father, after all, was a convicted murderer. No respectable family of that mid-Victorian—let alone any other—era would want a family tie with a convicted felon. Perhaps it was for this reason that the Donnelly boys and their sister cast a wider net in their romantic endeavors. To marry outside the parish was not unusual. To marry outside the faith, though not unheard of, was not at all common. The second generation in Canada of the Donnelly family, however, seemed to do both with more regularity than almost all the other families of St. Patrick's parish. There may, of course, have been another reason for this seeming anomaly, namely, the marriage in Ireland of their

Catholic grandfather to a Protestant grandmother.

Jenny's story is taken up by Jim Currie's younger sister, Catherine, who was eyewitness to some of the important events. Jim Currie was now back at his parent's home just outside the village of Glencoe near the railway tracks. Over in Biddulph, the slow realization came upon Jenny that she had to take decisive action. Packing a small bag, telling no one of her resolve and—despite the February weather—finding a pretext to make a trip to London, she suddenly left. From London she took the train westward. Alighting at the station in Glencoe, she set out along the tracks towards the Currie home. Inside, Catherine looked out the kitchen window and saw the lone figure trudging along the railway tracks toward the house. As it approached, the figure lurched into the ditch and continued walking in the line of the track but at the bottom of the ditch as if not to be seen. It was cold, but with little snow.

"Why, it's Janey Donnelly," Catherine gasped.

On opening the door, she and her parents could see that Jenny was in a high state of excitement. They thought it odd that she was carrying a small suitcase.

"Is Jim home?" she asked.

"He's lying down," the mother answered, motioning to a back room.

"I must see him," Jenny said excitedly.

The father, old Robert, probably guessed what was coming.

"Jim," he called out, "are you dressed?"

From the back room came Jim's voice. "I've just got my shoes off. I'll be right there."

He came out and stared at Jenny.

She looked directly at him. "Jim," she said, "we have to get married."[6]

Jim Currie was taken aback and his face flushed but she continued, "If you want me, it's now or never."

Here words failed everyone. In the uncomfortable silence, quick glances were exchanged all around as the reason for Jenny's sudden visit sank in.

Finally Robert Currie drew up to her and in a low voice asked, "Did my son give you his promise?"

"Yes, Mr. Currie, he did. Jim gave me his word."

He turned to his son. "Jim, did you give this girl your promise?"

"Yes, I did," he answered.

Old Currie quickly made up his mind. "Get your uncle's democrat," he said to Jim, "And get over to Bothwell right away. The minister there will marry you."

The father then sat down at the table and scribbled out a note. "Here," he said, "give this to him."

Jim quickly put on his shoes and overcoat and the couple left. They drove the uncle's wagon westward to Bothwell.

It was not long, however, before Mrs. Donnelly, accompanied by a couple of her boys, came banging at the door. As they burst in, Robert Currie seized a rifle from the corner with bayonet fixed at its muzzle.

"We ain't goin' to hurt no one," Mrs. Donnelly said as she eyed the bayonet. "I jist want my girl back."

"She's not here," Currie said.

"Where is she?"

"We don't know."

Catherine Currie had in the meantime run out the back door. Fearful for her brother's safety, she was hurrying across the frozen field to warn her uncle not to tell the couple's destination in case the Donnellys went over there to search.

Mrs. Donnelly growled at old Currie, "Misther, ye'd betther not lie to us. If ye do, ye maybe will git a reaper burned,"

Then one of her boys looked out the window and saw Catherine running across the field. The boys quickly rushed out of the house and easily caught up with her.

"Where's Jenny?" they demanded.

"Don't know," she answered.

"Where's Jim?"

"Don't know."

"You do so. Where did they go?"

Catherine thought quickly. "Over to Melbourne," she blurted out, motioning eastward.

The Donnelly boys ran back to the house, jumped into their rig with their mother and drove off eastward in the direction of Melbourne. It was, of course, in the exact opposite direction to where the fleeing couple was headed.

In the meantime, James Currie and Jenny arrived at the Episcopalian Church in Bothwell, where they were legally bound together as husband and wife. It was February 9th, 1874.

Jenny's new husband felt sorry for the way she had ruined her shoes walking along the railway track. He bought for her as a kind of wedding present a smart new pair.

Two or three weeks later, when Jenny felt that emotions back up home in Biddulph had cooled off and it was safe to try to make peace with her parents, she returned to Biddulph. Arriving first in Lucan, she found one of her brothers—probably Michael—and quickly won him over. She asked him to take her out to the homestead but insisted that her husband wait in the village.

Patrick Whelan, who lived across the road, happened to be in the Donnelly house when Jenny came in. Her parents loved their daughter dearly, but as she had caused them deep hurt by running off to get married, their reception of her was cool at first. Their welcomes were mixed with reproaches and expressions of disappointment at her leaving without taking them into her confidence. Jenny, knew, however, that they could not hold their spite for long, and before they could help themselves she would soon again be their favorite child.

To get a few items of clothing which she could not take in her hasty departure, she went into the little bedroom she shared with her mother. When she came back out, her father suddenly said, "Where did ye git them shoes?"

148

Patrick Whelan, who lived across the road from the Donnellys and witnessed the father's wrath following his daughter's runaway marriage.

"Jim bought them for me," she replied, a little apprehensively. She knew her father well enough to sense that there was trouble brewing.

"Give them heer," he commanded.

She dared not defy him. Slipping the shoes off her feet, she handed them over. Jim Donnelly seized them and quickly stepping over to the stove and lifting the lid, he thrust them into the flames. He clamped the lid down over them. Jenny cried out but did nothing. This was the old man's way of punishing his willful daughter and showing her how much she had hurt them. In later years, Jenny herself in order to show the depth of her feelings, would act in very much the same way.

Chapter 22

Life at Pratt's Siding

The small frame house at the rear of the big house was the home in Ekfrid Township of Jenny Donnelly and her husband from 1875 to 1878.

When emotions had calmed down, peace was eventually restored to the household and James Currie was accepted into the family. The couple returned to the Glencoe area where Jim found a small frame house in Ekfrid Township to set up his family. Later that year when spring had come, three of Jenny's brothers, John, Bob and Tom, came for a visit. They seemed still a bit angry about the elopement and said they were going to whip the man who had stolen their favorite away from her parents against their wishes.

"You've taken our kid sister and had your way with her," they told him. "We'll teach you not to play around with us like that."

Instead of beating him up, however, they joined him in the field. With their help, Jim Currie performed a whole week's work in a couple of days.

"The Donnelly boys mesmerized Jim," Catherine Currie recalled many years afterwards. "In his eyes, they could do no wrong."

Bob and Tom continued to visit Glencoe often to see their sister and new brother-in-law. They called him "Brother" and after work took him out to drink. Where there was drinking, there was fighting. In the Middlesex Returns of Convictions for this period, we find the note by William J. Simpson, a magistrate of the nearby village of Newbury, settling a charge of assault by James Currie upon one Joseph Hauley. For the same offence upon the same defendant, Tom Donnelly was convicted and fined one dollar.[1]

After three or four years Jim gave up the little frame house in Ekfrid and bought an acreage in adjacent Mosa Township where he decided to build a new home. During the months of its construction he moved his little family in with his parents on the family homestead outside Glencoe. They had to share the home with Jim's unmarried brothers and sisters. Jenny's introduction into the Currie family was not an entirely happy one for her in-laws did not unanimously admire her. Although Jim's sister, Catherine, admitted that she was a beautiful girl, she grew to dislike if not despise her. And Jim's oldest brother could not bear her to the extent that he would often leave the house rather than show his displeasure.

One day old Robert Currie sent Jenny along with his daughters Annie and Catherine out to the potato patch to pick bugs off the plants. Each of the young women was armed with a pail. As an incentive, old Currie had offered a small reward to the one who ended up with the most bugs in her pail. The girls began. From personal experience, I can tell the reader that the most efficient technique in picking potato bugs was to set down your pail, hunch over the rows and from plant to plant scoop as many bugs in to the other hand as you could before returning to dump them in the pail, which you then brought forward. Catherine and Annie had done this job before and quickly plunged forward along the rows.

After a while, Catherine noticed that her pail did not seem to be filling up as fast as it should. Keeping close watch, she discovered that when it seemed her back was turned, Jenny would deftly scoop a few bugs out of Catherine's pail and dump them into her

150

Jenny's two oldest children in front of the Pratt's Siding School are Robert, in lighter clothing second from left in front row, and Johannah, the smaller figure below the tree in the front row.

own. Catherine surreptitiously motioned to her sister Annie and, sure enough, she did the same with Annie's pail. The Currie girls then put their heads together and took action. Sidling up to Jenny as she crouched, they each stepped on one side of her skirt and held her down.

"We'll let you up," they said, "if you promise not to steal any more of our bugs."

She finally agreed to play fair and the potato picking continued, but the Currie girls never after trusted their new sister-in-law.

During the first years of her marriage, Jenny often grew homesick. She missed her father especially and had quickly forgiven him for burning her new shoes.

"It was always 'Pa this' or 'Pa that' until we all got sick of it," her sister-in-law Catherine said. "Even when they moved in to their new house, she was always picking up and going 'up home'. And if at any time she didn't go, she was always talking about going back 'up home to Biddulph.'"

Some of Currie's own family were willing to forgive Jim for marrying a Catholic—their own father, after all, was one himself—but they could not forgive Jenny's relentless opposition to non-Catholics. She insisted, of course, that her own children be brought up in her own faith. And that she had been married in a Protestant church bothered her a great deal. She began to nag her husband about it.

On one occasion Catherine was outside their house when she heard a great clattering in the kitchen. Rushing inside, she found her brother grappling with his wife near the stove. Jenny was holding down the stove lid to prevent her husband from retrieving an object that she had thrust into the flames. Later, Catherine learned it was the Protestant bible.

Finally, after relentless badgering, Jim Currie decided to satisfy his wife concerning their marriage.

"They made restitution to the church," their son Michael stated, "by renouncing their first marriage in public and getting married again by the priest."

Another incident, which Catherine Currie related to her own daughter Margaret had to do with a setting hen. Jim and Jenny had a

151

Jenny attended this church during her married life.

beautiful woman whose smile could beguile everyone.

"Whenever she was caught in some deceit, she would break into a winning smile and whoever had just been hurt would instantly go up and hug her," she said, "Oh, she could charm a person, all right."

It is difficult to see Jenny's life as a happy one. Following her flight from Biddulph into a runaway marriage, she must have crossed some evil genie that relentlessly brought her news of misfortune and tragedy from up home in Biddulph. In 1874 in the year of her own marriage, there were the shameful events of the Maggie Thompson affair trumpeted in all the district newspapers. Her brother Will was hard pressed to live down this much publicized scandal, and Jenny must have felt some reflected disgrace from the

Views of Wardsville where Jenny attended on Sundays and where she is buried. *(Courtesy of the late Stuart Nisbet)*

fine flock of chickens and Catherine asked for some of the eggs from the hen so that she could start her own flock. Jenny brought over a clutch of the eggs but when they were set under a hen, nothing happened.

"I can't understand that," Jenny said, "for I candled them myself."

Candling was a test for fertility made by holding the egg up to the light of a candle in a darkened room to see if its contents were still living. The remark may have been completely innocent but Catherine interpreted the incident as an example of Jane Donnelly's treacherous nature. She told her daughter that Jenny might have candled the eggs all right, but only after boiling them.

"She just didn't want my mother to have as fine a set of chickens as she did," Margaret said.

Like most of her family, Margaret admitted that Jenny, despite her faults, was a

ensuing public trials which the Victorian press so gleefully reported and its readers so eagerly devoured.

Then came the many stagecoach imbroglios of 1875, culminating early in the

152

Daughters of Jenny Donnelly, believed to be from left to right, Jane, Johannah and Margaret.

Items from the 1907 Glencoe *Transcript* reporting the social activities of Jenny's children.

following year with the brawl at Fitzhenry's tavern in Lucan, followed by the arrest of most of her brothers and, again, the widespread publicity of the so-called Donnelly Assizes in London. These trials made the name Donnelly a household word throughout southwestern Ontario. In 1877 came the mysterious death of her oldest

brother, James Jr. The controversy over the cause of his death lingers to this day. Did he die of consumption, inflammation of the lungs or from a gunshot wound? In 1878 her favorite brother, Bob, was sentenced to two years in Kingston Penitentiary. Bob had by this time married Jenny's sister-in-law, Annie, and had been spending more and more time with his wife in Glencoe. Then in December 1879 came the terrible news of the stabbing death of her brother Mike in Waterford. In this case, Jenny roused herself from her shock by temporarily taking a house on Fifth Avenue in St. Thomas within a couple of doors of Mike's distraught young widow who had been left with two infant children. Jenny herself had young children but she had a husband and his sisters to help look after them.

In St. Thomas in mid-January, Jenny harbored her mother who suddenly appeared one day as if fleeing from some trouble back up in Biddulph. Following quickly on her heels came the constable with warrants for both her mother and brother Robert. Fresh out of prison, the latter had brought his mother to St. Thomas but fled, and Constable James Carroll had to be content with taking Mrs. Donnelly alone as prisoner. Jenny insisted on accompanying her and then hurried back to St. Thomas. Only a few days later came the greatest blow of all.

One can hardly imagine the effect on this young woman of the news of the murders of her father, mother, brothers and cousin by a mob of their close neighbors. She survived this and the ordeals of the court hearings. But the verdict rendered by the jury on February 3rd, 1881 finding James Carroll not guilty of her mother's murder was a bitter pill to swallow.

Thereafter, along with her brother Will, she lived for the divine retribution that was promised. Let us hear it in the words of William Donnelly himself:[2]

> After Carroll and the rest of the prisoners were turned loose on the world again, my sister Mrs. Currie was sitting crying in Crown Attorney

Hutchinson's office, when Mr. Irving said to her, 'Do not cry, my dear woman, there is a just God who sees all and who will try the case without lawyers or jury, and He will give you ample satisfaction in the way of retribution before ten years passes.'

Jenny returned to St. Thomas and then to her burgeoning family in Mosa Township. Except for attending Sunday Mass in the closest Catholic church at the nearby village of Wardsville, she went out rarely. Her pastor from May 1878 until 1881 at Wardsville was Father Michael J. McGrath. It is ironic that she would therefore have received spiritual sustenance and listened to sermons preached from the pulpit by a man whose brother during his very pastorship plotted against and helped to kill her parents and brothers.

Along with her siblings, she respected and admired her brother Will's quick intelligence and sharpness of wit. While Will was alive, she would oftentimes confer with him about the great family tragedy. They clipped news reports concerning the fates of members of the hated Peace Society of Biddulph and in the margin wrote little notes about them.

For the rest of Jenny's life, she kept close to her home and kept her children close to her. The first-born was Robert who lived from 1875 to 1943. He joined the railway as an acting baggageman, lived in Bothwell in 1903 and then became a brakeman on the Wabash Railroad. He eventually became a conductor, married and lived in Windsor

Jenny Donnelly spent most of her life and raised her 12 children in this house in Mosa Township.

where he raised a family. I exchanged many e-mails with his son, also named Robert.

Johanna was the second child of Jenny and she lived from 1876 to about 1944. She was a very good student and on one occasion at S. S. #2, Mosa achieved 100% on an arithmetic test. She married in 1903 a Biddulph boy named Zackariah McCormick, had several children, Mary Ellen, Stephen, John and Zackariah, and for a time lived in Lucan while her husband operated the Queen's Hotel. Her sisters Margaret, Jane

Original floor in the kitchen of the Currie house in Mosa Towsnhip.

and Mary Ellen visited her often in Lucan and on at least one occasion, in 1904, even her mother came for a visit. Zack eventually lost the hotel—one story says it was in a poker game—and they moved to London. They lived on Oxford Street where Zack was a bar tender for a while. They also lived on Princess Street and Lyle Street and Zack became a commercial traveler for a time and then a warehouseman. By about 1919 they had moved to the Windsor-Detroit area and may have fallen on hard times. Zackariah was a watchman in 1941 and was living on Cass Avenue in Detroit. A story is told that Johannah's brother, John Currie, went to Detroit in about 1944 trying to find his sister but could not and concluded that she may have met with foul play.

James William Currie was born in February 1879. He was of slight build and at the age of 22 won the men's foot race at a Glencoe picnic. He did not marry but loved

The three youngest of Jenny's children in this photo of Pratt's Siding School class are: Mike, second from right in rear row; Clara, centre in middle row; and Pat, seated at right end of front row.

his dogs and stayed on the Currie farm, which he worked his entire life, taking great pride in his horses and crops. He was a gentle man of quiet manners and disposition and a tobacco chewer but, according to his nephew Robert, with a wonderful laugh that lit up his face. He died in his 91st year at the Newbury Hospital and I remember seeing his fresh grave in Wardsville.

Margaret was born in September 1881, became a nurse and did not marry. In 1937 she became depressed, possibly over some conflict with one or two of her brothers, and committed suicide at the home of her brother John in Glencoe by taking strychnine.

Jane was born in March 1885, became a dressmaker and lived for a time with her sister Johannah in London. In October 1912 she married Mike Egan of Sarnia, went to live with him there and later in the Windsor area where they raised a family. She died in 1973.

Mary Ellen was born in August 1887, also became a dressmaker and joined her sisters in London. For three years she worked at Smallman and Ingram's store in London but in 1914 she became fatally ill and went home

to her parents, the only one of Jenny's children to die in her mother's lifetime. Her death certificate ascribes her death to tuberculosis of 9 months' duration.

John, who was born in August 1889, also got a job on the railway as a telegraph operator and in 1911 was living in Bothwell. He eventually returned to Glencoe where he married Maude Helen McCracken in 1921 and may have been a town councilor for a time in the 1930s. They had no children. He died in 1960.

Anna was born in January 1892, graduated as a nurse in 1917 from St. Joseph's Hospital in Chatham where she spent the rest of her life. For years she worked for Dr. Jim Rutherford, a general practitioner in that city. She did not marry and died unexpectedly in 1936 from partial obstruction of the bowels due to adhesions following acute gall bladder trouble with gallstones.

Catherine was born in July 1894 and was called Cassie as a young girl and later Kate. In 1912 she accepted a position at Smallman & Ingram's in London and in 1915 married Alexander McKay, a glass beveller. A

Jenny Donnelly in the year that she died.

in October 1984 in the Newbury Hospital after spending some time in a nursing home.

Clara Gertrude was born in August 1899 and died of pulmonary congestion, probably tuberculosis, on February 4th, 1919.

The last child of Jenny, Patrick Leo, was born in October 1902 and also became a telegraph dispatcher for the Canadian National Railway. By 1937 he was living in Chatham where he remained the rest of his long life. He married Celestine Ruth (Sally) McManus and had a family of three daughters and four sons. Pat was already four years retired from the railway when I met him and his wife in 1971. She died in 1991 and Pat himself died in Chatham in 1994.

Jenny stayed close to her home in Mosa Township in the house her husband built for the family in 1878. The children attended Pratt's Siding School and the community where the Curries lived was known for years as Pratt's Siding. As mentioned, Jenny did go back to visit her daughter Johannah in Lucan on one occasion and likely the only time, in 1904. It was then that someone asked her to go see an elderly woman in the Catholic Settlement who was lying on her deathbed. Jenny knew she was the widow of one of the vigilantes who had murdered her family. She refused to go.

"She just wants to confess to me about the guilt of her family," she said "and so relieve their souls. I will not give them the satisfaction. Let their souls burn in hell."

daughter, Jennie, was born in August 1917 but lived only a few days. Catherine died of consumption in 1925.

Michael Thomas was born in March 1897. He too joined the railway as a dispatcher for the Grand Trunk, later the Canadian National Railway. He married Mary Quigley in 1923 and had a son and two daughters but was estranged from his wife and children for the last several decades of his life. When I met him, he was living in the house outside Glencoe on the farm in Ekfrid Township where the family had moved in 1912 and where his mother had died. He himself died

In 1912, the Curries sold their farm in Mosa Township and moved to a house on a fifty-acre farm in Ekfrid just south of the village of Glencoe. Here Jenny died in 1916. Her husband and the children who had not yet left home continued to live there for many years. The youngest daughter, Clara, died three years after her mother. Mike and Pat reached their manhood on this farm and stories are told by their neighbours of their thinking of themselves as "lady-killers" who, when they went out to attend local dances were "dressed up to the nines". They eventually married and left their older brother Jim to continue to farm the place. He quietly boasted of getting three crops off the land in one season. Jim never married. Jenny's husband Jim Currie eventually died in 1931. Mike Currie, after becoming estranged from his wife and young family, moved back in with Jim on the home farm. I met him there in 1971, the year after the death of his older brother. Not long after, Mike was removed to a nursing home and the house was either razed or burned to the ground.

By most accounts, some of Jenny's boys were a rowdy lot although Jim and Pat were not.

"Bob could lick anyone," Glencoe old-timers recalled, adding that Jack and Mike were the most pugnacious.

The Glencoe clerk, Bill Diamond, related: "I once saw Jack in a fight in which his opponent had Jack's ear in his teeth."

A story is told of Mike enlisting in the Royal Canadian Mounted Police, but his recruiting days ended with his knocking down the instructor.

Patrick Currie married Sally McManus and I was fortunate to know Sally's best friend, Mary Walter. She told me that when she first went to their house in Chatham, Pat appeared to be very hostile.

"Are your people from up in Biddulph?" he asked her gruffly.

"Why, yes," Mary replied, "my mother was Theresa Whelan. They lived across the road from your grandparents. They watched your uncles grow up from boys."

"Were they involved in killing my people?"

"No, of course not," Mary said, "Why, they were always friendly with them. They knew your mother very well."

"Well," said Pat, "we'll see about that. I'll check it out in Glencoe."

Pat must have consulted his mother's clippings, for the next time Mary went to see the Curries, Pat met her at the door and welcomed her in.

Chapter 23

Bob Versus The Army

On All Fool's Day in 1878, fate played a cruel joke on Bob Donnelly. On that day Justice Adam Wilson sentenced him to serve two years in Kingston Penitentiary. Within a few months of his entering the prison, his family was petitioning to have him released. A host of Lucanites as well as many others signed their petition.[1] As Bob had been convicted of shooting at Constable Everett of Lucan with intent to commit murder, the grounds set forth were "that the evidence adduced at the trial was conflicting, several witnesses positively stating that the said Donnelly was several miles away at the house of his father, at the time the said shooting took place." The petition went on to state:

> That we are well acquainted with the circumstances attending the said shooting and believe the same was not done by the said Robert Donnelly.

Although Bishop John Walsh of the London diocese signed the petition, after his signature he added the salient words "in view of the fact that Everett the Prosecutor has reason to entertain grave doubts of his Guilt". Everett, on his part, had made a sworn statement that he no longer thought it was Robert Donnelly who had taken the potshot at him and that he now conscientiously believed him to be innocent.

While the petition had probably been forwarded to the government before the coming to St. Patrick's Parish of Father John Connolly, its existence was brought to his attention soon after his arrival. Whether this was done by the bishop himself, who may have suggested to Connolly that it presented a timely opportunity to make a good beginning in the troubled parish, Father Connolly quickly made it known that he would use whatever influence he had to free Bob. As it happened, that influence may have been considerable for the government in office in Ottawa at the time was that of John A. Macdonald. In Macdonald's cabinet was Hector Langevin who, like Macdonald, was one of the Canadian Fathers of Confederation. John Connolly knew Langevin personally. He happened to be the member of parliament from the riding of Dorchester in Quebec in close proximity to the parish of St. Athanase where Connolly had served as parish priest for the previous seven years before coming to Biddulph. But either Langevin had more important matters with which to concern himself or the petition was felt by the legal authorities to be without merit. It came to nothing.

As it turned out, Robert Donnelly was released early in any event on grounds, as he claimed, of good conduct. He was discharged on December 11th, 1879 after serving not quite 21 months of his two year sentence. The authorities may have moved on compassionate grounds to enable him to attend the funeral of his brother killed in Waterford, Ontario two days before. Immediately after his brother's funeral, Bob conveyed back to St. Thomas his brother's widow, Nellie, and his own sister, Jenny, who had taken a house two doors away from the bereaved widow. But by January 11th, 1880, as noted in his diary by William Porte, Bob was back at his parents' home on the Roman Line, having returned to the homestead to attend the wedding of Martha Keefe to Michael Quigley, both old friends.

There was something unusual about this wedding, which came to pass on January 15th, 1880. It took place against the wishes of Father Connolly and probably for that reason the wedding rites were performed in the Donnelly Schoolhouse rather than at St. Patrick's Church. The priest had decided to make a visit to his old parishioners in Inverness-St. Athanase, Quebec and had told the couple to postpone the wedding until his return.

From the front corner of the Keefe house, where the wedding guests watched the barns burn in January 1880, the Grouchy Ryder farm buildings lay across the fields at the centre of the far horizon.

Determined to be married with or without the parish priest, the couple obtained the services of an outside priest named Peter Feron. He came and performed the ceremony, apparently on the understanding that he would not be usurping the regular priest's function if the wedding took place at the Donnelly Schoolhouse instead of the church. It may well have been this breach of ecclesiastical etiquette, which upset Father Connolly, for when he returned and learned that the wedding had taken place in his absence, he was angry.

"Damn the wedding, and damn the schoolhouse," he is reported to have said, "And damn the gaudy little bride."

Well over a hundred years after this, Joe Quigley, grandson of the wedding couple, said to me, "Priest or no priest, I would have bopped him in the nose for saying that about my grandmother. She was not like that at all but as fine a woman as you could meet and I am proud of her."

Following the wedding, the bride's family threw a celebration at the Robert Keefe farmhouse. It went into the early morning hours of the next day. Four of the Donnelly brothers, William, John, Robert and Thomas, attended the celebrations. Early in the morning while festivities were in full swing, someone looked across the fields and noticed a fire in the distance. The barns of Grouchy Ryder, plainly visible and less than half a mile from Keefe's, were ablaze. The music stopped and the wedding guests crowded out on the front lawn for a better look.

There is an apocryphal story that one of the Donnelly boys, standing in the crowd, is reputed to have said, "Oh, this will be the end of us." Sure enough, the boys were the first persons suspected of setting the fire— except that there were far too many wedding guests to provide alibis for them. Still, it would not have been too difficult for someone to steal away from the festivities, set the fire and return in less than half an hour. Suspicions against one of them, Bob, were

159

Mary Ryder, who attended the Keefe wedding celebration, is shown here many years later on the Grouchy Ryder farm, with her husband and grandson.

heightened when it was discovered that the very next day he had lit out from Biddulph to return to St. Thomas. And he took his mother with him.

That was enough for Grouchy Ryder. It is true that his own daughter, Mary Ryder, had attended the wedding celebration at Keefe's and knew that the Donnelly boys were there, too, but in Grouchy's eyes, who but the guilty parties would up and flee the scene of the crime so quickly?

And it appears that the alibis provided by the wedding guests did not cover Bob, for when James Carroll arrived in St. Thomas on January 18th, he had in his possession not only a warrant for the arrest of Mrs. Donnelly but one for Robert as well. When Carroll showed up, however, Robert was not to be found. The answer Carroll and Chief Fewings of St. Thomas received on inquiring after him was that he had "gone to Michigan to work in the woods". Two weeks later, however, when the news of the tragic deaths of his family reached him, he quickly surfaced in St. Thomas and was in Lucan within a day or two, arriving shortly after his sister Jenny.

Bob stayed around in Lucan for a while after the funerals. On February 9th it was reported that "Robert Donnelly remains in the village, but takes no active part in the proceedings now going on". His personality was unsuited to police work. If anything, he created more ill will than good by his presence. Two or three times that month he went out to visit the scene of the murders "just to see where they had been burning". The first time, Joe Whelan came from across the road presumably to extend his sympathy. Another time, Bob claimed to have found one of the murder weapons—an elm club about three feet long squared on one end and whittled on the other as if for a handle—about a hundred and fifty feet from the house site in the direction of the schoolhouse. The business end of this club was smeared with blood. Bob also assisted in finding a pair of overshoes hidden in a manure pile on the Maher farm. This discovery resulted in the arrest of Mrs. James Maher and the hired man James Shea. The members of the Biddulph Peace Society deeply resented the arrest of the woman who was then with suckling child. All of this evidence worked up by Robert Donnelly came to nothing and the two suspects were soon released.

When Mrs. John Kennedy died in March 1880, Bob borrowed his brother Will's horse and buggy to go over to pay his respects to the Kennedy girls and their father who were all friends of the Donnelly family. The London *Advertiser* reported the result:[2]

> Robert Donnelly left the buggy some distance from the house whilst he went in, and upon his return found that the rig had been broken to pieces. It seems as if the troubles in Biddulph are not yet over.

Another report later stated that the first had been false.

As the preliminary hearing against the Biddulph prisoners commenced in London, Bob was in the courtroom. During the testimony of Johnny O'Connor, he was sitting among the spectators when Hugh Macmahon for the defense caught him nodding to the witness whenever the boy made a strong point against the prisoners. On Macmahon's motion, the court ordered him ejected.

During the remainder of the year 1880, Bob Donnelly continued travelling between Lucan, St. Thomas and Glencoe. The middle of April found him living near the railway tracks in Lucan in one of the two adjacent houses of Michael O'Connor near the east end of Francis Street. With him was his wife, Annie. They slept three in a bed with a woman named Kate Waun, also known as Johnson or Johnston, and alleged by Bob's enemies to be a woman of ill repute.[3]

On the Sunday before, Bob Donnelly had stomped into the Donnelly Schoolhouse where Father Connolly was holding a service and noisily nailed to the wall one of the government posters offering a reward for the apprehension of his family's murderers. When the priest protested that this was not the proper place for such a demonstration, Donnelly replied, "I think it's the proper place all right, for you got all the rest of the murderers around you here."

Following the first trial of James Carroll—concluded in the fall of 1880 as a mistrial due to the jury's failing to reach a unanimous verdict—Bob Donnelly moved back to Glencoe. The move was not without mishap for the London *Advertiser* of October 28th, 1880 reported:

> While Mr. Robert Donnelly was passing through the township of Adelaide on Friday last, on his way from Lucan to Glencoe with a load of furniture, he met with an accident by which his load was upset, one of his horses killed, and considerable damage done to the contents of the wagon. He made out a bill of $200 against the Council, and at a special meeting yesterday a compromise was effected for $92 cash. The mishap occurred through a defect in the road on Robbins' hill.

Again, however, Bob was soon back in Biddulph where, with his surviving brothers, he took an active interest in the homestead. Robert and Patrick wanted to rebuild the house immediately and to commence ploughing as soon as the weather permitted but brother William was uncertain. Their sister, Jenny, it appears, did not care one way

or the other. Her whole life, totally occupied by her burgeoning young family, was centred on her house and farm in Mosa Township. Eventually the brothers agreed to rent the land to Michael Feeheley for a term of six years. Shortly after, however, while Feeheley was visiting friends in Saginaw, Michigan, he died unexpectedly. In the end, the brothers built a two-storey frame house which was completed by the beginning of 1882 and they rented the farm to an old friend, John Kent, a Protestant.

Bob Donnelly returned to Glencoe where he took up the occupation of teamster and, perhaps because of his previous experience with the Adelaide Council, proved a litigious one. Over the years, he brought several actions against municipalities for non-repair of roads and bridges. In 1884 he billed the Ekfrid Council $3 for damage to his wagon while getting off Coulthard's Bridge on the Longwoods Road. The following year he obtained a judgment of $50 damages against Mosa Township for injury to a horse.

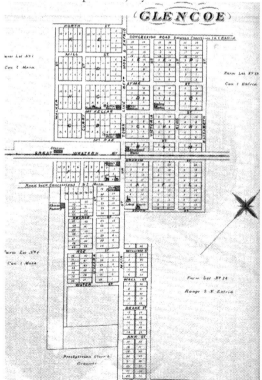

From Page's *Atlas of Middlesex County,* 1878.

Following the conclusion on February 3rd, 1881 of the second trial of Carroll in London with a Not Guilty verdict, Bob Donnelly confronted his family's enemies in both the Western and City Hotels in that city. As they celebrated the acquittal, Donnelly stood staring at them "offering to buy all you murderers a drink". No one took up the offer. Later in the year in Lucan, Robert tried to pick a fight with Jim Carroll by jostling him on the sidewalk in front of Bernard Stanley's store and taunting him with the words, "You can tell by that man's shoulders that he's a murderer." Carroll refused to react, but five minutes later Donnelly came up behind and threw a shoulder at him which almost knocked him off the sidewalk. Carroll then went off to lay a charge of assault but his friends persuaded him to drop the matter.

Then in October 1881 on the information of Francis Morrison West, William and Robert Donnelly were charged with attempting to burn down the Stanley and Dight Mill in Lucan. Patrick and Cornelius Carty and John Kent were also charged. In the end, the testimony of West was not believed and the defendants found not guilty.

Following this escapade, Robert Donnelly returned to and settled down in Glencoe with his wife. Together they informally adopted his brother Michael's child, James Michael Donnelly. Glencoe, with a population then of between ten and twelve hundred, accepted him in the community. The townspeople admired him for his energy, hard work and enterprise. As a teamster, it was reported, "He says he can't do half the work he can get." And when the Glencoe constable was dismissed, Bob applied for the position. While he was rejected as town constable, he appears to have got himself appointed for a brief period as a county constable, for despite his past he was then on good terms with Charles Hutchinson, the long-time county crown attorney. The latter, for example, wrote to his brother William on April 24th, 1884:

I had a visit from your brother Robert the other day, and was glad to see him looking so well.

Being Bob, however, he was soon in the midst of controversy. On the evening of July 2nd, 1884, a row broke out at the Simpson House in Glencoe and Bob was sent for. He waded into an unruly mob, which was milling about in the street. A young stranger to the village whom he shoved aside, held what was termed a slung-shot and with it attempted to strike Donnelly. Bob hit the man over the head with his baton and knocked him unconscious.

The Glencoe *Transcript* of July 3rd, 1884 reported the incident:

A young man named Charles Burchell, formerly a brakesman on the Grand Trunk Railway, was severely injured last night at the hands of an assailant whom he alleges to have been Robert Donnelly, county constable . . . The blow must have been a heavy one as Burchell was rendered insensible, in which condition he remained nearly all night, and it is possible the injury sustained may yet prove serious.

When crown attorney Hutchinson learned that the victim was said to be lingering between life and death, he was angry. He telegraphed Malcolm Leitch, a tailor in Glencoe who was also a justice of the peace:

Is man dead? Has Donnelly been arrested?

Although Hutchinson ordered that a warrant be issued for Bob's arrest, among the constables who did not appear to want to arrest him was his own brother, William, who was by then the village constable. William had taken possession of the slung-shot for evidence and assured the crown attorney that his brother would not flee. Hutchinson chided him that he must do his duty. Will Donnelly waited, however, until his brother had nursed the victim back to health in his own home and only then brought Bob in. Although the case against him was disposed of, Bob was soon sacked as constable. Even then, however, his older brother occasionally called upon him for assistance as a temporary deputy.

Early in 1884 the Glencoe *Transcript* began to report the doings of a peculiar new religious movement that had come to southwestern Ontario. On March 20th of that year it stated: "The Salvation Army will attack Strathroy on the 23rd inst." On April 3rd it reported: "The Salvation Army is meditating an attack on Wardsville." Glencoe's turn finally arrived in early June of that year when the newspaper reported:[4]

> The Salvation Army made an assault on the camp of the Evil One in Glencoe on Sunday morning, and the sound of drums, cymbals and tambourines, and the shouts of Captain Fisher and her six or eight soldiers scattered disorder and confusion through the streets sufficient to convey the impression that hades itself had broken loose.

Armies are militant, and when it came to saving souls, the Salvation Army was no different. It was loud and brash. Its members did not steal off quietly to worship in respectfully hushed tones but went blaring about the streets with loud horns and booming bass drums. Its first meetings in Glencoe were held at the Town Hall, a frame two-storey building of about thirty by forty feet which had been built in the fall of 1872. In front of it was a platform from which crowds could be addressed.

Notwithstanding the derisive nature of its reports on the antics of the Army, the *Transcript* editor seemed on the whole to look with favor on the new organization. "The army so far have been successful in Glencoe," it stated the following week after several more meetings had been held,[5] "and while some are opposed to their mode of worship, the general opinion is that they are the means of doing much good."

But those who were opposed to them happened to be the upper class establishment of the town, insofar as Glencoe could be said to have had social classes. This circle of society viewed the Army as not quite respectable. In that Victorian age, the idea of

young women going out in the streets with uniforms and brass bands to convert the wayward appeared outlandish.

Then there were the fears of the elders for their youth "some of whom are already ornaments and the pride of the family, deluded and frightened into making confessions of sin before the public, which serve to goad others on to do likewise"[6]. It was said that "this Salvation Army business has had a blasting and withering influence on the youth of this village."[7] The upwelling of animosity amongst the town's respectable citizens forced the minister of the Methodist church to write a letter to the newspaper disclaiming support for the Army.

Robert Donnelly, still a favorite with the respectable citizens of the town, took his cue from them. This class of men included Nathaniel Currie, the unofficial founder and several times reeve of the village; John Orange, land developer and councilor,

War Cry was the Salvation Army's newspaper.

assessor of the tax roll and chief of the fire department; Wilmot Swaisland, described as a starchy English banker; Malcolm Leitch, master tailor and justice of the peace; and John A. Leitch, cheese factory owner and village councillor. Whatever these respectable citizens thought was right had the support of Robert Donnelly, and it was not long before he and the Army collided.

Soon some of the boisterous youths of the village—one might say Bob Donnelly's young flock of admirers—began to harass the new group. Among the youths was a lad from Biddulph named Johnny Ryan while another was young John Orange, Jr. Others were youths or young men named Joseph Hillman, Colin McKellar, Daniel Thody, John McIntyre, William Cochrane, Duncan McDonald, George Riddell, Donald McRae, Peter Smith and Alex Finlayson. Another cohort of Donnelly was the recently graduated veterinary surgeon who had shortly before begun to practice his profession in Glencoe named Edward A. Blackwell. As in

Biddulph, Bob Donnelly proved again that the family could inspire the fiercest loyalties among those whom they befriended. John N. McCracken of Sarnia, whose family was one of the first to settle in Glencoe, wrote:[8]

> My grandfather once said that his uncle David McCracken (1853-1897) used to go out drinking with one of the Donnelly boys (probably Bob) when they came to Glencoe. [He] once told his father, Nathan McCracken, "'If ever you need my help, my coat will be off for you in a minute' . . . .

At first the actions of the foes of the Army were cloaked in darkness. "A number of young men have of late been making night hideous by their howling Salvation songs and various other unseemly noises," it was reported[9] in the town newspaper.

By day, Bob Donnelly was conducting business as usual. At the same time that the Salvation Army was soliciting subscriptions for the purchase of a drum, Donnelly was drawing a hundred boxes of cheese at one load from John Leitch's cheese factory to the

Detail from a Robert Harris painting of a Salvation Army band parading in full cry.

railway station. On this job he used his second team of heavy horses, a matched span 16 hands high weighing about 24 hundredweight, four and six years old respectively. Now becoming the opportunistic man of business, he offered to

Glencoe determined not to be outdone. At the regular weekly meeting of the Army in Glencoe on the night of Friday, September 26th, 1884, one of the youths from Donnelly's gang entered the room. He disrupted the meeting. The captain of the

The Lucan detachment of the Salvation Army in front of its newly built barracks on the Main Street and still standing in 1964.

sell them to the highest bidder.

One night in September, the newspaper reported, a gang of young people had caused a great ruction. They were "allowed to hold high carnival at all hours of the night in the most populous parts of the village" shouting "volumes of profanity as made Main street notorious on Monday night."[10] The report commented that these people should not be excused simply because they were well dressed and not strangers to the town.

When it was reported that in nearby Wardsville the Salvation Army had a hard time holding its audience at the Saturday night meeting after a "nasty boy placed a skunk in the barracks,"[11] the young people of

Army seized the youth by the collar and threw him out, "landing him outside the hall door."[12]

Up to this time, the Salvation Army had held its services in a meeting room in the Town Hall, which they designated as "the barracks". And when marching through the streets it was to the beat of one or two tambourines. Such sound did little to assault the ears of passers-by who watched bemusedly as they passed. By November 1884, however, the Army had raised enough funds to raise the decibel levels. "If the devil cannot be 'licked' he is bound to be frightened," it was jocularly printed, for "shot and shell was the order of the afternoon."[13]

Near the town of Glencoe lived the Squires family. They were lovers of music and embraced the new religion. They let it be known to the townsfolk that the Army proposed holding a full-scale demonstration consisting of a torch-light procession followed by a "jubilee" in the Town Hall and that thereafter it proposed to hold meetings on Sundays. To Bob Donnelly and his youthful cohorts, the announcement was a call to arms. Sure enough, on November 20th, 1884, it was reported:[14]

> A number of young men who should know better disturbed the quietness and order at last Sunday's Salvation Army meeting, and also made the streets a perfect bedlam with their hooting, swearing, etc. These young men are known . . . .

Then on Christmas Day the Glencoe paper carried the following item:[15]

> Bad boys sprinkled pepper on the stove in the Town Hall Sunday evening while the Salvation Army meeting was in progress. The result was a good deal of sneezing.

Nevertheless, on February 26, 1885 the *Transcript* reported that the Salvation Army had held four meetings on the previous Sunday headed by Mr. William Smith, leader of the Hallelujah Band. The Army was becoming so successful—said to have 120 converts since coming to Glencoe—that it intended holding meetings every Friday as well as Sunday. In addition, it would be building new barracks near the Methodist church on Concession Street.

Towards the end of May, the new barracks was just about complete. The Army would open the new building "by holding one of their notorious devil paralyzers", the newspaper said, adding ominously that "the boys have already laid in a stock of firecrackers in anticipation of the event."[16] The boys referred to were, of course, Bob Donnelly's gang of young troublemakers.

Another small item reported that someone had tried to light fire to the new barracks but the ball of carpet rags soaked in coal oil had failed to ignite.

A few days later, the newspaper reported that the Salvation Army had held the banquet and "hallelujah hurricane" which had opened the new barracks as scheduled:[17]

> The hurricane was kept up all night, and consisted of singing and praying. The soldiers were not disturbed in their banquet, which was allowed to pass off quietly, but towards morning some boys on the outside of the barracks created quite a racket, breaking in the door panels and smashing windows, besides making night hideous with their yelling.

Throughout the summer the Army continued its campaign. "The Hallelujah Band has brought a number of hardened sinners to the penitent form in Glencoe," it was reported.[18] When some of the converts resented being called hardened sinners, the newspaper replied:[19]

> When people stand up before crowded meetings and confess what ungodly lives they have led and how hardened in sin they were, applying to themselves such terms as "the vilest of the vile," "servants of the devil," "hell-deserving sinners," etc., we think the press is fully justified in alluding to them as "hardened sinners".

View of Main Street, Glencoe.

166

Chapter 24

Emma's Tribulations

In September, 1884 the Glencoe *Transcript* reported that the Army had stepped up its campaign with a vigorous new local leader from, of all places, the village of Lucan:

> Lieut. Rees, of Lucan, has been appointed to the Glencoe station of the Salvation Army, and meetings are now held every evening.

Although Emma Rees was named as lieutenant, her rank on coming to Glencoe was captain. She was said, probably unfairly, to be buxom. One Glencoite, Charles Tom, described her as "a very powerful looking woman, and I would not like to tackle her myself."[1] Because many of the members of the new movement were of the fair sex, those who opposed them in Glencoe would not only make such disparaging remarks but add innuendoes about the young men who were joining up as soldiers. One of them, Kenneth McKenzie, became a drummer in the Hallelujah Band. He was forced to answer in open court that he was "not casting sheep's eyes at any person—had no sheep's eyes to cast"[2] Another, Walter Squires, had to state in open court that he was "not mashed on Emma Rees".[3] Edward Skill was another volunteer but, as we shall see, may have felt otherwise.

Miss Rees soon came to know the kind of place she had been assigned to when the following item was reported in the village paper shortly after her arrival:[4]

> A couple of roughs got into a row on Main street, Monday, and one of them knocked the other through the glass front of Rockett's store.

The Rockett family members were supporters of the Army which often held its street services in front of their store on the main street.

Emma Rees

The first direct confrontation between Bob Donnelly and Emma Rees took place that same month, on Saturday, October 10th. While the Army was conducting its usual march on the streets in Glencoe, it ran into Bob Donnelly's youthful gang, including Peter Smith, Colin McKellar, George Riddell and William Hillman. And among the youths was not only Bob Donnelly himself but his wife, Annie, along with a young child who was probably Bob's nephew, young James Michael, son of Michael killed in Waterford. Members of the Army claimed that Donnelly and his group had deliberately obstructed their path. Mrs. Donnelly alleged that Emma Rees struck her on the shoulder with a tambourine and pushed her and the child off the sidewalk. Emma Rees said Bob Donnelly swore at her. Moreover, he quickly rushed off to the justice of the peace, Malcolm Leitch, who he knew would be sympathetic to his case. Emma Rees was hauled up before him and Leitch convicted her of an assault on both Hillman and Mrs. Donnelly.

Indignant at the result—especially when another justice of the peace, Robert Hannah, failed to convict Robert Donnelly on her counter-charge—Emma Rees paid the fine under protest and then complained to the crown attorney in London. Charles Hutchinson was sympathetic. He advised her to appeal the convictions and she did. Then he wrote to Leitch.[5]

"I can't imagine that either in this case or the Donnelly one, there would be any willful unprovoked aggression on the part of Miss Rees," he stated. "I am sure that if the Salvation Army people were left alone and not disturbed and annoyed, there would be no trouble."

Hutchinson also chided Hannah for his disposition of the case against Donnelly. And he wrote to Constable William Donnelly under date of October 17th, 1885 as follows:[6]

> I hope you will believe that my sympathy for your family is not exhausted, altho' I disapprove highly of some recent proceedings to which I propose to direct your attention. I now particularly refer to the conduct of your brother Robert, in which I fear you are to some extent backing him, towards the Salvation Army people. Whatever you may think of their methods they are endeavouring to do good, and have accomplished much good here and elsewhere. At any rate in a free country they are entitled to protection and must have it fully accorded to them.

And then the crown attorney added some words which showed he may have been getting some real insight into the events leading up to the early morning of February 4th, 1880 in Biddulph, when he continued:

> Robert is apparently pursuing a similar course to that which led to such fearful consequences in Biddulph, and I hope he will desist, as I intend to see the law upheld if possible.

Hutchinson concluded:

> I write this in a friendly spirit and hope it will have a beneficial effect upon Robert and all others acting with him or for him.

The Glencoe Railway Station, now standing derelict, where Bob Donnelly continued to harass Emma Rees upon her return from London.

William Donnelly was deeply hurt by the words of this letter, insinuating as it did that the horrible fate delivered to his murdered people was partly of their own doing. It was only many months later that he could bring himself to allude to it.

The crown attorney viewed the Salvation Army as "harmless religious enthusiasts (many of them women)"[7]. He told their captain that "I have also warned the Donnellys to desist from their evil ways, and trust you will be let alone in future. If not, do not offer resistance, but come to me and I will see that you are protected."[8]

In London, Emma Rees laid charges against Robert Donnelly and his companions before Robert Hannah. They were arrested the following Saturday, came up for trial in the city, were convicted and fined five dollars each. Bob Donnelly, however, took the occasion to make Emma Rees better acquainted with the character of his family. With the devil smoldering in his eyes, he followed her around the city and—without actually committing a physical assault—pranced circles around her. He jeered at her, mocked her and insulted her with raucous, lewd and obscene language she had never before heard. "I will send you to the cooler," he threatened, "and cut your heart out." The intimidation and insults continued on the train all the way back to Glencoe and even after her alighting at the station.[9]

Shaken, Emma Rees again wrote to the crown attorney and Hutchinson replied:[10]

> I am sorry you had so much trouble and were so much annoyed by that unfortunate man Robert Donnelly, who is his own worst enemy.

He told her, however, that in the line of work she had chosen to pursue, it was one of the crosses she had to bear.

The course of justice crept slowly along. Captain Rees, not to be deterred awaiting her appeal to come on, held an Army meeting on the evening of Sunday, November 30th. Young Colin McKellar broke into the hall. Pretending to sing, he shouted and hooted instead. The captain asked him to leave. He refused. She attempted to push him out the door but he resisted. Completely exasperated, she slapped him on the face with her open hand. McKellar immediately rushed off and laid a charge of assault before the sympathetic justice of the peace in the nearby village of Newbury, William J. Simpson.

It was well known that Simpson was not in sympathy with the Army. He quickly issued a summons and it was served as fast. Emma Rees again wrote to the crown attorney to complain, as well as to discuss the impending appeal. Hutchinson replied on December 3rd, 1885:[11]

> Is Robert Donnelly worth anything, if you should succeed with your appeal? You would in that case get judgment against him for your costs, but unless he has property you would recover nothing, and be at all the expense of the appeal.

Robert Donnelly was, of course, worth something. Not only did he own a couple of houses in the village, he was a prospering teamster. During working hours, he was with his teams and wagon busy with many jobs including hauling cheese from the cheese factory, hauling loads of stone and gravel for the village streets and, in winter, hauling ice from the village pond and selling it not only to the shopkeepers and businesses of the village but to the townspeople for their homes.

Hutchinson also wrote to Simpson in Newbury suggesting that the McKellar charge against the Army captain was improper as Miss Rees should not "be held responsible for a mere slap on the face which probably the young man richly deserved"[12] and that it should be McKellar himself who should be charged with disturbing the religious services. He advised Simpson to adjourn the case. Just to be sure, he sent a telegram to Rees in Newbury advising her to get the case postponed.

As was demonstrated in the case of James Grant of Granton when dealing with the case of John Donnelly for perjury in 1879, justices of the peace in Middlesex County were willfully independent creatures who did not always bow to the advice of the county crown attorney. The Newbury J.P. not only convicted Emma Rees, he opened up and silently read to himself the telegram addressed to her. He did not deliver it to her until after she had been fined. When Hutchinson learned this, he was furious. He angrily told the J.P. that the case would be appealed and asked why he had the temerity to open the telegram addressed to the defendant. In his reply, Simpson expressed annoyance at the tone of Hutchinson's letter. But the latter berated the magistrate for his willfulness, lack of Christian tolerance, bigotry and wrongful judicial conduct. He also made Colin McKellar pay back to Emma Rees the amount of the fine that Simpson had imposed.

In the meantime, the appeal by Rees for assaulting Mrs. Robert Donnelly came up at the Quarter Sessions Court. The convicting magistrate, Squire Leitch of Glencoe, had in the meantime died. Upon Bob's wife failing to appear, the appeal was allowed and the conviction quashed. Not only did Emma Rees seem vindicated but now new charges against the young men of the village were pursued. Young Colin McKellar was arrested on four charges of disturbing the Army and

The Wesleyan Methodist Church in Glencoe, beside which the Salvation Army built its ill-fated barracks.

Alex Finlayson was convicted of assaulting William Virtue, one of the Army soldiers.

Hutchinson wrote to Rees on December 22nd, 1885 to tell her that the lawyer whom he contacted on her behalf thought there would be no difficulty in getting back from the estate of the deceased magistrate the money fine, which he had levied against her. He also wished her a Merry Christmas.

Shortly before the old year ran out, the Salvation Army barracks in Glencoe burned to the ground. The *Transcript* commented on the fire in its issue dated the last day of 1885:[13]

> It is generally believed that the fire was the work of an incendiary, though there is no actual proof that such was the case nor did the appearance of the fire when first discovered give that impression. The only ground for the incendiary theory is in the bitter animosity which has manifested itself between the members of the army and several parties who were either opposed to their movements or for want of other means of occupying their time amused themselves by disturbing the army's meetings and otherwise annoying its members.

But the crown attorney himself had no illusions about the cause of the fire. It was, he said "undoubtedly the work of an incendiary."[14]

The Salvation Army was undeterred. The new year of 1886 saw it resuming its services out of temporary quarters. Not only did their street parades continue, they were adorned with an attractive new Cadet who stood second in command to Emma Rees. Carrie

Misener, the new recruit, quickly showed her mettle. She, too, was soon charged with an assault. Her brother paid the fine but she appealed the conviction.

Notwithstanding the winter weather, the Hallelujah Band scheduled an open-air meeting for the evening of Tuesday, January 19th. The reason it was open air, Cadet Misener declared, was that the Army had no barracks to hold it in. That evening it was about eight o'clock, with the village street lamps lit and the moon shining, when eight to ten members of the Army gathered at the home of William Virtue where Emma Rees boarded. Besides their two female leaders, the group included Walter, Fred and George Squires, Mrs. Filmore, Edward Skill, Kenneth McKenzie and John Hitch. Marching out in formation to the beat of the tambourines and drum, they approached Simpson's Hotel.

Suddenly out of nowhere, Bob Donnelly and his gang of youths appeared.[15] Dancing and gesticulating, they fell in behind the marchers. When they reached the hotel, the Army drew themselves into a circle at the side of the road "between the sidewalk and the waggon track". As they began to sing, Donnelly and the youths mockingly joined in with "ribaldry and obscenity" and their loud and raucous voices soon drowned out the Salvationists. Colin McKellar blew cigar smoke into the face of Emma Rees, and when Bob Donnelly gave him the nod, he forcibly bumped into her. Then the others began to buffet the soldiers as they tried to maintain the ring. Bob Donnelly jumped inside the circle and began prancing about. "Don't give them a show," one of the boys cried out. This started Donnelly whooping at the top of his voice. The others quickly joined in.

"That isn't half a try," Bob shouted, "Can't you do better than that?" And he raised the decibel level a few notches higher.

A large crowd of bemused onlookers had by this time gathered, among them John Orange, Jr., accompanied by his father. The senior man, thinking at first to avoid or prevent a commotion, drew back, but he was soon drawn into the fun and began shouting with the others. At last the Army retreated in confusion.

The following evening, the Army tried again. Gathering once more at the Virtue house, they marched out. Again, Bob Donnelly and his gang of youths quickly appeared and followed them. When the Army reached the Adams store on the main street, they tried to form a circle but the gang, shouting and swearing, jostled them and threw themselves between the soldiers. One of the rowdies, Alex Finlayson, was a little drunk. He knocked the drum out of the hands of Walter Squires. Another, Colin McKellar, threatened to slap the drummer's mouth while young George Riddell was said to have "kept damning it off almost all the time".

"Look at the — cranks," he kept saying. Another youth, the Army people later

Author's sketch of Bob Donnelly, including his signature, when he chose to write it instead of making an "X".

testified, came up behind the captain and "swore something fearful. He took God's name in vain."

Finally, when Emma Rees gave the command to stop singing and make a strategic retreat, the soldiers had to fight their way through the rowdies. Again the Oranges, father and son, were present. While they had not shoved into the ring like the others, they joined in the raising of the disturbance as the Army pushed through the crowd. When they had regrouped and began to march off, Bob Donnelly and his boys fell in behind them shouting, jeering and jumping about.

Emma Rees turned around and confronted Bob Donnelly to his face, "Why don't you stop this?" she said.

"I can't do that," he shouted at her, "I'm paid for it. We're all paid for it. And if we're all arrested, why I'll pay their fines."

The straggling Army made its way back to the Filimore house and went inside, followed to the gate by the jeering crowd of Donnelly and his youths. After Mr. Filimore came out and spoke to them, the noise subsided.

Once more on the following evening, Thursday the 21st, the Army tried again to hold an outdoor service. With Emma Rees in the lead beating on the first tambourine followed by Carrie Misener beating on the other, they marched out into the street. Kenneth McKenzie, beating the drum, followed the two women and next came seven or eight soldiers. As they passed Walker's Hotel, Bob Donnelly suddenly appeared from a side street.

"I've got a big crowd tonight," he shouted and, sure enough, the marchers saw behind him a group of 150 to 175 persons. Not all were sympathizers of Donnelly and his boys but word had got around that much fun was to be had of an evening on the streets of Glencoe and most of the crowd, coming from miles around, had come to view the anticipated rumpus. The gang did not disappoint them.

This time Bob Donnelly and the youths scampered in front of the marchers, first

Ed Skill, who had been one of the Army soldiers in Glencoe, and his wife, Emma Rees, circa 1918, Toronto.

stepping along in front of them mimicking their gait and then suddenly halting to disrupt the ranks. The Army finally managed to reach the front of Rockett's store where they were allowed to form the usual ring. Upon Emma Rees giving the order, "Sing out," the gang joined in. They shouted, swore and jostled. A general melee broke out. When someone jabbed Rees on the shoulder from behind, she wheeled around and with a chop of her right hand struck out. The blow landed on the face a Strathroy youth named Daniel Thody. It staggered him. He fell back and melted into the crowd.

"By the looks of Thody afterwards," said a bystander, noticing the left side of the youth's face quickly swelling up, "I thought she knocked him silly."

The crowd now extended from McAlpine's Hotel to Foster's barbershop. Emma Rees happened to spy among the onlookers the reeve of the village. Nathaniel Currie, she thought, was enjoying the proceedings when he should have been invoking the law to their defense. And, in truth, Currie later admitted he considered the goings on "a regular jollification".

When Rees pushed her way over to speak to him, she found young George Riddell standing in her way. Taking hold of him by the throat, she flung him aside.

"For God's sake, sir," she cried out to the startled reeve, "do something to stop this rowdyism."

When Currie recovered his composure, he replied, "Other people have rights on the street as well as the Salvation Army."

"Yes," she said, "but we have the right to worship here without being molested."

The reeve told her to make complaint in due form in the morning and he would deal with the parties according to law. Exasperated at his attitude, she turned and ordered a retreat. Once again the Army withdrew in disarray.

172

Chapter 25

An Abominable Outrage

On Sunday January 24th the Army marched out once more from the Virtue house. They were again disrupted and had to retreat. This time Emma Rees went not to the reeve or the local justices of the peace but to London where she laid formal complaints. Summonses were issued and two county constables, Hodge and Brown, went out to Glencoe and arrested several of the youths including Colin McKellar, both the elder and younger Oranges, Daniel Thody, Duncan McDonald and John McIntyre. They took them to London where they were bailed out. The constables had also wanted, but did not get, Bob Donnelly, George Riddell and John Ryan.

That day Constable Brown had gone down to the village pond where he met Robert Donnelly teaming ice.[1] Perhaps because the constable would have had to deal with Donnelly's horses and rig, he did not attempt to arrest him on the spot and Donnelly obligingly gave the constable a ride back downtown. But then he disappeared from sight.

Having been given the slip, a couple of days later the constables returned. This time they brought with them an additional member of the force named Crawford. Constable Hodge arrested Riddell and took him off as Brown and Crawford went over to Bob Donnelly's house. They entered. As Donnelly was not there, they sat down to wait.

In a little while Robert Donnelly, accompanied by the lad Ryan stepped inside. Donnelly had an axe in his hand.

"We are here again, Bob," Brown said, "And I want you."

Donnelly stiffened. "You can't get me this

Bob Donnelly's house in Glencoe where he was confronted by the constables.

morning," he said. Ryan turned and ran off but the axe in Donnelly's hand gave the constables momentary pause. The hesitation was enough to permit Donnelly to turn quickly and run out, slamming the door shut behind him. Constable Brown jumped up from his seat and ran after him. Donnelly fled around the corner of the kitchen, dropped the axe in the front yard and kept running.

"Stop, you —, or I'll blow your brains out," the constable shouted.

Donnelly ran around the north side of the next house and out through a gate on to O'Mara Street. Brown, waving his revolver, ran after him.

"Halt," he cried and pulled the trigger.

Bob was only about fifty or sixty feet ahead. The bullet whistled past his ear but he kept running. When Brown reached the corner of Concession Street, he came to a halt and shouted: "One, two, three—stand.

Donnelly kept running and got away. The constables spent the rest of the day ferreting about the village. They could not find Donnelly but managed to take Ryan into custody.

Following this escapade, Bob Donnelly kept out of the way for several days. He did manage to find the opportunity, however, to lay a charge against Constable Brown for shooting at him "with intent to disable or at least do some other grievous bodily harm".

With Bob in hiding, the Salvation Army in Glencoe was able to conduct its services in the street almost without incident. Still, brickbats thrown from the crowd of onlookers struck two of the soldiers, Samuel Squires and Kenneth McKenzie.

Eventually Bob Donnelly, still in hiding, surreptitiously contacted his brother, the town constable, and asked him to try to settle the charges laid against him by Emma Rees. Will got in touch with Hutchinson. "The evidence is so strong against all and especially Bob," Hutchinson wrote Will,[2] "that there will be no difficulty in obtaining convictions in all the cases and I shall certainly press all to

the bitter end unless Bob and the lads will listen to reason and make the best amends in their power." He ended by telling Will he would drop all charges if the defendants would plead guilty to one charge and be punished accordingly. In addition, all must give security to keep the peace for twelve months.

When Will delivered this message, Bob and his cohorts balked at the offer. "I am sorry the young men are so stiff-necked," wrote Hutchinson to William Donnelly,[3] "I suppose it is due to their backers who have apparently more money than wit."

When cases of those who had been arrested came up, some of them did plead guilty but the others decided to defend. They retained the boorish defense counsel, Tom Essery. All were convicted. Meanwhile, Bob Donnelly remained at large. Finally, on February 22nd, 1886, Charles Hutchinson wrote to Will Donnelly:[4]

I had hoped you would have prevailed upon your brother to surrender. He can not surely expect to defy the law always.

Hutchinson concluded by saying that he now enclosed the warrants for the arrest of Bob and expected Will to do his duty as a county constable. He added:

I of course know that your brother is within reach, & that you can have no difficulty in doing as requested . . . I am sorry to be driven to this but there seems no alternative. Your brother has brought it on himself and you.

The letter resulted in quick action. William Donnelly arrested his brother and took him to Hutchinson's office. But they brought with them a letter from Emma Rees, which Will had taken the precaution of obtaining. It stated that she wished to have Bob dealt with leniently. He pleaded guilty and was accordingly fined five dollars and costs for disturbing the Army on January 14th. And upon his entering into a bond in the amount of $400 to be of good behavior for twelve months, all other charges were withdrawn. As the costs were $12, Bob

Donnelly got off with a payment of under twenty dollars.

The next day, however, Will Donnelly served a summons on Emma Rees issued by the Newbury magistrate, William J. Simpson, on the charge of assaulting young Daniel Thody. When she complained to the crown attorney, Hutchinson was angry. He advised her to appeal at once if convicted, especially as the trial was to be held before a justice of the peace who had previously shown animosity towards the members of the Army.

Then on Friday, February 26th, 1886, the case against John McIntyre and Duncan McDonald for disturbing the Army at Glencoe on January 27th came off before Squire Hannah in London. Bob Donnelly gave evidence for the defense and was cross-examined by county crown attorney Hutchinson as follows:[5]

> Q.—Are you the famous Bob Donnelly of Biddulph?
>
> A.—I am Robert Donnelly of Biddulph. There is no famous about it.
>
> Q.—Well, are you the infamous Bob Donnelly?
>
> A.—I am Robert Donnelly, but my character is as good as any one's here.
>
> Q.—How many times have you been convicted?
>
> A.—You have the books here. I cannot tell.
>
> Q.—Were you ever convicted of feloniously shooting Constable Evaretts [sic] of Biddulph?
>
> A.—Don't you know?
>
> Q.—It doesn't matter what I know. Answer the question.
>
> A.—I was convicted, but you had reason to know since that I was innocent.
>
> Q.—You were sentenced for that?
>
> A.—I got two years in the penitentiary, but got out for good conduct in 21 months.
>
> Q.—Did you get people to swear alibis for you?
>
> A.—No.
>
> Q.—Was your reputation good in Biddulph?
>
> A.—We always paid 100 cents on the dollar—that's the kind of people we were.
>
> Q.—Were you not compelled to leave—driven out of the township?
>
> A.—No.
>
> Q.— Have you not frequently disturbed the Army at Glencoe?
>
> A.—I have joined in the service. I would give $50 to have you see them one night; you would be disgusted with them.
>
> Q.—Were you not convicted of disturbing the Army?
>
> A.—I did plead guilty to one charge and others were dropped against me. A few dollars wouldn't go far in that crowd—pointing to the county constables.
>
> Q.—Were the defendants inside the ring?
>
> A.—I could not see whether they were or not.
>
> Q.—Did you have a buggy there that night?
>
> A.—No.
>
> Q.—Did you have a horse there?
>
> A.—Yes; I had a horse and cutter.
>
> Q.—Did you drive against or through the ranks to break them up?
>
> A.—Certainly I did not. I laughed and sang with them. I was trading horses with a man.
>
> Q.—And that's as true as all the rest you said?
>
> A.—Do you think I am perjuring myself?
>
> Mr. Hutchinson— I am convinced of it.

Hutchinson was not finished with Donnelly yet. In his closing argument to the magistrate, he stated:

> The defendants had the evidence of those who had been convicted of similar offences to that they were charged with, and the statements of that man of infamous character and world-wide notoriety, Robert Donnelly, of Biddulph, whose crimes were mainly responsible for the dragging down of the decent members of his family to the position of social outcasts, and were in a large degree responsible for their murder.

Those were strong words indeed by the county crown attorney. The defendants were convicted.

The case against Emma Rees for assaulting Daniel Thody came off in McRae's Hotel in Glencoe on Saturday, February 27th, 1886. Presiding over it was William J. Simpson of Newbury who had asked Nathaniel Currie of Glencoe to sit with him. On hand was a large crowd of spectators including Bob Donnelly, no doubt grinning from ear to ear. A lawyer named W. Horton,

McRae's Hotel, first building on the right, where one of the many trials of
Emma Rees took place.

who had not long before opened an office in Glencoe, prosecuted. Emma Rees, the defendant, did not have a lawyer.

The following will give the reader an idea of the flavor of the proceedings.[6] A witness, Charles Tom, testified, "Saw defendant collar George Riddell. She was quite on her muscle that night. Saw her choke Riddell." What immediately followed this answer, was reported thus:

> Miss Rees then appealed to the magistrate and asked to have the protection of the Court the same as if she were conducting the defense as counsel. She objected to Mr. Horton asking if she was on her muscle that night. She did not consider the question a respectable one.
> Mr. Horton—There is such a thing as muscular Christianity.

Again, when another witness for the prosecution, Duncan McDonald, was on the stand the questioning went thus:

> Duncan McDonald - . . . Thody is not a bad sort of coon. I don't think he'd strike a lady at least.
> Mr. Horton—Perhaps he would rather kiss a lady than slap her?
> Witness—I suppose so, but I don't know how it would be with Salvation Army lasses. I think he would rather not.

The report does not say so, but one can imagine the guffaws these questions and answers would have elicited from Robert Donnelly. Then Bob himself took the stand and his testimony was reported as follows:

> Robert Donnelly—Remember the night the Army was in front of Rockett's store, January 21st. Was in the crowd. Am pretty near always there. Saw Emma Rees there. I'll never forget her. Saw Thody. He was standing 4 or 5 feet from me. Emma Rees and Thody were about two feet from each other. I think Thody was standing on her left. There was a great many tapping Miss Rees that night. Thody did not tap her that I saw. Saw her slap Thody on the face. Could not hear the noise; was enjoying myself too well.

The questionable defense which Emma Rees decided upon was to deny the blow altogether. Not surprisingly, it failed. The magistrates not only imposed a fine of $2 and costs of $11.45 or fifteen days in jail, but refused to accept bail to allow her to appeal. Constable William Donnelly carted her off to the London jail. Within an hour of her landing there, Charles Hutchinson learned of her incarceration. Furious at Magistrates Simpson and Currie, he had her released immediately. Advising Rees to sue for damages, he wrote to them wondering where they had obtained their "antiquated law" and told them they would live to regret their bad judgment. And in the end, they did, but more on that later.

In the meantime, Bob Donnelly's charge against Constable Brown for shooting at him came up before County Judge Elliot in February 1886. At the end, although he warned the constable not to repeat the action, the judge found him not guilty. In March, the Glencoe council passed a by-law prohibiting "the ringing of bells, blowing of horns, shouting and other unusual noises, or noises calculated to disturb the inhabitants of the village." The ringing of church bells or the village bell was excepted.

Things remained relatively quiet in Glencoe for several weeks, save for a few small disturbances such as the old trick of sprinkling of hot pepper on the stove during the Army's indoor services. It was probably a prank such as this at which fifteen-year-old Billy Cochrane was caught. Emma Rees told Hutchinson she did not wish to prosecute the lad because of his youth. Nevertheless, the crown attorney wrote him a letter warning him to leave the Salvation Army alone or he would "act harshly" against him. The letter read in part:[7]

> Don't let Bob Donnelly or anyone else get you into trouble. They will be willing enough to do so, & won't care how much trouble you get into so long as they are not caught themselves.

In the spring the Salvation Army found new premises on the main street when the milliner vacated her rented shop two or three doors north of the McKellar House and relet the premises to the Army. It was a big mistake. Occupying the upstairs room in the building was Dr. Edward A. Blackwell, the young veterinary surgeon from Napanee who had graduated from the Ontario Veterinary College in 1878 and set up business in Glencoe. He had quickly become a crony of Robert and William Donnelly who often called on him for professional services in connection with their business of horse-breeding.

The Army took possession of its new premises in May. Within a matter of days on a Saturday night, the front window of the new barracks was smashed in. The following night the place was again broken into and this time[8]

> The Cadet's trunk carried off and deposited on the track, about half a mile west of the station, in such a position that the first train coming along would smash it to pieces.

Although the night switchman discovered it in time to save it from destruction, letters and

papers from the trunk were scattered along the track.

What happened next must have been felt by the newspaper editor to be so abominable that no public report of the next three incidents was made. They involved the depositing during the night on three different occasions—each successive incident being more loathsome in its extent than the previous one—of human excrement in the new premises of the Salvation Army. First, Emma Rees and her cadet walked into the new barracks and discovered a quantity of human waste on the floor. They were sure the filth had been dropped down the stove pipe from Blackwell's room overhead. A few days later, someone threw in a quantity of excrement "sufficient to defile the walls as well as the floor".[9] A day or two after that, so much more dung had been flung in that it

The McKellar House is Glencoe's only hotel to survive as such to the present day.

seemed the contents of an entire outhouse had been deposited in the former millinery shop.

By this time Emma Rees was close to a nervous breakdown. She went to Hutchinson and laid charges against Blackwell on the grounds that he alone had access to the room upstairs. The newspaper first reported that this charge was against Robert Donnelly as well as the veterinarian but it later corrected its mistake. Obsessed with gathering evidence, Emma Rees could not bring herself

177

Tom Donnelly

The words are instructive. They make apparent that the views of the county crown attorney, so sympathetic to the Donnelly survivors during and immediately after the trials of the Biddulph vigilantes, and who acted at those times as almost a surrogate father to them, had come a long way. But in addition to those strong words, there was more. The letter continues:

> He and his brother Tom who was slain with the others, were the cause of all the trouble there, which terminated in that terrible tragedy.

Hutchinson had had a few years to think about it and there was now no doubt in his mind as to the real reason for the massacre of the Donnelly family. His letter goes on to show what insight he had got into the Biddulph affair:

> Unfortunately for Glencoe, Bob and his brother William, who also escaped, finding Biddulph too hot for them, settled in that hitherto quiet village & for some time lived there quietly, without attracting much attention. But the S.A. invaded the locality, and this proved too much for the restless spirit of Bob Donnelly. Why he should have felt constrained to molest these poor innocent people I can not say, but the fact is that he organized and led a gang of young roughs to disturb the S.A. religious services & to give the members of the Army every possible annoyance. They could obtain no protection in Glencoe. It was just as it used to be in Lucan. Well disposed people were afraid to interfere & the roughs had it all their own way.

to ordering a cleanup of the premises. Finally the board of health ordered it. Blackwell was convicted. When he appealed, Charles Hutchinson felt compelled to write on June 25th, to the deputy attorney general in Toronto:[10]

> I enclose a letter from Miss Emma Rees Captn of the S.A. at Glencoe. It refers to the last of a series of outrages more or less abominable, which have been committed by a party of roughs at Glencoe headed by the notorious Bob Donnelly, who one might almost properly say "unhappily" escaped the massacre of the family in Biddulph some few years ago.

In order to try to put an end to the persecutions, Hutchinson procured the services of a detective named J. W. Foster. He went to Glencoe covertly to try to find evidence but in about a week returned almost empty-handed. The crown attorney forwarded his meagre report to Toronto with the following commentary:[11]

> These Donnellys are the survivors of the famous Donnelly family of Biddulph, the only two [*sic*] remaining, & unfortunately as full of mischief as ever. They are following precisely the same course that led to the celebrated Biddulph murders in which all the other members of the family were murdered. Such

was the public feeling in Middlesex, that it was found impossible to obtain the conviction of the murderers, notwithstanding the clearest evidence, direct & circumstantial.

Again, after a few years' reflection and experience, there seemed little doubt in the mind of the county crown attorney as to where the blame principally lay for the Donnelly massacre.

In September 1886, Emma Rees, having been given a leave of absence to recuperate from a nervous breakdown, left Glencoe for good. Before she left, however, on Hutchinson's advice she sued the JPs Simpson and Currie. The case dragged on for many months but she proved dogged in her pursuit of justice. Goodspeed's *History of the County of Middlesex* published in 1889 summarized the final outcome starting at page 556:

> In May, 1887, the case of Emma Rees . . . against Justices Simpson and Currie, was carried to the assize court,—charges being unlawful arrest, and improper or malicious imprisonment. The action was dismissed without costs. Later the case was carried before the Queen's Bench at Toronto, where an order for a new trial was entered. This lady lieutenant won her suit, the original judgment costing the local justices about $700.

Emma Rees continued her work with the Salvation Army at various postings in Ontario. One of the Glencoe soldiers, Edward Skill, followed her and in 1892 they were married in Chicago, Illinois. Later still, they settled down in Toronto and raised a family of at least five children. Emma may have had a break with the Army in later years and did not often talk of her days in Glencoe but on a rare occasion she did tell her daughter Grace that as a young woman she had "had trouble with a certain bad family" but she did not mention the family's name. She died in Toronto in 1946.

A new captain, Grace Hill, replaced Emma Rees in Glencoe. Cadet Carrie Misener married a young and prosperous Glencoite and fellow Salvationist named William Rockett and settled down to married

life. And not only did the Salvation Army begin to build new barracks in the village, they obtained from a judge in Toronto a decision which pronounced that they had every right to beat their drums on the street

Charles Hutchinson, who eventually came to realize the lengths to which the Donnellys would go in pursuit of their ends.

notwithstanding the by-law of the local municipality. News of the judgment apparently did not reach the ears of the Glencoe constable, William Donnelly, for shortly after, in the first week of December that year he confronted the Army which[12]

> Undertook to "raise the dead" . . . —those being the words they shouted as they sailed down the street with coat tails flying and drums beating—but the dead did not raise—oh, no! The living, however, did not relish the racket . . . .

When Constable Donnelly arrested Richard Thompson, one of the Army soldiers, the new captain Grace Hill, interfered. Thereupon the constable's brother, Robert Donnelly, came to his rescue.

179

The Donnelly brothers hustled the two members of the Army down the street and into the lock-up.

A newly appointed justice of the peace named Wilson quickly tried the defendants, holding the hearing in one of the Glencoe hotels. Although the occasion was one of fun and merriment for the likes of Bob Donnelly, the venue did not sit well with the newspaper reporter, who complained:[13]

> Crowding into a small room, making the atmosphere fetid and almost stifling—where prisoner, witness and spectator are jumbled together in a confused mass, inhaling the foul breath of the tobacco chewer, and it may be having the mind poisoned with the vulgar remarks of some half-drunken spectator, whom it is impossible to point out in a crowd . . . .

Emma Rees, in later years.

Richard Thompson was found guilty and fined but "the lady captain, who was charged with interfering with officer Donnelly while making the arrest, was also taken before the Squire, but was acquitted as the evidence did not prove the charge."

The matter did not rest there, however, as the Army now laid charges of assault against the Donnelly brothers.[14] It was alleged that the defendants had grasped Thompson and the woman very rudely.

In December "the Grand Jury returned a true bill against Robert and William Donnelly for assault and a second bill against Robert Donnelly upon a similar indictment." The first case against both brothers was tried before a jury in mid-December. For the defense,[15]

> it was contended that the Army was occupying the whole of the sidewalk pushing other people off and otherwise disturbing the peace, for which they were arrested by the defendants, and that no unnecessary violence was used towards Thompson or the woman.

The newspaper reported that in his charge to the jury, the county court judge William Elliot "spoke strongly against the accused, but the jury did not see it that way and returned a verdict of not guilty."[16]

The second charge against Robert Donnelly alone was put over to the next sessions. Eventually, before the case came on, the crown attorney agreed to allow Bob to enter into a recognizance to appear when called upon and that was the end of the matter.[17] Thus concluded Bob Donnelly's campaign against the Salvation Army in Glencoe.

Chapter 26

The Prodigal's Return

For well over a hundred years Lucanites resented the association of their village with the Donnellys. Most respectable Lucanites despised the family for bringing ill-fame to the village by their shenanigans while they were alive. As far as they were concerned, the Donnellys were a fringe family who had little to do with the important affairs of the place.

Mabel Stanley was born in 1878, daughter of the justice of the peace, William Stanley, who had many dealings with the Donnellys. She put it this way in a letter she wrote in 1963:[1]

> Who the H---- is this Kelley? . . . I resent the attitude he takes that the whole of Lucan were terrorized. The village people of the right sort, or as Sarah Turner the negro used to put it, "De Quality" meaning the Armitages, the Stanleys, the O'Neils, the Foxes, the McCosh's, Hodgins, Atkinsons and dozen more families, went about their business as usual, and if the Donnelly gang tried anything they were promptly put in their place by plain language.

The mill, photographed here about 1897, was built to replace the one lost in Lucan's first "reign of terror" in 1877. It, too, burned down.

Before the tragedy, the notoriety that the Donnellys brought to the village was confined to southwestern Ontario, but with their murders it spread nation-wide. When the newspapermen descended upon the village flinging their notebooks and prying questions in all directions, many Lucanites recoiled in exasperation. Upon a journalist approaching Big Bernard Stanley in his store on Main Street, the shopkeeper lashed out. "We've done this thing ourselves," he said, "And we want none of you London reporters or police to come out here and blackguard our town again."[2]

Along with other villagers, Big Bernard felt strongly that the notorious Donnellys were not part of Lucan at all. It is true that for the few short years they ran their stagecoach line out of the village, several of the boys boarded within its limits and a couple of them even brought their child brides to live there. But they did not stay long. William Donnelly himself lived for only short periods of time in the village. Although after the second trial of Carroll, all three of the brothers were found residing in Lucan, they soon departed. By 1882 all of them had left: Will for Ohio, Pat for Thorold and Bob for Glencoe.

Ten years later, the return of Bob Donnelly to the Lucan area raises questions about the coincidence of the second great fire period in the village. Although the townsfolk called each period—perhaps with some exaggeration—a reign of terror, their descendants have sometimes confused the two. The first occurred during the height of the stagecoach wars. In roughly the first half of 1877, suspected arsonists destroyed Sylvanus Gibson's woodworking mill, James Byron Hodgins' blacksmith and wagon shop, Pieper &

Hogg's flax mill, James Maloney's wagon shop, Judge and Cook's blacksmith and wagon shop, the stables of the Central Hotel and the Fitzhenry Hotel in its entirety.

The second reign of terror occurred shortly after the return of Bob Donnelly from Glencoe. Fire seemed to follow Bob wherever he went. During his ten-year sojourn in Glencoe, which is dealt with in previous chapters , Bob had two fires: the first destroyed one of his two houses and the other a year later his stables.

The 1890s reign of terror by fire in Lucan began with an incident reported by the local newspaper in November 1892 within a short time of Bob's arrival:[3]

> Postmaster Porte, of Lucan, seems to have one enemy in that place; that is, if the fire in the stable attached to the house was the work of an incendiary a few nights ago.

The blaze was discovered before it could do much damage but the event did not augur well for the future. In March, stables belonging to the Western Hotel on William Street burned to the ground. The hotel was then being operated by John Whelan.[4] Although two horses and a cow died in the 1893 blaze, the villagers were able to turn out in force to save the hotel itself and other nearby buildings. Whelan's loss was said to be a thousand dollars; his insurance covered only $150. The fire had been set deliberately.

Bob Donnelly soon settled into the homestead and set about raising sheep. His forty ewes gave birth to seventy lambs in April that year. "Strange to say," a news item reported,[5] "one of the ewes had a fine lamb [and] fourteen days afterwards she gave birth to twins, which are living and doing well." In June, Thomas Simpson of Mooresville sheared the wool off fifty sheep on the farm.

Then on August 22, 1893, fire destroyed the Royal Hotel[6] at the corner of Main and Water Streets in Lucan along with the residence, stables and outbuildings of a Mrs. Brown. The following month a fire burned down a small unoccupied building in the rear

Bob Donnelly, from an 1880 souvenir card in the author's possession.

of the premises owned by Patrick McIlhargey on the main street. This time the fire brigade rushed out and confined the flames to the building itself. Though it was of little value, the newspaper report stated that because of its close proximity to the stables and driving house of the Queen's Hotel[7]

> It was almost by a miracle that a terrible conflagration in the business portion of the village was prevented.

On an early morning in January 1894, fire destroyed the butcher shop of Downing Brothers and the veterinary office of Doctor Tennant.[8] Although there was doubt about the cause of this fire, there was no doubt about another that same day. Someone deliberately set fire to the stable of George Hodgins. A week later the stable of Sam McLean on Frank Street suffered the same fate. While McLean was able to rescue a pair of cows from the burning building, two horses died in the flames.[9]

Thomas A. Webb, the baker, lost two horses in Lucan's second "reign of terror" in the 1890s.

the usual weekly fire occurred. This time the barn and stables of Mr. Chisholm were destroyed by fire at the hands of an incendiary.

In December that year, the stables of the Western Hotel burned down again. The guests of a party in progress at the hotel lost their harness in the flames but managed to save their horses.[14] Then, just before Christmas, Constable John Bawden thought he had the culprits. He arrested four young men and brought them before justices of the peace, Armitage and O'Neil, who committed them for arson. Although the four spent the holidays in London jail, they were discharged when no evidence against them could be worked up.[15]

In 1895 there were two big fires, both deliberately set. The first in January consumed the elevator and store house of R. S. Hodgins containing 5,000 bushels of barley.[16] The second in July destroyed the grain warehouse of Stanley and Dight.[17] Then came a couple of smaller fires the following year in which a former photograph gallery was damaged and a few weeks later entirely consumed.[18] The building was owned by the widow of the late Albert Goodacre. The fire brigade managed to save Charles Haskett's adjoining furniture warerooms and Leonard Fox's drygoods store and dwelling house.

Then in July 1896 the driving sheds and new stables of the Central Hotel again burned to the ground. Alex McFalls, the new hotel proprietor, lost a new buggy and a cutter along with some harness, robes, oats and hay. The village baker, Thomas A. Webb, had been renting a stable room from McFalls and lost two horses although the Lucan fire

Alarmed, the village council offered a $500 reward for the detection of the firebugs and assigned eight or more special night watchmen to patrol the streets.[10] The night patrols, however, could not prevent the burning down of the stables of the Central Hotel in the middle of February. The proprietor, Robert McLean, managed to rescue the horses from the flames.[11] Not long after, the long-time hotel proprietor decided he was too old to live through another reign of terror in Lucan. He leased the business and retired to Michigan.

A few weeks later the newspaper reported:[12]

About 10:15 p.m. last Thursday night Mr. Hawkshaw was attracted to his stable by seeing a blaze resembling a candle under the corner. He discovered a ball of rags saturated with coal oil burning. It had set fire to the boards around. One pail of water put out what might have swept away a third of the town. A reward of $600 is offered for the scoundrel who did this.

Fires continued throughout the summer. The Lucan correspondent for the Exeter *Times* wrote:[13]

If things continue as in the past, Lucan will soon pass from the scene. On Monday night

183

brigade was able to save his adjoining bakery.[19] The fire also singed but did not destroy William Porte's stables and John Armitage's dwelling house. Lucan council again offered a reward for the conviction of the firebugs, this time set at $800. As events turned out, however, this second reign of terror had run its course.

Again, perhaps by coincidence, Bob Donnelly at this time leased out the homestead and returned to Glencoe. When inside of a couple of years he did come back to Lucan, he was to remain a resident of the village more or less permanently for the rest of his life. Upon his return, he decided to emulate his two surviving brothers by going into the hotel business. In 1901 he and his nephew Jim, the 22-year-old son of Mike, purchased the Western Hotel on William

Street.

Years later, I met Emma Mawson who worked for the Donnellys at the hotel when she was an eighteen-year-old. She had been employed by the McKees in Denfield and when they bought the Queen's Hotel in Lucan, she said, she came over with them. When a disagreement terminated the relationship, however, she went over to await the train to take her back to her home in McGillivray Township. She stopped only for a quick meal at the Western which, because it stood almost across from the train depot, was sometimes known as the Station Hotel. A few days later, young Jim Donnelly came to her home in a buggy. They needed help in the dining room, he explained, and offered to take her back to Lucan if she would work for them. Emma agreed, went back with young

The Western Hotel at the west end of William Street was purchased by Bob Donnelly and his nephew, James Michael, in 1901. They sold it to John McFalls, shown here seated at the front door, in 1905.

184

Jim and stayed with the Donnellys for two years.

Bob Donnelly and his wife Annie proved to be kind employers. They kept a watchful eye on Emma and the other young woman who worked with her in the hotel. If the girls went out to fetch water from the pump which stood in front of the building and remained too long in conversation with the young men of the village who gathered there, Bob would wave them back in.

"We're running a respectable place," he told them. "We won't have you wagging your tongues with the boys."

As was the custom in those years, Bob, Annie and Jim lived in the hotel along with the hired help. On a Sunday, Bob and his wife would take Emma out for a drive. After stopping at the graveyard beside St. Patrick's church, they would drive north along the Roman Line.

"They showed me the farm where Bob's parents were killed," she told me, "and there was a big flat stone at what had been the front door where one of the brothers had died. Bob was just about my height, five foot and eight inches or so, with an average build, wavy hair and good looking. He could not bend the little finger on one hand. And he would get very agitated when any of the Tooheys or Ryders came into the hotel, walking back and forth in the hallway, very tense but saying nothing."

A couple of others who knew Bob Donnelly in those days were Harold B. Hodgins and Harry Clinton Ryan. I met the former in London, the latter in Toronto. Each confirmed that Bob had indeed permanently injured the little finger in his right hand but, according to Ryan, he had sustained the injury in a fight with a son of one of the vigilantes.

After about four years in the hotel business, the Donnellys sold the Western Hotel to John McFalls in 1905 and moved into a little white frame house on south Main Street. Many stories are told of Robert Donnelly's later life in Lucan. For example,

as the former members of the Peace Society of Biddulph who remained in the community one by one died, he is said to have attended each of their funerals and was the first to throw a shovelful of dirt upon the coffin. At the same time he would mutter, "There goes another of the bastards to hell."

Sophia McIlhargey knew Bob Donnelly well in those days. She and her parents had always been on good terms with the family. The McIlhargeys showed me a ring and watch chain which Bob had given Sophia's brother, Zackariah. Sophia often told the story of Bob rushing out of church as soon as the Sunday mass was about to finish and scurrying across the road to the sheds where the parishioners had left their buggies and horses. Bob would be waiting as the rest of the churchgoers filed out. Just as one of the marked men of the Peace Society was crossing the road, he would start up his horses and drive them furiously at the startled man, reining in the horses only within inches of the discomfited victim.

Sophia's niece, Catherine, told me of another incident which occurred at one of the annual St. Patrick's Church picnics. Towards the end of the day, someone asked who was going to take the priest back to the rectory. Another answered, "Oh, Bob Donnelly said he would look after that."

Old Martin McLaughlin, standing nearby with his son, said, "Oh, we can get somebody better than that." Bob Donnelly was not far off in the crowd and overheard the old man. He thereupon accosted McLaughlin and directed a volley of oaths at him, accusing him of being a murderer and cursing him to the day of his death.

As the young McLaughlin accompanied his father out the gate, the son turned to his father and asked him, "Dad, did you have to take that from Donnelly?"

Old McLaughlin's silence and bowed head told the son what he had long suspected. He left his father's home and never returned.

James Collisson was born in Biddulph in 1875. His family, too, was always on good terms with the Donnellys. Collisson became a lawyer and practiced law for many years in Edmonton, Alberta from where he wrote of the following incident during his youthful days in Biddulph and Lucan:[20]

> One day I was getting my mail in the post office and a young fellow who was waiting on me, who knew me, threw me out a post card and told me to read the back. I turned it over and written in red was, "Dear Mr. — when you go to church on Sunday and bless yourself with your bloody hand, think of the poor Donnellys who you sent to their death without any chance

of repentance."

The card was, of course, addressed to one of the vigilantes and was written either by Robert or Patrick Donnelly or, more likely, one of the latter's children. Many similar stories are told of the brothers' anger.

On June 15th, 1908, Bob Donnelly's final sojourn in Lucan was interrupted by his committal to the London Insane Asylum. Harold Hodgins said he got "weak in his mind" but stories within the family have it that his nephew was afraid he would do his

Bob Donnelly and his wife Annie lived out their final years in this little white frame house which still stood on the Main Street of Lucan when we first visited the village in 1964.

wife harm. One morning Annie awoke with her husband's hands around her throat. "Now look," Jim told her, "he is going to kill you, or at least hurt you. We have got to do something." Jim Donnelly therefore had his uncle committed. The asylum authorities diagnosed his condition as melancholia. They kept him for over a year, finally releasing him on October 30th, 1909. Bob Donnelly returned to Lucan and once in a while relapsed into a depression when he might disappear for a day or two. He died in his little white frame house on Main Street on June 14th, 1911.

His brother Patrick came from the Niagara Peninsula to bury Bob. Shortly after the funeral, Pat wrote to the Lucan *Sun* as follows:[21]

> Permit me . . . to extend my sincere thanks to the citizens of Lucan and surrounding country for the respect and sympathy shown at the death and burial of my deceased brother . . . . I assure you I dearly love the land of my

birth—with all its faults I love it still.

> When I looked around and saw the vast concourse of people of every walk of life—clergymen of different denominations, doctors, lawyers and merchants—I arrived at the conclusion that those who are left as well as the departed ones must without a doubt retain the respect of the whole community at large in the misfortune that has befallen them.

Robert Donnelly was buried in St. Patrick's churchyard on the Roman Line. Eight years later when his wife died, however, her last will directed her executor[22]

> To remove the remains of my deceased husband Robert Donnelly from the grave yard, at St. Patrick's Church, in the Township of Biddulph, and to re-inter the said remains in St. Peter's Roman Catholic Cemetery, in the City of London . . . .

The executor was Robert's nephew, James Michael Donnelly, described in the last will as a hotel-keeper in Kincardine. Annie Currie Donnelly also directed that

> The caskets of my said husband and myself shall be enclosed in steel shells . . . .

These instructions were complied with and Robert Donnelly and his wife, Annie, now lie in St. Peter's Cemetery in London, the plot also containing the remains of James Michael Donnelly and William Donnelly's older daughter Jo-Anna.

Bob Donnelly was buried the second time under this stone at St. Peter's Cemetery, London.

Chapter 27

Grandma Bell

The two earliest hostelries of Biddulph were kept by black Americans of African descent. The blacks, escaped slaves or descendants of slaves, formed the first permanent settlement of the land of Biddulph. They came in about the year 1829. The founder of the settlement was a charismatic black man, himself escaped from slavery, named Israel Lewis. From Cincinnati, Ohio, he led a group of five or six families—joined by about ten more families from Boston—to the then recently opened Huron Tract in Upper Canada. Here the group entered into a bargain with Thomas Mercer Jones of the Canada Company to purchase the entire Township of Biddulph with the intent of distributing its lots to blacks fleeing from the United States. Only 956 acres, however, were actually taken up by deed, and were parceled out in portions of 25 and 50 acres to the various black families scattered along the London-Goderich Road running from the Sauble River to the London-Biddulph townline.

The road from London to Goderich was then but a trail through the forest marked with blazes by the axemen in the party of John McDonald, the land surveyor of the Canada Company. When in 1831 James Ingersoll took up the contract to clear that section of the road, he hired the blacks in Biddulph to cut the line through the bush. After completing that job, they cleared on their own contract another six miles. Then they went back to clearing the woods on their original parcels around their humble hewed log cabins set helter-skelter in the little glades with their exterior chimneys of clay and slats.

Soon after its founding, Austin Steward, a well-educated and idealistic one-time slave himself, visited the black colony, as he called it. On the very day he arrived, he persuaded a meeting of the settlers to name the place Wilberforce after the great English proponent of the abolition of slavery. Later in that same year of 1830, Steward moved his family in. He attempted to take charge of the settlement which he saw needed guidance. A board of directors with Steward as president dispatched Nathaniel Paul and Israel Lewis to England and the United States respectively for the purpose of raising funds for the education of the children of the settlement. Both trips turned out worse than useless.

Lewis transformed his crusade into a pleasure trip, sending back funds not to the board but to his confidant, Benjamin Paul, for his own private purposes. Steward described the latter as "a friend [of Lewis] wearing the sacred garb of a minister of the gospel" who on one occasion attempted to bribe Steward with a promise of $250 "out of the collections for the colony".[1] Furthermore, wrote Steward, whenever Benjamin Paul made a trip to the States, Israel Lewis and his family

commissioned [him] to purchase a long list of expensive articles, which the poor colonists were seldom able to buy; and he generally returned to them richly laden with goods, purchased with money given to the poor, sick, and destitute in the colony.[2]

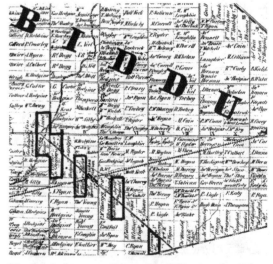

The lots in heavy outline on this 1862 map, along the London-Goderich Road near the later site of Lucan, were the only ones that the Canada Company transferred to the Wilberforce blacks.

188

Salome Squawker, wife of the first Peter Butler, appears to have been the only one of the original black settlers to have been photographed.

one occasion Lewis attempted to kill him by trying to ambush him in McConnell's Dismal Swamp while on his return from London. The swamp he referred to was in the immediate vicinity of McConnell's tavern near the intersection of the London-Goderich Road and the town line between Biddulph and London Townships, part of the great cedar swamp stretching into the ninth concession of Biddulph after which the Irish Catholics named their Cedar Swamp Schoolhouse a decade or so later.

Steward described Lewis as "the founder of the Wilberforce colony" and a man, though born into slavery, of prepossessing personal appearance and a "manner and address easy and commanding". He possessed a high intellect, taught himself to read and write and became an eloquent speaker. But, according to Steward, he could not govern his animal passions and turned his considerable gifts to avarice, pride and ambition. He eventually left Wilberforce and died a pauper in a Montreal hospital.

Austin Steward probably opened the first hostelry in Biddulph. How it happened is best described in his own words:[4]

> From the time I first settled in Wilberforce, my house had ever been open to travelers and strangers, but a conversation I happened to overhear, led me to take a course different from what had been at first intended. I was at a public house about twenty miles from home, when I heard the landlord advising his guest to eat heartily, for, said he, "you will find nothing more worthy of your attention, until you reach Wilberforce. When you arrive at that settlement, inquire for A. Steward, from the States, and he will give you a meal fit for a prince." I began to reflect on the subject and concluded, inasmuch as people would send company to me, it would be better to make some preparation for entertaining them. I had plenty of furniture, and all I needed was a larger supply of food, to commence keeping a tavern. This was easily obtained, and I opened a public house which was well patronized.

Nathaniel Paul who had been dispatched to England did not much better. He returned with no funds but with a lengthy claim against the settlement for expenses incurred on his trip. He also brought back his new white English bride and set her up in his one-roomed log house in Wilberforce. Steward describes meeting her as follows:[3]

> . . . we were immediately ushered into the presence of Mrs. Nathaniel Paul, whom we found in an inner apartment, made by drawn curtains, carpeted in an expensive style, where she was seated like a queen in state,—with a veil floating from her head to the floor; a gold chain encircling her neck, and attached to a gold watch in her girdle; her fingers and person sparkling with costly jewelry. Her manners were stiff and formal, nor was she handsome, but a tolerably fair looking woman, of about thirty years of age; and this was the wife of our agent for the poor Wilberforce colony!

Israel Lewis had also returned without funds for Wilberforce. He and Steward were soon at loggerheads. Steward claimed that on

The Wilberforce settlement languished, however, when the Irish Protestants poured in and surrounded its lands. Then, on the

189

Austin Steward, born a slave but freed by his mistress, on the very day of his arrival in the little black settlement inspired the inhabitants to name it Wilberforce.

Kelley wrote of Old Jim Donnelly and three of his sons, John, Mike and Tom, riding their horses up to the little log house of Grandma Bell. Kelley describes her as a centenarian teacup reader and states in his careless way that she was the last of the colored colony which had settled in Biddulph many years before.

"I see blood on the moon," Grandma Bell tells Mr. Donnelly and his boys when they insisted on her telling them their future, "I see death, Mr. Donnelly, death for you, death for your wife and sons here! I see death for all of you—soon and terrible!"

Turning from fancy to something more factual, there was indeed a Grandma Bell in Biddulph at the time of the Donnellys and she was reputed in 1876 to be 104 years of age. Her name was Rosanna and she was the widow of William Bell. Bell was the other tavernkeeper of the black settlement of Wilberforce and one of the blacks whose barns, stacks of grain and stock were burned back in 1848.

When Rosanna Bell died in November, 1878, she may well have been the last of the original black settlers. But she was then not yet a centenarian but only 87 years old. The scene by Kelley—right out of the American Wild West—never happened at all but Kelley's writing of it puts him at his pulp-fiction best.

William and Rosanna Bell's tavern at the Sauble and Austin Steward's at or near the site of Lucan were but a distant memory when in 1982 my wife and I travelled there not only to experience but to participate in the greatest country fair that ever came to Old Biddulph. The week-long event, called the International Plowing Match, had never before been held in the township. To accommodate it, temporary streets were laid out in the countryside on the outskirts of Lucan village. The entire site covered an area of over one hundred acres with dozens of huge tents, acres and acres of farm machinery, agricultural displays, demonstrations and enclosure after enclosure

night of October 9th, 1848, some of the white settlers burned the barns and crops of three of the blacks, Ephraim Taylor, Daniel Turner and William Bell. Government rewards for capture of the perpetrators were offered but there were no takers. Friction between the blacks and the white settlers continued to the extent that the Sauble Hill was jokingly referred to as Bunker's Hill. When the Canada Company refused outright to sell them any more lands, most of the black families eventually drifted away and the settlement shrank. A few like the Butlers remained, however, and as a result there are descendants of the Wilberforce colony living in Lucan to this day.

In Chapter 13 entitled *Blood on the Moon* in the book *The Black Donnellys*, Thomas P.

of farm animals. Several hundred thousands of visitors were expected.

Longtime reeve of Lucan, Ivan Hearn, told me himself that when the ploughing match was being planned months in advance, the officers of the event came to a meeting with the local officials. They laid out their enthusiastic plans for the naming of the streets: Donnelly Avenue, Vigilante Boulevard, and so on. The local officials were horrified. They would have none of that, they said, and there was no further mention of the Donnelly story as far as the official International Ploughing Match was concerned.

My wife and I, however, had arranged in advance for a little bookstand in one of the tents along with a small display of Donnelly artifacts and photographs. Our little display was the only sign in evidence at the ploughing match that the community had anything to do with the Donnellys. On each successive day the numbers of persons who stopped at our little display grew larger and larger. As I expected, a great many of those claimed a distant relationship to the Donnellys. One young boy aged ten said he was a seventh cousin. There were also several genuine informants. Others who stopped bore names which I knew belonged to the Catholic Settlement of Biddulph. One day two elderly ladies of the Ryder family stood in front of the display and held a quiet but earnest conversation. "Mother wouldn't have liked this," said one. I said nothing but knew that their mother was Mary Ryder. Mary had

Behind the classical portico and brick veneer of this little building which stood on the Main Street of Lucan until 1965 was said, by good authority, to be the original log schoolhouse of the Wilberforce blacks.

191

been at the Keefe wedding celebration in January on the night that the barns of her father, Grouchy Ryder, burned and which started the train of events that led to the massacre of the Donnellys about three weeks later.

Some viewers expressed surprise that the Donnelly story had finally come out of the closet, so to speak, and put on display in public. "When did they open this up?" was an expression heard a few times that week. And one young fellow came up in a belligerent manner and demanded to know if we had got permission from the township authorities to do this.

Several individuals from a distance volunteered the information that the only attraction that had drawn them to the plowing match at all was the Donnelly story. Most of them were surprised to find on their arrival in Lucan that there was no museum. And they could not believe that the congregation of St. Patrick's Parish was at that very time planning to raze the old church.

If the International Ploughing Match brought thousands to Lucan, it recalled another event almost a hundred years earlier that also attracted a huge crowd to the village. This was the visit of the Prime Minister of Canada, John A. Macdonald, on December 16th 1886. The old warrior in his waning years had taken the train to make one last journey across the country he had helped to create.

He eventually arrived at Lucan. Everybody of importance in the village and township was on the temporary platform in the Drill Shed to see little Ida Porte present the Grand Old Man of the Conservative Party with a bouquet of flowers. On that platform stood several members of the Peace Society of Biddulph including James Toohey, Martin McLaughlin and Patrick J. Dewan. And one of the speakers was Jim Carroll's old friend, Timothy Coughlin, still member of parliament for the riding of North Middlesex.

During the proceedings the makeshift grandstand broke down, sending the spectators sprawling in all directions. Because everyone was bundled up in winter greatcoats, no one was much hurt. Old John A. was wildly cheered, for Conservatism had reigned supreme in Lucan and Biddulph ever since the acquittal of Carroll for the murder of Judith Donnelly. According to local wisdom, William Ralph Meredith, as one of the defense counsel as well as leader of the provincial Conservatives, made Liberals or Reformers in the riding anathema for generations.

James Collisson, the Biddulph Old Boy who became a lawyer in Edmonton, wrote:[5]

> . . . Carroll was brought up again . . . this time he was defended by William Meredith . . . who was then head of the Orange Order, and this Jury acquitted him. Every Juryman was challenged except Orangemen. For years afterwards no Liberal or Reformer could get a vote in Biddulph, as they claimed the Conservatives saved him.

And, went the oft-repeated platitude: "Why, you could get a dog elected in North Middlesex after the second Carroll trial, so long as it was a Conservative."

Our little booth at the International Plowing Match at Lucan was the only sign of the Donnellys in 1982.

Chapter 28

Tavern Stories

While Will Donnelly once referred to Lucan as "the village of saints", outside wags would irreverently refer to it as Lucifer. Thanks to the vivid imaginations of those outsiders it remains, after all, a haunted place. Ghosts of the Peace Society can easily be conjured up and be seen to walk its sidewalks. Did I just then almost catch a fleeting glimpse of the long black-robed frame of John Connolly drawing up his arm to hide the Roman collar around his neck and casting a guilty glance back as he flitted around a corner?

If the ghosts of the Donnellys haunt Lucan, they would be to my mind especially palpable on the sites of their favorite retreats—the old hotels and taverns of the place. There were, after all, at least ten such

hotels although few have survived to the present day. What happened to William Madill's old British Hotel, Henry and Leonard Hodgins' old Lucan House, Charlie McRoberts' old Dominion, William Walker's Maddock House, John Carroll's Royal, Alex McFall's Queen's, Bob McLean's Central, Hugh McPhee's Revere, Sam Flannery's Dublin House, William McLaughlin's Australia House and Joseph Fitzhenry's tavern?

When we first visited the village, the Queen's and the Central hotels still stood brooding over the main street. The Queen's was one of the favorite haunts of the Donnellys, especially after Fitzhenry's burned down, whereas the Central was the one they probably had the least to do with. Its longtime owner, Robert McLean, was as respectable as a tavernkeeper could be in that Victorian age. He frowned on Catholic patrons, especially the more disreputable ones like the Donnellys. That, of course, did not prevent Hugh McKinnon's earlier

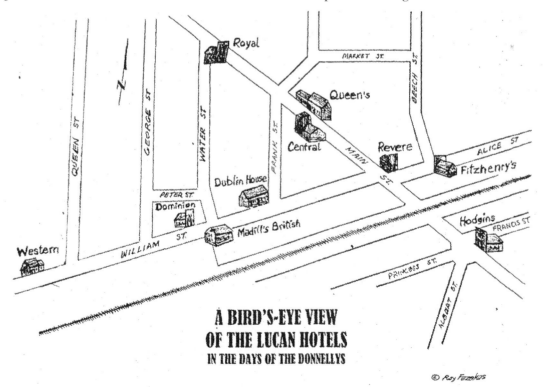

A BIRD'S-EYE VIEW
OF THE LUCAN HOTELS
IN THE DAYS OF THE DONNELLYS

© Ray Fazakas

At least seven of the hotels shown in this sketch were operating in the 1870s.

193

vigilante group holding Mike Donnelly prisoner for a few days in one of its rear second-storey bedrooms.

The old Central finally died in a fire in our day. Its brooding hulk stood staring bleakly out on the street for two years more before it was finally demolished to ground level in 1997. Before the Central burned, its then owner gave me a grand tour of the place from top to bottom and as a keepsake allowed me to remove a small but ancient dresser from one of the rear bedrooms of the second storey. Now, the Donnelly Museum stands on its site.

The first of the several hotels in the village—aside from that of the blacks—appears from the records to have been Henry Hodgins' Lucan House, built on the corner of Main and Francis Streets, perhaps as early as the 1840s. It may have been originally of log but by 1861 was a storey and a half brick tavern. In 1863 Henry Hodgins sold the hotel to Leonard Hodgins who carried on until March of 1866 when the hotel burned down with almost all its contents. All that was saved were "two feather ticks".

William Madill's British Hotel was also one of the earliest. When I began looking into the Donnelly story, no one could tell me where it had stood. Investigation revealed that it sat on the south side of William Street on Lots 14 and 15, very near the station and close to siding tracks of the railway. On the night of Wednesday, February 8th, 1865 the hotel caught fire, apparently from the sparks of a nearby locomotive. Villagers rushed to the scene and managed to save half the furniture and the stables but the tavern itself burned to the ground. Some attributed the fire to a defective chimney in the bar-room but most blamed its too close proximity to the tracks. Madill resolved to rebuild and did so, but moved the location to the other side of the street at the west corner where it meets Frank Street. Madill had hardly opened at his new location, however, when he died. The hotel was closed for several months before being eventually taken over by George

William Walker built and for many years operated the Western Hotel near the railway station. He once had a row on the street with Tom Donnelly.

(Dublin) Hodgins who renamed it the Dublin House.

As with the early hostelries, many of the other buildings along the streets have been razed and rebuilt since Judith Donnelly trudged the hardwood planks that served as sidewalks in front of the shops. When I tried to discover where Lucan's old Dominion Hotel had stood, I learned that its site had disappeared into the mists of time. No one in Lucan had the faintest idea where it might have stood. Its exact location had to be dug out of the records. The Dominion was one of the three or four hotels strategically located on William Street to pick up passenger trade from the Grand Trunk station. It appears to have been built and continuously owned by one, Charlie McRoberts, although it was leased out to others at different times.[1] Located like its competitors near the railway station, I finally was able to place it at Lots 78 and 79 immediately east of Sylvanus Gibson's planing mill on William Street. For the last four or five years of its existence the village fathers, despite the fact that its owner was

Hugh McPhee was always on good terms with the Donnellys, who ran their stagecoach out of his stables at the rear of his tavern, the Revere House. His wife, Rebecca, was sister to William Walker of the Western Hotel.

serving on the council, refused to grant it a liquor license. As a result, liquor being at that time and for generations after the lifeblood of the tavern business, its clientele dwindled. Then at about half past two in the early morning of Friday, August 1st, 1879, the old Dominion burned to the ground.

Based on suspicion alone, Charlie McRoberts blamed the burning of the hotel on the Donnellys. There was no question he held a grudge against the family. Following the conviction of Bob Donnelly in the spring of 1878 for shooting at Constable Everett, McRoberts voted in council to pay the law firm of Becher, Street and Becher $20 for assisting in the prosecution of the case against Bob.[2] Why the grudge?

Will Donnelly in 1880 may have been referring to Charlie McRoberts when he said sarcastically:[3]

> About twenty-five years ago an Englishman moved in on a Canada Company lot adjoining Biddulph, and built a house upon it. A gentleman, who now uses more of the sidewalk in Lucan than he pays taxes for, coveted his farm, and took a gang of Biddulphers and threw a lot of trees on the house, smashing it to pieces and frightening the poor stranger so that he ran away with his life. This noted

bushwhacker then erected a shanty on the farm, and remained on it for a number of years, until the Canada Company put himself and his furniture, which amounted to a table and an ox-yoke, out on the road.

It is the reference to the sidewalk which suggests McRoberts may have been the person referred to. While the sidewalk in front of some of the stores on the main street of the village consisted merely of a pair of one-foot planks laid lengthwise, McRoberts had demanded a four-foot wide sidewalk at village expense in front of his home on Princess Street. The rest of the council, however, demurred. Charlie eventually compromised the matter by agreeing to pay for the labor as long as the village purchased the lumber and nails.

And as a juror on the inquest into the burning of Michael O'Connor's house in the village one night in April 1880, Charlie McRoberts proved less than impartial. Crown Attorney Charles Hutchinson wrote that McRoberts was especially hostile to the witnesses who attempted to state in their testimony that the burning had been arson. "He was quite offensive in his manner to the witnesses," Hutchinson wrote,[4] "cross-examining them in a manner to indicate his distrust of everything they said." And David McRoberts, Charlie's brother, not only gave evidence to the jury on this inquest but sat on it as well.

Robert Hill O'Neil was one of the important men of the district in its early days. He served for years as reeve of Biddulph. When Lucan was incorporated in 1872, he was the first reeve of the new village. Besides being a justice of the peace, he also opened the first bank. Although his attitude towards the Donnellys differed from that of the Stanleys, he was well connected to the latter family for he had married a sister of Bernard and William Stanley while his own sister had married their brother, Thomas W. Stanley.

The Donnellys usually found Robert Hill O'Neil especially obliging and a friend in need. A later newspaper account said of him:[5]

> During the years of trouble through which Lucan passed, Mr. O'Neil seems to have been able to keep the goodwill of the entire community notwithstanding the fact that most of his neighbours suffered in some way through the awful scourge of fire in which nearly every resident of the place had some of his buildings burned; Mr. O'Neil came out with a record of not a single fire . . .

Robert Hill O'Neil's brother-in-law, Big Bernard Stanley, was the grand potentate of all Lucan. As its most affluent citizen, he built the biggest store, the biggest warehouse, the biggest mill and the biggest house in the

Big Bernard Stanley in his later years.

village. His grand home on the north end of the main street that he completed in 1869 at the enormous cost of $8,000 had a bathroom on the second floor with hard and soft running water in every room, a normally unheard of luxury for a village house of those days. At the house-warming party there were 80 guests.[6] Big Bernie had only two grandchildren. The daughter of his only granddaughter let me copy the many photographs he had taken of the house, both inside and out, as well as the many pictures of his family.[7]

The oldest building in or about Lucan today is the old McIlhargey Tavern standing near what had once been the southern outskirts of the village. Built in the summer of 1850, its red bricks were uncharacteristic for the district and were made in a special yard specifically set up for that purpose with clay dug from a pit across the road. It contrasts with the pale yellow brick of most of the other buildings of the area.

Several early inquests were held inside the McIlhargey tavern. The upstairs storey was originally one big room that was used as a dance hall. Pat Laverty told me that his wife's grandmother, Jane Ann Hodgins, always claimed that the first dance she ever had was a jig with Will Donnelly in that ballroom. Patrick McIlhargey—the family pronounced the name "Michael Hardy"—was the first proprietor of the tavern.[8]

Patrick McIlhargey knew all of the Donnellys well. Following their murders in 1880, Charles William Kent, an affluent land developer in London who was also a friend of the family, received the following letter from Lucan:[9]

> I suppose you have heard of the taking away of the Donnellys and the reason why. When men commit crimes and use their influence to escape punishment then it is the duty of the publick [sic] to take the law in their own hands and punish the guilty. The Donnellys murdered and robbed and burned and still managed to escape justice. You murdered poor Howie [sic]. It was a cold-blooded murder. You bribed lawyers and doctors and jurimen [sic] and by

The McIlhargey Tavern on the outskirts of Lucan was built in 1850 and remains one of the oldest buildings in the community. In it were held dances and inquests in the early days.

period in 1876 when many of them had been arrested following the ruction at Tom Ryder's wedding celebration at Fitzhenry's Tavern. The mother, Mary, whose maiden name was Hastings, was a good friend not only of Mrs. Donnelly but especially her sons, some of whom likely boarded with the family at their home during their stagecoaching days. The oldest O'Connor girl, Bridget, was an accomplished seamstress and often did sewing for the Donnellys. And, of course, it was their middle boy, young Johnny, who was the only survivor of the massacre at the homestead.

them mens [*sic*] escaped the gallows which you well deserved . . .
(Signed)
VIGILANCE.

The reference to "poor Howie" was to James Howe who was fatally struck down in a scuffle between Biddulphers named Hodgins and Collins on May 24th, 1876 in which Rhody Kennedy was also involved. Jim Howe lived in a log house within a stone's throw of the old McIlhargey tavern. Both still stand at the time of writing (the year 2010).

Before leaving the subject of Lucan taverns, it would not be out of place to mention the shebeen house that Johnny O'Connor's parents once ran in the village. Shebeen here is used in the sense of a little local drinking place, often illicit, which was fairly common in the country places of Ireland in the nineteenth century.

Like the McIlhargeys, Kents and Nangles, the O'Connors of Lucan were always on friendly terms with the Donnellys. The father, Michael, better known as Mick, had driven stage for the brothers for a short

In 1874 the London *Advertiser* in its North Middlesex column under Lucan reported the following:[10]

A groggery with imposing interior has just made its appearance on one of our principal streets. An alluring shingle, invitingly extended, holds out inducements to heated pedestrians to draw nigh and partake of the fluids in vogue, commencing at "shanty gaff" (a mixture of pop and beer) and ending with "whiskey straight". And all this is done in broad day, and that too without a licence. Is the miserable offender aware that on the same street, on either side, and opposite him, reside, respectively, the village clerk, last year's inspector, this year's inspector, and two clergymen? Look out, Mickey, your time is short.

The License Inspector himself, William W. Lee, wrote to county crown attorney Hutchinson:[11]

Complaint has been made to me that a person in this village named Michael Connors keeps an unlicensed groggery. The chief complainant who is a respectable man says he can prove

Henry Ferguson, of Birr, was at one time one of the Donnellys' favorite Justices of the Peace.

that Connors disposes of liquor and that men in state of intoxication frequent at the place—I visited the house in my official capacity and found a bar with bottles, glasses, whiskey, wine and pop. I notified Connors and his wife that he was liable to prosecution but he and she bade me defiance and stated that they would keep liquor for their boarders. After waiting some days or weeks to see if the business would be given up I visited the place today after receiving information that there was a drunken brawl in the house last Sunday morning when I found everything as I found it before and Connors and his wife again bade me defiance . . . .

In due course, Mick O'Connor was hauled up before Squire Henry Ferguson, the justice of the peace at Birr. He and a fellow magistrate convicted O'Connor of selling liquor without a license and imposed a fine of twenty dollars. This is how the Exeter *Times* reported the case:[12]

A Lucan Episode.

1 Now it happened that there dwelt in the village of Lucan a certain man named Michael, and he was named after a great archangel.

2 And Michael did commune with himself thus: "My health is growing feeble and the desire for work is not what it once was, but my friends are many and thirsty, so I shall open a shebeen."

3 Now this thing was not only against the law, but was an abomination in the sight of many people, who said "we must put this thing down, lest peradventure our fathers and our brothers be enticed therein."

4 And the house was called the "Good Intention Inn."

5 But the saying of a certain wise man that hell was paved with good intentions stirred up the friends of temperance, and an officer of the law, to wit, Wm. W. Lee, License Inspector, was ordered to his duty—and he did it.

6 And he brought Michael before the judge, even the Buss, and charged him with selling the spirit of rye, even ancient rye, and the fermented juice of the corn.

7 Then the judge cried with a loud voice "art thou guilty" and Michael replied "how am I to know until thy servant heareth the evidence."

8 Then the prosecutor called Samuel and James and John and Daniel and David, and these all testified to the truth of the charge.

9 And the judge pronounced him guilty and ordered him to pay into the treasury thirty-two sheckles of silver or to be banished from Lucan for many days.

10 And so the law was vindicated and the transgressor was a sadder if not wiser man.

The prisoner was placed into the custody of Constable Rhody Kennedy, but on making their way to the London jail Kennedy was apparently drugged and the warrant of committal illegally altered to show the fine as having been paid. Upon recovering his senses, however, Kennedy had only a pittance of money on his person and the prisoner was gone.

The Corporation of the Village of Lucan sued the Birr magistrate, Henry Ferguson. The case rumbled on for a year. The Exeter *Times* in September 1875 realized that it had gone on for so long that a summary of the

The Western Hotel in 1906 with a crowd of Lucanites gathered to watch the slaughter of a deer. The man in front with the bowler hat is "Red Bill" Stanley.

events was needed for its readers. It stated that William W. Lee, Inspector of Licenses[13]

> Lodged an information with Mr. Ferguson, who is a Justice of the Peace, against M. Connors for selling whiskey without a licence. The magistrate would not take the case except he received a deposit as security for costs, which deposit of $12.80 the inspector paid him. Connors was then summoned, tried and fined, but the fine not being paid he was arrested and afterwards set at liberty by the constable on payment of $13.50, ten of which he paid Ferguson. Connors was afterwards rearrested and served a term in jail. The Corporation demanded the repayment of the deposit.

In the end, the judgment went against the Birr magistrate but not for the full amount claimed.

These, then, were the hostelries of Lucan village both legal and illicit. Besides those already mentioned, there were in the early days of Biddulph at least ten or twelve other hotels or taverns outside the village bounds but within the township. All were familiar to the Donnellys. Cuthbertson's Commercial stood at Mooresville, Glendenning's and Flanagan's at Flanagan's Corners while at the Sauble Hill were George Hodgins' Stonehouse Tavern and the hotel of Thomas W. Stanley. South of Lucan was Bob McLean's British Exchange with Andy Keefe's two-storey hotel at the Catholic Church Corners. The Keefe Hotel, often erroneously thought to be at Elginfield corner, was built by Andy Keefe but operated by him for a short time only. In Granton were William Middleton's Ontario House and James P. McIntyre's Central Hotel.

Chapter 29

Connolly's Career

In February 1980 I had told Bob Gibbons of CBC-TV that I could not participate in any filming for television until the existing film option on my services had expired. Frankly, I thought I would never hear from him again. When the time came, however, Bob called me. We soon had our heads together and with his help I wrote the one-hour dramatization for television entitled *The Donnellys of Biddulph*.[1] Then, with Bob as producer and director, we began filming.

One of the locations was a three-day shoot at St. Patrick's Church and Cemetery in Biddulph. In the first week of September in that year of 1980, our caravan of vehicles conveying actors, equipment, crews and props rolled up to the church. Many months earlier, I had contacted the parish priest,

Father Joe Finn, for permission to film on the grounds. As the caravan of trucks and vans drove up, I went over to the rectory to let him know we had arrived.

"Oh, everything is fine," Father Joe said, "Just carry on."

A little while later as the costumed actors were stretching their legs and the crew was unloading the props from the trucks in front of the church, I saw Father Finn approaching. On his face was a small frown.

Drawing Bob and me aside, he said, "Look, I've had a little flak from some of the parishioners."

We wondered what he was about to say. Perhaps we would not be allowed on the grounds after all. He relieved us, however, with the words, "Don't worry. Just go ahead and do as you had planned. But remember. If anybody asks you, this is a story about the early pioneer days, right? And whatever you do, just do not mention THAT NAME."

We knew, of course, what name he meant. We chuckled and were nodding in

Shooting the Donnelly story at St. Patrick's Church in September 1980.

200

understanding when just as Father Finn had finished speaking, I looked up to see directly behind him two of the prop-men lifting from one of the big trucks the huge full-sized replica of the Donnelly tombstone which had been made up for the purpose. Emblazoned across its front in huge letters was THAT NAME.

The three days of filming, however, went

building commenced in 1850 and completed the following year. Nine years later the new brick church was erected and the old frame building was relegated to use as a school. The rectory was built ten years after the church.

In addition to the church and rectory, there is another brick building on the church grounds from the nineteenth century. In

John Connolly is at the top right hand corner of this portrayal of the pastors of Inverness-St. Athanase, Quebec.

off smoothly. On the last morning, Father Finn again came out to see us. This time he was smiling broadly. "One of my parishioners is so mad at me for letting you come here in the first place," he said good naturedly, "that he's reported me to the bishop. So please finish up and get the hell out of here."

A couple of years later, Father Finn was instrumental in saving old St. Patrick's parish church on the Roman Line of Biddulph when some of the parishioners wanted to replace it with a modern building.[2] The original frame church had been a humble

1885 Father John Connolly raised the money to erect a new brick school and it stands on the grounds today as a monument to the tenure of the ill-fated priest. The new school was completed just in time, for in February of the following year an arsonist set fire to the original frame church building then serving as a school and burned it to the ground.

St. Patrick's in Biddulph was the second charge of John Connolly as a parish priest. He had been born in County Sligo, Ireland about the year 1829 and went to school at St. Charles' College in Tuam followed by

Father Connolly's school built in 1885 on or adjacent to the site of the old Andy Keefe tavern.

ordination studies in Maynooth that he continued in Paris, France.[3] About 1864 he arrived in Quebec where he completed his theological studies and was ordained. For some years, he was a professor in one of the diocesan colleges where he had the distinction of teaching a student who in later years became the chief justice of Canada. In 1871 when the first parish priest of St. Athanase in the County of Inverness about 40 miles southwest of Quebec City, fell off a ladder and broke his leg while building the rectory kitchen, the bishop appointed John Connolly to become the second priest in charge of the parish.[4]

In his seven years' sojourn in Inverness-St. Athanase, he made the acquaintance of the local member of parliament, Hector Louis Langevin, a close associate of John A. Macdonald and also one of the Fathers of Confederation. Robert Harris, the Prince

Edward Island artist who painted the famous portrait of the Fathers, had earlier in his career sketched those accused of murdering the Donnellys. In that Fathers portrait, Hector Louis Langevin is seated at Macdonald's right elbow.

Shortly after his arrival in Biddulph and in an attempt to have Robert Donnelly released from penitentiary prior to expiration of his term, Connolly contacted Langevin, then a prominent member of the federal cabinet. The attempt was made in order to gain the confidence of the Donnelly family but its failure proved an ill omen to the subsequent relations between them and the priest.

Following the tragedy, the priest was asked about the so-called Property Protective Association which he had founded by having his parishioners sign the declaration in the church. His position as reported by the newspapers was as follows:[5]

> Father Connolly states that a short time after his arrival in his present mission, he ascertained through the means of his sacred calling that there was a society already in existence in the settlement, and that upon learning the purport of its intentions, he formed another committee, the principles of which were so modified that any person under his spiritual jurisdiction could become members of the same without violating the enactments of any law, human or divine.

The priest did not reveal the purport of that first society's intentions, but he did acknowledge to Patrick Donnelly his own reasons for starting the new one. From Thorold Patrick wrote to the crown attorney:[6]

> Having learned through the papers that you wish to prove that a society existed in Biddulph independent of the one Father Connolly formed, I wish to inform you that such is the case. Those are the rev. Gentleman's statement to me on two different occasions. He said there was a society existed in Biddulph previous to his coming there. [H]e obtained this information t[h]rough the confessional and to modify the one in existence he established the one which he has already tendered to Mr. Mcma[h]on. He said if he undertuck [*sic*] to

cruch [*sic*] out the one they had formed by setting himself against it, it would only prosper all the more for he said if you want a thing to prosper just trample on it. He also said they drifted away from the one he had formed, back to the old one, but he could not help that. He said he was of the oppion [*sic*] that when he formed his society, that eventfully [*sic*] the other would die out. I am prepared to sware [*sic*] to this information and I think if you will call on the rev. Gentleman for a witness he will not refute my statements.

Father Connolly maintained that he had never attended any meetings of the society. Which society he meant he appeared not to specify—whether it was the one that he had formed or the other one into which it evolved or which had existed before his arrival. Presumably it was the one that he had formed as it cannot be imagined that he would countenance the other one let alone attend its meetings.

Whatever may have been the case, however, there was at least one of his parishioners who contradicted him, as appears from a letter written by Charles Hutchinson to Æmilius Irving:[7]

Pat Bennett says that he was at the last meeting in the Cedar Swamp School house shortly before the Murder; & that Father Connolly called in while the meeting was in progress— the meeting seemed to be divided—he thought one section seemed to wish not to let the other know what was going on—they entered into an ante room at the back—they wouldn't let him & some others know what they [were] at—so Bennett left, while Father Connolly was still there—the meeting was held at night . . . Wm. Donnelly was in today and gave me the above memo . . . .

Father Connolly's part, if any, in the conspiracy to murder the Donnellys was not pursued by the crown authorities and while there may have been suspicion there was probably little direct evidence. The priest himself was, in my opinion, more a victim of his own bad judgment and the evil intentions of his parishioners than his own.

There have always been, of course, those who were prepared to believe the worst of

anything that had to do with the Church of Rome. The following memorandum, for example, written by one, W. A. Shannon, states:[8]

A man born in the Lucan area who lived there at the time of the tragedy, was about the age of 25, and who was . . . an Irish Roman Catholic . . . told me in private (as a close friend of his) that it was the local priest who . . . planned the whole affair, coached them in his own home and according to opinion by the more observant, gave them communion beforehand, and led in person the gangsters to action, in the understanding they were not committing any wrong since they were God's chosen vessels to avenge the enemies of God's church . . . .

And the London *Advertiser* printed the following:[9]

A paragraph appears in the columns of the Globe today to the effect that their special reporter stated that in an interview with a

Father John Connolly

leading resident of the village he (the resident) said "There is no doubt that it was the members of the Vigilance Committee that killed the Donnellys. The Committee were organized for

NO OTHER PURPOSE

Than to make war against them. When the priest denounced them in church the feeling against the family became intensified to such a degree that I firmly believe the Committee thought it would be no crime to kill them." And further, in reply to the reporter, said "It is my firm conviction that

THE PRIEST KNEW WHAT WAS GOING TO TAKE PLACE.

If it had not been for him I do not think the murder would have occurred."

The *Advertiser*, to its credit, did not believe the opinions of that leading citizen of the village, whoever he may have been.

Far more credible evidence of the whereabouts and state of mind of the parish priest, in my opinion, is the recollection of Michael James McCormick, the seventeen-year-old son of storekeeper Stephen McCormick, who lived not far from the church. On the evening of February 3rd, 1880, he remembered clearly that a pale moon shone "with a light skiff of snow on the ground" as he and a few neighboring lads assembled at St. Patrick's rectory, the home of Father Connolly, to meet with the priest for the purposes of organizing a debating society or some similar social group.[10] News of the tragedy the following morning put an end to the incipient organization.

Connolly remained at St. Patrick's for several years in uneasy peace with his parishioners and his soul. That he felt some guilt for the commission of such a serious crime within his parish, there seems little doubt. James Collisson grew up near the church during Father Connolly's pastorship following the tragedy. Over seventy years later, following a legal career in Alberta, he wrote from Edmonton:[11]

One night my father asked Father Connolly if he had any incriminating papers in the house, he went in and brought out a big bunch of papers which my father put in the stove

Theresa Whelan, in later life.

without looking at them. About 10 or 12 years ago a new rector of St. Joseph's College came here from Toronto. St. Joseph's College is affiliated with the Alberta University and is conducted by the Christian Brothers. When I was made acquainted with him he asked me if I was any relation to Mike Collisson of Biddulph. I told him he was my father and asked him what he knew about him. "Oh," he said, "He was the man who burned the incriminating papers in Father Connolly's house." I could never find out from him where he got the information.

Within two or three years of the Donnelly tragedy, two more tragic events occurred in Father Connolly's parish—not anywhere near approaching the cataclysm of 1880 but troubling nonetheless. The first occurred on Christmas Day in 1880 at Grundy's Crossing north of Lucan when a train locomotive bore down upon and killed a leading member of the Peace Society, James McGrath. Killed along with him were his wife, brother and cousin. It was largely this accident that sustained the legend that each of the Vigilants who participated in the massacre of the Donnellys would soon die a violent death.

204

Then in 1883 another prominent member of Father Connolly's congregation, a young medical doctor named John Joseph McIlhargey, died suddenly. It seems that the young physician had fallen in love with a young lady whose religious convictions were not of the Catholic faith. Up to that time, the priest had been a close friend and confidant of the young doctor. But when strong suspicion arose that the young medical man had taken his own life, the Parkhill *Gazette* had the temerity to claim that the cause of the alleged suicide was the threat of excommunication the priest had made if he went through with a marriage to the non-believer. The priest denied it and demanded an apology from the newspaper. When it was refused,[12] Father Connolly sued for libel claiming $5,000 in damages. The case came on for hearing at the London Assizes in May, 1884 and the jury returned a verdict against the priest.

The Donnelly survivors ensured that the blot on his incumbency at St. Patrick's would not be forgotten when in 1889 they had erected on their family's grave plot the tombstone with the word "murdered" written after the names of each of the five victims.[13] During John Connolly's long

remaining sojourn in Biddulph, even before the erection of that marker, he could not pass between the rectory and the church without being reminded of the terrible blemish upon his career. Rarely did he allude to it but he must have felt bitter when the accusing words on the stone appeared. Finally, in January 1895 the bishop transferred him to Sacred Heart Church in Ingersoll. Here he took up residence with his widowed sister-in-law and her two daughters.

Although the congregation of St. Patrick's gave him a gold-headed cane in appreciation of his years of work in St. Patrick's parish, he was doubtless glad to shake the dust of Biddulph from his feet. Mary Mitchell Whelihan, daughter of Theresa Whelan, once said to me: "We had friends in Ingersoll who told us that Father Connolly there declared to his parishioners from the altar that the people of Biddulph had betrayed him."

In 1907 John Connolly in failing health, made a trip back to his native Ireland and two years after his return to Ingersoll, he died on September 24th, 1909.[14] Many of his former parishioners from Biddulph attended the funeral services which were conducted by a great host of priests and other church officials.[15] His worldly possessions he left to his two nieces, Mary and Sarah Connolly, and their mother.[16] They took his body to New Jersey for burial in the family plot.

Father Connolly lies beneath this stone marking the family plot in Belmar, New Jersey.

Chapter 30

The Dying Curse

On February 4th, 1893 William Donnelly, now settled down in Appin, was in a pensive mood. Collecting his thoughts, he took pen in hand and wrote:[1]

The Biddulph tragedy took place on Wednesday morning, February 4, 1880, and before the public can read this thirteen years will have elapsed since the memorable slaughter. But those years have each brought their terrible changes in Biddulph and if any of the living vigilants can look calmly back and notice the slaughter made by old 'Father Time' he must come to the conclusion that retributive justice has been busy at work, and the cold, relentless hand of death is almost on his own shoulder. Yes, in the thirteen years 34 persons, who were either directly or indirectly concerned in the slaughter have met their just deserts, and as none of them have been murdered, a direct visitation from Almighty

God must have been the cause. I will not be personal, but I will say several were killed by the London, Huron and Bruce train. More were found in bed without any apparent cause. More fell in to a well. More dropped dead. More died suffering the agonies of a mad dog, and a few are in the asylum, while the majority of those living are homeless and not worth a dollar, though well off thirteen years ago.

Will then recalled the words of Æmilius Irving, the chief prosecutor against Carroll, who told the grieving Donnellys immediately after the trial that divine retribution would give them satisfaction if the laws of man would not. Will's letter continued:

How true his words were all Ontario knows. Some of the broken and wasted bones of my family are in my possession and will be until justice is fully done. But if the next thirteen years will reap as large a harvest as the past thirteen has, I think justice will be done and those heartbreaking relics may be laid away quietly to rest.

Did subsequent events prove the truth of the prediction of the chief prosecutor? To answer this, one must first identify those upon whom retributive justice was supposed to have wreaked its revenge.

In *The Donnellys Must Die*, Orlo Miller states that Sam Everett, the sometime Lucan constable, came as close as anyone to identifying those who were at the Donnelly homestead in the early morning hours of February 4th, 1880. I agree with Orlo.

Although an outsider when he first came to Lucan, Everett's rough and ready personality fit well into village street society and his constabulary experience did no harm in assisting him to gain the confidence, not necessarily of the Peace Society members themselves, but of those in the Catholic Settlement who knew of the bitter hatreds swirling within that community. The note to the crown attorney, in the handwriting of Everett, reads:[2]

List of names

Denis Henan
Mike Henan
John Henan

Æmilius Irving, the crown prosecutor, whose words of comfort to Jenny Donnelly were one source of the divine retribution to come.

Sam Everett's deadly little list of the participants in the Donnelly murders.

James Toohey Sen.
Do Harigan
John Thompson
John McGlochlin
John Ryder
Mike Carrol he killed the old woman
James McGraw
Wm. Casey J.P.
James Ryder
Dan Ryder
John Quigly
Pat Quigly
Ed Ryan
John Ryan
John Cain
Wm. Thompson
James Maher killed the Old Man
John Dorcey
John Bruin
John Lamphier
Pat Ryder and his two sons
Wm Feehley
John Ryan little Johney
Mike Madigan
Mike Blake
James Kelley
Pat Breen pres of the Committee
Pat Dewan
Ted Toohey

Along with the prisoners they were all there

There are thirty-two names on this list. When augmented with Pat Ryder's two sons and the six prisoners, the total is forty. There may have been a few omissions such as Martin Darcey, a second James Kelly, young

James Maher, James and Thomas Lamphier, Ned Sullivan, James Carrigan, James Heenan and Dennis Toohey. On the other hand, the inclusion of William Feeheley is to my mind questionable. While William was doubtless a sympathizer of the group and he and his brother James may have been accessories to the crime, I doubt whether William was a participant. The best evidence about his role is that he, in company with John Whelan and perhaps Mike Welch, Martin McLaughlin's hired man, watched from behind Whelan's fence across the road.

As already stated, the story of the curse on the Peace Society was given a great boost when on the Christmas Day following the tragedy James McGrath and three members of his family were killed on their return home from visiting relatives in McGillivray Township. James McGrath was so proud of his span of horses, a bay and a chestnut sorrel, that in the year previous he had challenged the train and beaten it across the tracks at Grundy's Crossing north of Lucan in McGillivray. A year later in 1880, at the same crossing, he challenged the train again but this time he lost.

The train locomotive smashed into the sleigh and killed James McGrath, his wife Rebecca, his brother Mathew, Jr., and his cousin Ellen Blake. A younger sister of James, Annie, managed to survive by jumping out of the sleigh before the train struck. Thrown out by the impact was Nellie, the small child of the McGraths and a mere babe in arms, who fell into a snow bank and was probably cushioned against serious injury by her swaddling clothes. The violent deaths of the known vigilante and his family gave life to the rumor that Mrs. Donnelly with her dying breath had cursed her killers and swore that all would come to a violent or tragic end.

Left at home on that night were the three young McGrath boys, Michael, John and William, aged seven, five and three respectively. They, along with their baby sister Nellie, were suddenly orphans. They went to live with their grandparents, the elder

The children of vigilante James McGrath, who were left orphans on Christmas Day, 1880.

brothers, Long Jim Toohey became the patriarch of his own large family. He became a very successful farmer and from 1891 to 1902 he served on the Biddulph Council and was reeve of the township in 1903. He acquired several hundred acres of land before he died in 1931. His son James became a Trappist monk and two of his daughters became nuns. His grandson Jim, son of Timothy, told me that the subject of the Donnellys was not discussed in the family.

"My dad just told me that it was never to be talked about," he said. "Once my dad went down to Iowa to visit his brother who was my Uncle Jim—Brother Anthony of the Trappists—who could not leave the monastery there once he had entered into it. On that trip he also visited one or two other families who had settled in Dubuque, Iowa after leaving Biddulph. He said that even though he had spent his whole life here on the Roman Line, he learned more about the

McGraths, and then with their Aunt Annie who had survived the crash.

The fate of another of the vigilantes, John Thompson, brother of Maggie and William, was also attributed to the curse. At one time John was a good friend of the Donnelly boys but gradually came to side with his brother and father in opposition to them. He was included in Sam Everett's list. John Thompson's end came by his own hand when on April 4th, 1899 he hanged himself with a chain. Years later his farm on the Roman Line near the church, lot 30 in the sixth concession, came into the possession of Hugh Toohey, son of Long Jim. Hugh married Julia Lauretta Dewan, granddaughter of another vigilante, Patrick J. Dewan. They farmed here for years until finally selling out and buying a place over on the Swamp Line. Hugh and Julia were both killed in a car crash in front of their house in 1969.

In contrast to the tragic ends of James McGrath and John Thompson was the life of James Toohey. The youngest of eight

Schoolteacher Ellen Blake, one of the victims of the train disaster of Christmas Day, 1880.

James Toohey and his second wife, Maria O'Meara, at their 1885 wedding. His first wife was Sarah Thompson, sister of Will Donnelly's old flame, Maggie.

death of his wife, Martin McLaughlin sold the farm in an auction sale held October 1st, 1919 and with the proceeds bought a house in Stratford, Ontario. In that house on Caledonia Street, he spent the last ten years of his life with his two spinster daughters, Temperance and Mary. The house was close enough to St. Joseph's Church for the old man to creak his aged bones a couple of blocks over to make penance for his tortured soul. Martin McLaughlin died in Stratford on April 9th, 1930.

Both daughters shared the family's guilty secret. They were old enough to know very well that their father had been out with his rifle on the night that John Donnelly was shot. On the witness stand, they both lied on their oath and testified that their father had been in bed. And they both carried the secret to the grave. Temperance died in 1936 and Mary in 1950. One wonders if their younger sister, Martha, learned the guilty secret from

Donnellys on that trip than he had ever known in his life."

In the Toohey family, the Donnellys were dead, buried and forgotten and the life of Spadey Jim Toohey—for it was he who was supposed to have clubbed Tom Donnelly over the head with Pat Quigley's spade—belied the myth of the curse.

The example of Martin McLaughlin also contradicted the myth. McLaughlin was born in Shinrone, County Tipperary, Ireland in about 1837 and came to Biddulph as a young boy. He grew up on the Roman Line but one farm away from the Donnellys. When he was about twenty, he married Anne McNamara and bought from his father-in-law the farm on the Swamp Line on which he remained for the next 62 years. Reputed to have been a good farmer, he built over the years a 36 by 56 foot barn with a large attached root cellar and room upstairs, a sheep shed, hog barn, large implement shed and a five-bedroom solid brick house. Here he raised a family of four girls and two boys. Finally, following the

Martin McLaughlin in front of his Stratford home, taken shortly before he died in 1930.

them for, being but two years old at the time of the crime, she was not asked to bear false witness. Martha became a Loretto nun and later a mother superior. Her religious name was Mother Mary Zita and she taught school in Guelph as late as 1950 and beyond.

The last of the Biddulph vigilantes to die was Jack Lamphier. John Joseph Lamphier, to give his full name, was the son of Anthony Lamphier and Margaret Crawford. He was educated in the Cedar Swamp Schoolhouse, then built of logs. Following his education there, he spent more time traveling than most other young farm lads of his time. At 24 he took a trip overseas for his health, returned home and then went to Arkansas for a short time. Back home again in 1880, he was 26 years old and a member in good standing of the Peace Society of Biddulph. Two years after the tragedy, he married Kate Carey, daughter of the baggage master at the Lucan

railway station. They left Biddulph and went to live in Iowa where Lamphier—now known as Lanphier—became a prosperous merchant in the small town of Lohrville.

One of his six children, Tom, joined the armed forces of the United States and at West Point was a football teammate of Dwight Eisenhower. The two remained cronies for the rest of their lives. After World War I, Tom Lanphier became an army air pilot and close personal friend of Charles Lindbergh. He claimed he was the only other person ever to fly *The Spirit of St. Louis* as Lindbergh wanted to see his plane from the ground and Lanphier was the only other pilot he would trust to fly it.

Tom Lanphier attained the rank of major and in 1928, while in command of an air base near Detroit, brought an airplane over to Father Hogan's Old Boys' Reunion at St. Patrick's Church in Biddulph where he gave a

Jack Lamphier, his wife Catherine Carey, both of Biddulph, and their family.

210

demonstration of flying. That exhibition was still talked about by the very old people in Biddulph when I first went there.

His son, Tom Lanphier, Jr., also became an air pilot. In April 1943 as a fighter pilot during the Second World War, he intercepted and shot down over Bougainville in the Solomon Islands the bomber carrying the brilliant Japanese commander-in-chief, Admiral Isoruku Yamamoto. Yamamoto had been the brightest star in the Imperial Navy and it was he who had planned the attack on Pearl Harbor. Tom Lanphier, Jr., thus became a genuine American war hero. His grandfather, the old Biddulph vigilante, eventually retired to Omaha, Nebraska and died a contented man in 1943. His great grandson of Omaha told me that what he remembered especially about him was that every once in a while he would proclaim, "By the blood of Lucan, who put the goat in the bed?" and then he would laugh uproariously.

Jack Lamphier's brother, Thomas, was at the time of the Donnelly tragedy married to Hanorah Ryder, daughter of Grouchy. Although not included in Everett's list, Thomas Lamphier was counted by Bill Donnelly as a victim of retributive justice when on September 8th, 1886 he was overcome by noxious gases in a well he was digging. He was almost rescued but fell back and either suffocated, died from the fall or was drowned at the bottom.

James Harrigan of the Peace Society lived from 1837 to 1895 and was for many years one of the school trustees of Biddulph School Section number four, popularly known as the Cedar Swamp School. Harrigan's son, Leo, was born in 1884. He purchased the Donnelly homestead in 1939 after James Michael Donnelly died the previous year and his sister, Catherine Crossman, put the farm up for sale. Leo bought the Donnelly farm for his own son, Joe Harrigan, and it was still in his possession when I first saw it in 1964. At that time I met Joe and his brothers, Frank and Jack. Leo Harrigan himself came to a tragic end two

years later when he died in a fire in his home on the old Harrigan homestead in June 1966. His son Jack and family were at that time living a few hundred feet away in the Cedar Swamp Schoolhouse. The old school served as their temporary home following the burning of Jack's own house on the Roman Line less than four months before. In this latter fire, Jack's youngest child and only daughter died. Her parents and eight brothers survived her.

Sam Everett stated in a roundabout way that three of Grouchy's sons were present at the murders. They were Grouchy Jim, the oldest boy and one of the six prisoners held for over a year in the London jail, as well as Patrick and Morris or Maurice. Although Michael was the second oldest boy, a few days before February 4th he had disabled himself by cutting his foot with an axe while felling timber for the new Ryder barn to replace the one alleged to have been burned by the Donnellys.

Young Grouchy Jim was a feisty young man. The following report appeared in the Glencoe *Transcript* on April 22nd, 1880:

> Two prisoners were brought to the County Jail on their way to the Central Prison and placed in the cells adjacent to those of Thomas and James Ryder, awaiting trial for the Donnelly murder. Upon learning who his neighbors were one of the travelers declaimed against them in no measured terms, saying that he had known the Donnelly boys, who were first class fellows. After the cells were unlocked next morning, James Ryder went to the man's cell and asked him to take back what he had said. Ryder then went into the cell and struck him with his fist, and kicked him in the ribs and stomach until he roared. Biddulph, it would seem, has taken possession of the jail.

After his release, Grouchy Jim apparently led an uneventful life. He farmed the old Farrell place in Biddulph for many years and then retired to London. The Brown sisters, great granddaughters of Grouchy Pat, told me their father, the son of Mary Ryder, often visited Jim on his trips to that city. Ed Brown told his daughters that their great uncle always seemed to wear a white apron around his waist after the manner of a bartender. Indeed, some of the Ryders believed he had kept tavern in Chicago for some years although they were mistaken. In fact it was Grouchy Jim's brother, Morris, who worked as a bartender in Chicago after drifting around the American West working on railroad construction and other jobs. Morris died unmarried in Chicago in 1941 and is buried in an unmarked grave in St. Gabriel Catholic Cemetery, Oak Forest, Illinois outside Chicago. His brother, Grouchy Jim Ryder, had died the year before in London. He, too, had never married and his estate was valued at $46,000, which was considered a substantial amount for the times.

At least a couple of the Ryder boys, Michael and William, went to San Diego, probably quitting Biddulph after their father,

Patrick (Grouchy) Ryder who had been widowed in 1883, took himself a new young wife in the person of Estella Creighton. She was 35 at the time and he was 63. He also made a strange kind of will leaving the homestead to his three youngest sons but to be held in trust until they attained the age of 65 years! The farm in fact ended up in the hands of his daughter, Mary Ryder, who married Edward Brown and the two brought up their daughters and son there and later passed it on to the son, Edward Brown, Jr.

Michael Ryder became a conductor on the San Diego electric railway where he later became a dispatcher. He married Corinne Phillips and they had no children. He returned at least once to the haunts of his boyhood in Canada and in 1927 went to see an old friend, Caleb Quigley, who was lying on his deathbed. Caleb's daughter, Lizzie

James Ryder, on the left, with his brothers, Will, and Michael, on the right. The woman is Michael's wife, Corrine.

Quigley, nursed her father in his last illness. Many years later, in May 1971 when she was then 79 years of age, she told me the story of that meeting. It took place just a few days before her father died. The house was a new one and she overheard the conversation between her father and Mike Ryder through the French doors that were still unglazed. The two were talking about the Donnelly murders, and she heard Ryder say:

> You know, Cabe, that you helped us many times by keeping watch over the Donnellys for us. And you know we were given permission by Father Connolly to do with them what we willed. He could not handle them. We had all gone to church the Sunday before. The Donnellys went on home but the rest of us stayed and talked with Father Connolly. That's when he told us he washed his hands of them.

William Ryder, the second youngest of Grouchy Ryder's boys, joined the armed services of the United States and spent his active life in the army. He served with Theodore Roosevelt in Cuba during the Spanish American War and served as an army recruiter in Washington, D.C. in 1930. Upon his retirement, he went back to San Diego where he died in 1960 at the age of 95.

Grouchy Pat's younger brother, Pitchfork

Caleb Quigley.

Tom, sold his farm and moved to Saginaw, Michigan in 1890. Shortly after he left, it was reported:[3]

> Robert Donnelly visited Biddulph on Monday and sold twenty tons of hay off the Donnelly homestead. He had the pleasure while there of noticing that the old log house, in which the gang accused of murdering his parents and brothers represented they played cards on the night of the tragedy, was a total wreck, and the late occupant [who] was one of those accused, had left bag and baggage to build up a new home in Michigan . . . .

The log house Bob Donnelly was referring to was, of course, Pitchfork Tom Ryder's on the Roman Line. Ryder settled his family in Michigan near Saginaw where it is doubtful that his sojourn was a happy one. In August 1898 his twelve-year-old son, Michael, was struck by lightning and instantly killed. In April 1901 his thirteen-year-old son, Valentine, drowned in the Saginaw River. Thomas Ryder himself died suddenly in 1904. He and his wife are buried in Calvary Cemetery, Saginaw.

Patrick Ryder, Jr., known as Young Grouch, married Lizzie Heenan in 1894. They soon separated when she went back to live with her brothers. Patrick himself was supposed to have drowned when on March 29th, 1903 he jumped into extremely cold water that brought on a fatal heart attack. He was 43 years old.

There seems little doubt that had Will Donnelly survived, he would have included both Tom Ryder and Young Pat Grouch among his list of victims of divine providence. He did include Michael McLaughlin, who was felled suddenly by a stroke in 1882. His wife Temperance had been called as a prosecution witness in the trial of James Carroll. Although she had grown up in close proximity to the Donnelly homestead and was the godmother of Johnny O'Connor at his christening, in the witness box she proved more helpful to the defense of Carroll than to his prosecution.

Chapter 31

In the Rockies

Buried in the little cemetery where St. Peter's Roman Catholic Church once stood just within Biddulph on its west boundary, are Roger Carroll and Catherine Maher, the parents of James Carroll. In 1980 Doug Hardy, an aficionado of the Donnelly story living in New Westminster, British Columbia, saved up a long time to pay for a once-in-a-lifetime trip to Ontario. Why Ontario? Because he wanted to visit Lucan and see the graves of the Donnelly family. Back in New Westminster, with my assistance, Doug located for me the last earthly resting place of James Carroll himself, native of Stephen Township and the man

Pictured here in 1880, James Carroll lived to be 64 and died with his boots off.

who led the Peace Society of Biddulph in the massacre of the Donnellys. Carroll lies below a stone bearing a simple inscription at bottom in which Doug found delicious irony. It reads: "Peace, perfect peace."

And it turned out that James Carroll was not blown to bits by dynamite in a railway construction accident as I stated in the first edition of *The Donnelly Album*. Johannah's curse proved ineffective in his case, for he died in a bed in St. Mary's Hospital in New Westminster. His last will, written only a few days before his death on May 14th, 1915, reads:

This is the last will and testament of me, James M. Carroll of the City of Revelstroke [*sic*] in the Province of British Columbia.

I hereby revoke former wills made by me at any time heretofore.

I hereby devise and bequeath all my real and personal property and estate whatsoever and wheresoever unto my two sisters Mrs. Margaret Kilcline of the City of Rossland and Mrs. Maddigan of the City of Revelstroke [*sic*] to be equally divided.

I hereby request that an account of one hundred & fifty dollars be paid to Mr. Maddigan before my estate is divided.

The Golden District property shall not be sold before two years from date.

And I hereby appoint Hedley Dart Executor to administer my estate in Golden District and also to look after the horses on St. Marys Range.

And I also appoint J. F. Armstrong of Victoria, B.C. executor to administer my estate called Durick Estate.

In witness whereof I have hereunto set my hand the fifth day of May one thousand nine hundred and fifteen.

The signature was in a shaky hand—not surprising in view of his death only ten days later—then struck out and re-signed in a firmer stroke. St. Mary's Range was a flat in the watershed of the St. Mary's River near Kimberley. Of the two sisters mentioned in Carroll's last will, Catherine was married to Michael Madigan, himself a Biddulph vigilante, and Margaret had married but was the widow of a Detroit man named Kilcline. Carroll himself had not married. While in

Biddulph, the Donnellys often sneered at him as a "queer fellow".

The requiem high mass at Carroll's funeral was conducted in St. Peter's Church in New Westminster by Father Beck, who also read the service at his graveside in the Catholic Cemetery.

A little over three decades earlier, William Porte laconically noted the departure of James Carroll from Lucan and Biddulph in his diary under the date of Saturday, May 26th, 1883 as follows:

> It would not answer to pass over the fact that James M. Carroll of Tragedy Renown left here on Friday the 25th on No. 4 to locate himself somewhere under the shadow of the Rockey Mountains in the Great Lone land. Won't he be lonely. Well, so be it.

The following year the Glencoe *Transcript* carried a little item about him as follows:[1]

> James Carroll, who figured so prominently in the Biddulph racket two or three years ago, is working on the railway out west. It is said that he scarcely eats anything, works only enough to provide himself with the necessaries of life, and holds out but little intercourse with those around him. He seems to be a victim of melancholy, and it is feared his reason is giving way.

Carroll kept his reason despite stories drifting out of British Columbia that he "seemed to be overshadowed by a guilty conscience and forebodings of evil."[2]

Jim Carroll spent the rest of his life in the East Kootenay district of British Columbia. He lived at different times at a small water-stop in the Rogers Pass area called Beaver as well as at Rogers Pass itself. He also lived at different times in St. Mary's, in Kimberley and in Revelstoke. He appears to have returned at least twice to the Biddulph and Lucan area, the first time in September 1884 when the London *Free Press* reported:[3]

> Jim Carroll, of Biddulph notoriety, has arrived from the Rockey Mountains.

Again, in the summer of 1886 the newspapers reported that Carroll had returned again to the city of London and was

From *A Short History of the Roger's Pass and Glacier Park* by Daem and Dickey.

also in St. Marys. He was then foreman of a C.P.R. construction party looking for carpenters to work on railway building in British Columbia.[4]

The Glencoe *Transcript* again referred to him in its issue of Thursday, January 13th, 1887:

> James Carroll, formerly of Biddulph, has started a general store at Roger's Pass, the highest pass in the Selkirk range of the Rocky mountains, with prospect of a good winter's trade. He writes that there has been a snow fall of over 30 feet, and that residents of the locality have witnessed several snow slides.

A Short History of Rogers Pass and Glacier Park by Daem and Dickey describes the place:

> It was an ugly little town, roughly built but in a priceless setting. It boasted a station, a boarding house for single men, stores run at various times by Jim Carrol who was also postmaster . . . .

215

Many years later in 1962 a pioneer woman named Mrs. Dow who lived at the Rogers Pass in the early days recalled that[5]

> . . . the mountain facing the CPR station was called Mount Sir Donald and the one behind the station was known as Mount Carrol. There was a general store . . . Jim Carroll owned the store and was also the postmaster with the post office occupying one corner of the store. He was obliging and well liked by everyone, later living in Kimberley where he passed away a few years ago . . . .

We know, of course, that James Carroll died not at Kimberley but in New Westminster. This makes me question whether this was the Jim Carroll of the Donnelly story, let alone the fact that "he was well liked by everyone" which, of course, is possible. The other question arising in my mind about this little account is, Was the mountain behind the station named after the vigilante?

During an election campaign in 1912, an Exeter man claimed he found Carroll working at carpentry in Golden, B.C. He was friendly but uncommunicative. He asked if Father Connolly was still alive. When told he had died some two or three years before in Ingersoll, Carroll wept.

That same year in 1912, when Carroll was in his sixties, he had a dispute with a former hired man, George Beattie, whom he had left in charge of his horse ranch at Beaver. Beattie, who had been hired at $40 a month, wrote Carroll during the latter's absence and I will quote from the letter as it will give the reader some idea of life on that ranch:[6]

> Beaver BC 4 July 1912
> J. M. Carroll Esq.
> Dear Sir,
>   I hope you made the journey in good time and find everything in good shape.
>   I have poulticed Jimmy's boot for a couple of days and he seems a bit better for it, although he is still lame. I have given him two good rubbings with the liniment.

View of Beaver, the later home of James Carroll, in the Selkirk Mountain Range of the Kootenay District of British Columbia. *(Copy permission of Provincial Archives of British Columbia)*

216

The chickens are all doing well and the big horn rooster's comb is all right again.

We have had three days rain and it has done a power of good the apple trees are splendid. The potatoes round the house are coming fine but not the ones in the field.

There is only about a dozen cabbage plants coming up but the turnips are doing fine. If it is dry I will start cutting tomorrow.

A party of surveyors went through our land from the Y. across the N.W. corner of the first clover patch and made a straight line for 6 mile creek. Through carelessness the[y] started a fire in the brush . . . but we soon got it out.

I sent in Connors machine but could not find the little wrench Do you know where it is?

Mr. Avery is asking me for a payment on the horse so I would be pleased if you could remit a cheque as soon as convenient.

I am
Yours faithfully
Geo. Beattie.

Beattie was asking for his overdue pay and Carroll's reply was:

I am in receipt of your last letter and would have answered before now but I was awaiting for a few days expecting to make a sale of mare and two colts for $275.00 but did not do so as the party wanted the stock for $258.00 [but] I could not let them go for less. I have put up $500.00 worth of Horses for [sale, and] expect [to] have a sale of some of them any day. I will send you $100.00 just as soon as I make a sale. I am working late and early endeavoring to get store finished as soon as possipple. I don't think that I can possiply get away before the 15th Aug. . . . Will you be taking the Horse or will you leave him until Winter or up to Christmas. Please let me know what you intend to do with him. Where are the R. R. surveyors. How is the Hay in the marsh . . .

Hoping you are well.
I remain
Yours truly
J. M. Carroll

Apparently the cheque did not come and in due course Beattie arranged to have a man take his place and left the ranch for Golden, B.C. He wrote again to Carroll requesting his money. Carroll, now back home on his ranch at Beaver, replied:

Yours re wages to hand.

Please let me know what you were doing from the 23rd June to the 15th Sept. I could not see that there was a day's work done between those dates. Now as you have put in claim for wages you no doubt take account of the fact that you are responsible for damages for negligence and nonperformance of duty which with other items totals close to $200.00 two hundred dollars.

I remain
Yours etc.
J. M. Carroll

Carroll again wrote Beattie on October 12th as follows:

I am writing to say that I received 5 chickens out of the 6 that you purloined from the Ranch. I cannot understand why you are not returning the Gun Field Glasses Watch and the Scarf Pin with the Anchor. I hope that these articles will be returned so as to avoid trouble.

When Carroll followed with another letter, Beattie made answer:

Golden BC   3 Nov 1912
J. M. Carroll

The person that told you the funny story about the field glasses must be having a fine laugh now because there is not one iota of truth in it. The field [glasses] were taken out of your house by a gentleman and were laying in a shack rented from Mr. Wilkinson and when he started to pack up and come away he found he had to hurry for the train and they were dropped into the grip along with other things.

The grip or whatever you call it was not opened by me although I admit I took the watch not from any purloining ideas I happened to see it lying on an old satchel and put it in my pocket and forgot all about it until I came to Golden & my brother took it and got it repaired. I have great pleasure in returning it repaired free of charge. Also the field glasses which your friend inadvertently took with him The same party had your gun killing gophers and came upon a porcupine & hit it with the gun which broke he has the gun at present and will return up when it is repaired. You spoke of me purloining your goods I do not think that you know exactly all that you write but we shall find out at the end of the month.

It will save you a good deal I expect if you square up with me before the case comes up after the way I worked for you without proper food and let you have the use of my horse without which you could have done nothing and for which you never even thanked me.

The gun will be returned as soon as William has got it repaired

G. Beattie

In due course the case was heard and judgment was given against Carroll for three and one-half months' wages less the value of the gun set at $5.

During his youthful days in Stephen Township, James Carroll's early troubles began when his mother, Catherine Maher, died and his father married again. The new wife was Catherine Glavin who had been born on a ship during the voyage across the Atlantic from Ireland in 1832. Her parents were John Glavin, Sr., and Margaret Lane. At the age of twenty-two she first married Thomas Riley who died of consumption in 1860 leaving her with three small children aged six, three and two. Ten years later she married Roger Carroll, the father of James Carroll.

Jim Carroll quickly grew to resent his stepmother and left the family home in Stephen Township. He went to Michigan. Here he obtained work in railroad construction and returned years later to lead the Biddulph Peace Society against the Donnellys. Meanwhile, Catherine Glavin quickly bore Roger Carroll two little girls— Hanorah in 1871, and Martha two years later. Not long after the birth of this second child, Roger himself died in 1873. Catherine Glavin is listed in the 1881 census of Stephen Township with three young men named Riley, presumably the sons from her first marriage, aged twenty-six, twenty-three and twenty-one. Also listed with her are the two Carroll girls, aged ten and eight, the daughters of Roger Carroll and half-sisters to James, the Biddulph constable. Finally, there is listed with Catherine Glavin Riley Carroll a little girl named Catherine Carroll, aged one year, also presumably her daughter but born long after the death of her last husband, Roger Carroll.

Carroll's marker in New Westminster, B.C.

Chapter 32

A Vigilante Interview

As probably in most cultures, in the Irish there is a deep sense of divine retribution suffered upon evildoers. Thomas D'Arcy Magee, in *A Popular History of Ireland*, published in 1863, wrote of the fates of the accusers of Father Nicholas Sheehy. Wrote Magee:

> The fate of their enemies is notorious; with a single exception, they met deaths violent, loathsome and terrible. Maude died insane, Bagwell in idiocy, one of the jury committed suicide, another was found dead in a privy, a third was killed by his horse, a fourth was drowned, a fifth shot, and so through the entire list. Toohey was hanged for felony, the prostitute Dunlea fell into a cellar and was killed, and the lad Lonergan, after enlisting as a soldier, died of a loathsome disease in a Dublin infirmary.

The theme was carried forward to the Biddulph tragedy. The popular legend repeated over and over is that every man of the Peace Society who participated in the butchery died a tragic death. For example, the newspaper obituary of Patrick Donnelly in the Thorold *Post* of Friday, May 22nd, 1914 reads in part:

> . . . one uncanny echo was the prophecy by Patrick that none of the alleged murderers would die in bed, which prophecy, strange to relate, was realized to its awful fullness, each one coming to a violent end.

If the origin of the legend was not the prophecy of Patrick Donnelly nor the prophetic words of Æmilius Irving spoken within minutes of the acquittal of James Carroll, then it was the curse that Mrs. Donnelly was supposed to have shrieked with her dying breath.

The individual named by Sam Everett in his list as Ted Toohey was Timothy, older brother of Long Jim Toohey. The nickname for Timothy was Thady or Thade which to

Timothy Toohey

the English ear sounds like Ted. Timothy was born in 1829 and was married to Grouchy's sister, Mary Ryder. He had served as a Biddulph councilor during the time that Jim Donnelly was in Kingston Penitentiary and for a couple of years after his return. He also served one year on the Middlesex County Council. It was Tim Toohey's two sons, Dennis and James—the latter known as the Younger to distinguish him from his uncle—who were involved with other young members of the vigilante families in the September 3rd, 1882 altercation on the Roman Line with John Kent and the Keefes.

A reporter of the Toronto *Globe* interviewed Timothy Toohey, who was not identified by name, a few days after the Donnelly murders. The interview was reported in the newspaper in its issue of Saturday, February 14th, 1880:

INTERVIEWING A VIGILANTE.
Until today there could not be found a member of the Vigilance Committee who

Patrick Breen

would submit to an interview . . . but this morning your reporter happened on a Vigilante who does not partake of the taciturnity of his brethren. The man in question is a characteristic Irishman, well up in years, and has lived in Biddulph since 1848. For years he served as a township councilor, and for one year he was a member of the County Council . . .

"You're a member of the Vigilance Committee, I believe," said the reporter.

"Yes, sir, I am, and will stick to it if I've got to go to the other world tomorrow."

"For what purpose was the Committee organized?"

"To maintain law and order, and put down the depredations that were going on in the township."

"How was it that the authorities could not do this?"

"Because terrorism reigned to such an extent that magistrates and constables were afraid to do their duty. Besides, no one in the township could be got to give evidence against the guilty parties, although there was no mistaking who the latter were. There was a time when I myself dared not speak for fear of the consequences. I was not fool enough, after

working hard all my life, to run the risk of having my barns and stables burned."

"Will you name some of the depredations of which you speak?"

"Cattle were stolen from the adjoining township of Blanshard, and left on the farms of innocent people in Biddulph. Barns and stables were burned, and robberies of grain and such like were frequent. You could not get down one-tenth of the transactions that occurred."

"Who got blamed for these deeds?"

"The Donnellys, although I do not think they were guilty of all of them, still they were implicated in a good many, but always managed to escape."

. . .

"Did you hold many meetings?"

"We met when anything happened, and we set about ferreting it out."

. . .

"Was violence ever proposed against any one?"

"No, sir," was the reply with emphasis. "The Committee was got up in good faith to keep down and ferret out crimes."

"Did the Donnellys join?"

"Not much. They knew that they were the principal cause of the Committee being formed."

"What was the last unlawful act the Donnellys were suspected of?"

James Lamphier

John Cain

"The burning of Ryder's barn. The Committee took it in hand, and knew that it was not a bit of use proceeding against any one else, for if the Donnellys did not burn the barns they were accessory to it."

"Then the Committee must have had strong feelings against family?"

"They did. Besides, the priest cursed them from the altar, and as Catholics we were bound to believe that the curse of a priest would prove true. In this case it has. Father Connolly cursed them again and again, and once said to the old woman that she would be made an example of in the ditch."

"Had Father Connolly anything to do with your meetings?"

"He had not; but he was the instigator of the Committee."

As already indicated, many of the vigilantes lived long and prosperous lives.[1] John Ryder, for another example, acquired several pieces of Biddulph land and quietly raised his family. He died in 1920. His wife, Kitty Casey, was a favorite of her brother-in-law, Grouchy Ryder, who mentioned her in his last will.

Nevertheless, several stories abound of the deaths of the vigilantes. Pat McGee related to me one or two. When in 1917 James Maher, Jr., was fatally hurt in the loft of his barn, he insisted that the priest climb the ladder to take his confession and administer the last rites. The implication was that he knew he was about to die and wished to confess his part in the Donnelly murders to save his soul from everlasting hellfire. When another of the vigilantes took sick, he said, the family locked the door to his room for fear that he, too, would make a deathbed confession.

When Big Anthony Heenan was found dead in his bed in January 1884, Bill Donnelly counted him a victim of divine retribution notwithstanding that Big Anthony was all of 65 years of age. And although he was one of the gang who had searched the Donnelly

Michael (Mooney) Blake

221

homestead for Thompson's cow, the elder Heenan was not considered to have been at the murders. Two of his sons, however, and a nephew were.

Patrick Breen[2] was considered to be one of the most intelligent members of the Peace Society. Well educated for a Biddulph farmer, he took a special interest in pedagogy beyond most school trustees and on one occasion formally addressed a meeting of educators in London. It was he who purported to give some organization to the Peace Society and wrote up its by-laws that were alluded to but not produced at any of the court proceedings.

At the time of the Donnelly murders, Big Pat Breen[3] possessed two to three hundred acres of land. After a lifetime of farming and raising a large family,[4] Big Pat Breen by 1910 had arranged a cozy retirement for himself, selling his farm to a son-in-law and moving to Masonville Corners, outside London, where he took up the duties of postmaster. A small country postmastership in those days was a lucrative and much sought after position. Unfortunately, however, the postal authorities soon after inaugurated rural mail delivery and on March 1st, 1914 closed the post office. Patrick Breen died on October 12th of the following year.

John Purtell, one of the six prisoners, upon his release married his first cousin, Mary Purtell, in London but not long after left the area and perhaps the country. By 1891 Mary was described in the census of that year as a widow and was living with her mother back in the Purtell hometown of Stratford, Ontario.

The next door neighbors of the Donnellys, William Thompson and his wife, Mary Carroll, had no children. By 1892 Thompson began to rent out his farm and started thinking of early retirement. By 1914, after almost forty years of marriage, he and his wife separated. When Bill Thompson died in 1929, he left an estate of $12,000. His last will, however, bequeathed his entire estate to his sister Maggie and sixteen nephews and

nieces. Mary Carroll died two years later and is buried in St. Patrick's Cemetery in the plot of her father, the "respectable" Mick Carroll. Bill Thompson himself lies in his parents' plot in the little graveyard at St. Peter's in Biddulph which used to be called, when the church stood there, "the front church".

John Heenan, another vigilante, quit Biddulph in 1893 and took his family to Detroit where he raised his children. He died there in 1928.

James Carroll's sister, Catherine, married Michael Madigan, himself a Biddulph vigilante, and his sister Margaret married a

John Kennedy

Detroit man named Kilcline. The sisters lived in Revelstoke and Rossland in British Columbia respectively at the time of Carroll's death. The constable's younger brother, Michael Carroll, married Anne Darcey and when she died the children of the union, Martin, Catherine, Cyril and James J., went to live with a relative on the Roman Line, Hannah Maher, who was married to Patrick Sullivan. Hannah was the daughter of James Maher whose sister, Catherine, was the mother of the Carroll boys including James, the constable, and his younger brothers, William and Michael.

I located James J. Carroll, son of Michael Carroll and Anne Darcey, in Michigan.[5] He had been born in Biddulph in 1894 and grew up there. His memories of his boyhood included the following:

> My grand-uncle Ned Maher lived right next door to the farm that Young Jim Donnelly occupied over on the eleventh concession. Ned Maher was a bare-knuckle fighter in his younger days and was well able to take care of himself. But he was completely free from trouble in Biddulph. When he heard that his sons were going to join the vigilance committee, he forbade them. "Just mind your own business," he told them, "and learn to take care of yourselves."

When Jim Donnelly, Jr., moved in next door, Ned Maher did not know he was a squatter but just assumed that his new neighbor had purchased the farm. As was the custom of the time, he took over a half bag of flour to help young Donnelly set up his new household. And when it came time for field work, they shared each other's implements such as plows.

James J. Carroll continued:

> . . . the eldest son of Ned Maher told me that when the land company kicked Donnelly off the place and sold it to this man whose name I cannot recall off hand he will never forget waking up one morning to the most forlorn sight he ever experienced. A young colt was running around the pasture squealing. It was the only animal alive in the field. All the others had their throats and bellies cut. It was done shortly before dawn because the colt was

running up and down the fence marking the boundary between the two properties. Everybody knew it was the Donnellys who had done this. They had warned this man that he would never raise anything on that farm.

This man who had taken over Young Jim Donnelly's place was completely ruined by the many misfortunes which befell him. Some time in the 1930s a son who was born on this farm

John Ryder

of this man came to the church at St. Patrick's. He said he just wanted to see the graves of the Donnellys. "These are the people who broke my father," he said, "not only financially, but they broke his heart. I just want to see where they are buried." He was shown the graves by the priest and caretaker, thanked them and left."

The ruined man was, of course, Joseph Caswell who had taken over Young Jim Donnelly's farm on the eleventh concession.

As a boy, James J. Carroll attended the Donnelly School and his recollections of Biddulph in the years not long after the Donnelly murders were vivid. Once, he said, he was up in a tree when two or three Biddulph farmers met under it. Keeping still, he heard them discuss who was present at the Donnelly house on the night of the massacre. On another occasion, he said, he was riding in a buggy on the Roman Line with Big Jack Kennedy when a stranger hailed them. He wanted to know where the Donnelly place was. As it happened, they were then directly opposite the homestead and Kennedy pointed to it. The stranger stared and wondered out loud why the people thereabouts would commit such a crime. He asked if any of those who were at the murder were still around.

Kennedy answered: "The Donnellys were robbing and stealing from everybody, and we just up and killed the sons of bitches."

Jack Kennedy and his brother-in-law, Will Donnelly, remained implacable enemies to

the end. When on May 30th, 1883 old John Kennedy, the father, died suddenly in one of the Granton hotels, Donnelly became convinced that his own son had poisoned him. As soon as he learned the circumstances of his father-in-law's demise, he was all for exhuming the body to prove the poisoning,

John Heenan and family

but Charles Hutchinson dissuaded him. The latter wrote on February 26th, 1884:[6]

My dear Mr. Donnelly,

I have consulted with Dr. Smith, one of the coroners for the county, as to the probability of detecting poison in the remains of a person who died so long ago as the 31st of last May. He thinks it very unlikely, as if it were a

224

vegetable poison all traces would be dispersed long ago. If there was any suspicion of foul play, action should have been taken at once. I fear it is too late now to do so effectually.

James Kelly—he whose horse was abused and whose complaint to the priest was instrumental in the latter's founding his property protective association—did die a premature death in 1882 leaving a widow with young children. They were assisted by

Patrick Cain

the Kennedys and the two families remained very close. A great grandson, Mike Kelly, told me that following Will Donnelly's death, Norah became reconciled with her brother's children and often visited them at the old Kennedy place. She also made visits to other friendly families in the Catholic Settlement. Mary Mitchell Whelihan recalled:

> I remember Mrs. Donnelly visiting us once. Her grandchildren, Ione and Jack Clay, were with her. Ione was the most beautifully strange child. But Mrs. Donnelly must have got out of

practice in farm ways for she broke her wrist milking one of the cows.

John Cain, who lived beside the Donnellys for many years, died in 1919. His younger brother, Patrick Cain, was a seventh son and therefore believed himself to be blessed in life especially when, in his youth, a gypsy fortuneteller predicted he was destined to wear brass buttons. At sixteen he left Biddulph to join relatives in Saginaw. In 1873 he joined the police and was assigned to "the roughest, toughest, fightingest spot in the Saginaws, none other than the Potter street area [where] the log trains would disgorge their human freight of lumberjacks . . . [and] where there were more fights to the square yard than anywhere else in the Saginaws."[7]

Here Patrick Cain, now spelling his name Kain, made his reputation as a tough cop. The day after the Donnelly murders, he rushed back to Biddulph to assist the vigilantes, including his brother John. Later, back in Saginaw, Cain helped his nephews, the Feeheley brothers, in resisting their extradition back to Canada. In 1883 Cain became Chief of the East Saginaw Police Force and later that same year became chief of the entire police force of the consolidated Saginaws. He retired in 1919 and died in Saginaw in 1925.

Most of the vigilantes lived out their normal life spans and died normal deaths. It is interesting to note that forty years after the tragedy, fully one-quarter of the members of the Peace Society of Biddulph were still hale and hearty.

How true, then, are these words in the Exeter *Advocate* of Thursday, February 10th, 1910, in which the Donnelly tragedy was revisited?

> It is a peculiar fact that all the persons said to have been connected with the tragedy, though many of them were comparatively young, scarcely any are living today, and many of them died a violent death.

Chapter 33

Friends and Allies

William Donnelly's letter of February 4th, 1893 about divine retribution on his enemies did not go unanswered. Soon after its appearance, a letter was sent by an unidentified writer to the St. Marys *Argus* that reads:[1]

I must protest against Mr. Donnelly's reckless assertion that the tragedy was a vigilante butchery . . . such reckless assertions are actionable . . . according to his own repeated statements both private and public . . . his extensive business in Biddulph prior to 1880 was worth $4,000 per annum to him . . . the local events of 1880 and 1881 destroyed that business which Donnelly & Co. operated from their headquarters at Whalen's Corner . . . What right has he to assert that certain persons who died in Biddulph and elsewhere since 1880 were directly or indirectly concerned in the slaughter referred to? . . .

But let us see how some of Mr. Donnelly's fast friends fared. His father-in-law, mother-in-law and sister-in-law died suddenly, the former in a hotel in Granton, the latter in Michigan; two of his friends were killed by cars in Michigan, another was crushed under a steam engine, another died from a paralytic stroke and one died raving.

The other record—5 persons who were vigilants have died, one of whom was suffocated by gas in a well, not by falling into it; an old man was over 70 years old, and whose sons were vigilants, died suddenly in his bed. These two cases which are outside the ordinary course of nature in the manner of people's taking off are all that can be charged

to the vigilants in the line of Mr. Donnelly's conclusions. The lamented victims of the Mail Road disaster he refers to must be left out of the reckoning as they had nothing whatever to do with either side further than to give evidence in court on behalf of Purtel who lodged in their house on the night of the tragedy . . . As regards the comparative wealth of both parties, the odds are largely in favor of the terrible vigilants and their friends.

The letter goes on to try to explain the real reason for the Donnelly tragedy. The words show to some extent the feelings that drove the members of the Peace Society to their murderous conclusion:

Prior to that memorable year a band of thieves and incendiaries infested Biddulph and the adjoining townships; neither life nor property were secure from the lawless depredations of that gang. People were obliged to stand guard with pitchforks over their property. Horses' throats were cut, their tails and manes cut off, cattle were hocked and otherwise mutilated, valuable horses were taken out of stables and driven about the country and rendered useless to their owners, property had been stolen or rather taken in broad daylight, dogs were shot at people's doorsteps, the air resounded with horrible oaths and blasphemies, scarcely a week passed without the heavens being made luminous with the glare of burning buildings, people were compelled to herd stolen cattle and feed the thieves till such time as they could dispose of them . . . .

The reader will note that the letter referred to tragic or unusual deaths suffered by friends of the Donnellys. Several of such deaths were those of the Keefes.

None of the sons of James Keefe, Sr., saw much future in Biddulph. Patrick J. Keefe was born the same year as Tom Donnelly. He was the first of the Keefes of the Roman Line to emigrate to the States but the prospects of a better life may not have been the only reason for his leaving. In an earlier chapter it was pointed out that one, William Thorpe, had laid a charge against him. The charge was of the rape of Thorpe's wife, Mary. Mary Thorpe made a sworn statement in the case that on Saturday, January 11th, 1879 a man using the name Smith whom she

Thomas Keefe's death certificate from Paris, France.

226

had never seen before but later discovered was Patrick Keefe came to her home in Fullarton Township, Perth County, in company with one, William McBride, and asked if her husband was at home. She said he was in back of the house chopping in the bush. They then left but in a few minutes Keefe returned. She went on:[2]

> He caught me by the arm and threw me upon the bed. He swore if I did not lay still, or if I said a word he would put a ball through me. I tried to get away and ordered him out of the house but he held me by the arm making the mark now shown upon the wrist. He then stripped my clothes up and violated my person. After getting satisfaction he got up and went out . . . .

Keefe appears not to have been arrested

on this charge for he was soon scouting out for land in Nebraska and not long after left to settle permanently at Jackson in Dakota County, Nebraska. Some other Keefes who had come out from Ireland had taken up land in that same area. Although he did return on an occasional visit to Biddulph, Patrick J. Keefe soon married, kept a saloon and had several children. But in 1891 he was killed in a train accident leaving his wife and four small children with the youngest only about a year old. His widow married the saloon's bartender, Jerry McBride, who helped bring up the children. One of them, Patrick, became a physician.[3]

By 1883 Patrick J. Keefe's brother Thomas was spending all his time between Biddulph and Nebraska, making trips to

This picture of Big Jim Keefe on an ox was taken during a scouting trip for new investment opportunities years after he had moved to the Iowa-Nebraska border area and had become affluent selling farm properties.

Europe and calling himself a liquor merchant. He, too, died prematurely when in 1900 he took fever and died in Paris, France. His body was shipped back in a coffin sealed with lead. Upon receipt of the sealed coffin in Biddulph, the family held a long discussion whether they should open it up to make sure it was Thomas's body that was inside, but in the end they left the coffin intact and it was buried at St. Patrick's. Thomas was unmarried.

The oldest son, Big Jim Keefe—he who along with Jim Jr. and Tom Donnelly had the brawl with Joe Berryhill during the stagecoach troubles—first went to live in Detroit where for a short period he operated a saloon. He soon came back and in 1884 claimed as his bride a popular London girl whom he had had his eye on for some time, Ann Jane Phillips.[4] The couple then left for the Iowa-Nebraska border country and eventually moved to Sioux City, Iowa, across

Big Jim Keefe in his later years.

the Nebraska River from Jackson where his brother had settled. Big Jim went into selling real estate and became a very successful salesman of farm properties. Selling property for a living came easier to him than farming and he made a lot of money from sales. He also became an astute investor and before long became quite well off. Two of his sons became lawyers and two of his daughters teachers. Jim Keefe apparently did not dwell on the past. His daughter recalled that he used to advise his children that if something bad happened to them, they were to go on with their lives. "Just forget it," he would say. It was not so much the words he used, she said, but the way he said it.

In the Iowa-Nebraska border area where Jim Keefe settled down, he adopted as his own middle name the maiden name of his mother and thereafter called himself James Quigley Keefe to distinguish himself from several other Keefes in the district bearing the same first name, for the most part his own relatives. James Q. Keefe spent his prosperous retirement years looking after his investments and enjoying life. On Christmas Eve in 1929 on his way to attend midnight mass, however, he was struck by an automobile driven by a youth and killed.

A younger first cousin of these Keefes was James Thomas Keefe, son of Robert Keefe, Sr. He stayed in Biddulph but also came to an untimely end. While transporting home a load of tile on a wagon, the horses bolted when they came to the little bridge on the Roman Line near where the last altercations took place in 1882 between James Carroll and the Keefes in the first case and the sons of the Biddulph Peace Society and John Kent and the Keefes in the other. The load became dislodged and fell on top of him.

"The animals became frightened," said the London *Free Press* report of Tuesday, October 28th, 1913, "and ran over half a mile, overturning the remainder of the load into the ditch. Mr. Keefe's injuries were confined to his head, his scalp having been almost completely severed."

Another cousin, John Keefe, was the son of Dan Keefe and grandson of the Biddulph pioneer, Matthew Keefe. John Keefe had been a good friend of Mike Donnelly and had acted as godparent to Mike's only daughter, Catherine, in 1876. Following the Biddulph tragedy, both the Dan and John O'Keefe families—they began to spell their surname with the Irish O'—moved to Saginaw. John obtained employment with the Flint & Pere Marquette Railroad. In my papers is a copy of the Saginaw newspaper clipping of his death on January 30th, 1889:

CRUSHED TO DEATH.
John O'Keefe, an Employe on the F. & P.M., Instantly Killed.
Slipped and Fell Between Two Freight Cars, and the Wheels Pass Over His Head—A Terrible Sight.

Another of those terrible accidents which have frequently shocked our readers of late took place about 9 o'clock yesterday morning, at the Sixth Street crossing of the F. & P.M., resulting in the crushing to instant death of a young yardsman named John O'Keefe.

O'Keefe was employed as a car inspector, and at the time of the accident was engaged in looking over a freight train which was being made up for the west, and while the train was in motion he attempted to board it catching between two freight cars just at the Sixth Street crossing. Unfortunately, he missed the bumpers, for which he had sprung, and there being no ladder on the end of the car for him to grasp he fell between them, his head striking the rail, and the next instant the wheels of the nearest truck had passed over him, crushing out his life and smashing his head into a shapeless mass.

As for Margaret, sister of Norah Donnelly, who was referred to in the letter answering Will Donnelly's allegations, her death was reported in the Glencoe *Transcript* of Thursday, April 30th, 1885 as follows:

A telegram from East Saginaw on Saturday says: "Last night the dead body of Miss Margaret Kennedy was found in the outhouse of Michael O'Connell, her brother-in-law. Miss Kennedy, aged 33, comes from Biddulph, Ontario. An autopsy is being held. Miss

Kennedy left the house at 8 o'clock last night, and her whereabouts were not known till her body was found. Death is supposed to have resulted from natural causes. The deceased was a sister to Mrs. William Donnelly, of this place."

Margaret Kennedy had, of course, grown up in the Catholic Settlement of Biddulph which extends from the Roman Line to three or four concessions east beyond the Cedar Swamp Schoolhouse towards the village of Granton but still within the Township of

Margaret Kennedy

Biddulph. Near Granton lived the two Caswell families—distantly related—neither of whom were friends of the Donnellys. Following the Donnelly tragedy descendants of the smaller family—headed by Joseph Caswell who had incurred the animosity of the Donnellys by taking over the farm left by Jim Donnelly, Jr., when he decamped to Michigan—and the larger Caswell family with its ten sons, spread far and wide throughout North America. Curiously, such descendants could not forget that tragedy and the infamous tombstone in the graveyard of St. Patrick's and they would often hark back to

Granton in this pre-1910 photograph appears much as it did in the time of the Donnellys.

the years that they and their forbears spent there.

John J. Caswell, for example, was born on board a ship out of Liverpool bound for America in 1848. His family settled first in other parts of Canada but eventually found its way to Biddulph where John J. Caswell spent his boyhood years on a bush farm near Granton. An older brother, Sam Caswell, had operated one of the earliest photographic galleries there, one of only two or three photographers who ever operated such an establishment in the village.

The ten Caswell boys of the larger family grew up and scattered throughout North America but in 1905 one of them, John J. Caswell above mentioned, retired to a prune ranch in California and died there in 1925. Five years before his death, he wrote his "Memories of Growing up in Granton". In this epistle, scrawled in pencil in a cheap schoolbook scribbler with a minimum of punctuality, grammar or spelling, he wrote:

> In 1851 my Father emigrated from Darlington to the township of Beddulph which has for many lear [sic] been known as a township of tyranny and murder . . . .

For two or three generations, after the death of Robert Donnelly, the tombstone in St. Patrick's stood unharmed, even neglected, and almost entirely ignored by the parishioners. The daughter of Theresa Whelan told me that during the years she was growing up in the first and second decades of the twentieth century, she often attended Mass at St. Patrick's with her mother but when I asked her about the Donnelly marker in those days she said, "We could not go over and look at that tombstone. My mother just would not have allowed it. You see, there were too many of that crowd still around and our going near the Donnelly stone might have been seen as sympathy for the family."

The marker was still standing there when in early August 1964 we first visited the church and cemetery. A little over a month later, however, the parish priest Father Francis J. Bricklin took decisive action. On Wednesday, September 11th, without telling anyone, he ordered workmen to dismantle the stone marker and remove it from the grave site. Only a few knew the new location of the pieces. They were in fact stored within a few feet of the graves themselves, as I was personally informed by one of the men who took down the stone, in a wooden shed on the church grounds.

230

As a result, but typical of almost anything connected with the Donnelly story, the abrupt removal of the stone became a matter of controversy. Some said it was taken to the church basement where it was smashed to smithereens. Others said the marker had been buried nearby but in unconsecrated ground. Others said the remains of the Donnellys themselves had also been removed: disinterred and reburied in the city of London. This last would not have been surprising for Robert's wife, Annie, had indeed had his remains removed from St. Patrick's graveyard and reburied in London.

Although the five victims of the February 4th tragedy remain in their original graves, however, it is true that following that event few families could be found in the Catholic Settlement who had anything good to say in the open about the Donnellys. One of them was the Keefe family who remained their staunch friends from beginning to end. Another, related by marriage to the Keefes, was ironically a Ryder family. They were known as the Buckshot Ryders.

There were two branches of Ryders in Biddulph, each descended from one of the two pioneer brothers, James and Patrick. Patrick came to be known as Buckshot Paddy and the nickname was passed down to his son Buckshot Jim who married Martha Keefe

and to his grandsons Buckshot Paddy and Buckshot Rhody. These Buckshots are sometimes confused with the family of Patrick (Grouchy) Ryder who was the son of the other pioneer, James. The confusion is perpetuated by the fact that Grouchy Ryder's son, Jim, was alleged to have wielded the shotgun that was used in the murder of John Donnelly. He is therefore sometimes erroneously referred to as Buckshot Jim.

Old Buckshot Paddy acquired his nickname during the events of the notorious Brimmacombe murder case in 1857. Born in Ireland about 1803, Patrick Ryder married

Cornelius Toohey, on the right, found the body of Richard Brimmacobe on the Roman Line in 1857. On the left is his brother, Long Jim Toohey. This picture was taken not long before both died in 1931.

231

Anne Mara and had at least nine children including six daughters, among them Catherine[5] and Rachel. Rachel married William Casey who in the year of the Brimmacombe murder lived on the road beyond the Roman Line extending into Usborne Township. Casey it was who helped Richard Brimmacombe raise his house but who at the raising got into a fight with some of the Devonshire English who were also on hand. When they beat him, Casey went out of his way to threaten not only the men who had assaulted him but Brimmacombe as well. Patrick Ryder, as Casey's father-in-law, was drawn into the dispute and also made threats against Brimmacombe on behalf of his daughter's husband. In February of 1857, not long after these threats were made, Cornelius Toohey, a young lad of seventeen, found the body of Richard Brimmacombe on the Roman Line near Patrick Ryder's homestead which was lot 24 in the sixth concession. It seemed obvious that he had been set upon and murdered.

"Has heard people say," young Cornelius testified at the inquest,[6] "that they thought themselves that Patrick Ryder had done it."

It is true that suspicions immediately fastened upon Ryder and William Casey as well as the latter's brother Patrick Casey as all three had been seen near the scene of the crime. Charges of murder were laid against them and warrants for their arrest issued. Two English constables named Thomas Bissett and James Balkwill went out to arrest Ryder. While the constables were on horseback, they hired a sleigh and driver at the Catholic Church Corners in order to convey the prisoner back with them. The owner of the sleigh was the hotelkeeper, Andy Keefe, who assigned his barman Michael Ryan to be driver. For good measure, Keefe himself went along with the constables to point out Ryder and to see what would transpire.[7]

When the little party arrived at Ryder's homestead, the constables left the sleigh and horses on the road and walked up the lane.

Catherine Ryder was ten years old when she saw her father send the English constables scampering down the road with a blast of buckshot.

Ryder's log shanty was in darkness. After a few moments of repeated knocking on the door, Ryder's voice came from inside. "Wait until I put my pants on," he yelled, "and then I'll let you in."

Ryder put on his pants but instead of opening the door he appeared at the window. "What do you want?" he asked.

Constable Bissett replied that they wanted to come in. The English accent of the constable doubtless told Ryder they were not there on a friendly visit. He left the window and they heard him walking about inside for a few moments. When he re-appeared at the window, the constables thought they caught a glimpse of a gun in Ryder's hands. Bissett asked him again to open the door.

Ryder then swore a big oath, the constables later testified, and said, "I will put the contents of what I hold in my hand into you if you do not leave my premises."

232

Bissett and Balkwill turned and went back towards the road. Ryder came out of the shanty and followed them close behind.

"I will shoot you," he repeated as they reached the road, "if you do not leave."

"I will not leave the road," said Bissett.

Ryder then went up to the head of the horses and seized the reins. He swore again and said, "You shall not go until you show me what is your authority to come after me."

"I will do as I mind on the Queen's highway," the constable replied.

Suddenly Ryder noticed the driver of the sleigh who was quietly sitting on the seat and recognized his fellow Catholic. "What, Ryan, is that you?" he said, "What business have you got here?"

While Ryder was thus distracted, Bissett thought he had an opportunity to seize him and began to edge forward but Ryder quickly swung around and pointed the gun at him. This seemed to give the other constable, James Balkwill, an opportunity but he hesitated and did nothing. Later he lamely explained that he was in the act of pulling off his gloves in order to put a better grip on Ryder but thought better of making a move for fear that Ryder would pull the trigger and kill his fellow constable.

Then Andy Keefe who had so far remained silent cried out, "Don't shoot, don't shoot, or you will kill one of us, sure."

Ryder, still at the head of the horses, began to back them up. "Stay away," he warned them, "if any of you take another step, by God, I will fire."

The constables were not entirely sure what happened next. But they were unarmed, they later said, and the arrest was not working out as planned. Ryder did not stop them from turning to leave but before they had gone very far they thought they saw Ryder run across the road in order, they surmised, to raise a mob against them. They reported hearing behind them as they drove off the loud report of a gunshot. Others say that they scampered down the road as quickly as they

could and that they not only heard but felt some of Ryder's buckshot.

The story of Ryder's singlehandedly driving off the hated English constables and peppering them with buckshot was gleefully told and retold in the Catholic Settlement for years afterwards. As a result of this incident, Patrick Ryder and his progeny were ever after referred to as the Buckshot Ryders.

The Buckshot Ryders always remained friendly with the Donnellys. As we have seen, in the summer of 1882 Buckshot Jim Ryder had an altercation with James Carroll when Carroll's horses broke into Ryder's field. There followed the squabble on the little bridge on the Roman Line when Big Jim Keefe and his brother were struggling with a young horse they were attempting to break in and Carroll seized the reins. Again, on September 3rd, 1882 occurred the great row of gun-shooting into the air and stone-throwing between John Kent and the Keefes on one side and the youthful gang who were for the most part the sons of the vigilantes on the other. William Porte noted the last affray in his diary:[8]

> Row on Carroll's bridge on the 6 & 7 Concession Biddulph between Kent—Tom Keeff & Pat Sullivan on one side—Hugh & Jim Toohey & Pat Ryder Jr. on the other. Stones thrown & Revolvers fired but no one much hurt. Warrants out by both parties about 20 in all.

At the time of this altercation, William Donnelly was living in Rendville, Ohio but he wrote to Charles Hutchinson about it as follows:[9]

> I learned all about the row between Kent and the Keefe boys & the gang & am sorry to see Kent & the Keefes in trouble . . . the reason they are at Kent is because he had nerve enough to go in amongst them to work our old homestead. But I hope the thing will turn out all right & the Vigilants be stop[p]ed in some way. If not I feel satisfied they will burn Kent & the Keefe families in their houses . . . .

This time Will Donnelly was wrong. The Kents and Keefes were not burned and their

The Robert Keefe house on the Roman Line.

houses survived into our time. The Keefe house that Will feared would be burned stood about a mile north of the Donnelly homestead. The Keefes had raised its hewed logs in 1860[10] during the time that Jim Donnelly was serving his term in Kingston. By then many of the original rude shanties of the Roman Line were almost twenty years old. By replacing the shanty with a building then considered grand and spacious—a house of squared logs with two storeys—the Keefes were simply emulating many of their neighbors. As Robert Keefe and his wife Mary Ryan, like the other Keefes, were always on good terms with the Donnellys, in all likelihood the older Donnelly boys helped with the raising of Keefe's house.

Immediately south of the Keefe house was the homestead of Mick Feeheley, whose mother was a Keefe. Mick had married Bridget Cain. It was Bridget's younger brother John who had finally taken over the old Michael Maher farm from which Jim

Donnelly had been ousted. While the Donnellys tolerated young Cain, Mrs. Donnelly in particular nursed her resentment over having lost one-half the family's original homestead and bore no good feelings towards him.

After the turn of the century, John Cain fell on hard times and had to sell the farm. News of its sale to Bob Donnelly was set out in a little item from the Exeter newspaper of January 9, 1907:[11]

> Messrs. B. and J. M. Donnelly have recently purchased the south half of Lot 18, Concession 6 of Biddulph Township from Mr. John Coyne [*sic*] for $2,550. This gives the Donnellys a farm of one hundred acres.

When the deal was concluded, Bob Donnelly proclaimed that "the deed jumped up and kissed me."[12]

Before that, however, Bob Donnelly rented the homestead in the early 1890s to one, Alfred Digman, which resulted in another misadventure to an ally of the family.

234

Bob Donnelly and his nephew Jim in a photograph dating from the first decade of the twentieth century, shortly after the erection of the large barn in background. Both it and the rebuilt house have survived into our time.

In March 1893, Buckshot Jim Ryder had driven in to Lucan with his thirteen-year-old daughter, Maggie, and his sister, Mary, who had married the schoolteacher Stephen Patten. In the village, Ryder met Digman and they had some words, apparently not of a friendly nature, about a horse trade. Later that day as Ryder was returning home and passed the Donnelly homestead, he heard Digman calling taunts out to him. Furthermore, according to young Maggie, he jumped up on a manure pile and exposed himself as he waved his hat in the air and called Buckshot "a papist son of a bitch".

Ryder was infuriated at the other's crude conduct. He stopped the horses, alighted from the conveyance and challenged Digman to come out on the road. Digman for his part dared Ryder to come to him. Ryder then rushed into the yard and the two men grappled and fell to the ground. Mrs. Digman ran out of the house and pulling Ryder off her husband cried out, "Kill him, Alfred, or I will."

Digman then produced a knife or had it given him by his wife. Both parties were badly stabbed in the ensuing affray but Buckshot's wounds were especially severe. His daughter drove him home as he bled from his arms and hands. He took several weeks to recover. Digman was sentenced to nine months in jail for the assault.

The Kennedy boys, Joseph, Rhody and John, were at one time cronies of the Donnelly brothers although Rhody and John became bitterly opposed to them following the marriage of their sister Norah to William Donnelly. Rhody Kennedy left the district before the Donnelly story came to its bloody climax in February 1880. He apparently went to the United States, for under date of Wednesday, February 12th, 1879 William Porte noted in his journal:

> Wrote Ephraim Butler to East Saginaw today in re Rhody Kennedy.

And again on June 12th of that year he made the entry:

> Wrote Peter Cody re Rhody, Penconning P.O., Bay County, Michigan. Recd June 18/79 a letter from Peter Cody & sent it same day to H. Macmahon, London. Did not know the exact place of his whereabouts but think a trip out

on the Jackson & Lansing railroad for about 50 miles would find him.

Wrote Mr. Macmahon July 28/79 to say I would go after Kennedy but my expenses must be paid.

And then under date of October 17th, 1879 Porte made the following diary entry:

Wrote Peter Cody today re Rhody.

After this, Rhody Kennedy was lost. Off and on for years my friend Randy White made efforts to locate him throughout the United States and tracked down many leads without avail. Then one day he turned up the following item in the London *Daily Free Press* of Saturday, January 8th, 1887:

Roady Kennedy, formerly of Biddulph, has sworn out a warrant at Tawas, Mich., charging Thomas Murphy with the murder of his brother Joseph in September last. Kennedy was killed in Murphy's house. Kennedy claims to have evidence that Murphy was an accomplice of Harvey and his wife in the crime.

Author's sketch of Robert Donnelly.

This item and follow-up research by Randy located Rhody Kennedy in Wisconsin. From there he went to East Tawas, Iosco County, Michigan to determine the fate of his long-lost older brother Joseph. He learned here that on September 15th, 1886 in a farm house near a place called Alabaster in Iosco County, Michigan, Joseph Kennedy—a big man six feet tall or near that and weighing two hundred pounds, described as "a dissipated, quarrelsome fellow"—was shot twice with a Winchester rifle by Charles Harvey, a disreputable character in and around Tawas City in that county. Kennedy had been quarreling with Harvey and his wife. The two dragged Joe's body to a nearby swale and there buried him face down in a hole about two and a half feet deep with his feet a little higher than his head and barely covered with dirt. The body was discovered three months later. Harvey later confessed to this homicide and was sentenced to five years in Jackson State Prison for manslaughter.

When Bob Donnelly returned once more to live at the homestead, he had the old stable of his father's rebuilt into a fine medium-sized bank barn which stands to this day. The granary erected a few years before may also have been raised on a cement foundation at this time. Buckshot Jim Ryder was a neighbor further along on the Roman Line and his sons, Buckshot Paddy and Rhody and his daughters attended the Donnelly School. Mary Mitchell told me that when the Ryder boys grew up they were always coming over and never seemed to be tired of bringing up the subject of the Donnelly tragedy discussing over and over again how it happened and who was present at the home of the Donnellys on that fateful night.

Chapter 34

A Tramp Letter

Many have wondered why no one was ever convicted of the February 4th massacre of the Donnellys. John Doherty, who witnessed a crowd of the vigilantes approaching the Donnelly house on that fateful night, could not be persuaded to testify. Others who probably could have given similar damning testimony were John Whelan, John Walker and William Blackwell. Blackwell, for example, told the Whalen's Corners schoolteacher, Frank Morley, on the very day of the killings that he had looked out and seen a gang of about twenty-five men marching down the road away from Will's house immediately after John Donnelly had been shot. Some of the men, he said, were dressed in women's clothing and some had clothing thrown over their shoulders. Blackwell did not repeat his statement to the police.

Shortly after the beginning of the first trial of James Carroll in London, Charles Hutchinson received word from Berlin (later renamed Kitchener) in Ontario that a young railway tramp had called on a house on the outskirts of that city occupied by the Young family and asked to borrow the *Globe* newspaper. The man was about twenty or twenty-two years old, thought Mrs. Young, with very red hair. He was about five feet eight or nine inches tall and "looking sick enough to die". He was not like the class of tramps that hang around there, she said "nor at all like a man one would be afraid of." The foot of Mrs. Young's garden came to the bridge over the railway tracks which the family took as a shortcut into town. Later that same day as Mrs. Young was walking along those tracks, she happened to spy that same man under the bridge. He was reading a letter. In his haste to depart, the man dropped the letter and Mrs. Young went over and picked it up. As it seemed to have significant reference to the Donnelly murders, the Youngs immediately forwarded it to the Middlesex Crown Attorney in London.

The letter, written in a tortured hand and with a few parts missing due to the paper having been slightly torn, reads:

> Lucan August 14
> Dere Mike
> i had a notion to begin with yi are a darn fool to go to try and get money out of Mcobthlin wife as if it wasent hard enouf for her to get along you had better be after trying to get it out of bill donnaly he semes to have lots   Mike sure if you sit yer foot in London before it is all over you will be aristed and get us all in a nice durn fus bill donnaly thinks like every one here that you are in the stats instead of here that night and if you did tell you could only tell on them that is in gal for I sware by the holy Jeezus [page 2] that I never [paper torn] purtel nor bill [paper torn] you could not have eather it was that durn Jim Carall and McLoughlin and Kanada and X that we sen going in the old donnalys house and you needent get us in to a scrape or yerself for them for all Father Connors or all the money in the hole consarn wont hinder them from swinging than to bust [out?] Jim done it all and ought to he was so smart he thought that cul Connors will be a big man after a while you bet but you better have the duckbillacke as well as the duckague if that is what you have for a while longer then come to London or Lucan tramping among the duck [page 3] [paper torn] them all [paper torn] can tell yet but will soon the old fellow is not so bad as that now don't make a fool and an ass of yerself because ye have it in head yer going to dee divil adu will ye do this many day but if you want a call from someone ye will turn spout I send this from London good by and kep a good hart Sure it will soon be all over and ye will be better of then you will if you spout rite as soon as ye get this yers Bill rite to London next time

It was not long before two tramps whose descriptions resembled that given by the Youngs were picked up, one in Berlin and the other in Guelph. Will Donnelly went over to both places. In Berlin, he took Mrs. Young over to the jail to look at the man there. She

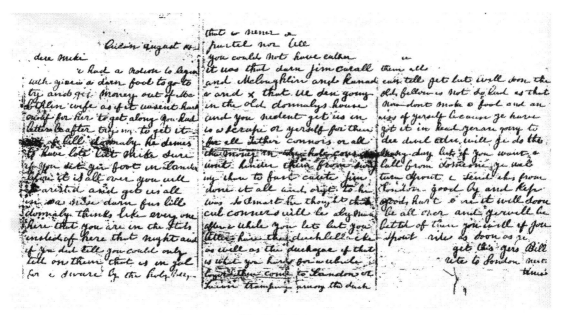

The Berlin letter

said immediately it was not the man she had seen with the letter even though he had red hair and resembled him quite a bit. Will reported on his visit to Guelph in a letter dated November 9th, 1880 that he wrote to Hutchinson as follows:

> The man in Guelph is very much of the same description but larger and the hair not so redd [*sic*]. He is so near the man we want that I consider the Chief at Guelph done exactly right in looking after him. The man will give no satisfactory account of himself and it seems to me *I know him well* [italics added]. Bill Whalen and Bill Feehely are gone to the States. They bought their tickets for Saginaw.

I find it curious that William Feeheley left for Saginaw about the same time the letter was found—its discovery was quickly made known in the community and leaked to the prisoners and their friends by Jailer Henry Fysch—and I have a hunch that "dere Mike" in the Berlin letter is Mike Welch, the sometime hired man of Martin McLaughlin. The latter referred to Welch only once during his testimony and that was in cross-examination at the first trial of Carroll in the fall of 1880. It was in answer to questions by one of the Crown lawyers. The evening

edition of the London *Advertiser* report of Friday, October 8th, 1880 reads:

> Martin McLaughlin, sworn—. . . on that Tuesday night I was at the barn where a cow was calving, and was there about an hour.
>
> To Mr. Magee—I was out about an hour at ten o'clock; after that I went to bed; Mike Welch, my hired man, and my family were in the house that night . . . slept in the front room downstairs that night; Welch slept in the kitchen part . . . .

Because of the several references to McLaughlin and his wife in the letter and because it was William Feeheley and John Whelan who stood behind Whelan's fence and saw the gang enter the Donnelly house, I suspect that the writer of the Berlin letter was William Feeheley and that it was addressed to Mike Welch. Welch may have been with them behind the fence. Mike Welch was more or less a transient and had been in Biddulph for a short time only. As such, Will Donnelly may well have seen him casually, perhaps once only, and for that reason thought about the tramp who resembled him that he "knew him well" but could not place him.

Again, Mrs. Young stated that the tramp she saw with the letter looked "sick enough to die" and the letter refers to the addressee as having some sort of sickness such as "duckbillacke" or "duckague". And there is clear reference to seeing three of the prisoners, namely, Jim Carroll, McLaughlin and Kennedy entering Old Donnelly's house. At the top of page two, the writer appears to be stating something like "we did not see nor could you have seen Purtell or Bill" there. The "Bill" referred to may have been Bill Thompson or, at a stretch, William Casey as these appear be the only two members of the mob bearing that given name. Of course, the letter was not part of the court record.

Aside from this letter, the testimony of men like Doherty, Whelan, Walker and Blackwell, would have served to corroborate the testimony of Will Donnelly which, except for the sworn word of the young lad O'Connor, stood alone. Of course, Donnelly's evidence was tainted—perhaps not in the strictly legal sense but in the public mind because of the family's criminal record. It was considered to be of insufficient moral worth in the minds of a Middlesex jury in 1880 to hang twenty or more men. The independent testimony of those other men, however, could possibly have tipped the balance.

Then there was the case of Luke Nangle. In February 1880, Nangle was working as a hired man for Jim Toohey. Charles Hutchinson wrote to Æmilius Irving in January 1881 about Nangle's possible testimony at the upcoming trial:[1]

> Luke Nangle told Charles Nangle and John Grace that in the morning after [the] murder he saw Toohey dressed in women's clothes and taking them off in the stable—Toohey had a black eye (this can be proved by Jas McLaughlin, Daniel Keefe and Patrick Keefe and Patrick Donnelly). He can prove that there were several meetings of part of the vigilance committee at Toohey's house including [the] night of the Ryder fire and the murder—when their windows were screened with bed quilts
> . . .

Hutchinson added words implying, however, that Nangle would not be a willing witness.

He was served with a subpoena but declared that he would sooner leave the country than be forced to give evidence against the Peace Society. His testimony was never heard in court.

There were those in the community, on the other hand, who always maintained that no evidence of any kind would have resulted in a conviction. Elgin Schoff was born in 1852 and grew up at Flanagan's Corners which in the mid-1870s became Clandeboye. His father, Daniel Schoff, was postmaster there for 42 years. Elgin Schoff, being of the same age as the Donnelly brothers, remembered them well. For one thing, they drove their stagecoach through Flanagan's Corners to Exeter.

"You couldn't have got twelve jurors in Middlesex County to convict anybody for murdering the Donnellys," said Schoff, "no matter how many trials you'd had."[2]

When in the 1930s his words were recorded, Elgin Schoff was an elderly retired lawyer living in Toronto. "There were a great many things happened before; barns and stacks burned, animals maimed, Flanagans shot, and the magistrates of Lucan afraid of the Donnellys and doing nothing. After the murders there was no more of it."

Schoff's opinion pretty well sums up the local feeling on the subject. He went on to say, however, that although the Donnelly story went underground in Lucan and surroundings, it was not forgotten elsewhere. "It's funny," he added, "how the interest in that case persists. I've been in most parts of Canada, and wherever I've been, from here to Dawson City, people have asked me about the Donnelly murder."

I believe, with Elgin Schoff, that from the beginning there was little chance of a conviction. We know that at the time of the trials the authorities undertook the dubious task of canvassing prospective jurors. The notes of the canvassers are extant. Typical of the results was the recorded opinion of Samuel Moore who farmed lot 22 in the third concession of West Nissouri. The notation opposite his name reads:[3]

> Said we have our private opinion but it would look hard to hang those men on that boy's evidence. A good man, but not recommended.

And notwithstanding their expressions of the desire to do justice based on the evidence, eventually all the jurors who acquitted Carroll on his second trial for the murder of Judith Donnelly came around to the same conclusion.

A bartender in the Revere House in the 1870s was one, Richard Tapp. Out of the blue one day I received a letter from his great grandson. Richard Tapp was born in 1854 in North Molton, Devonshire, England and came to Canada in about 1872. He died in 1948, before any of the books on the Donnelly story had been written. This is Richard Tapp's recollection of the Donnellys:

> I worked in the Exeter-Lucan area for 10 years and was handy man for a Lucan hotel owner for a while. When working there I found a body in the hotel barn. Bob Donnelly was accused of the murder and I had to testify at the trial. The Donnellys were terrorizing Lucan at this time and one of them told me to keep my mouth shut or I'd be killed.

This incident is described in chapter 23 of *The Donnelly Album.* The Donnellys—not Bob but his brothers Young Jim and Tom—were indeed suspected of having killed poor Clark for his money. Like others who relied on their memory years after the events, Tapp could probably not distinguish between so many Donnelly brothers but the body in the hotel barn was that of Daniel Clark. Notwithstanding the suspicions of some Lucanites, Dr. James Sutton gave it as his opinion that the few wounds on the body were of no consequence in causing death and that Dan Clark had died of natural causes. The enemies of the Donnellys thought otherwise. And so, apparently, judging from the above passage, did Richard Tapp. It should be mentioned also that James Sutton was the Donnelly family's doctor.

Richard Tapp, in his later years.

240

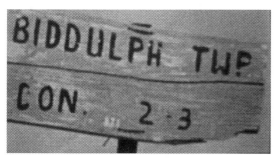

Photographed by the author in 1964, these old Biddulph Township road signs have long since disappeared.

Whatever their reputation, the Donnellys could not be characterized as lazy. Whether this was a result of an attempt to compensate for their tainted status as a family headed by a convicted murderer, or simply a case of being blessed with an emergent and seemingly boundless energy, can be argued. Some readers may have seen a book which was published a few years ago called *Greenbank,*[4] a local history of a little town of that name northeast of Toronto. Its author, W. H. Graham, one morning was looking at the Biddulph Agricultural Census for 1871 and made a brief little informal study that he passed along to me. He compared the Donnellys' farming output to about a dozen of their neighbors. Graham's little essay does not pretend to be profound or deep, but it says something about the Donnellys which pretty well everybody agrees with. When it came to work, they were not slackers.

I will quote Graham's own words: "A superficial run-through . . . produces some idea of the Donnellys' economic situation. They were right at the bottom as land owners. The average holding was 95 acres (median 75) and they had 50 acres . . . In agricultural returns they were highly individual. They report spring wheat at 20 bushels per acre. The next closest is 12, the average 9. They were either some farmers or creative estimators.

"Among the people showing, as the Donnellys do, 2 acres of garden or orchard, the average yield of apples is 39 bushels. The

Donnellys is 50. They report roughly the same amount of barley and oats as other farms the same size, but just twice the amount of peas. And potatoes! Other farms the same size report 40 to 80 bushels of potatoes, the Donnellys report 300.

"The Donnellys were either industrious or highly imaginative in the wood lot—everyone else reports 25 to 50 cords of firewood, they claim 200."[5]

It is true that the Donnellys as folk heroes are alive and well. In this connection, I am reminded of the time when I went to speak to the inmates of the Burtch Correctional Centre near Burford, Ontario. The inmates of this penal institution were older boys and young men who had run afoul of the law. The room where I spoke was huge—I think it was the dining room—and it was crowded. Every member of the audience listened with rapt attention to what I had to say on the Donnelly story even though it could be fairly said that they were a captive audience.

What struck me during the question period following my talk, was how these young people sympathized with the murdered Donnellys. When the subject of the church officials removing the original tombstone from the churchyard came up, these young people were outraged.

"If they do this to them when they are dead," one young man stood up and said, "Just think of all the mean things they would have done to them when they were alive."

From all parts of the room came murmurs of approbation with this view. But then the young man continued, "What did they do anyway that was so bad"—and there was a pregnant pause before he added—"besides murder, I mean?"

The entire room exploded with laughter.

241

Chapter 35

Court Weapons

A reader in Ireland once took umbrage at me for writing in *The Donnelly Album*: "In accordance with the general rule in nineteenth century Ireland, [James Donnelly, Sr.] was much shorter than his Protestant neighbors."

My authority for this statement is none other than William Carleton, acknowledged to be the pre-eminent chronicler of the Irish peasants of nineteenth century Ireland before the great Famine—those very Irish who came to settle in Biddulph, Canada. Carleton, the son of a County Tyrone Catholic tenant farmer, was born in 1794 and died in 1869. In *The Party Fight and Funeral* he wrote:[1]

> Both parties arranged themselves against each other, forming something like two lines of battle, and these extended along the town nearly from one end to the other. It was curious to remark the difference in the persons and appearances of the combatants. In the Orange line the men were taller, and of more powerful frames; but the Ribbonmen were more hardy, active and courageous. Man to man, notwithstanding their superior bodily strength, the Orangemen could never fight the others; the former depend too much upon their fire and side-arms, but they are by no means so well trained in the use of the cudgel as their enemies. In the district where the scene of this fight is laid, the Catholics generally inhabit the mountainous part of the country, to which, when the civil feuds of worse times prevailed, they had been driven at the point of the bayonet; the Protestants and Presbyterians, on the other hand, who came in upon their possessions, occupy the richer and more fertile tracts of the land; being more wealthy, they live with less labor, and on better food. The characteristic features produced by these causes are such as might be expected—the Catholic being, like his soil, hardy, thin and capable of bearing all weathers; and the protestants, larger, softer, and more inactive.

In the fighting between factions and parties in Ireland, guns were rarely used. In the United States, on the other hand, the

William Carleton

country became awash with firearms[2] following the American Civil War, and they were not uncommon in the Catholic Settlement at the time of the tragedy. Attempting to identify the types of guns that were used at the shooting of John Donnelly, however, can be a challenging exercise.

One gun, which was probably a rifle or carbine, shot a bullet that went through John's pelvic area and lodged in the window casing or wall behind him. Will dug this bullet out of the woodwork and gave it to Chief Williams. A rifle of Martin McLaughlin's was taken from him on February 5th. McLaughlin claimed he had obtained it in Missouri while visiting his brother Ambrose who had gone to settle in Iowa some years before. This rifle held seven cartridges—one in the breech and six in the magazine that was in the stock of the gun. The name of the manufacturer was not stated but it may well have been a .56 calibre Spencer rifle or carbine that was manufactured in the U.S.A. from 1860 to 1869. The Spencer was the first successful magazine repeating rifle. It shot rim-fired cartridges and was "the most widely used carbine of the American Civil War."[3]

London police chief William T. Williams and Detective Enoch Murphy compared the bullet found by Will with a bullet taken from a cartridge found in McLaughlin's gun. They thought the two were very similar and that the rifle itself had been fired not long before. If it was McLaughlin's gun used to shoot John, which in my opinion was quite likely, only one shot was fired out of it—this

obtained possession of another gun of McLaughlin's, a revolver that was handed over to him by the hired man, Mike Welch. Welch had been given it by Mrs. McLaughlin the day her husband was arrested. It appears, however, that nothing further was done about this revolver although the police authorities continued to keep it until after the trial. Although the police had taken possession of or inspected several other guns in the township, these three were the only firearms kept by them for the trials as Chief

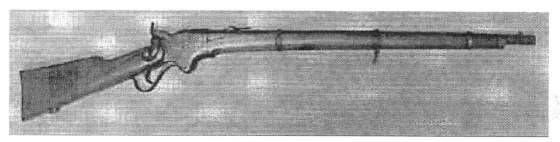

A Spencer carbine

according to the evidence. The empty shell cartridge had apparently not been ejected as there was no sign of a spent shell casing at the scene which would no doubt have been mentioned had any been found.

In connection with McLaughlin and the gun, there are two or three curious points which seem not to have been followed up by the police but which should be mentioned. First, in addition to his stating that he picked up the rifle in Missouri while visiting his brother, McLaughin is also reported as stating that he acquired a rifle in Biddulph in the previous November. Second, McLaughlin's daughter, Mary, testified that her father's gun was always kept hanging on a nail over his bed, yet it was found by the police on the day following the killing of the Donnellys lying on a dresser in the bedroom. And, third, after the trials when Charles Hutchinson and Æmilius Irving were exchanging letters about the former prisoners requesting their guns back, they referred to McLaughlin's rifle and revolver as well as Ryder's revolver. Chief Williams had

Williams was of the opinion that all the other firearms they had found in Biddulph had not been fired recently.

The second gun[4] used to shoot John—the propellants from it hit the chest area—was a musket, shotgun or rifle. It was a muzzle-loading firearm and, on that night at least, expelled small pellets. These were, in Will Donnelly's opinion, smaller than regular buckshot and more like the pellets used for shooting ducks. The paper wad used in the muzzle was a piece of the Catholic *Record* newspaper about the size of an adult hand. Because of the makeshift nature of the load, I suspect that the powder was not a capsule of measured grains such as one that had been manufactured and would be available for purchase. I believe the charge was simply poured from a receptacle like a powder flask or horn. This gun, whether a musket, shotgun or rifle, was never recovered by the police authorities.

The witnesses William Donnelly, William Blackwell and Martin Hogan all testified to another gun firing four to seven more shots

243

in the little laneway between the houses as its holder was passing from the door where John had just been shot towards the roadway. The shots came in rapid succession and two of the three witnesses referred to them as revolver shots. It was most likely a revolver and could very well have been the revolver belonging to the Ryders which Chief Williams took possession of at the Ryder house. It was a seven-shooter and had been, in his opinion, recently fired. Again, it could have been of a manufacture such as a Smith and Wesson but the brand name was not stated in any of the testimony. It, too, was released back to Ryder after the trials along with McLaughlin's rifle and revolver.

In civilized society, disputes are settled not by firearms but by other means such as a resort to the courts. The many books, plays and television documentaries on the Donnelly story have spawned at least three such disputes which resulted in copyright lawsuits. I write this not as a lawyer, however, but as one who was involved in two of those lawsuits.

In 1984 Pagurian Press Limited wrote me asking if they could use some of the illustrations from my book, *The Donnelly Album*, for a proposed new edition of Thomas P. Kelley's *The Black Donnellys* for which Pagurian then held the rights. I readily agreed, subject only to the conditions that I receive (1) an appropriate credit adjacent to each picture, and (2) a small, almost nominal fee, for each of the images they proposed to use. I did not hear from Pagurian again. They certainly heard from me, however, when I walked into a bookstore one day and picked up the new Pagurian edition of *The Black Donnellys*. There on the front cover and throughout the book itself were several of my illustrations. Of the 27 illustrations used by Pagurian, 26 were copied straight out of *The Donnelly Album*. The Pagurian illustrations were drawings only but a glance could tell immediately from where they were copied. Quite naturally, then, I instituted a lawsuit for infringement of copyright not only against

Pagurian but also against Christopher Ondaatje, the financier, whose name appeared on the book as publisher.

The case rumbled on for many weeks as lawsuits tend to do until one morning I opened the Toronto *Globe and Mail* and found a large photograph of Mr. Ondaatje, smiling broadly as he presented an award to Pierre Trudeau along with the sum of $50,000 which accompanied it. I confess that the photograph and accompanying article got under my skin. I immediately called the local newspaper. "We'll send a photographer right over," said the reporter after interviewing me. Next day my own photograph appeared in the Hamilton *Spectator* along with a write-up of my case against Pagurian and Ondaatje. The item was reprinted by at least one other newspaper, the London *Free Press*.

Within a day or two, my copyright lawyer in Toronto called me. "Ray, I don't know what you've done," he chuckled, "but Pagurian and Ondaatje want to settle your case as quickly as possible."

Terms satisfactory to me were soon reached, a settlement was agreed to and that was the end of the matter.

The basic law of this field is that a literary or artistic work can only be copied by the rightful owner of the copyright who in most cases is the one who created it. Any other person can only copy *with permission*. This concept of permission is often lost sight of by writers. They often confuse it with attribution—which is another matter altogether and which I will address a little later.

The second lawsuit concerning the Donnelly story of which I am aware, was an action in 2002 brought by Theresia Winkler against Sam Roy and certain corporations owned or controlled by him. Theresia Winkler, of Toronto, was the last landlady of Thomas P. Kelley when he died in 1982, a few days after the death of his wife. Mrs. Winkler claimed to be the owner of the copyright in Kelley's two books, *The Black Donnellys* and *Vengeance of the Black Donnellys* by virtue of inheritance pursuant to Kelley's last will. She had registered her claim under the Copyright Act.

Sam Roy and the corporations, on the other hand, claimed to have obtained an assignment of those rights from Kelley some time before he died. They had also registered their claim. The Court summarized the publication history of Kelley's books and referred to him in his later years as being "impecunious". The defendants alleged in their lawsuit that in 1968 Kelley had granted to them an option to acquire the royalty rights to his two books and that this option was later exercised by one of the corporations in consideration of "a one-time payment to Mr. Kelley". The judgment does not refer to the amount of that payment because, strictly speaking, it was not material to the result.

In the judgment, the Federal Court of Canada held that because of the assignment of the royalty rights by Kelley, Sam Roy and his corporations did indeed own the royalty rights to Kelley's books. The result, however, was not a total defeat for Mrs. Winkler in that the Copyright Act contains a provision that any assignment of royalty rights by a creator in his or her lifetime is only effective for a period of twenty-five years following the death of the author. After that, the rights revert to the author's estate. As it turned out, Mrs. Winkler was the sole beneficiary of Thomas P. Kelley under his last will and therefore the royalty rights reverted back to her in the year 2007.

It is here useful to address the requirement of registration. In the Winkler case, both Sam Roy and his corporations and Mrs. Winkler quite rightly registered their claims and thereby, on the face of it, kept them alive. It is worth noting, however, that one who *creates* a literary work does *not* have to register. The creator does not have to register anything in order to acquire copyright. *It arises by virtue of its creation alone in the right of its creator.* This is such a simple concept that some find it difficult to grasp.

In addition, the concept is sometimes blurred in the minds of artists such as songwriters who register their works under associations such as SOCAN—The Society of Composers, Authors and Music Publishers of Canada—which collects and distributes performing and other credits.

Several years ago an unscrupulous person who shall remain nameless got hold of a screenplay I had written on the Donnelly story. He called me on the telephone and asked if I had registered the screenplay. "No," I replied, "I did not," for I knew full well that as its creator I owned the copyright without having to register it and that my name as the copyright owner appeared on the cover page. The caller seemed astounded that I had not registered. I took it from our conversation that he was familiar with registration of songs by songwriters but was confusing this with copyright. He quickly said goodbye and I never heard from him again. A little while later, however, I did hear by chance from a television producer in Toronto who claimed to have seen a screenplay on the Donnellys allegedly written by that same person who had called me. It turned out that he had simply torn off the cover and copyright page with my name on it and replaced it with one showing himself as author—thinking he would thereby reap the supposedly immense rewards.

When discussing copyright, a question is often put to me such as, "But if the person uses your stuff and says that he got it from you, is that not okay to avoid a charge of plagiarism?" This question addresses the concept of attribution and the simple answer to the question is, No. A university professor or school teacher who marks essays and other student works is concerned with unattributed ideas, expressions, thoughts or words of another. This is plagiarism. In the field of academics, attribution is all-important as such passing off without attribution is intellectual dishonesty. Most such teachers are usually knowledgeable enough about the subject to be able to quickly spot the plagiarisms and deal with them accordingly. In the commercial field, however, it is not *attribution* that is required but *permission*.

In Canada, the federal Copyright Act deals with plagiarism as an infringement of copyright. It protects the creativity of one person against the appropriation of that creativity by another. Attribution in this context is irrelevant. The Copyright Act of Canada, which is a complete code of copyright in our country, makes no mention of attribution for that reason. What it deals with is permission. Copying by a second author of the literary activity of a first author

without the latter's permission is an infringement of copyright. Such copying can be word for word, or "by colourable imitation"—which I personally like to think of as "disguised copying"—or by other means such as the appropriation of the first author's sentence structures, patterns of thought, expressions and concepts.

The third lawsuit was my case in the year 2005 against Peter Edwards as author and Key Porter Books Limited as publisher. The book in question was entitled *Night Justice: The True Story of the Black Donnellys*. I was able to demonstrate that the offending author copied extensively from my works, *The Donnelly Album*, *In Search of the Donnellys* and the booklet, *Legend of the Roman Line: The Donnellys of Biddulph*. Such copying was substantial and accomplished in all three of the ways mentioned, namely, word-for-word, by colourable imitation and by appropriation of sentence structures, patterns of thought and expressions and concepts.

In the result, I obtained from the court a judgment as follows: (1) a declaration that the offending work did indeed infringe copyright in my works, (2) an injunction prohibiting further sales of the offending work and other dealings such as the sale of subsidiary rights, (3) an order for destruction of all copies of the offending book in the warehouse of the publisher's distributor, and (4) an order for payment of a sum of money by way of damages and costs.

None of the above purports to be nor should it be taken as legal advice for which, of course, the reader should consult a lawyer.

Court File No. T-178-05

FEDERAL COURT

Toronto, Ontario,   Date: 5 October 2005

Present: Madam Justice Judith Snider

BETWEEN:

RAYMOND LESLIE FAZAKAS

Plaintiff

- and -

PETER EDWARDS and
KEY PORTER BOOKS LIMITED

Defendants

JUDGMENT

UPON MOTION IN WRITING dated September 30, 2005, on behalf of the plaintiff in this action, Raymond Leslie Fazakas, for Judgment on consent;

AND UPON reading the motion record filed on behalf of the plaintiff and the consent of the defendants by their solicitor;

1. **THIS COURT DECLARES** that the literary work, *Night Justice: The True Story of the Black Donnellys*, authored by the defendant, Peter Edwards, and published by the defendant, Key Porter Books Limited, has infringed the copyright in the literary works authored by the plaintiff, namely, *The Donnelly Album*, *Legend of the Roman Line: The Donnellys of Biddulph* and *In Search of the Donnellys*.

2. **THIS COURT ORDERS AND ADJUDGES** that the defendants, their officers, servants, agents and employees are enjoined from further sales of or other dealings with the work entitled, *Night Justice: The True Story of the Black Donnellys* including the sales of any subsidiary rights thereto.

3. **THIS COURT ORDERS AND ADJUDGES** that the defendant, Key Porter Books Limited, shall destroy all copies of the work entitled *Night Justice: The True Story of the Black Donnellys*, which are presently in the distributor's warehouse.

4. **THIS COURT ORDERS AND ADJUDGES** that the defendants shall pay to the plaintiff the sum of $36,000.00 by way of damages, inclusive of costs.

"Judith A. Snider"
Judge

The judgment obtained by author against Peter Edwards and Key Porter Books Limited.

Chapter 36

Fraudsters and Fakes

No matter on which side one's sympathies fall, it seems that everyone wants to be connected in some small way with the Donnelly story. Over the years when addressing groups on the subject, I was often surprised at how frequently this phenomenon occurred. On one occasion in Welland, Ontario during the question and answer period following my little talk, a man put up his hand to speak.

"My grandfather lived two lines away from the Donnellys," he said, "And he gave evidence at the trial. His name was John Herbert."

There was no need to question the veracity of the man's story for John Herbert is mentioned in *The Donnelly Album*.

In a moment, another man raised his hand.

"My grandfather lived on the Donnelly farm right after the massacre," he said "And I've got a picture here to prove it."

From a brown envelope he pulled a large photograph. "This is a picture of my grandfather, John Kent, and his family," he said. "They farmed the Donnelly homestead after the tragedy and here they are standing in front of the house which was rebuilt on the farm. The site of the old house which was burned down on February 4th, 1880 is to the right in the picture."

I had seen the picture before. The photograph he held is again in *The Donnelly Album*. The picture the man held was a better reproduction. He let me copy it and it is reproduced in this book.

Then a third man stuck up his hand and said proudly, "That may be all very well, but my grandfather was in the story, too, and he was killed by the Donnellys."

And, sure enough, this man turned out to be a grandson of Richard Bryant who in 1876

Richard Bryant, the stage proprietor, who lost his life during the stagecoach rivalry with the Donnellys.

assumed ownership of one of the Lucan to London stage lines that ran in competition with the Donnellys. Soon after commencing his new business, a wheel fell off his stagecoach and Bryant was thrown to the ground. Several weeks later he died from the injuries thus sustained in the accident.[1]

Whether on one side or the other, all of the speakers were proud to have had a grandparent associated with the Donnelly story.

While over the years many individuals have come forward claiming to be related to the Donnellys of Biddulph, ironically the legitimate descendants of Jim and Judy Donnelly rarely take the initiative in identifying themselves. "You usually have to dig them out of the woodwork," I have often said.

One claimant was Kerry Donnelly from Ireland who presented himself to Londoners in 1980 as a genuine "Black Donnelly". In September of that year he was introduced to the Glencoe Historical Society and remained for a short time a minor local celebrity. I had

Patrick O'Donnell, at right front, alias Kerry Donnelly, during his brief period of fame as a Black Donnelly, with Orlo Miller, in front, and Sherwood Walters, at left rear. The other man is the latter's cousin.

met him earlier that month. Our meeting took place in, of all places, the churchyard of St. Patrick's in Biddulph. It was during our final day of shooting of *The Donnellys of Biddulph* by the television crew of the Canadian Broadcasting Corporation.

Striding boldly in amongst the crew, the slight young man with rust-colored hair confronted the director Bob Gibbons and demanded to know what we had done with his family's tombstone. Bob was momentarily taken aback at the disruption. The crew was on a tight schedule and as my role as writer was superfluous to the day's activities anyway, Bob turned to me and said, "Ray, talk to this young man" and went on with the shooting.

The young pretender had brought with him a little delegation: another young man and a young lady friend. I approached them.

"Would you mind telling me who you are?" I asked innocently.

"I'm Kerry Donnelly," he announced firmly holding crossed arms against his chest in a belligerent manner.

"Oh, and what is your connection to the Donnellys buried here?" I asked, knowing full well that if his name was Donnelly he

could not have been a descendant of our Roman Line Donnellys.

There was a slight bristle in his reply but he was obviously prepared for the challenge. Without another word he reached into a pocket of his blue jeans and pulled out a small piece of paper that he flourished at me. This document was intended to put all doubt to rest. I looked at it closely. It purported to be an original birth certificate but it was obviously only a photocopy. Worse still, it had been tampered with, and none too expertly at that. Part of the surname had been painted over with whiteout that had been typed over. Whatever it had been originally, the surname now read "Donnelly".

I tried not to betray my amusement as I scanned the document. "And who is that?" I asked, trying to keep my face expressionless and pointing my finger at the name on the altered birth certificate.

"That's my grandmother!" he declared grandly, as if this pronouncement put the matter beyond all further question.

"Oh," I went on, "and who is she to these Donnellys?"

"What do you mean?" he demanded with a touch of scorn—or was it fright—at my audacity in even daring to question his standing in the matter.

"Well," I continued inquiringly, "which one of the Donnellys buried here is she related to, and how?"

I now got the distinct feeling the young man had hoped the questioning would not go this far. A slight shift of his body position betrayed his uncertainty. His two companions also shifted uncomfortably on their feet. For a moment he did not answer. Then, his eyes swiftly darting like a trapped animal, he suddenly looked straight at me and, holding his breath, blurted out: "It was

248

This is neither Jim Donnelly, nor his wife with a friend, as some have alleged.

This is neither the Western Hotel in Lucan nor William Donnelly in the buggy, as alleged.

through Bridget. I am descended through her."

Barely able to control my bursting out in a loud guffaw, I murmured, "Interesting," then turned and quickly walked away. A short distance away, I turned to look at the trio. They seemed totally discomfited and I felt embarrassed for them.

A few weeks later, I noticed a little news item in the paper which read:[2]

> A native of Northern Ireland who claims he's a descendant of Canada's notorious Black Donnellys may have an easier time convincing people of his roots nowadays. Patrick O'Donnell, also known as Kerry Donnelly, came to Canada recently to research his famous ancestors. But now research has been interrupted for a time—Donnelly's been sentenced to five months in prison in London, Ont., for passing bad cheques.

The little faker also seems to have run up a few long distance telephone bills back to the Ould Sod on the account of a certain Donnelly expert whose memory of him is not too kind. This man's opinion of Kerry Donnelly, alias Patrick O'Donnell, is not printable in polite language.

This was not the first alleged Donnelly from Ireland who sought me out. John Kinsella, a friend and sometime neighbor, promised to bring over some evening a genuine Black Donnelly from Ireland. John had a great sense of humor but eventually in 1968 he came along to my house with a young man in tow named Frank Donnelly. The latter hailed from Northern Ireland. This was not surprising as there are probably more Donnellys in County Tyrone in the province of Ulster than anywhere else in the country. Frank claimed that his forebears were the genuine Black Donnellys. And where did "black" come from? Simple. They originally came from Coal Island in County Tyrone. According to Frank, legend had it that one of the Coal Island Donnellys had bushwhacked a land agent and shot him dead with a blunderbuss. As a result, he had to flee Tyrone for Canada. Of course, I did not believe a word of it.

Aside from posing individuals, there are many spurious photographs of the Donnellys. Some of these, which I call the Gallery of False Photographs, I have included in this chapter. And how do I know they're false? It is mainly because I was in more than one instance a witness—but only a witness and not a party—to their being concocted up. The two perpetrators of these shams shall go nameless. They are both deceased and I do not name them in deference to the feelings of their surviving relatives.

John Flanagan, proprietor of the hotel at Flanagan's Corners founded by his father, had been the financial backer of his brother Patrick Flanagan, Jr., in the stagecoach rivalry with the Donnellys. Following those turbulent years, John Flanagan continued as

This is not James Donnelly, Jr., as alleged.

Flanagan, Sr.. Although very popular, she had reached the age of thirty years and was still a spinster. Then an old beau, William J. Cain (changed to Kain in the United States), who had emigrated to Texas and had made a small fortune as a real estate broker came back and claimed her. When they were married in 1882 even William Porte was so surprised at the unexpected event that he made an entry of the marriage in his diary. The couple took a lavish honeymoon trip to Europe and on their return settled down in Dallas, Texas.

While he may not have been a complete fraudster or a charlatan, in the end John Flanagan proved to be less than scrupulous when in 1890 he absconded with the township funds. It was some time before it was discovered that he, too, had headed to Texas where he settled down in Waco and later in Hillsboro between Dallas and Waco.

This is not James Donnelly, Sr., as alleged.

an important member of the community, now known as Clandeboye, not only as proprietor of an apparently thriving hotel and general store but also as the township treasurer and division court clerk. His sister Marion, better known as Buby or Babe, was the youngest girl in the family of old Patrick

This is not Bridget Donnelly, as alleged.

250

This is not Tom Donnelly, as alleged.

This is not Norah Kennedy nor her brother John, as alleged.

This is not Johnny O'Connor, as alleged.

Window sign in Hillsboro, Texas, in the store operated by the sons of John Flanagan, formerly of Flanagan's Corners in Canada.

A curious postscript to the Flanagan story is that his sons, Pat and Will, operated a store in Hillsboro, Texas, for many years. Its location came to be known as "Flanagan's Corners". John Flanagan never returned to Biddulph. He died in Texas in 1922 and his sons and daughter are all buried at Hillsboro in that state.

251

**This alleged photograph of William Donnelly and his wife, Norah, is really that of
Norah's sister, Sarah, and her husband, William Mansbridge.**

Chapter 37

Final Thoughts

To clarify certain matters about which questions have been put to me over the years, I should here like to set out a number of final thoughts, conclusions and opinions arrived at after close to fifty years of studying the Donnelly story.

* * *

There is little or no evidence that the so-called feud was imported from Ireland. It began, in my opinion, on the Roman Line with James Donnelly's quarrel with Patrick Farrell over land, the loss of one-half of his original homestead to Michael Maher, and the subsequent murder of Farrell. For those who disagree with me, I have one question: what is your evidence?

* * *

The animosity between the Donnellys and their long-standing and more recent enemies had nothing to do with Blackfeet and Whitefeet. Some authors on the subject misunderstand the true meaning of the word "factions" in Irish history. For those who wish to learn more about factions within Irish peasant society in the nineteenth century, I direct them to the works of William Carleton and in particular *The Battle of the Factions* and *The Party Fight and Funeral* in his *Traits and Stories of the Irish Peasantry*.

* * *

The introduction of the term "Whiteboys" into the Biddulph troubles is a misreading of Irish history. The Whiteboys were not a faction in its proper sense but a term applied to a widespread agrarian protest movement, mostly defensive in nature, whose actions were usually prompted by innovations in agrarian practice such as enclosure of common land, tithe collection, increases in government cess or tax exactions and the like.

* * *

The significance of "Sheehy's Day" in the history of St. Patrick's Parish in Biddulph is so small as to be practically meaningless. My reason for including a chapter on Sheehy in this work is to let the reader decide.

* * *

Almost all of those pioneers who emigrated from Ireland to settle in the Catholic community of Biddulph were relatively well-off tenant farmers or the sons and daughters of medium or large landholding tenant farmers. They were not of the impoverished cottier class, landless day-laborers or even small-holding farmers. If one insists on dividing them into Blackfeet and Whitefeet—an exercise with which I disagree as it has little or nothing to do with society in Biddulph—almost all of the Biddulph farmers, including the Donnellys and their ultimate enemies, would have been Blackfeet.

* * *

The murder of Patrick Farrell was not "an unlucky stroke given in liquor", as the Donnelly family would have us believe, but an almost premeditated and deliberate killing. The conviction of Donnelly for murder was well supported by the evidence.

* * *

The personality of Mrs. Donnelly (familiarly and usually called Judy or Judith by her closest friends rather than the more formal Julia or Johannah), nee Magee, was indeed the cause of much of the later trouble between the Donnellys and their neighbors. Many who knew her called her "a hellion".

* * *

The root cause of the failure to obtain the conviction of James Carroll for the murder of Judith Donnelly notwithstanding the clearest of direct and indirect evidence, was the bad

By the time the children of the vigilantes had grown up, the story of the Donnellys had gone underground. Shown here are some of those children. From left to right they are, in rear, William Dewan (1868-1936), James Cain (1869-1896), John Maher (1870-1940) and John Bennett (1864-1931). In the middle row are Hannah Maher (1863-1921), Annie Cain (1872-1955) and Mary Maher (1872-1969). In front is Catherine Maher (1866-1957).

reputation that the Donnelly family had earned for itself over the years. Not only was the head of it a convicted murderer but also the boys' shenanigans on their own account, particularly in the relatively short period of the stagecoach rivalry between them and Hawkshaw, Flanagan, Bryant and others, had branded them as disreputable. Because of this bad reputation, the jury did not *want* to convict.

* * *

The death of Michael Donnelly at the hands of William H. Lewis in the bar-room of Slaght's Commercial Hotel in Waterford, Ontario was a premeditated killing for which, as the editor of the Waterford *Star* believed, Lewis should have been convicted of murder. It had nothing, however, to do with the troubles in Biddulph.

* * *

Almost everyone within the Catholic community in Biddulph knew at the time who the murderers of the Donnellys were.

* * *

The citizens of the village of Lucan, ninety per cent of whom were Protestants, were well aware that there was trouble brewing between the Donnellys and some of their neighbors within the Catholic Settlement but they were quite content not to know the details and to keep out of it altogether.

* * *

The story of the shameful lynching of the Donnellys in 1880 was soon after its occurrence so suppressed within the community in both the Catholic and Protestant portions as to be almost completely obliterated from the consciousness of the people who lived there

254

in the first half of the twentieth century and even into our own day.

* * *

The journals of William Porte, while interesting, are largely over-rated as a source of information on the Donnelly story. They contain little which cannot be found in much greater detail elsewhere. Porte did not generally set down private confidences in his diaries but kept such secrets to himself.

* * *

The political interference in 1881 by the Ontario premier and attorney general Oliver Mowat which forced the crown authorities to abandon the case against the Feeheleys (which the local Crown authorities hoped would lead to the ringleaders) was alluded to briefly by Orlo Miller in *The Donnellys Must Die*, by me in *The Donnelly Album* and in greater detail and at some length by William Butt in his doctoral thesis, *The Donnellys: History, Legend, Literature*. A recent writer's claim that he discovered this aspect of the

Donnelly story which was previously unknown is humbug.

* * *

Vengeance of the Black Donnellys by Thomas P. Kelley is a pack of nonsense exceeded only by Nate Hendley's book published in 2004 surprisingly entitled *The Black Donnellys*.

* * *

Just as I have found in the original sources not a single reference to the family having been called in their lifetimes "the Black Donnellys"—as Thomas P. Kelley would have us believe—so have I not found in those sources anyone ever having said in their lifetimes that "The Donnellys Must Die"—as Orlo Miller had it.

* * *

There is little doubt that the story told by Johnny O'Connor from first to last—from what he said sitting on the knee of Detective William Hodge the day following the massacre to his testimony at the inquest, the

Cast of the Donnelly family in the 1980 television production written by the author.

Three of the Fathers of Confederation here depicted figured marginally in the Donnelly story. They are John A. Macdonald, Hector Langevin and Oliver Mowat. The painting was done by Robert Harris, who also sketched several members of the Peace Society earlier in his career.

preliminary hearing, the first and the second trial of Carroll—was consistent and truthful from beginning to end.

* * *

Many writers churn out screenplays based on the Donnelly story. Years ago I wrote one myself. It must have had some merit as twice it was stolen from me by unscrupulous persons who attempted to pass it off as their own.

* * *

In the year 2005, I was personally involved in five television documentaries which were then in course of preparation on the Donnelly story. Most but not all came to fruition.

* * *

To this day the Donnellys can arouse the most intense passions. The Ottawa *Citizen* ran an article on the Donnelly story in its February 5th, 2005 issue to which a reader responded:

256

Your Donnelly story of February 5 repeats the same libels and slanders which have been printed about the noble Donnellys for the past 125 years . . . The Donnellys only crime was being Catholics who had friendship with Protestants . . . The Catholics who murdered the Donnellys were of the Protestant hating brand of Catholic . . . I hope the name of the Donnellys can be cleared and honoured for the beautiful people they really were.

* * *

With the recent discovery that the mother of James Donnelly came from not only a Protestant family, but also a family supporting the Orange Order at that, many little loose ends of the story have fallen into place.

* * *

The opening of the Donnelly Museum in Lucan on May 1, 2010 was a small watershed in the history of the Donnelly story as well as that of the community now known as the Township of Lucan Biddulph.

* * *

The author in his Donnelly Room many years ago when it was but a corner of his basement.

Notes

Chapter 1 Kelley's Revival

[1]Incidents in the early life of Thomas P. Kelley are related by him in a book about his father, Thomas P. Kelley, Sr., entitled *The Fabulous Kelley* published in 1968 by Simon & Schuster of Canada Ltd., and republished in 1974 by General Publishing, Don Mills, Ontario.

[2]That one-week show in Exeter made such a strong impression upon an eight-year-old local boy named Earl Heywood that he decided then and there to become a stage performer. Earl spent the rest of his life on stage as a magician and country and western musician known in his heyday as the Gene Autry of Canada. In later years he wrote and performed *Tales of the Donnelly Feud*.

[3]When I obtained copies of the letters written by Thomas P. Kelley they were in a private file kept by Ed Phelps, then librarian at the Regional Collection, University of Western Ontario (hereafter, RC, UWO).

[4]Kelley may also have consulted Goodspeed's *History of the County of Middlesex* published in 1889.

[5]The story had in fact been written up from time to time in *MacLeans Magazine*. In the issue of November 1, 1930 *The Donnelly Case* by J. Lambert Payne is immediate and gripping. Payne in 1880 was a youthful newspaper reporter in London and therefore quickly on the spot both at the scene of the crime in Biddulph and in Lucan. When writing in 1931, however, he relied for the most part on memory and with the lapse of some fifty years it is understandable that a few factual errors crept into his account. *The Vigilante Massacre* by Magistrate S. Tupper Bigelow is in the June 1, 1950 issue of the magazine (reprinted July 26, 1956). Magistrate Bigelow told me his article was based on contemporary accounts in the London and Toronto newspapers.

[6]It was later called the Regional History Collection and was then renamed the J. J. Talman Regional Collection after historian, James John Talman, 1904-1993.

[7]Spencer Sceli, who later changed his name to Armitage-Stanley, was born and grew up in Lucan. During his entire life he took a great interest in local history. He contacted me soon after my interest in the Donnellys began and assisted me greatly in getting to know the Protestant families of Lucan and Biddulph as he was related to a great many of them.

Chapter 2 The Scene of the Crime

[1]Despite misinformed writers who put the location of the tavern at the Elginfield corner, there is no question that it was here at the Catholic Church Corners close to the church itself. Those writers were misled by the fact that in early days the post office address of both the church and the hotel was Elginfield.

Chapter 3 Jim the Father

[1]This record was obtained for me by Mary Panton who said that a copy was made available by the curator of the Correctional Service of Canada Museum in Kingston, Ontario. He informed her that the original is in the National Archives in Ottawa.

[2]Toronto *Globe*, March 30, 1880

[3]Notes of the testimony of witnesses given at the inquest are preserved in the National Archives of Canada in Ottawa catalogued as Record Group 5, Cl. Vol. 529, no. 1653, 28 pages.

[4]The trial notes bear the Ontario Archives reference RG-22-390 file 33.1, 400-408. The reader should be warned, however, that to the unpracticed eye the handwriting can be formidably difficult.

[5]On that date it printed a portrait of William Bawden, the recently deceased reeve of the town.

[6]RC, UWO

Chapter 4 Mother Judy

[1]Miller, *The Donnellys Must Die*, Macmillan, Toronto, 1962, 135

[2]Arnold A. Hodgins to Orlo Miller, February 1, 1965 (RC, UWO)

[3]Others were less temperate in their descriptions of Mrs. Donnelly. For example, the daughter of William Stanley, tells the story of her mother coming to live in Lucan

shortly after her marriage to the Lucan JP. She inquired of the household's servant girl, Harriet Coughlin, about the woman she couldn't help noticing out on the street in front of their house. "Oh," replied Harriet, "that's a vicious old woman whose husband has been sentenced to seven years for manslaughter." (Mabel L. Armstrong to Spencer Armitage-Stanley-Sceli, January 10, 1963, now in RC, UWO).

[4]Cosens (ed.), *The Donnelly Tragedy 1880-1980*, Phelps, London, 1980, 15

[5]Hamilton *Spectator*, February 11, 1880

[6]London *Advertiser*, May 23, 1881

[7]His information before Justice of the Peace Peters, October 16, 1878 (RC, UWO)

[8]Toronto *Globe*, February 11, 1880

[9]Margaret Corbett Grover to Mildred Diamond, wife of the clerk of Glencoe, and others

Chapter 5 Land and Religion

[1]*Irish Roots*, 1994, No. 1, 6

[2]Another version of the land dispute, also apocryphal, has it that Donnelly was a tenant of the land sold to Maher by Grace and refused to vacate upon termination of his tenancy because of the landlord's refusal to compensate him for the improvements Donnelly had made over the years. This version, however, fails to take into account the role of Patrick Farrell in the affair.

[3]For example, of the approximately one hundred or so Catholic families listed in the 1881 Biddulph census, only about three have the given name Robert whereas over fifty have the name James.

[4]I am indebted to Jeff Thomas, of Waterdown, for bringing this to my attention.

[5]His age is variously given but a perusal of the censuses of 1861, 1871 and 1881 seems to indicate 1815 as the approximately correct year.

[6]Randy White, of Toronto has been very successful in tracking down the Ashburys in Canada. A stonemason named John Ashbury died on February 1, 1876 in Fergus, Ontario. The death certificate states his age to be seventy-five years and eleven months, which

puts his birth in the year 1800 at Borrisokane, Ireland. Adjacent to Roscrea, not far from Borrisokane, is a townland named Ashbury and on it the respectably large and old Ashbury House. I cannot suppress the suspicion that the townland and house may have had something to do with the English soldier-actor named Joseph Ashbury whose career began with his participation in the capture of Dublin Castle in the days of Cromwell and went on to the reign of Queen Anne decades later. In his day a career combining acting with soldiering was not unusual. He was well-known both in England and Ireland and one of the favorites of James Butler, 12th earl and first duke of Ormond who was lord lieutenant of Ireland at three different times. In Ormond's hands was a huge power to grant lands to his favorites and my suspicion is that this is how Ashbury House came into being.

[7]Three of the nephews ended up a little further afield in the cities of St. Thomas, Ontario, Cleveland, Ohio and Sacramento, California.

Chapter 6 Toohey Trouble

[1]McGrath, *Interdenominational relations in pre-famine Ireland*, in the volume, *Tipperary: History and Society*, Dublin, 1985, 256 at 276.

[2]Nenagh *Guardian*, Supplement, March 9, 1839

[3]As might be supposed, however, the North Tipperary migrants did not bring with them the Gaelic language for at least in that part of Ireland the ancient language had gone into misuse. What those migrants spoke was English with traces of a Gaelic memory.

[4]It is reconstructed from the depositions of witnesses in the ensuing law case of O'Flynn v. Toohey (RC, UWO).

[5]They left behind in Biddulph a few female members of the name who had married into other families of the parish such as the Tooheys, Heenans and Quigleys. Some of the others who left for the American Mid-West, most notably Iowa and Nebraska, at this time or not long after included the bridal couple

themselves, the Sherlocks, and some of the Lamphiers and Keefes.

[6]Both relied on the basic work of the Frenchman, Joseph Nicephore Niepce, who made the first prototype of a photograph as early as 1826 or 1827 for which the exposure time was eight hours.

Chapter 7 The Last Donnelly

[1]RC, UWO

[2]Tom and Margaret Newman were kind enough to give me not only a copy of that letter to Jack but also the original of the latter's reply to them.

[3]I remember passing through Detroit since 1971 but have not visited there since then, to my recollection, and therefore do not know if the time differential still exists but suspect it does not.

[4]John William Donnelly, to give his full name, was born in Glencoe, Ontario on December 23, 1884 and baptized in Bothwell.

Chapter 8 Tales From Toledo

[1]London *Free Press*, January 10, 1913

[2] London *Free Press*, January 15, 1913

3Alice O'Hearn Donnelly died within days of the end of the nineteenth century. Her obituary in the Grand Rapids *Tri-County Bulletin* of January 2, 1900 states that she settled with her husband Peter Donnelly on the Washington Township homestead in 1849 and not 1844 as stated in *A History of Northwest Ohio*.

[4]Toledo *Blade*, May 5, 1881

[5]This assumes that the date in Norah's letter as published is 1858 and not 1853—the final digit is not perfectly legible and may possibly be a three instead of an eight.

[6]Toledo *Blade*, March 4, 1932

Chapter 9 The O'Connors

[1]Louis Raycraft told me O'Connor had gone to Michigan and came back to Lucan once only and that for a short two hours as he waited for a connecting train. Bill Burns told me that according to Patrick Kelly of the Roman Line he died in California. Fred Dobbs said O'Connor had visited his father in 1933 or 1934 and was then living in Winnipeg but Dobbs also told Sherwood Walters that he came back in 1931 from Detroit. An Ontario Provincial Police constable stationed at Lucan said he had gone to Ohio. Spencer Armitage-Stanley-Sceli said he was a farmer near Detroit. Mike Currie said he ran a bar at Detroit. Bill German said he was a barber in Detroit and came back to visit in the 1930s or 1940s. Walter Fults told me that he remained in Lucan and lived to a ripe old age. Norman Harris said he once lived in Hamilton. Kate Ryan said he died in Toronto. Dan Brock thought he died in Paris, Ontario. Eric Hodgins thought he might have gone to Dakota. Others said he went to live in Moose Jaw, Saskatchewan, or Alberta, or Quebec—and so on.

[2]As explained elsewhere, the nickname Buckshot was sometimes understandably but erroneously applied to the Jim Ryder who allegedly wielded the shotgun that killed John Donnelly.

[3]Stott (ed.), *Passing Into Oblivion: The Diaries of William Porte, Lucan, Ontario 1864-1898*, 265

[4]On this date John O'Connor was in fact twenty-two years of age although, to be fair, the family did not reckon true ages correctly. The O'Connor children's true ages can be ascertained from baptismal records. During the reporting of the tragedy in 1880 and 1881, the newspapers attributed various incorrect ages to him. It seems a bit curious to me that Porte, the village conveyancer, would mention O'Connor's attaining his majority, and I suspect it may be because it indicated to him, as a conveyancer, that he was now able to have a deed made out to him. His spending an hour with Porte, without mention of the tragedy, indicates to me he was there on business of a kind which might involve the transfer of property. He probably also arranged for Porte to collect the rent from the tenant and remit it to him from time to time.

[5]*Op. cit.*, 314.

[6]If the reader is wondering why I simply did not check the land registry office records for the transfer, it appears that while Mick

O'Connor registered the deed to his home parcel on Francis Street, he did not register the deed to the second lot and neither did John. This practice of saving the cost of registration was not unknown in those days.

[7]There is a seaman in the 1900 U.S. census who is enumerated as John O'Connor, aged 35, born June 1865, mate on a ship apparently docked in the harbor at Duluth, Minnesota, whose both parents were born in Ireland. The residence of John O'Connor's siblings in Duluth at this time is very near to the docks of that city. Again, in the 1910 U.S. census there is a John O'Connor listed in a boarding house in Cleveland, Ohio as age 52, engineer on a steamboat, with both parents again born in Ireland. Judging from the several other references to steamboats on the page, the residence of that person is also close to the dock area of Cleveland as was the residence of the John Connors who died there in 1936. It is possible these entries all refer to the same person. It must be pointed out, however, that the birthplace of the first-mentioned is noted as Connecticut and the second as Detroit.

[8]Exeter *Times*, June 2, 1881

Chapter 10 Tipperary At Last

[1]This ancient round tower was supposed to be the very one from which Red Hugh O'Donnell, imprisoned by the officials of Queen Elizabeth I, escaped on Christmas Eve in 1591.

[2]Despite the name, a townland does not necessarily mean that there is a town associated with the area just as our township does not imply a town or other urban area.

[3]The baronies of Clonlisk and Ballybritt in those days formed part of County Tipperary but were later transferred to King's County, now known as County Offaly.

[4]The problem with this is that there are other places in the country which claim to be the centre of Ireland.

[5]Nenagh *Guardian*, August 18, 1841

[6]Thomas G. McGrath, *Interdenominational Relations in pre-famine Tipperary*, in the volume,

Tipperary: History and Society, Dublin, 1985, quoting from a letter by Peel, 256 at 276.

[7]In its issue of October 20, 1844

[8]State Paper Office, Dublin, Outrage Reports, 1842, 27/183393

[9]In a letter to the editor of the Nenagh *Guardian*, October 10, 1838

[10]A large landholding was a farm of one hundred acres or more, keeping in mind that an Irish acre was equivalent to 1.62 statute acres of the English and American systems.

[11]It is strange how the label has stuck to this day. Patrick Donnelly of Moatquarter in Ireland, who lives opposite the road from the spot where James Donnelly married Judith Magee, related to me how his family is still to this day referred to in pub talk as "land grabbers" even though they have resided in Dunkerrin parish for a hundred and fifty years or more.

[12]Thomas G. McGrath, *op. cit.*, 272

[13]Report from the Select Committee on the State of Ireland, 1831-32, British Sessional Papers, vol. xvi, 171

[14]Alfred Scott Garrett to Orlo Miller November 18, 1959, RHC, UWO. Mrs. Clay was Jo-Anna Donnelly, daughter of William Donnelly.

Chapter 11 Borrisokane

[1]Curiously, from my point of view, one of its principal patrons in the nineteenth century was a family named Biddulph.

[2]It should be pointed out, however, that historically there were in the barony of Longford, County Galway, distinctly separate septs bearing the names Donnelly and Donnellan.

[3]Greyfort has a close connection with families in Biddulph Township, Ontario named Owens and Maloney, both being near neighbors of the Donnellys on the Roman Line.

[4]Nenagh *Guardian*, May 18, 1939

[5]My contact in Dublin sent me on loan some of McLysaght's handwritten notes for perusal. The venerable genealogist died in 1986 at the age of 99 years.

[6]Edward McLysaght, *Irish Families*, Allen Figgis, Dublin, 1978, 248

[7]Richard Berleth, *The Twilight Lords*, Knopf, New York, 1978, 248

[8]Michael Menon Donnelly was born in 1899, the son of Michael Donnelly (1850-1917), Lord Mayor of Limerick City in 1904-05, whose father, John Donnelly was, the author at present believes, a brother of James Donnelly, Sr., of Biddulph.

[9]*Op. cit.*, 122

[10]John O'Donovan, *The Tribes and Customs of Hy-Many*, Dublin, 1843, reprinted 1972, footnote on page 40

[11]Sean P. O. Cillin, *Travellers in Co. Clare 1459-1843*, Galway, 1977, 2. John J. W. Donnelly refers to a similar map attached to the second volume of the Irish State Papers in the reign of Henry VIII.

Chapter 12 Tumbrikane

[1]This Michael was the father of Michael Menon Donnelly, the elderly gentleman whom we found in Dungannon. In 1901 also living in the townland of Tumbrikane were Mary Farrell, aged 70, and her two sons, John and Daniel, aged 35 and 30 respectively, which may lend some credence to the suggestion that Jim Donnelly and Patrick Farrell who died at his hands were related.

[2]While his parents probably lived in Borrisokane, other evidence indicates they may also have lived in the town of Shinrone or in the townland of Irishtown or even in the parishes of Kilbarron, Terryglass or Lorrha. All are places not far from Borrisokane itself.

[3]King's County, Barony of Clonlisk, Primary Valuation of the several Tenements Comprising said Barony, 1851

[4] Nenagh *Guardian*, February 3, 1844

[5]William Nolan, *Patterns of Living in Tipperary, 1750-1850*, in the volume, *Tipperary: History and Society*, Dublin, 1985, 288 at 315

[6]My surmising was wrong. The name of this ancient Norman castle built around 1200 was *Castrum Phillipi*, or Phillip's Castle, see Cunningham, *The Anglo-Norman Advance into the South-west Midlands of Ireland, 1185-1221*.

[7]As I later learned, the small stone tower was not of medieval origin at all but a decorative garden or field piece built in the fashion of the day in the eighteenth or nineteenth century by the then owner of the Busherstown estate.

[8]Another family in the parish closely associated with the Magees was that of Tobin. A John Tobin was hanged at Tullamore in 1835 for an attempt on the life of a landlord's agent.

[9]The fact that most if not all of James Magee's several children had the means to emigrate to Canada or Australia despite his small holding suggests to me that Magee's principal occupation may have been that of a tradesman or schoolteacher rather than that of a small farmer.

[10]State Paper Office, Dublin, Outrage Reports, 1839, 26721C

[11]State Paper Office, Dublin, Outrage Reports, 27/6623

[12]State Paper Office, Dublin, Outrage Reports, 30798C

[13]As reported in the Nenagh *Guardian*, August 1, 1840. The sponsor of her claim before the Grand Jury was a Mr. Stoney who was either Thomas George Stoney or Robert Johnston Stoney, both descended from Cromwellian officers. The seat of the former was at Kylepark, where Darby Slevin resided. Robert Johnston Stoney lived at Killavalla House, where we had taken our bed-and-breakfast lodgings in 1978 and visited again in 1988. Both Stoneys were on friendly social terms with their large landholding Donnelly tenants. They were of the most influential of the Borrisokane Protestant gentry class at the time as well as being two of the largest landlords in the vicinity of Borrisokane.

Chapter 13 What About Sheehy?

[1]Ballyporeen is today noted for the fact that in 1829 there was baptized at its Catholic chapel the great grandfather of a president of the United States of America, one Ronald Reagan.

[2]For much of the story of Nicholas Sheehy I have relied on Chapter XVIII of W. P.

Burke's *History of Clonmel* published in Waterford without a date but apparently in 1907 and reprinted in 1983 in Kilkenny (hereafter cited as Burke). Burke for the most part relied on a previous publication, *The United Irishmen*, by R. R. Madden, Dublin, 1857.

[3]Burke, 371

[4]Quoted in Burke, 372

[5]Burke, 376, citing Curry's *Civil Wars*, 1810 ed., 569

[6]Burke, 378, citing *Exshaw's Magazine* for May and June, 1766

[7]Burke, 376

[8]Burke, 391. The National Library of Ireland also sent me a copy of this letter on microfilm in 1969.

[9]Maurice J. Bic, *The Whiteboy Movement in Tipperary, 1760-80*, 148 at 161, quoting another work unidentified but perhaps the Freeman's *Journal*, in the volume, *Tipperary: History and Society*, eds. Nolan and McGrath, Dublin, 1985.

[10]*Twilight of the Ascendancy*, Bence-Jones, London, 1987, 10

[11]Nenagh *Guardian, July 17, 1841*

[12]*Ibid.*

[13]*Ibid.*

[14]Nenagh *Guardian*, February 10, 1844

Chapter 14 Faction Fighting

[1]The notice was apparently placed on the pump by Hanorah Darcey, daughter of Patrick Darcey and Margaret Cain: London *Free Press*, September 8, 1880. Darcey was a vigilante sympathizer who stood surety for James Feeheley in 1881.

[2]Roberts' paper is entitled *Caravats and Shanavests: Whiteboyism and Faction Fighting in East Munster, 1802-11* and is found in the volume, *Irish Peasants: Violence and Political Unrest, 1780-1914*, eds. Samuel Clark and James S. Donnelly, Jr., U. of Wisconsin, 1983.

[3]*Ibid.*

[4]Kevin Whalen, *The Catholic Church in County Tipperary 1700-1900*, in the volume, *Tipperary: History and Society*, Dublin, 1985, 215 at 218

[5]In and around Nenagh there were bodies of Blackfeet and Whitefeet who were involved in a labor dispute in the shoe industry. The Blackfeet cooperated with Brian Consedine, a master shoemaker who was a budding industrial capitalist employing lesser skilled tradesmen to manufacture boots on a larger scale than most cobblers. The Whitefeet claimed he was an exploiter of labor and that the Blackfeet were scabs who worked for less than the going rate. This labor dispute had little to do with James Donnelly.

[6]Galen Broeker, *Rural Disorder and police reform in Ireland, 1812-1836*, London & Toronto, 1970, 7

[7]Samuel Lewis, *Topographical Dictionary of Ireland*, London, 1837 (Reprint, 1984), Vol. II, 106

[8]Report from the Select Committee on the State of Ireland, 1831-32, British Sessional Papers, vol. xvi, 471

[9]*Ibid.*

[10]W. R. LeFanu, *Seventy Years of Irish Life*, London, 1914, 312. There were 12 pence in the shilling.

[11]London *Free Press*, June 24, 1880

[12]London *Free Press*, June 29, 1880

Chapter 15 The Nature of an Oath

[1]Set out in the book by Rev. John Gleeson, *History of Ely O'Carroll Territory or Ancient Ormond Situated in North Tipperary and Northwestern King's County*, Ireland, Gill, Dublin, 1915, 171. Only a portion of the words are here included.

[2]Nenagh *Guardian*, April 28, 1841

[3]Nenagh *Guardian*, August 17, 1842

[4]Proceedings of the committee reported in the Nenagh *Guardian*, August 7, 1839

[5]Nenagh *Guardian*, September 1, 1838

[6]Nenagh *Guardian*, August 25, 1838

[7]State Paper Office, Dublin, Outrage Reports, 1838, 19203C

[8]Nenagh *Guardian*, March 25, 1843

[9]*Ibid.*

[10]Records variously render it as Derrenvoohala, Derenvohela, Derravohala and so on.

[11]Nenagh *Guardian*, October 20, 1838

[12]Nenagh *Guardian*, October 24, 1838

[13]Nenagh *Guardian*, August 2, 1841

[14]Nenagh *Guardian*, July 2, 1842

[15]Nenagh *Guardian*, June 1 and 8, 1842

[16]Nenagh *Guardian*, March 25, 1843

[17]His coming to Canada has not been firmly established but has been variously put by earlier writers as somewhere between 1842 and 1845.

Chapter 16 Bridget's Secret

[1]In the steerage passenger list, all unmarried females over the age of eleven are marked down as "spinster".

[2]London *Advertiser*, April 5, 1880

[3]Unlike the letter from Michael, the letter from the parents was not printed but simply referred to in London *Advertiser*, October 1, 1880.

[4]As stated later in the text, I had actually discovered Bridget and Michael in 1982 on the microfilm of the parish register of Terryglass and Kilbarron made by the Church of Jesus Christ of Latter Day Saints but I had set them aside because, with nothing else to go on, there seemed too great a discrepancy in the age of Bridget between that shown in the register from what was carved on the grave marker in Canada.

[5]In the small square in front of this church, now becoming derelict, had stood on September 30th, 1803, a wooden platform and gallows upon which the Irish patriot and martyr, Robert Emmet, had been hanged, drawn and quartered.

[6]By personal communication with author.

[7]By personal communication with author.

[8]www.census.nationalarchives (2009)

[9]A close relative of Captain Stoney was Thomas George Stoney, the principal landlord of the Donnelly families in the Borrisokane area. He was an improving landlord who established a model agricultural school on his estate at Kylepark and was very generous in granting work under drainage schemes to his smaller tenants during the famine years. This probably contributed to his bankruptcy in 1851. See *Irish Roots*, No. 38, 2001 2nd Quarter, 20 at 21.

[10]This is not Martin McLaughlin of the Peace Society but his father.

Chapter 17 Affairs of the Heart

[1]*North Middlesex Argus Review*, Friday, Feb. 10, 1871

[2]*North Middlesex Argus Review*, Friday, Apr. 21, 1871

[3]*Ibid.*

[4]Ellen had been born a Hodgins.

[5]By personal communication with author.

[6]Anne Donnelly Newman to Scott Garrett, undated (RC, UWO).

[7]By personal communication with author.

[8]Thomas P. Kelley to Ed Phelps, June 19, 1974 (RC, UWO)

[9]Thomas P. Kelley to Ed Phelps, June 1974 (RC, UWO)

[10]The lock of hair passed by inheritance to Kelley's last landlady who as far as I am aware still has it.

[11]This letter and the research abilities of Randy White led to the discovery of Maggie Thompson's eventual fate.

[12]One of the saddest letters I ever received was from the nephew of Ignatius Clarke, one of the children of Nellie Hines from her second marriage. It recounted how Nace, as they called him, died of a broken heart after learning of his mother's connection to the Donnellys, about which she never saw fit to tell him.

[13]R C, UWO

[14]Glencoe *Transcript*, July 16, 1885

Chapter 18 Village of Saints

[1]Some papers such as the London Jail record sheets at RC, UWO suggest that it was Michael, and not William, Donnelly who was charged with this burglary.

[2]Charles Hutchinson to Æmilius Irving, April 1, 1880 (RC, UWO)

[3]William Donnelly to Charles Hutchinson, June 16, 1880 (RC,UWO)

[4]Charles Hutchinson to Æmilius Irving, July 2, 1880

[5]Reported in the Toronto *Globe*, March 11, 1880

[6]London *Advertiser*, February 28, 1881 copying from the Toronto *World*

[7]Reported in the London *Advertiser*, March 7, 1881

[8]Letter March 4, 1881 (RC, UWO)

[9]William Donnelly to Charles Hutchinson (RC, UWO)

[10]Exeter *Times*, December 14, 1882

[11]Huron *Expositor*, July 15, 1881

[12]As reported in the Exeter *Times*, October 20, 1881

[13]London *Free Press*, October 11, 1881

[14]October 10, 1963 (RC, UWO)

[15]Hutchinson Papers (RC, UWO)

[16]His father, Obediah Washington Everett, was a manufacturer of chairs and cabinets. Obediah was a Canadian patriot who knew and corresponded with William Lyon Mackenzie, sympathized with the rebels in 1837 and even went so far as to name his son after one of them, the blacksmith Samuel Lount, who was hanged following the rebellion in Upper Canada. In 1866 Samuel Lount Everett married Margaret Catherine Ashbaugh of Ancaster.

[17]London *Advertiser*, March 1, 1877

[18]Stott (ed.), *Passing Into Oblivion: The Diaries of William Porte, Lucan, Ontario 1864-1898,* 116

[19]Hutchinson Papers (RC, UWO)

[20]*Ibid.*

[21]*Ibid.*

[22]Quoted in the London *Free Press*, October 11, 1881

[23]*Ibid.*

[24]Exeter *Times*, October 20, 1881

[25]*Ibid.*

[26]London *Free Press*, October 12, 1881

[27]Much of it from West's testimony given in great detail at the preliminary hearing as reported in the Exeter *Times*, October 20, 1881

[28]*Ibid.*

[29]London *Free Press*, October 11, 1880

[30]*Ibid.*

[31]*Ibid.*

[32]October 13, 1881 (RC, UWO)

[33]*Ibid.*

[34]London *Free Press*, October 13, 1881

[35]Reported in the London *Free Press*, October 11, 1881

[36]As reported in the London *Free Press*, October 13, 1881

[37]London *Free Press*, October 15, 1881

[38]Exeter *Times*, November 17, 1881

[39]Toronto *Globe* December 24, 1883

[40] The political interference by government was alluded to by Orlo Miller in his *The Donnellys Must Die* (1962) and by the author in his *The Donnelly Album* (1977) and in greater detail and at length by William Butt in his doctoral thesis *The Donnellys: History, Legend, Literature* (1977). The 2004 claim by a recent writer that he alone uncovered this is humbug.

Chapter 19 The Feud A-Fizzle

[1]London *Free Press*, September 5 and 18, 1882

[2]London *Free Press*, November 24, 1974

[3]London *Free Press*, September 8, 1882

[4]Porte Diary, Sunday, September 3, 1882 (RC, UWO)

[5]Porte Diary, Thursday, October 19, 1882 (RC, UWO)

[6]Alice McFarlane to author, December 2, 1967

[7]Toronto *Globe and Mail*, November 20, 1946

Chapter 20 Constabulary Duties

[1]April 5, 1882 (RC, UWO)

[2]Referred to in a letter by Charles Hutchinson to W. J. Gerald, April 21, 1882 (RC, UWO)

[3]October 2, 1882 (RC, UWO)

[4]William Donnelly to Charles Hutchinson, September 12, 1888 (RC, UWO)

[5]Glencoe *Transcript*, April 26, 1883

[6]Glencoe *Transcript*, July 2, 1885

[7]Glencoe *Transcript*, July 9, 1885

[8]Glencoe *Transcript*, July 16, 1885

[9]Glencoe *Transcript*, July 23, 1885

[10]The Glencoe *Transcript* was so enthralled with the horse that on April 16 and again on September 17 in 1885 it published Lord Byron's lineage and an account of the many races which he ran.

[11]London *Free Press*, November 8, 1887

[12]The hotel was at the corner of Main and George Streets in Bothwell.

[13]London *Advertiser*, December 15, 1887 copying from the Glencoe *Transcript*

[14]London *Advertiser*, March 13, 1888

[15]London *Advertiser*, July 19, 1888

[16]July 9, 1888 (RC, UWO)

[17]Glencoe *Transcript*, March 14, 1889

[18]Glencoe *Transcript*, September 29, 1892

[19]As reported in the Exeter *Times*, September 20, 1894

[20]Norah Donnelly Lord to Orlo Miller, June 21, 1954 (RC, UWO)

Chapter 21 Courtship of Jenny

[1]The source for much of what is related in this chapter and the next is of necessity anecdotal but the stories of Jenny were told by those who knew her or their mothers and fathers who knew her personally. They include her own sons, Michael Thomas Currie and Patrick Leo Currie; her nephew John William (Jack) Donnelly; her sister-in-law, Catherine Currie and the latter's daughter, Margaret Corbett; family friend, Catherine McIlhargey; near neighbor, Theresa Whelan, and several others who specifically requested their names not be put in print. Regrettable as that is, I felt the reader would feel less cheated by including the material without perfect attribution than omitting it altogether.

[2]Some family members spelled the name Curry.

[3]This appears to accord with the record of the 1861 census that puts her age on her next birthday as 5. The 1871 census on the other hand lists her age as only 14 on her next birthday and as the census was taken on April 4th that year, this would put her birth year in 1857. The Hamilton *Spectator* of February 7th, 1880 described her as "now only in her 23rd year" which puts her birth date in 1858, the same year as on her monument. But upon the booking of her father into the Goderich Jail on May 7th, 1858, he is stated to have eight children. If she had indeed been born in October, it would have to have been before 1858. On balance then, the evidence seems to come down to ascribing October 1856 as the time when Jenny was born.

[4]It was in McGillivray Township where Will Donnelly's old flame, Maggie Thompson, had been born and raised.

[5]As "ea" by the Irish of that time was pronounced the same as the "a" in Janey, the latter and Jeannie in Stephen Foster's song are pronounced alike.

[6]The implication in Jenny's words seems to be that she was pregnant but they may have signified only a moral compunction to wed now that they had become intimate. Be that as it may, it must be pointed out that her first child, Robert, was born on March 21, 1875, over a year after the couple's marriage. The registration of this birth, however, was not made until 63 years after the event.

Chapter 22 Life at Pratt's Siding

[1]Returns of Convictions, Middlesex, 1876 (RC, UWO)

[2]Exeter*Times*, February 9, 1893

Chapter 23 Bob Versus The Army

[1]A copy of this petition was given me by the Lucan clerk but I understand the Regional Collection (UWO) also has a copy.

[2]London *Advertiser*, March 29, 1880

[3]In reality, she was Catherine Caroline Waun from West Williams Township near Parkhill who married Alexander Johnson but may have been separated from him at the time.

[4]Glencoe *Transcript*, June 12, 1884

[5]Glencoe *Transcript*, June 19, 1884

[6]Glencoe *Transcript*, September 25, 1884

[7]Glencoe *Transcript*, February 4, 1886 quoting Josiah Blackburn in the London *Free Press*

[8]To author, May 17, 1981

[9]Glencoe *Transcript*, July 31, 1884

[10]Glencoe *Transcript*, September 18, 1884

[11]Glencoe *Transcript*, September 25, 1884

[12]Glencoe *Transcript*, October 22, 1884

[13]Glencoe *Transcript*, November 20 and 27, 1884

[14]Glencoe *Transcript*, November 24, 1884

[15]Glencoe *Transcript*, December 25, 1884

[16]Glencoe *Transcript*, May 21, 1885

[17]Glencoe *Transcript*, June 11, 1885

[18]Glencoe *Transcript*, January 15, 1885

[19]Glencoe *Transcript*, January 22, 1885

Chapter 24 Emma's Tribulations

[1]Glencoe *Transcript*, September 10, 1885

[2]Glencoe *Transcript*, March 4, 1886

[3]*Ibid.*

[4]*Ibid.*

[5]Glencoe *Transcript*, October 29, 1885

[6]October 20, 1885 (RC, UWO)

[7]October 17, 1885 (RC, UWO)

[8]Hutchinson to E.F.B. Johnston, Deputy Attorney-General of Ontario, June 4, 1886 (RC, UWO)

[9]October 17, 1885 (RC, UWO)

[10]Donnelly's conduct on this day was apparently described in a letter by Emma Rees to the crown attorney which I was unable to locate and have had to rely on William Butt's account in chapter 9 of his Ph.D. thesis, *The Donnellys: History, Legend, Literature*, 1977, UWO, at page 343.

[11]October 21, 1885 (RC, UWO)

[12]December 3, 1885 (RC, UWO)

[13]December 4, 1885 (RC, UWO)

[14]Glencoe *Transcript*, December 31, 1885

[15]Hutchinson to E.F.B. Johnston, Deputy Attorney-General of Ontario, June 26, 1886 (RC, UWO)

[16]The events of the January 1886 confrontations on the streets of Glencoe between the Salvation Army and Bob Donnelly and his gang of youths are reconstructed from the testimony of the witnesses at the trials of the defendants as reported in the Glencoe *Transcript*, February 11, 18 and 25, 1886.

Chapter 25 An Abominable Outrage

[1]The attempted arrest of Bob Donnelly is taken from the testimony of witnesses in the case against the constable reported by the Glencoe *Transcript*, March 4, 1886.

[2]February 18, 1886 (RC,UWO)

[3]February 19, 1886 (RC,UWO)

[4]February 22, 1886 (RC, UWO)

[5]London *Free Press*, February 27, 1886

[6]Glencoe *Transcript*, March 4, 1886

[7]April 5, 1886 (RC, UWO)

[8]Glencoe *Transcript*, June 3, 1886

[9]The events relating to the defiling of the Army's premises with human waste are described in letters by Charles Hutchinson to Emma Rees (June 12, 1886), Miss J. E. Schoff (June 15, 1886), Emma Rees (June 19, 1886), Oliver Mowat, Premier and Attorney-General of Ontario (June 21, 1886) and E. F. B. Johnston, Deputy Attorney-General of Ontario (June 26, 1886) (RC, UWO)

[10]Hutchinson to E. F. B. Johnston, July 16, 1886 (RC, UWO)

[11]Hutchinson to E. F. B. Johnston, July 16, 1886 (RC, UWO)

[12]Glencoe *Transcript*, December 2, 1886

[13]*Ibid.*

[14]Glencoe *Transcript*, December 16, 1886

[15]*Ibid.*

[16]Glencoe *Transcript*, December 23, 1886

[17]Glencoe *Transcript*, December 8, 1887

Chapter 26 The Prodigal's Return

[1]Mabel Stanley Armstrong to Spencer Armitage-Stanley-Sceli, January 19, 1963 (RC, UWO)

[2]Reported in the London *Free Press*, October 11, 1881

[3]Exeter *Times*, November 10, 1892

[4]Exeter *Times*, March 8, 1893. It was this same Whelan who lived across the road from the Donnellys in February 1880.

[5]Exeter *Times*, May 4, 1893

[6]Stott (ed.), *Passing Into Oblivion: The Diaries of William Porte, Lucan, Ontario 1864-1895, 394* and the Exeter *Times*, August 24, 1893. The proprietor for many years, John F. Cain, later purchased William Walker's old Western Hotel on William Street. His naming this hotel the Royal has confused some researchers.

[7]Exeter *Times*, September 21, 1893

[8]Exeter *Times*, January 11, 1899

[9]Exeter *Times*, January 18, 1894

[10]Exeter *Times*, January 25, 1894

[11]Exeter *Times*, February 14, 1894

[12]Exeter *Times*, April 12, 1894

[13]Exeter *Times*, July 19, 1894

[14]Exeter *Times*, December 13, 1894

[15]Exeter *Times*, January 3, 1895

[16]*Ibid.*

[17]Exeter *Times*, July 25, 1895

[18]Exeter *Times*, May 7 and June 11, 1896

[19]Exeter *Times*, July 16, 1896

[20]James T. J. Collisson to Miss M. Turner, September 2, 1952 (RC, UWO)

[21]Lucan *Sun*, June 29, 1911 (RC, UWO)

[22]Copy preserved at RC, UWO

Chapter 27 Grandma Bell

[1]Steward, *Twenty-two Years A Slave and Forty Years A Freeman*, Rochester, 1857 (Reprint, 1969), 148

[2]*Ibid., 156*

[3]*Ibid., 160*

[4]*Ibid., 120*

[5]James T. J. Collisson to Miss M. Turner, September 2, 1952 (RC, UWO)

Chapter 28 Tavern Stories

[1]John Nelin was proprietor shortly after Confederation while the last operator was William Deacon.

[2]London *Advertiser*, June 13, 1878

[3]Toronto *Globe*, September 10, 1880

[4]Hutchinson to Æmilius Irving, May 11, 1880 (RC, UWO).

[5]Undated newspaper clipping in a scrapbook of Spencer Armitage-Stanley-Sceli which he loaned to me and which I believe is now in RC, UWO.

[6]North Middlesex Review, January 29 and February 6, 1869

[7]It is curious that I managed to get possession of the family photographs of his only other grandchild and thereby ended up with almost all of Bernard Stanley's family photographs either as originals or copies.

[8]In Montana, you can find the name of his cousin on a stone monument on which are carved the names of all the soldiers who fell with Custer at the Little Big Horn.

[9]Hamilton *Spectator*, February 23, 1880

[10]London *Adverister*, August 9, 1874

[11]William W. Lee to Charles Hutchinson, September 16, 1874 (RC, UWO)

[12]Exeter *Times*, October 1, 1874

[13]Exeter *Times*, September 2, 1875

Chapter 29 Connolly's Career

[1]The film was telecast on the national network in the spring and summer of 1982 and a few times since on local television channels.

[2]It is now a designated heritage building under provincial law. I understand that one parishioner, who shall remain nameless, was so angry at the decision not to tear down the old church and replace it with a modern building that he has never since set foot inside the old church.

[3]As set out in his obituary in the Ingersoll *Chronicle and Canadian Dairyman*, September 30, 1909 and *The Catholic Record*, October 9, 1909.

[4]Letter from Quebec Archives to author, May 3, 1993

[5]Hamilton *Spectator*, February 7, 1880

[6]Patrick Donnelly to Charles Hutchinson, March 12, 1880 (RC, UWO)

[7]The letter is undated but appears from its position in Hutchinson's bound letter-book containing copies of his letters to be January 15, 1881.

[8]Undated (RC,UWO)

[9]London *Advertiser*, February 14, 1880

[10]Note made by Alfred Scott Garrett (undated), Orlo Miller papers (RC, UWO)

[11]James T. J. Collisson to Miss M. Turner, September 2, 1952 (RC, UWO)

[12]St. Marys *Argus*, May 22, 1884

[13]Bob Donnelly is noted ordering the stone in the Glencoe *Transcript*, March 14, 1889

[14]Stratford *Daily Herald*, September 27, 1909

[15]Ingersoll *Chronicle and Canadian Dairyman*, September 30, 1909

[16]Probate file papers which I understand are now at the Ontario Archives

Chapter 30 The Dying Curse

[1]Exeter *Times*, February 9, 1893

[2]RC, UWO

[3]London *Free Press*, October 24, 1890 quoting from the Glencoe *Transcript*

Chapter 31 In the Rockies

[1]In its issue of Thursday, September 25, 1884 quoted from the Winnipeg *Times* of the previous Thursday

[2]A.S. Garrett note to Orlo Miller, Miller Papers (RC, UWO)

3London *Free Press*, September 4, 1884

[4]London *Advertiser*, Saturday, May 29, 1886 and St. Marys *Argus*, Thursday, June 3, 1886

[5]Printed in the Western Weekly Supplement (British Columbia), Wednesday, October 17, 1962

[6]The exchange of letters between Beattie and Carroll are in British Columbia Archives, Golden County Court, George Beattie (plaintiff) vs. J. M. Carroll (defendant), reference GR2222, Box 1, File 75/12.

Chapter 32 A Vigilante Interview

[1]Patrick Breen lived to be 71, John Cain and William Casey to be 74 each, James Feeheley to be 75, Dennis Heenan to be 67, John Heenan to be 76, Michael Heenan to be 74, James Maher, Sr., to be 74, John McLaughlin to be 81, Martin McLaughlin to be at least 92, John Quigley to be 80, Patrick Quigley to be 86, Sideroad Jim Ryder to be 63, his nephew Grouchy Jim Ryder to be 84, John Lamphier to be 89, Patrick (Grouchy) Ryder and James Lamphier to be 84 each, James Toohey to be 86 and Michael Blake to be 82. Timothy Toohey died of "organic heart disease" at the age of 78. John Ryder died in 1920 at the age of 81 years.

[2]Big Pat Breen was so called to distinguish him from his first cousin of the same name who was called Little Pat. Both were Biddulph vigilantes. Big Pat was George's son while little Pat was Edward's son. George and Edward, along with an apparently younger brother who was also named Pat, were the pioneer patriarchs of the Breen family of Biddulph. The last-mentioned Patrick appears not to have married in the parish and perhaps it was he, described as of Lake Shore, Port Stanley, who married Mary Elizabeth Maher, the daughter of Michael Maher, in St. Thomas in 1877. Maher was referred to as "the late architect of St. Louis" and not therefore the Michael Maher who ousted James Donnelly Sr. from the south half of his homestead plot in 1856. George Breen, father of Big Pat of the Peace Society, and his brother Edward, both died in middle age leaving large families. George was killed by runaway horses on the Proof Line Road in 1864 and Edward died five years later. George and his wife, Margaret Carey, had chosen as their homestead Lot 30 in Concession 9 of Biddulph but the family had acquired additional adjacent land.

[3]There may be a connection between George and Edward Breen of Biddulph and the Breens of Port Stanley and St. Thomas, perhaps through their brother, Patrick, mentioned in the last note. There is no doubt that the Breens of Port Stanley and St. Thomas were of the same family as the Breens of the Donner Overland Party. On its way to California the Donner Party got stuck in the Sierra Nevada Mountains in the winter of 1846-1847 and almost all—some say all—those who survived resorted to cannibalism. Among the survivors were Patrick Breen and his family all in a tolerably good state of nourishment. This Patrick Breen, who may have been related to George, Edward and Patrick of Biddulph, was born in 1795 and married Margaret Bulger in Canada where their first two children were born in 1831 and 1832. As late as 1858 his mother, Mary Breen, lived in St. Thomas with some of her other children and was then quite elderly. In 1861 we find a Mary Breen, aged 99, living with the George Breen family in Biddulph. If this Mary is the same in both instances, then the link to the Donner Party Breens is more obvious.

[4]One of Big Pat's sons named George Edward after his grandfather and uncle (although he sometimes called himself George Clement) grew up and married Ellen (Nellie) McGrath, the babe in arms who survived the railway accident at Grundy's Crossing on Christmas Day in 1880. They lived in Saskatoon.

[5]The grandson of John Cain, Frank Clear of Detroit, was kind enough to tape an interview of James J. Carroll for me and provide me with a transcript of the tape. Carroll had been a prosperous business man of Detroit and was then retired.

[6]Hutchinson Papers (RC, UWO)

[7]Extract from *Diary of a Department, A History of the Saginaw Police Department* by Freeman Coats, 1965.

Chapter 33 Friends and Allies

[1]Reprinted from the St. Marys *Argus* in Exeter *Times*, March 30, 1893

[2]Indictments, Ontario Archives

[3]John Toohey, a descendant of Timothy Toohey of Biddulph, who came to our house for a visit from the American Mid-West a few years ago, claimed that he had been delivered by Dr. Patrick Keefe.

[4]Grouchy's son, Michael Ryder, married Corinne Phillips but as far as I am aware the two girls were not related.

[5]Catherine Ryder married Joe Lawrence who made a small fortune in Manitoba and returned to London, Ontario where he claimed to have purchased the first automobile in that city. Catherine survived her husband and died a wealthy woman. She was buried out of the Catholic cathedral in London but the officiating priest refused to come to the graveside.

[6]Public Archives of Canada, Manuscript Division, RG 5, Cl, vol. 529, no. 1653

[7]The event is reconstructed from the depositions of the witnesses in the case of Q. v. William Casey, Public Archives of Canada, Manuscript Division, RG 1, Cl, vol. 544, no. 369

[8]Porte Diary, September 3, 1882 (RC, UWO)

[9]Letter dated October 2, 1882

[10]It is noted in the 1861 census as "Log 2 sty"

[11]This item was reprinted in the Exeter *Times-Advocate*, January 22, 1997 in the column *Back in Time*.

[12]Letter by Alfred Scott Garrett November 18, 1959, Orlo Miller Papers (RC, UWO)

Chapter 34 A Tramp Letter

[1]Letter undated but apparently January 15, 1881 (RC, UWO)

[2]Newspaper clipping undated but apparently 1932 in the scrapbook of Dora M. Armitage, Lucan

[3]RC, UWO

[4]Graham, *Greenbank*, Broadview, Peterborough, 1988

[5]In *From This Side of Heaven: Determining the Donnelly Murders*, University of Toronto Press, 1999, author Norman Feltes develops an elaborate Marxist dialectic argument on a related theme.

Chapter 35 Court Weapons

[1]*The Works of William Carleton*, 1881, republished 1970 by Books for Libraries Press, New York, Volume 2, page 762 at 784

[2]See Bellsiles, *Arming America: The Origins of a National Gun Culture*, Knopf, New York, 2000.

[3]Newark, *Illustrated Encyclopedia of the Old West*, Gallery Books, New York, 1980, page 237

[4]*The Catholic Record* (London) newspaper of October 22, 1880 argues, however, that both shots which hit John Donnelly may have come from a double-barreled type of gun with one muzzle having a rifle bore loaded with a bullet and the other a musket-like bore loaded with shot. I find the argument unconvincing for several reasons.

Chapter 36 Fraudsters and Fakes

[1]London *Advertiser*, August 10, 1876

[2]Hamilton *Spectator*, December 24, 1980

Chapter 37 Final Thoughts

Reader's Notes